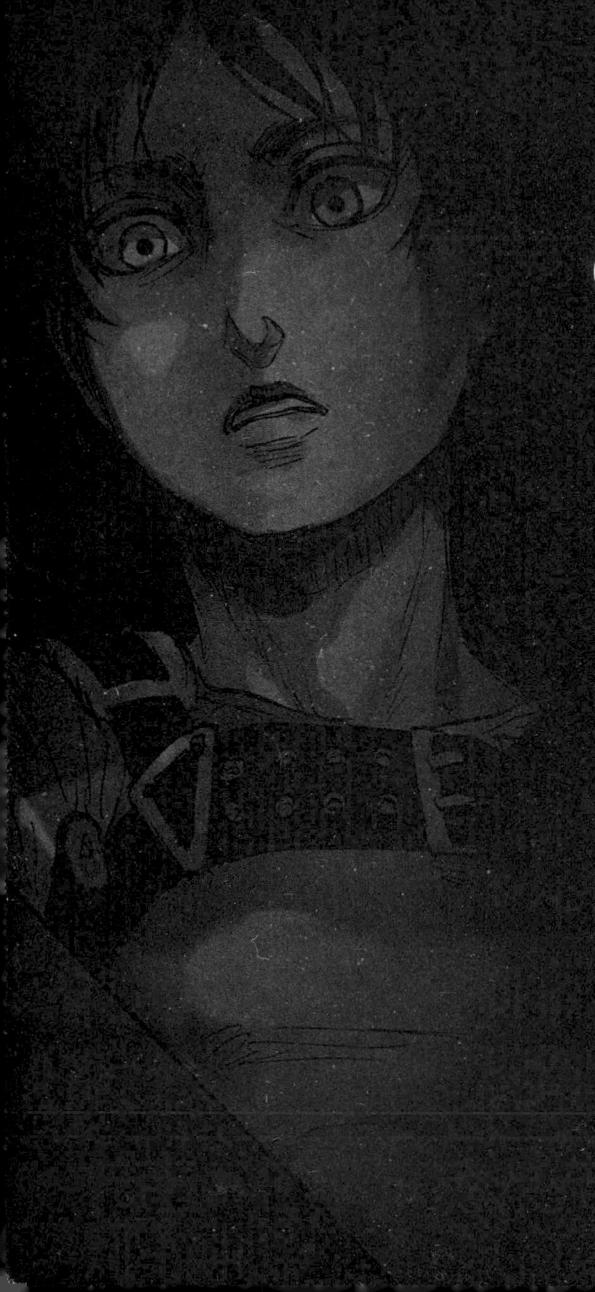

ATTACK ON TITAN 21

HAJIME ISAYAMA

"Attack on Titan" Character Introductions

104th Corps

raduated at
e top of her
aining corps,
ikasa is a
ghly talented
ldier. Her
arents were
urdered
efore her
yes when she
as a child,
t Eren saved
er life. Since
en, she has
ade it her
ission to
otect him.

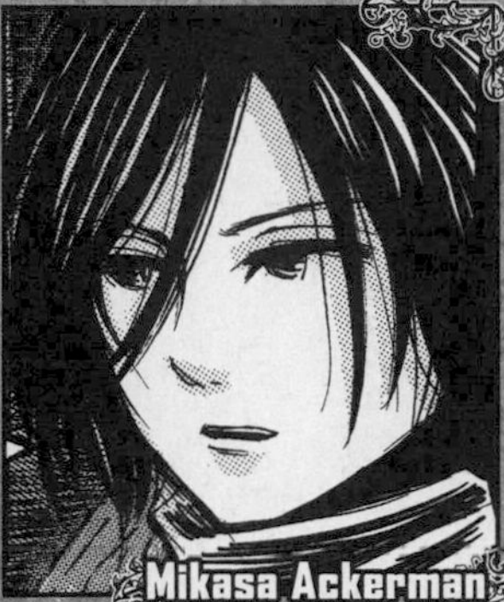
Mikasa Ackerman

Eren joined the Survey Corps out of his longing for the outside world and his hatred of the Titans. He has the power to turn himself into a Titan, but its origins are unknown.

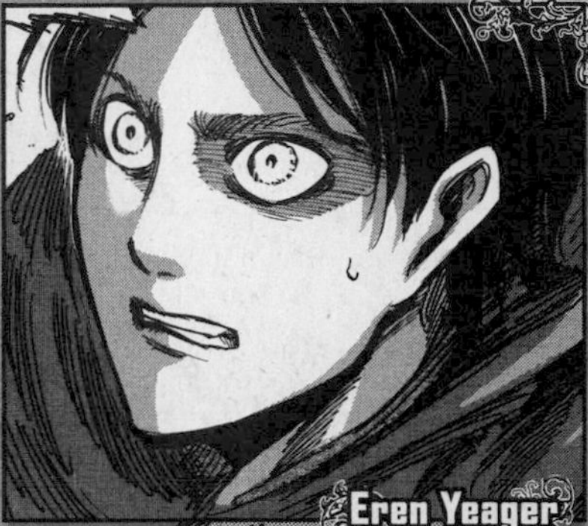
Eren Yeager

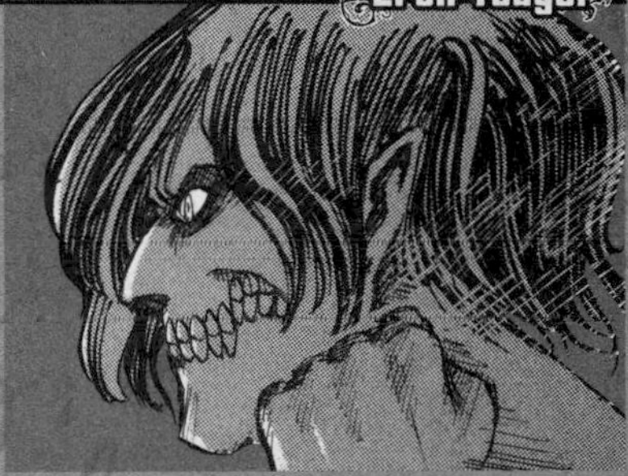

en and Mikasa's
ldhood friend.
ough Armin isn't
letic in the least,
possesses both
arp observational
wers and keen
ight, and he
ibits an
raordinary ability
develop
ategies.

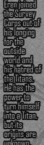

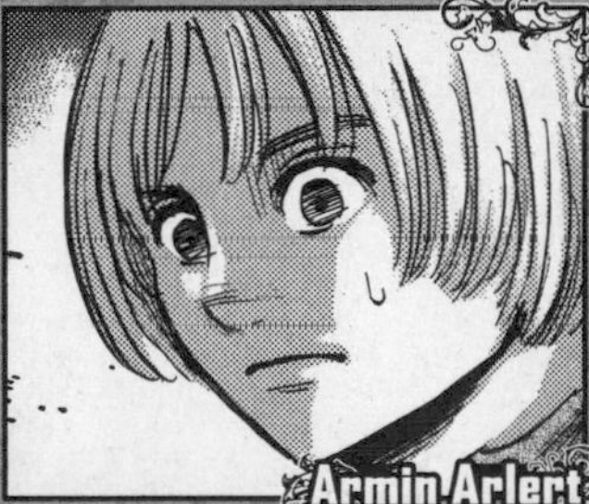
Armin Arlert

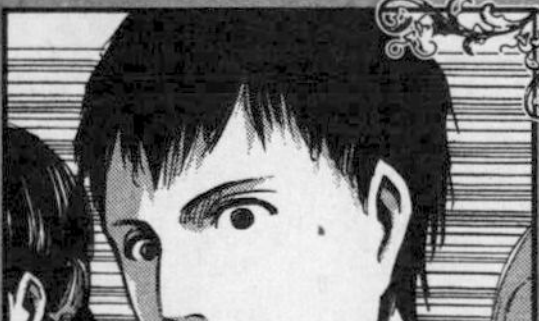
Bertolt Hoover

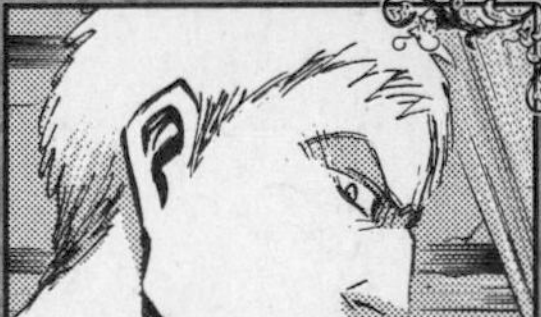
Reiner Braun

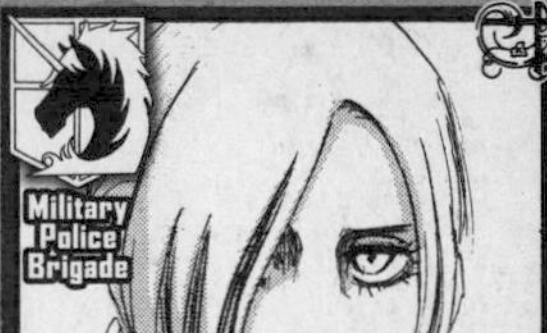
Military
Police
Brigade
Annie Leonhart

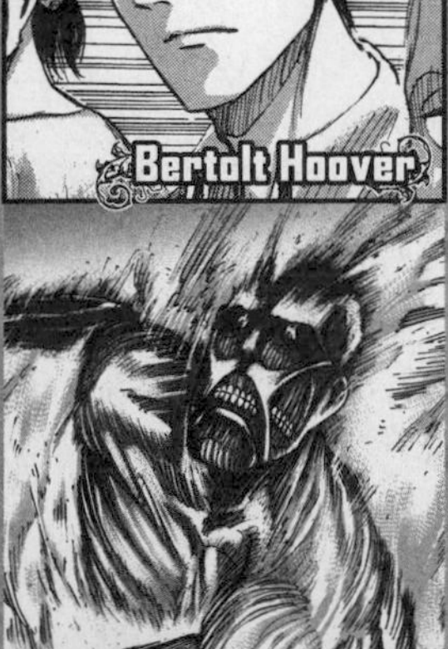
The Colossus Titan

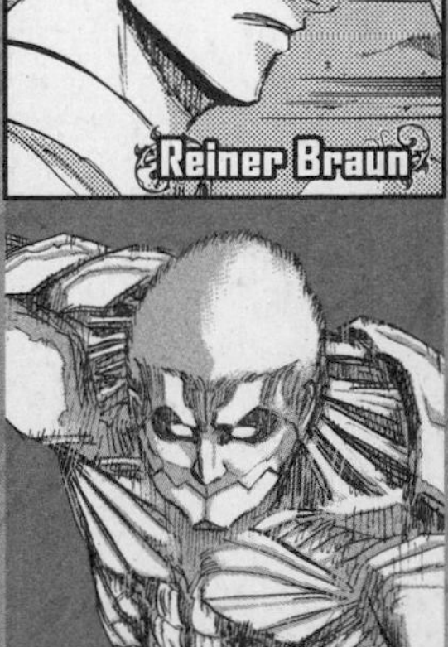
The Armored Titan

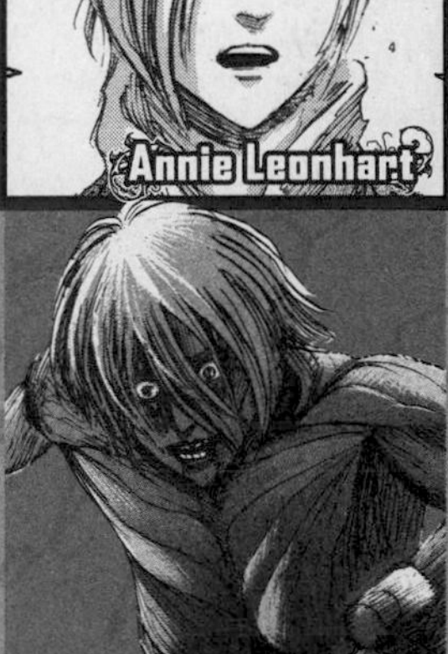
The Female Titan

Survey Corps

Soldiers who are prepared to sacrifice themselves as they brave the Titan territory outside the walls.

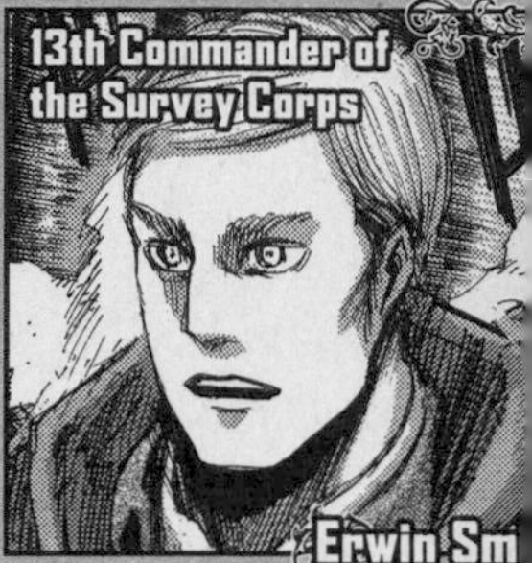

13th Commander of the Survey Corps

Erwin Smi

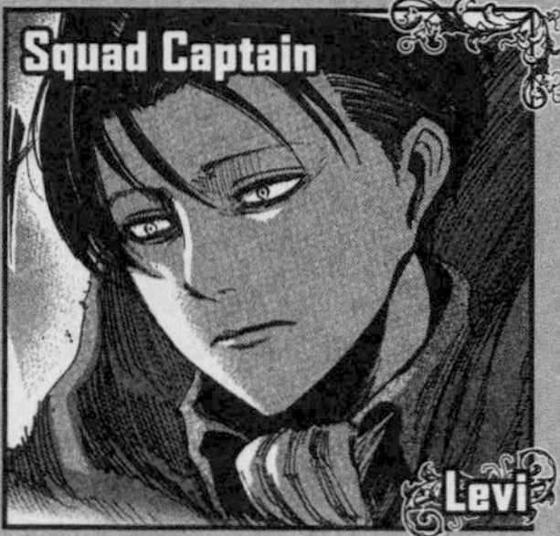

Squad Captain

Levi

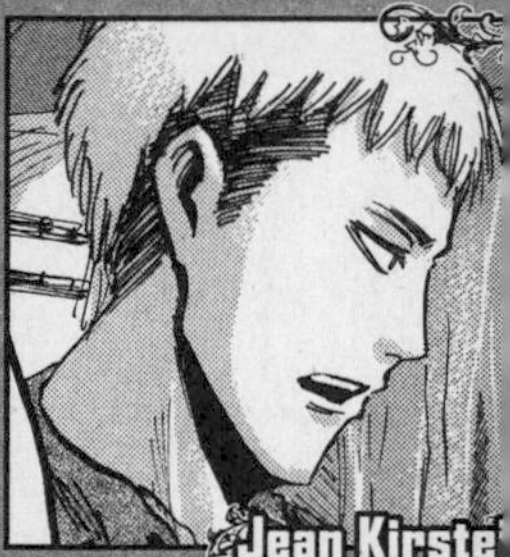

Jean Kirste

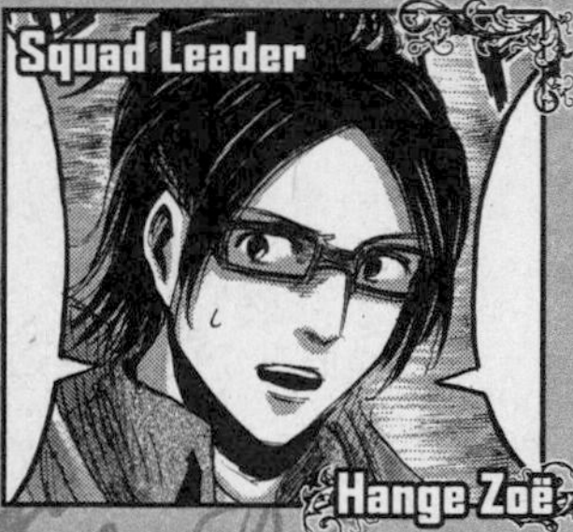

Squad Leader

Hange Zoë

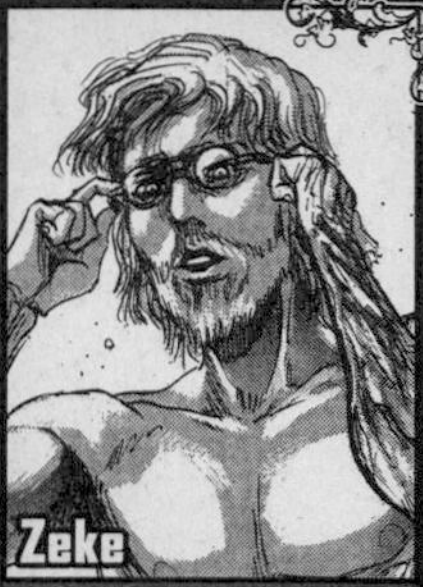

Zeke

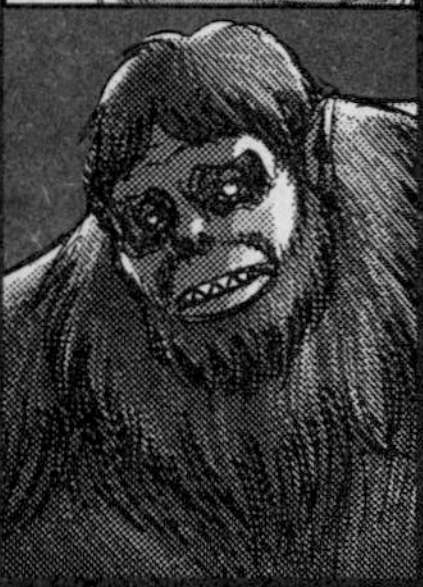

The Beast Titan

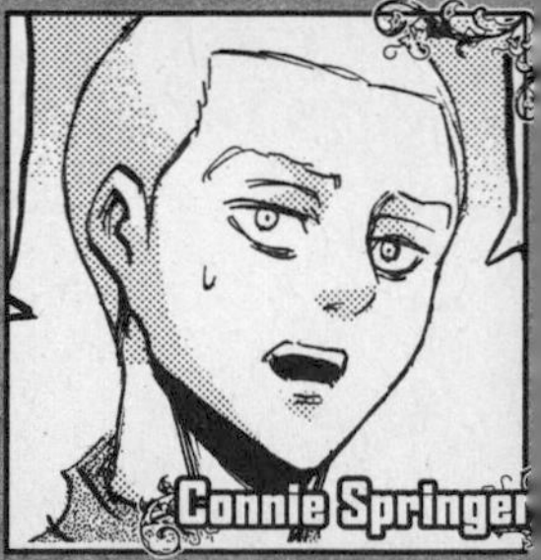

Connie Springer

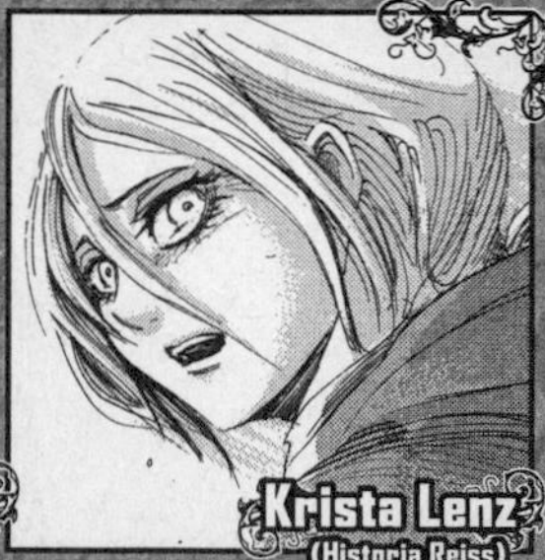

Krista Lenz

(Historia Reiss)

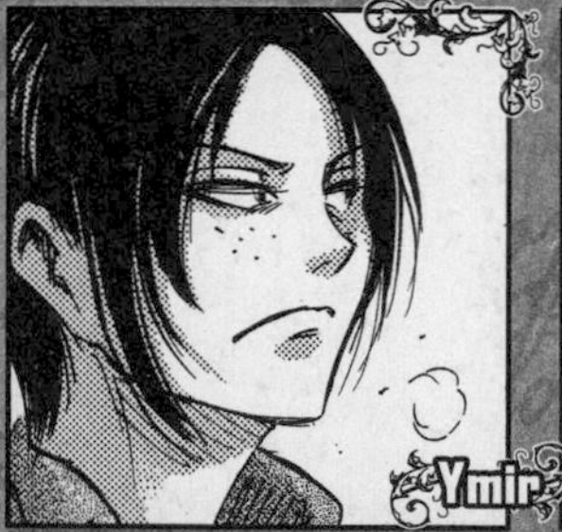

Ymir

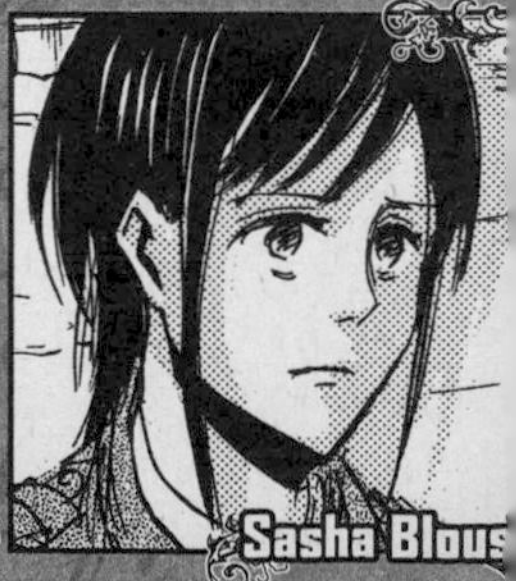

Sasha Blous

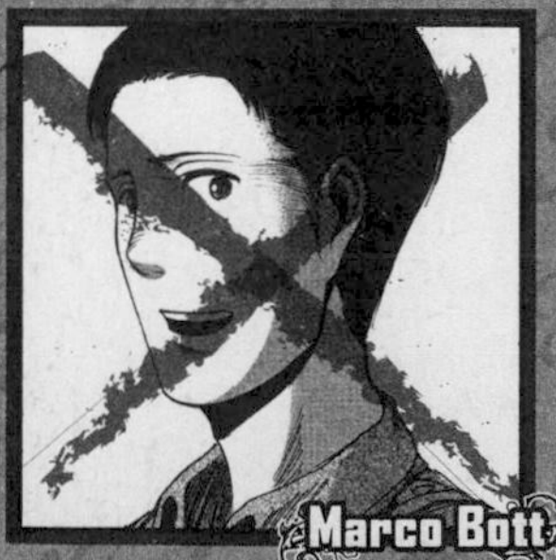

Marco Bott

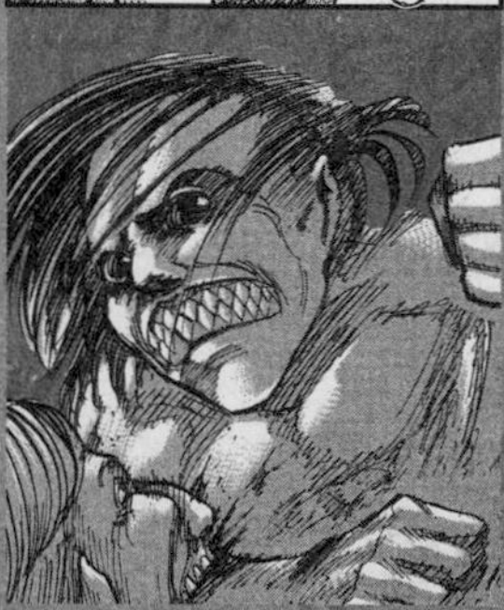

ATTACK on TITAN

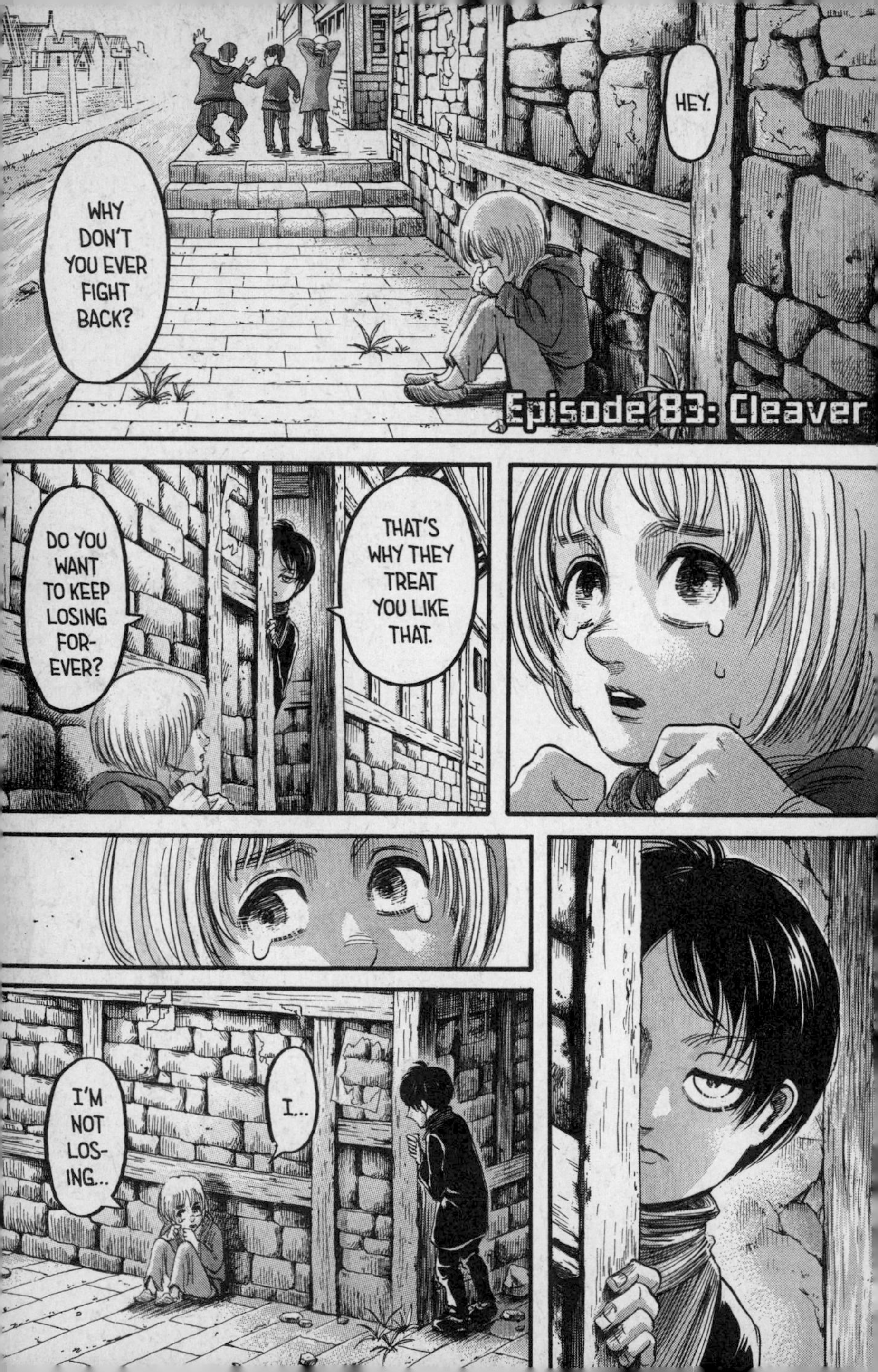
HEY.
WHY DON'T YOU EVER FIGHT BACK?
Episode 83: Cleaver
THAT'S WHY THEY TREAT YOU LIKE THAT.
DO YOU WANT TO KEEP LOSING FOR-EVER?
I...
I'M NOT LOS-ING...

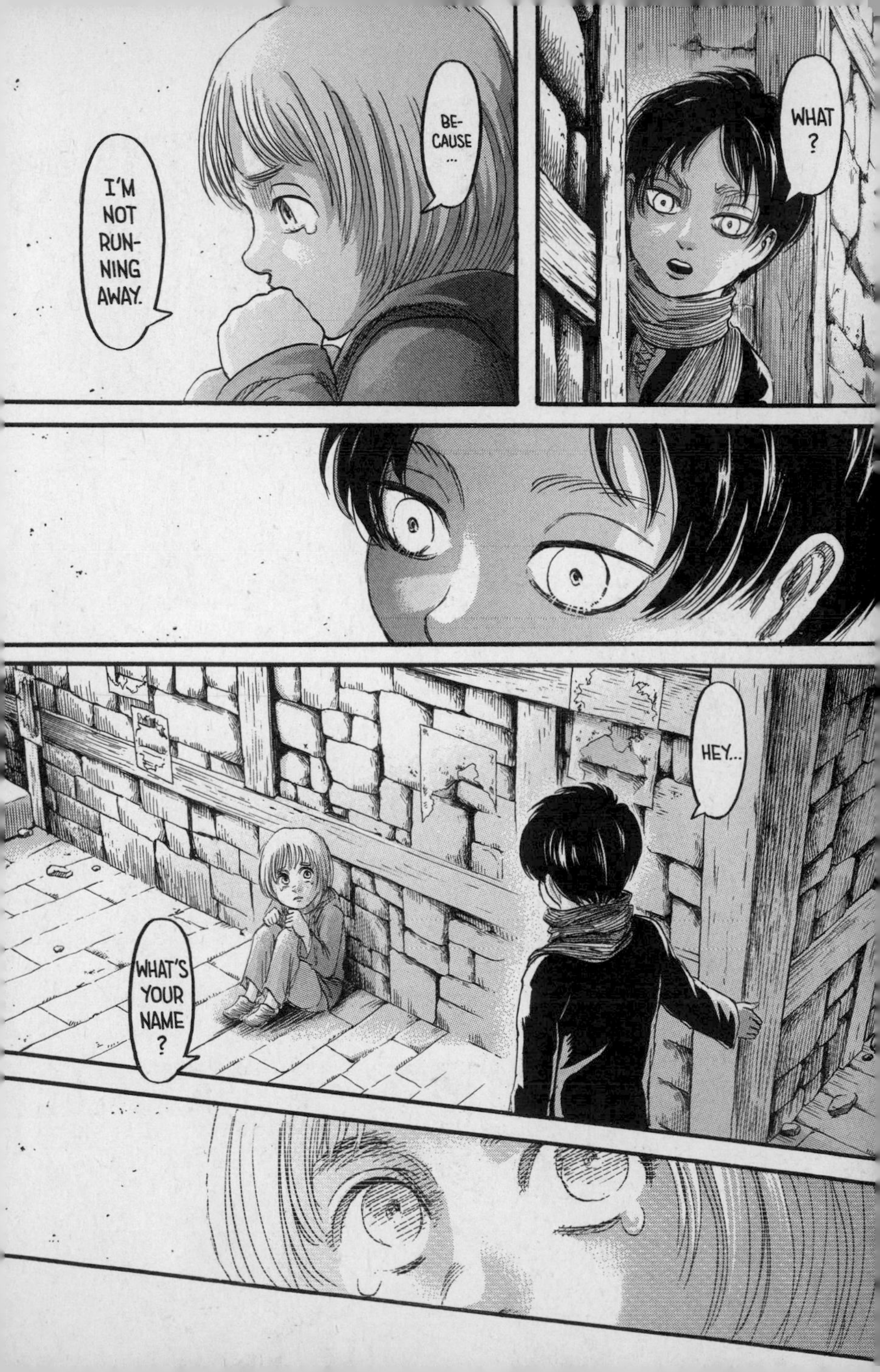
WHAT?
BE-CAUSE...
I'M NOT RUN-NING AWAY.
HEY...
WHAT'S YOUR NAME?

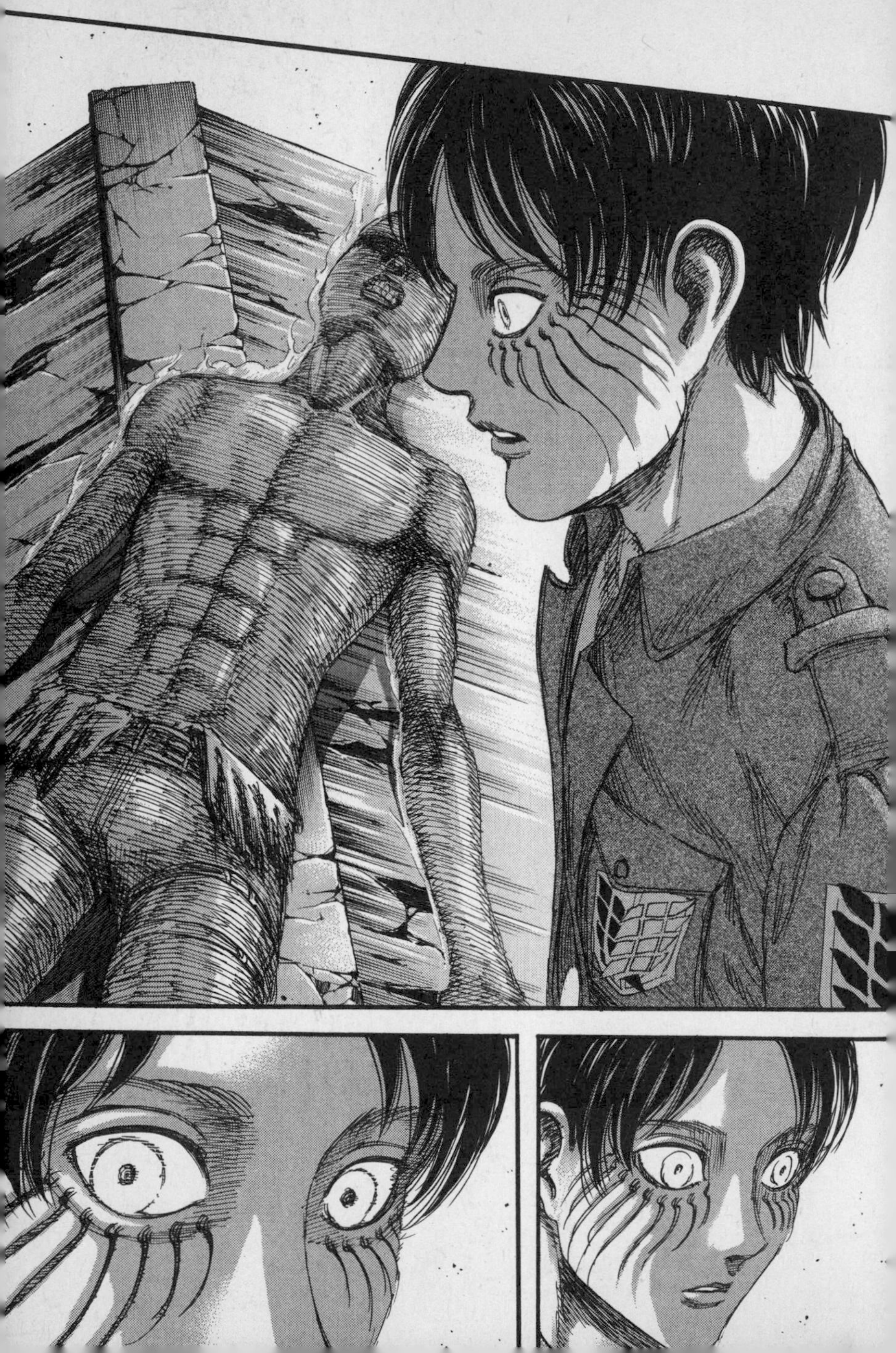

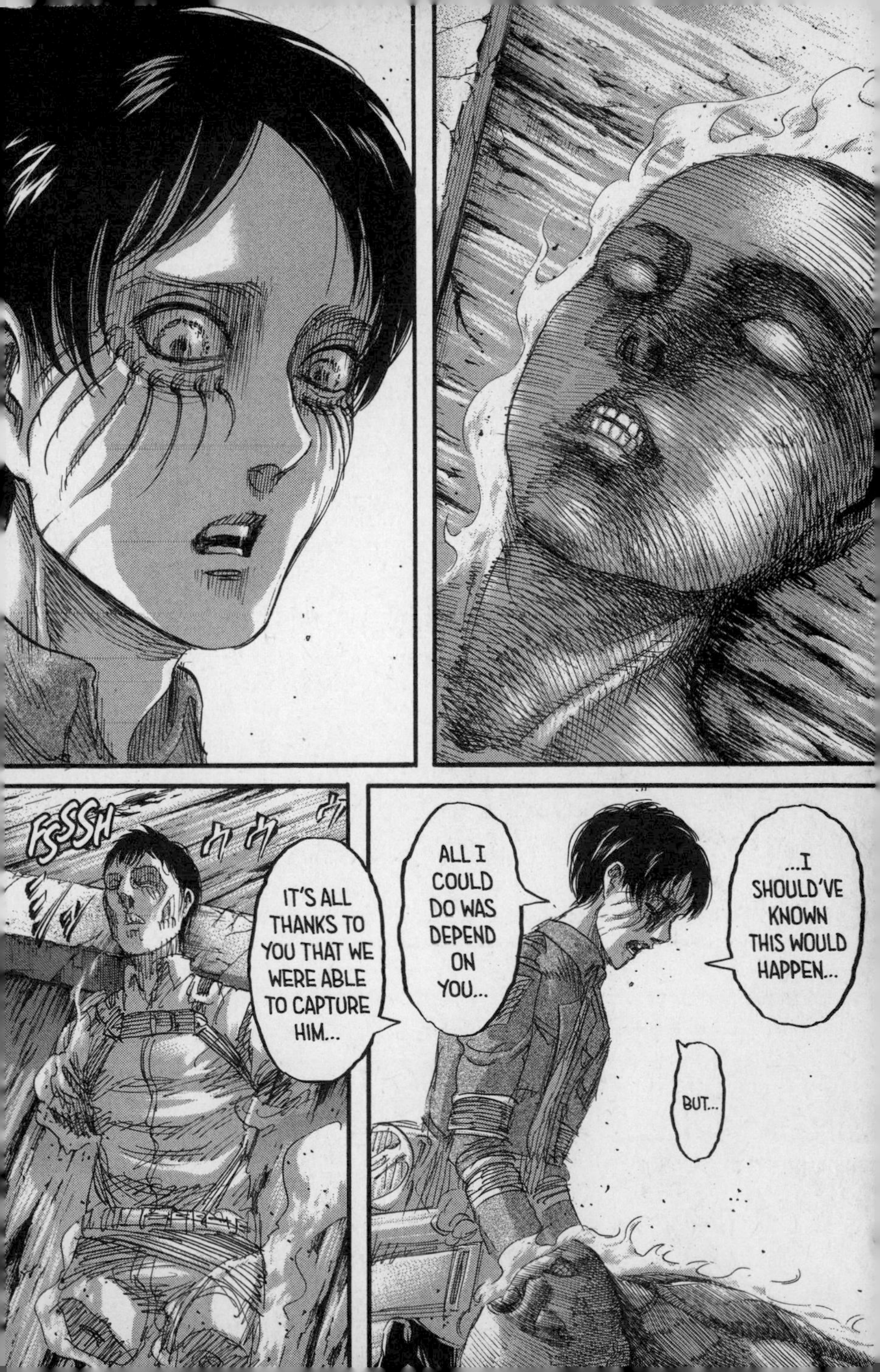
...I SHOULD'VE KNOWN THIS WOULD HAPPEN...
ALL I COULD DO WAS DEPEND ON YOU...
BUT...
FSSSH
IT'S ALL THANKS TO YOU THAT WE WERE ABLE TO CAPTURE HIM...

...RUN AWAY...?

WHY DON'T YOU EVER...

ARMIN...

BL... BOOOM

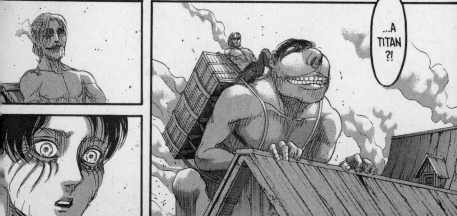

...A TITAN ?!

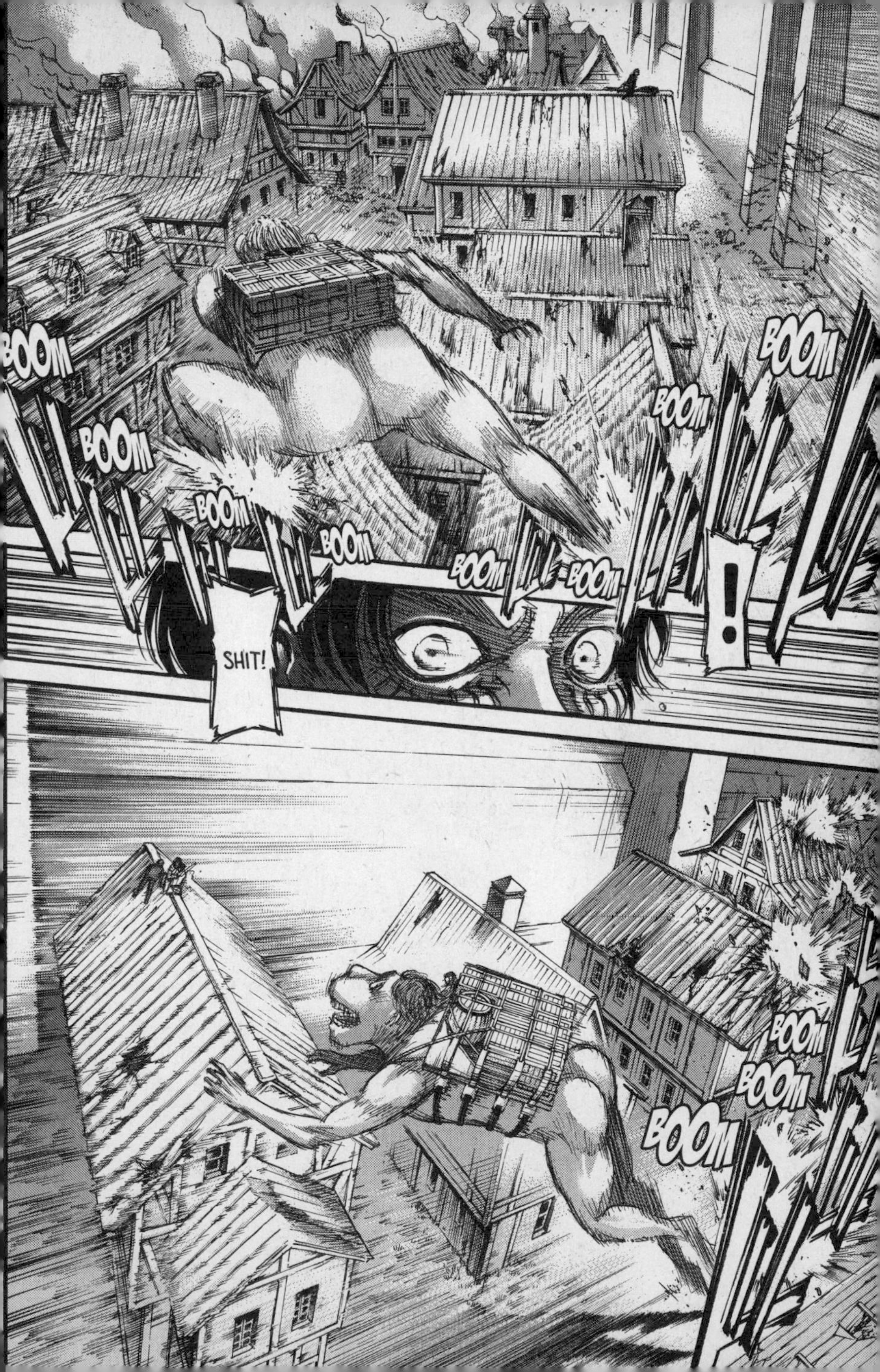
BOOM
BOOM
BOOM
BOOM
BOOM
BOOM
BOOM
BOOM
!
SHIT!
BOOM
BOOM
BOOM

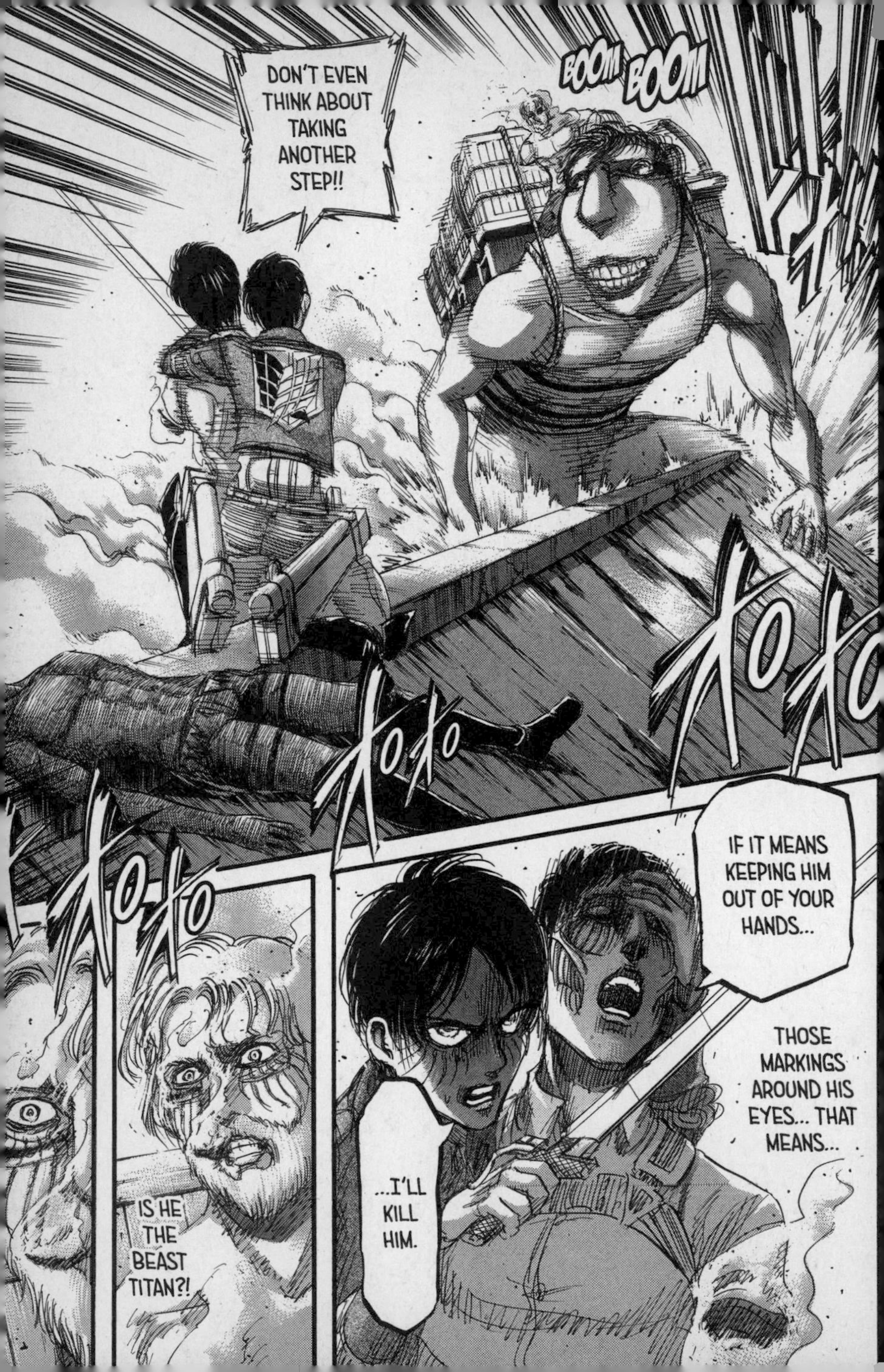
BOOM BOOM
DON'T EVEN THINK ABOUT TAKING ANOTHER STEP!!
IF IT MEANS KEEPING HIM OUT OF YOUR HANDS...
THOSE MARKINGS AROUND HIS EYES... THAT MEANS...
...I'LL KILL HIM.
IS HE THE BEAST TITAN?!

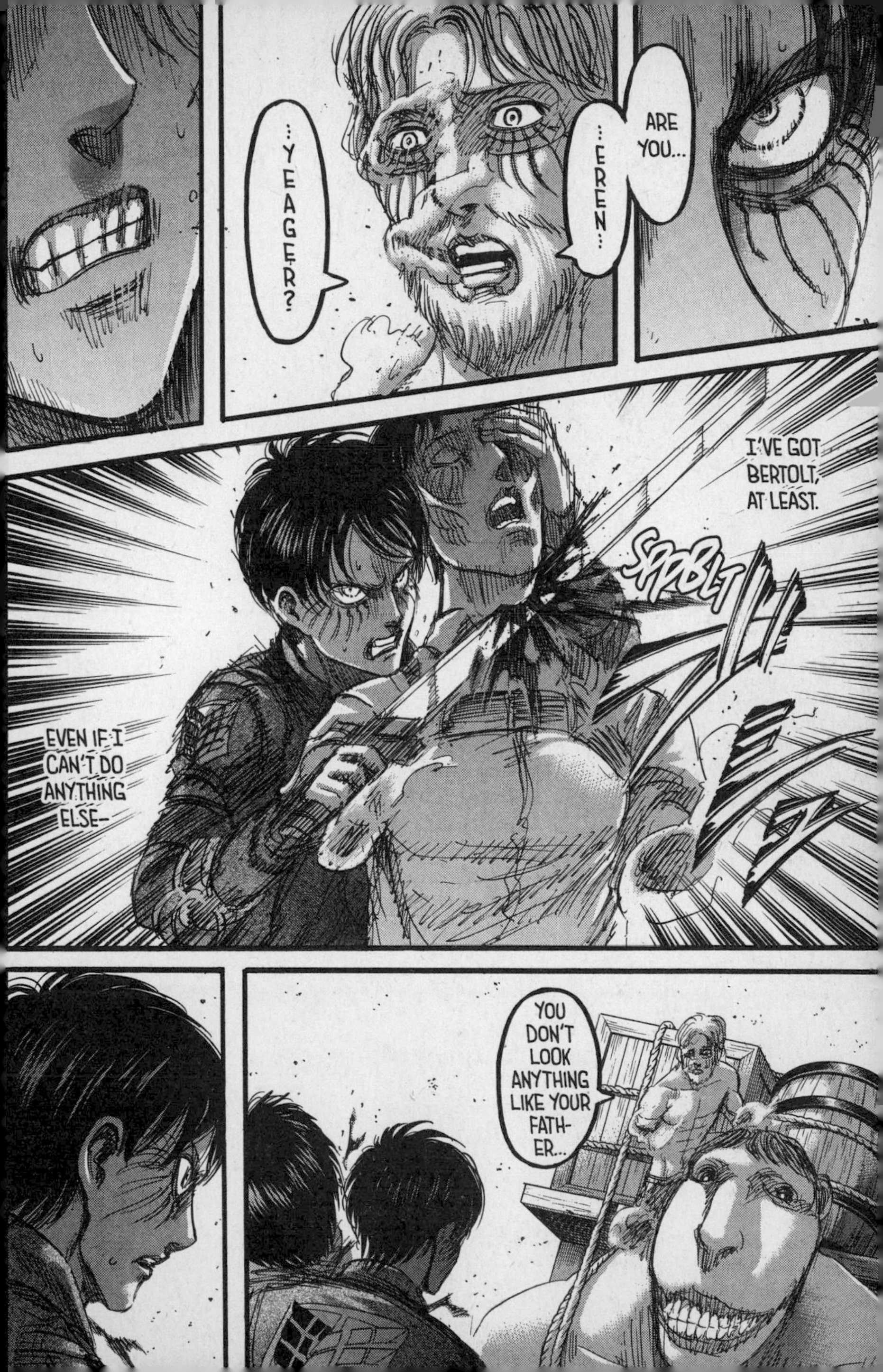
ARE YOU... ...EREN...
...YEAGER?
I'VE GOT BERTOLT, AT LEAST.
SPBLT
EVEN IF I CAN'T DO ANYTHING ELSE-
YOU DON'T LOOK ANYTHING LIKE YOUR FATH-ER...

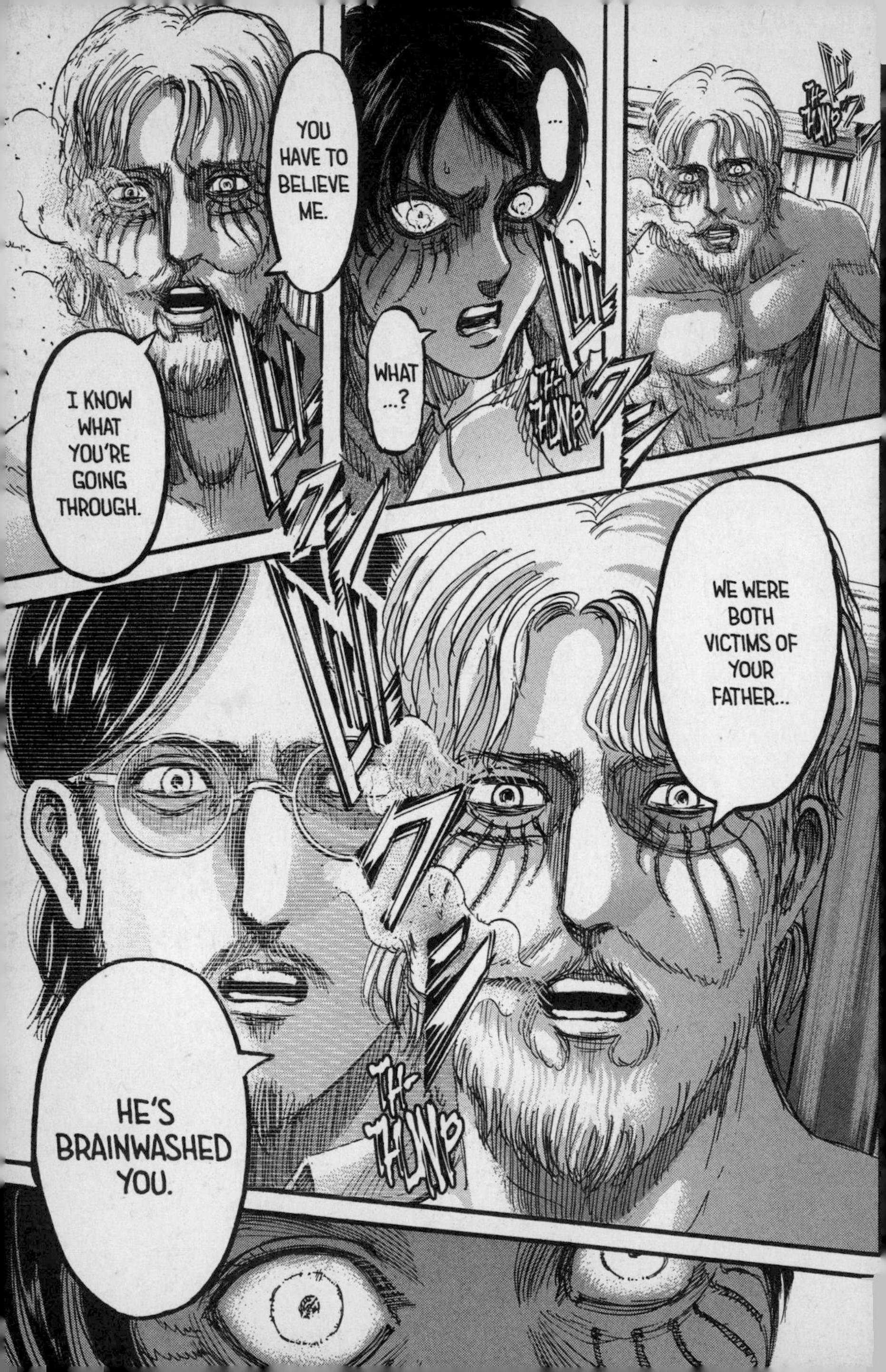
TH-THUMP
...
WHAT ...?
TH-THUMP
YOU HAVE TO BELIEVE ME.
I KNOW WHAT YOU'RE GOING THROUGH.
WE WERE BOTH VICTIMS OF YOUR FATHER...
HE'S BRAINWASHED YOU.
TH-THUMP

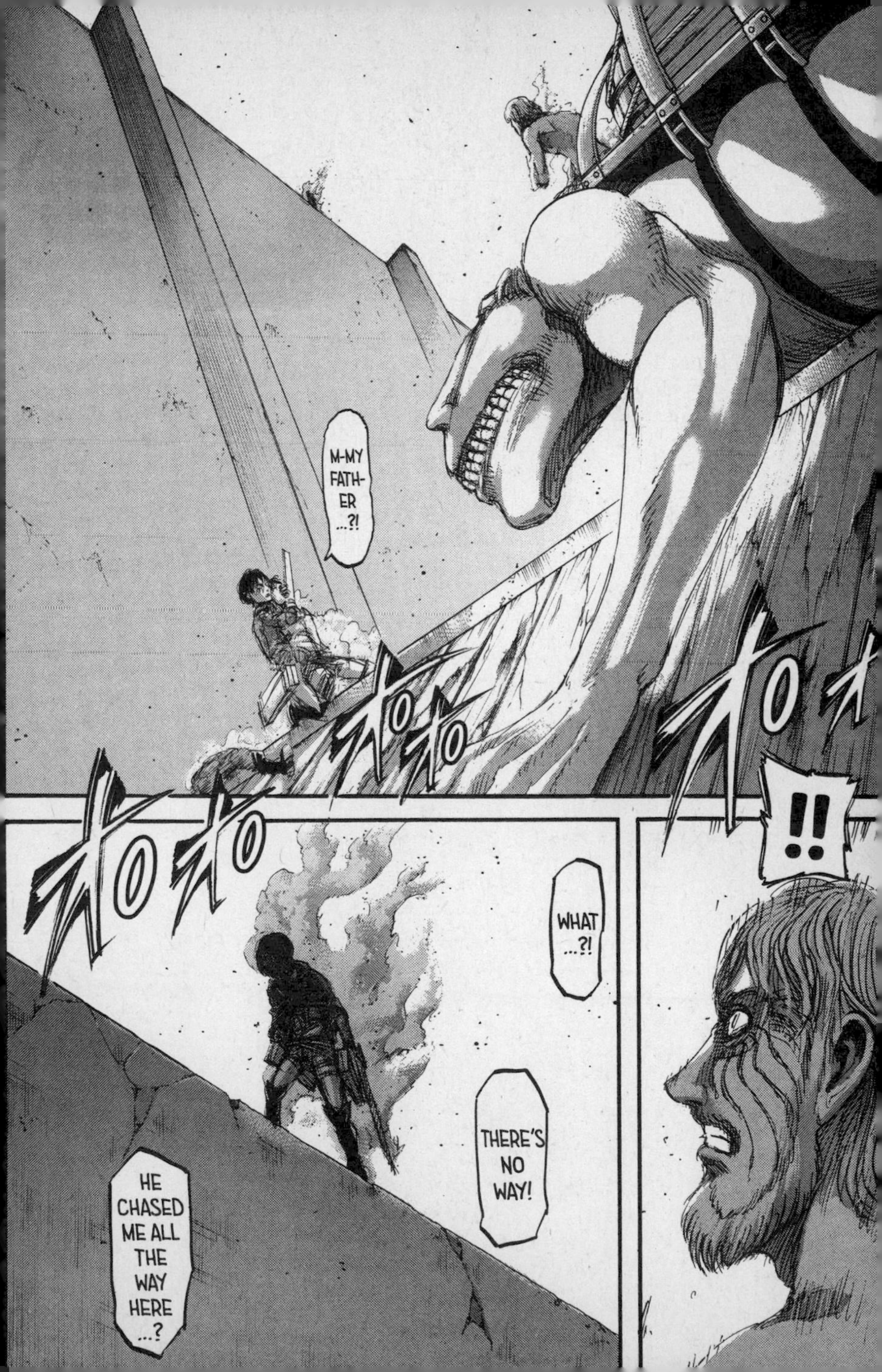
M-MY FATHER-ER ...?!
!!
WHAT ...?!
THERE'S NO WAY!
HE CHASED ME ALL THE WAY HERE ...?

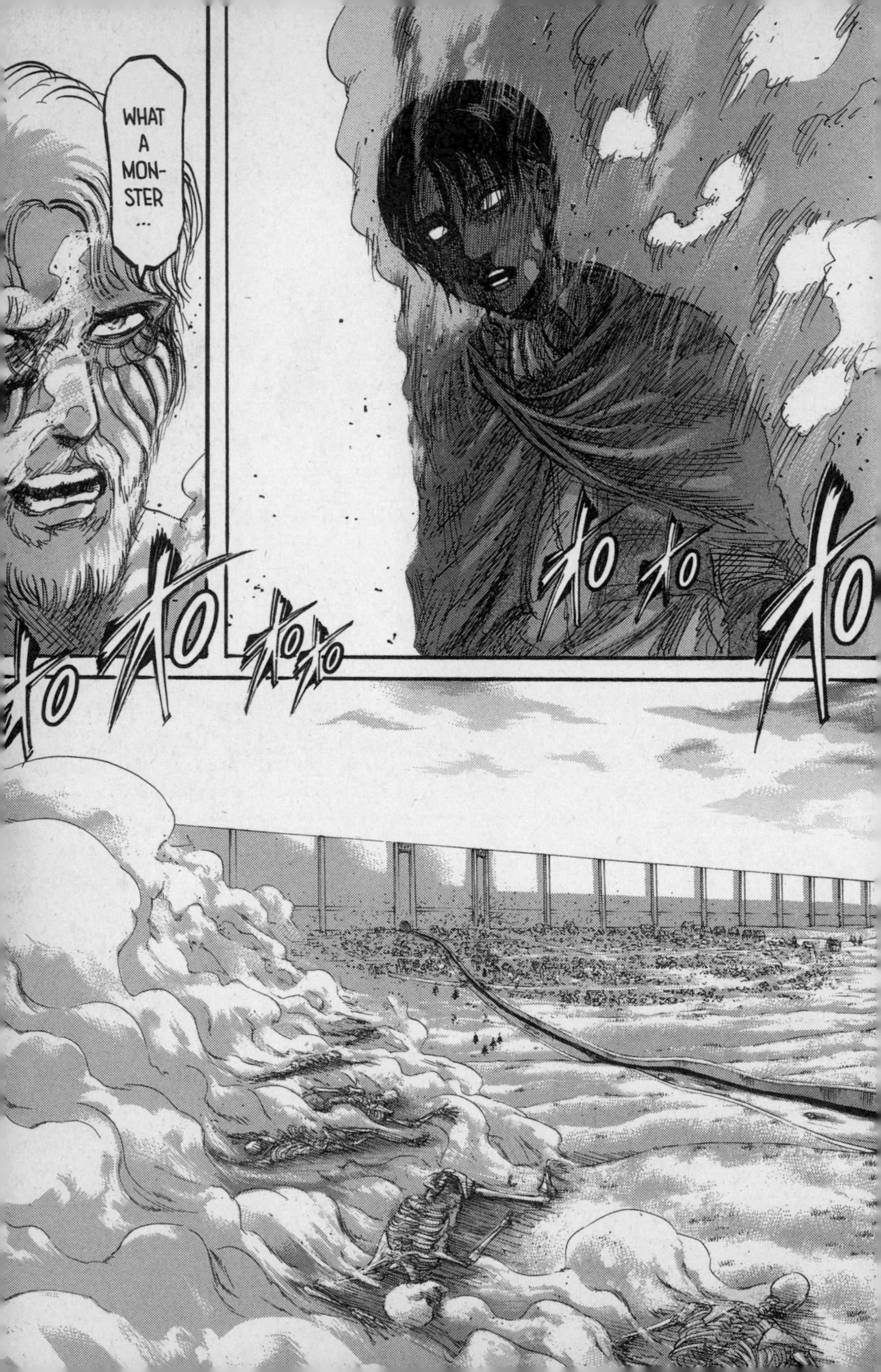
WHAT A MON-STER ...

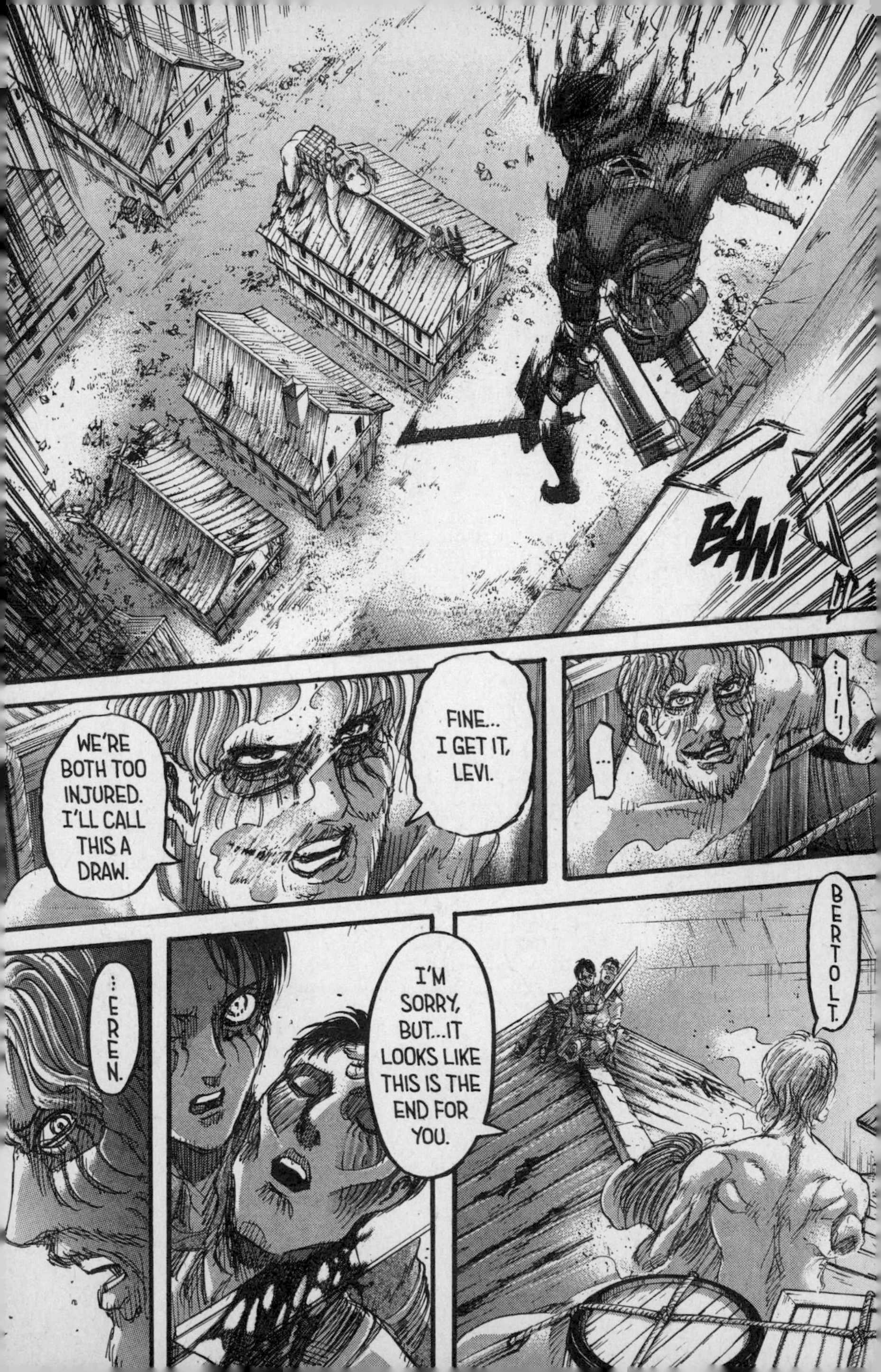
BAM
...!!
...
FINE... I GET IT, LEVI.
WE'RE BOTH TOO INJURED. I'LL CALL THIS A DRAW.
BERTOLT.
I'M SORRY, BUT...IT LOOKS LIKE THIS IS THE END FOR YOU.
...EREN.

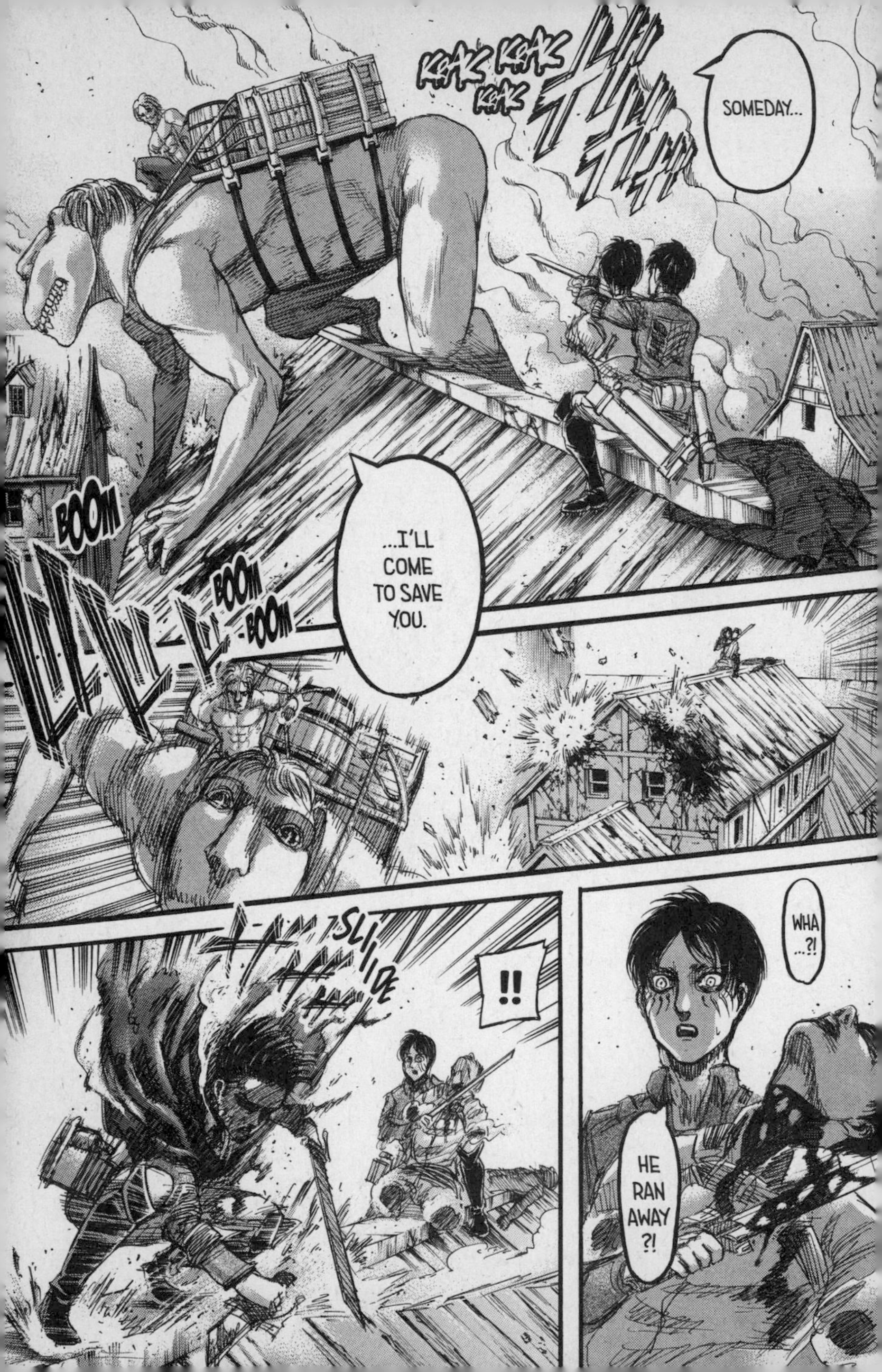
SOMEDAY...
...I'LL COME TO SAVE YOU.
BOOM
BOOM
-BOOM
WHA ...?!
HE RAN AWAY ?!
!!
SLIIIDE

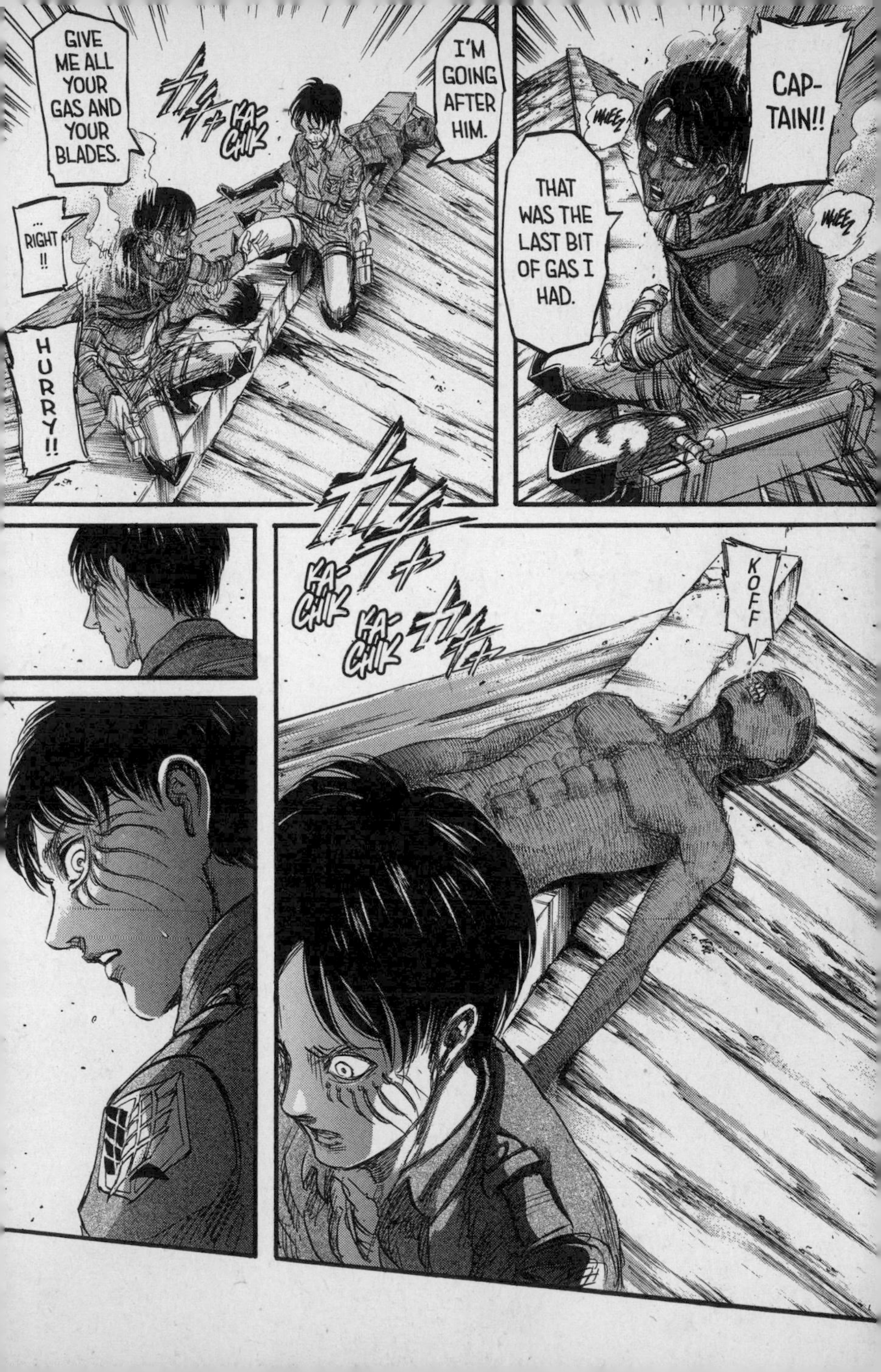
CAP-TAIN!!
WHEEZ
THAT WAS THE LAST BIT OF GAS I HAD.
WHEEZ
I'M GOING AFTER HIM.
KA-CHIK
GIVE ME ALL YOUR GAS AND YOUR BLADES.
...RIGHT!!
HURRY!!
KA-CHIK
KA-CHIK
KOFF

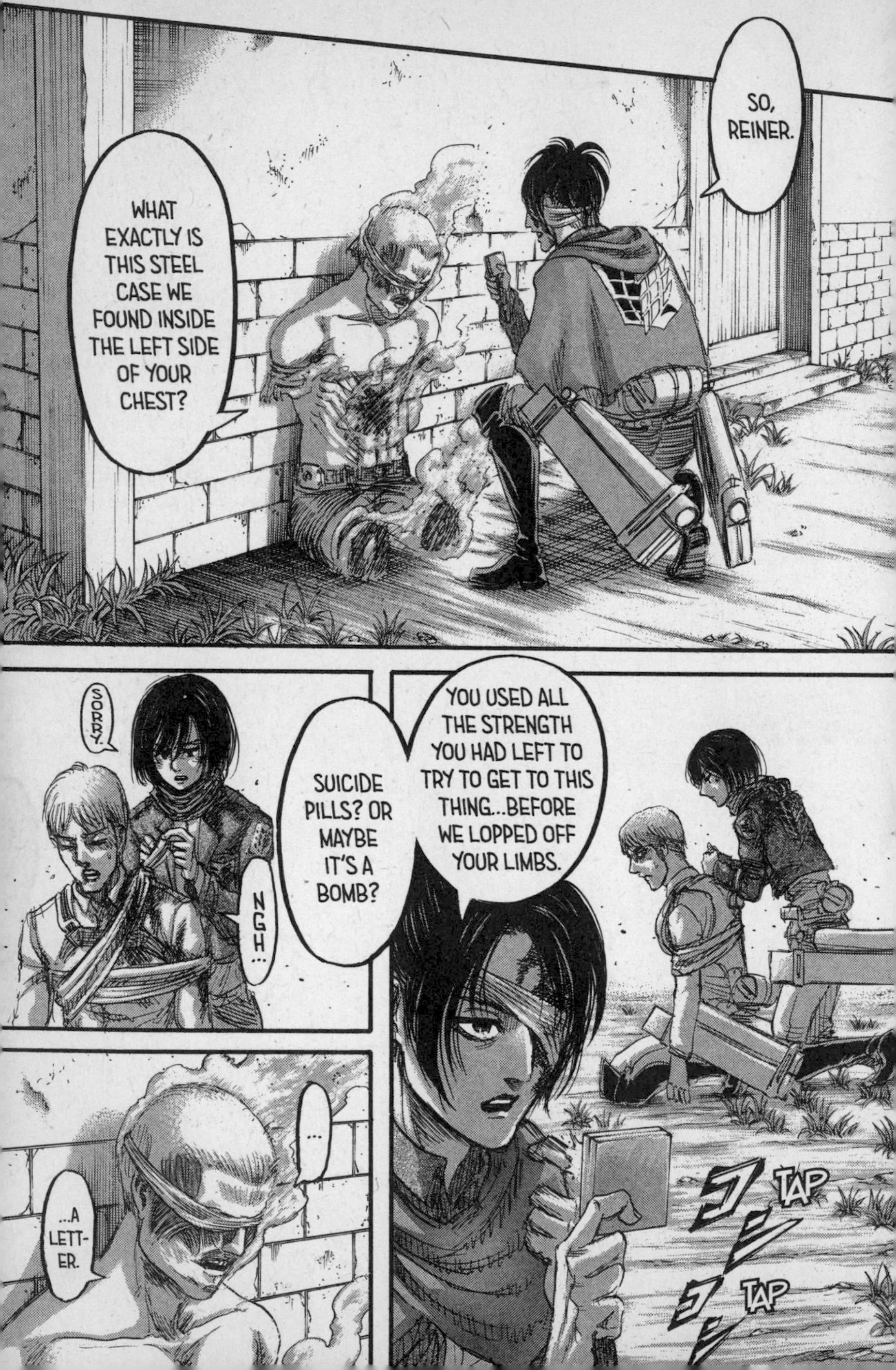
SO, REINER.
WHAT EXACTLY IS THIS STEEL CASE WE FOUND INSIDE THE LEFT SIDE OF YOUR CHEST?
YOU USED ALL THE STRENGTH YOU HAD LEFT TO TRY TO GET TO THIS THING...BEFORE WE LOPPED OFF YOUR LIMBS.
SUICIDE PILLS? OR MAYBE IT'S A BOMB?
TAP
TAP
SORRY.
NGH...
...
...A LETT-ER.

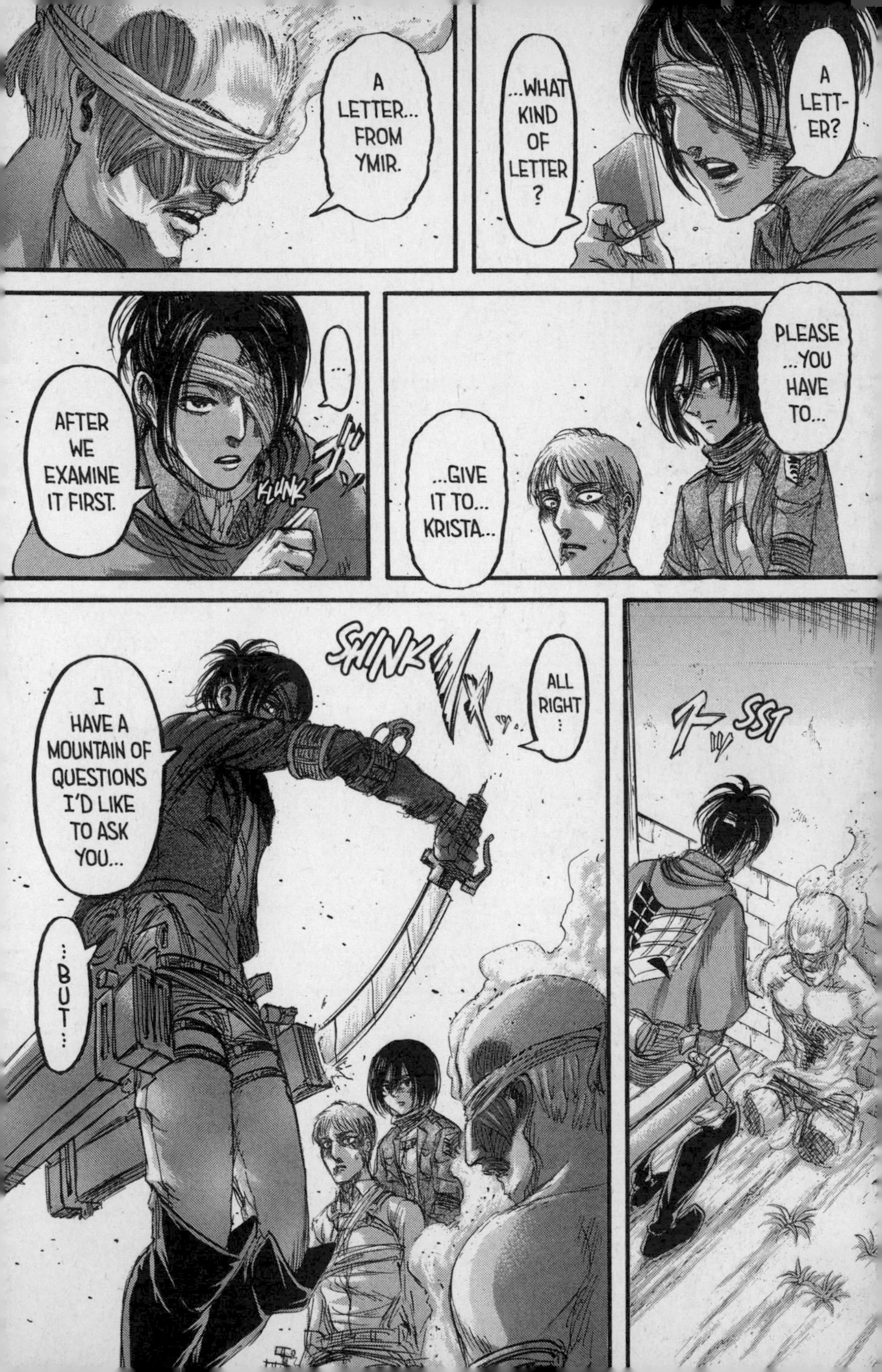
A LETTER?
...WHAT KIND OF LETTER?
A LETTER... FROM YMIR.
PLEASE ...YOU HAVE TO...
...GIVE IT TO... KRISTA...
...
KLUNK
AFTER WE EXAMINE IT FIRST.
SSST
SHINK
ALL RIGHT...
I HAVE A MOUNTAIN OF QUESTIONS I'D LIKE TO ASK YOU...
...BUT...

I WON-
DER...

YOUR MOUTH SEEMS TO BE AS HARD AS ARMOR.

...WILL YOU TELL US WHAT WE WANT TO KNOW?

THAT MAKES THIS JOB EASIER.

:THANKS.

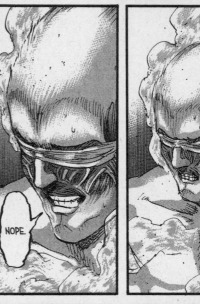

NOPE.

GRRK...

SHOVE

...WAIT, PLEASE!

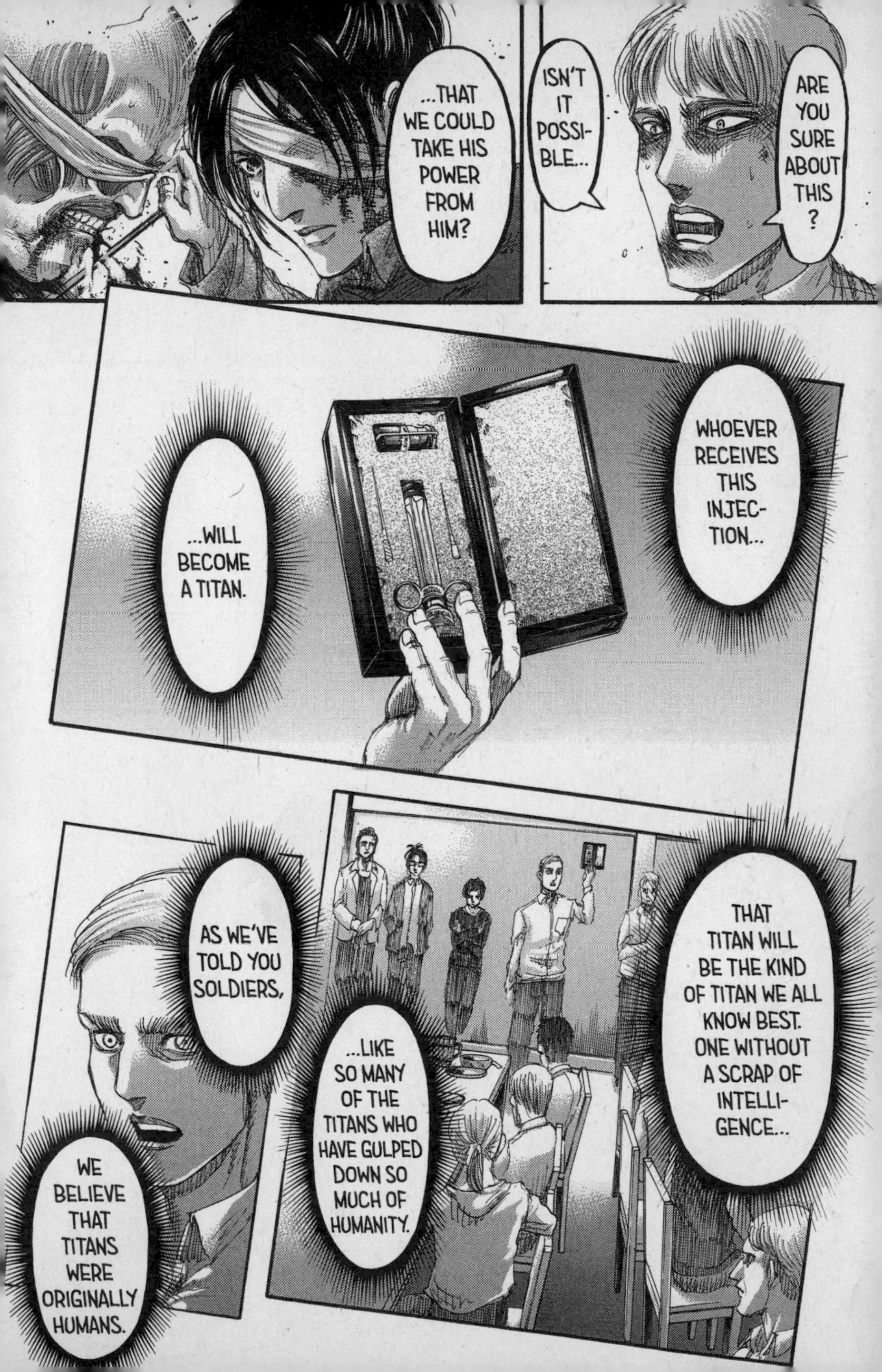
ARE YOU SURE ABOUT THIS?
ISN'T IT POSSIBLE...
...THAT WE COULD TAKE HIS POWER FROM HIM?
WHOEVER RECEIVES THIS INJECTION...
...WILL BECOME A TITAN.
THAT TITAN WILL BE THE KIND OF TITAN WE ALL KNOW BEST. ONE WITHOUT A SCRAP OF INTELLIGENCE...
...LIKE SO MANY OF THE TITANS WHO HAVE GULPED DOWN SO MUCH OF HUMANITY.
AS WE'VE TOLD YOU SOLDIERS,
WE BELIEVE THAT TITANS WERE ORIGINALLY HUMANS.

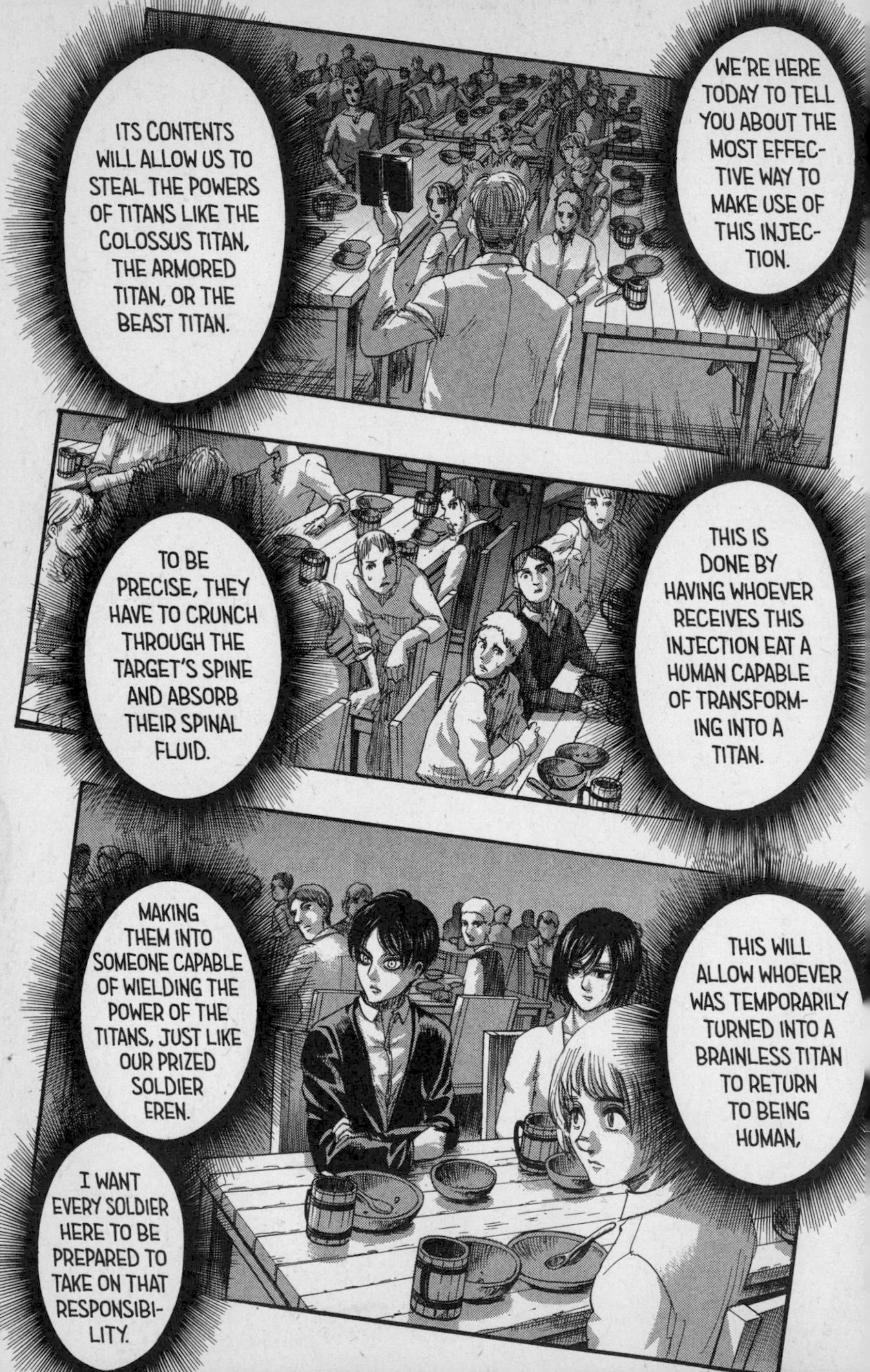
WE'RE HERE TODAY TO TELL YOU ABOUT THE MOST EFFECTIVE WAY TO MAKE USE OF THIS INJECTION.
ITS CONTENTS WILL ALLOW US TO STEAL THE POWERS OF TITANS LIKE THE COLOSSUS TITAN, THE ARMORED TITAN, OR THE BEAST TITAN.
THIS IS DONE BY HAVING WHOEVER RECEIVES THIS INJECTION EAT A HUMAN CAPABLE OF TRANSFORMING INTO A TITAN.
TO BE PRECISE, THEY HAVE TO CRUNCH THROUGH THE TARGET'S SPINE AND ABSORB THEIR SPINAL FLUID.
THIS WILL ALLOW WHOEVER WAS TEMPORARILY TURNED INTO A BRAINLESS TITAN TO RETURN TO BEING HUMAN,
MAKING THEM INTO SOMEONE CAPABLE OF WIELDING THE POWER OF THE TITANS, JUST LIKE OUR PRIZED SOLDIER EREN.
I WANT EVERY SOLDIER HERE TO BE PREPARED TO TAKE ON THAT RESPONSIBILITY.

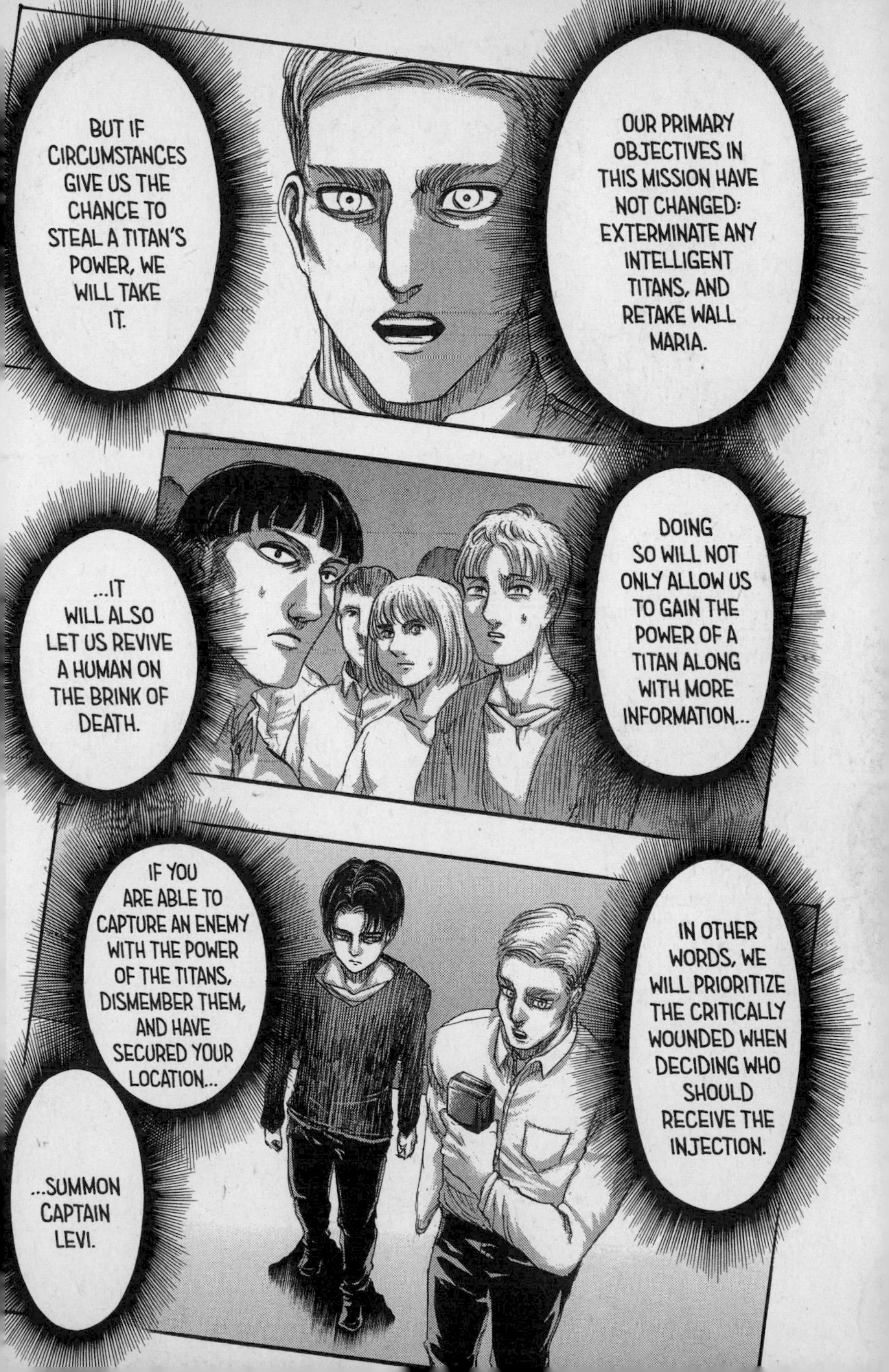
OUR PRIMARY OBJECTIVES IN THIS MISSION HAVE NOT CHANGED: EXTERMINATE ANY INTELLIGENT TITANS, AND RETAKE WALL MARIA.
BUT IF CIRCUMSTANCES GIVE US THE CHANCE TO STEAL A TITAN'S POWER, WE WILL TAKE IT.
DOING SO WILL NOT ONLY ALLOW US TO GAIN THE POWER OF A TITAN ALONG WITH MORE INFORMATION...
...IT WILL ALSO LET US REVIVE A HUMAN ON THE BRINK OF DEATH.
IN OTHER WORDS, WE WILL PRIORITIZE THE CRITICALLY WOUNDED WHEN DECIDING WHO SHOULD RECEIVE THE INJECTION.
IF YOU ARE ABLE TO CAPTURE AN ENEMY WITH THE POWER OF THE TITANS, DISMEMBER THEM, AND HAVE SECURED YOUR LOCATION...
...SUMMON CAPTAIN LEVI.

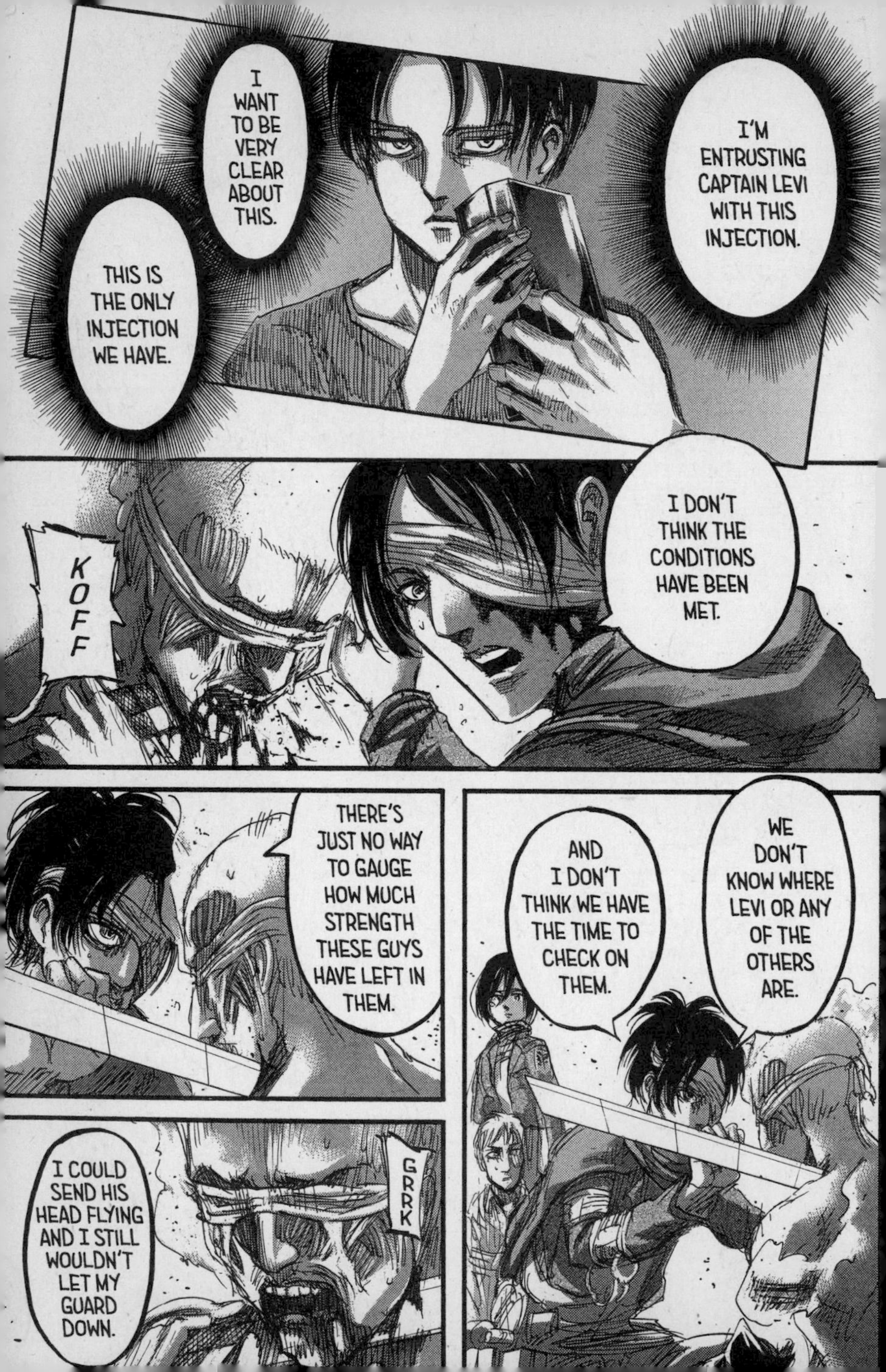
I'M ENTRUSTING CAPTAIN LEVI WITH THIS INJECTION.
I WANT TO BE VERY CLEAR ABOUT THIS.
THIS IS THE ONLY INJECTION WE HAVE.
I DON'T THINK THE CONDITIONS HAVE BEEN MET.
KOFF
WE DON'T KNOW WHERE LEVI OR ANY OF THE OTHERS ARE.
AND I DON'T THINK WE HAVE THE TIME TO CHECK ON THEM.
THERE'S JUST NO WAY TO GAUGE HOW MUCH STRENGTH THESE GUYS HAVE LEFT IN THEM.
GRRK
I COULD SEND HIS HEAD FLYING AND I STILL WOULDN'T LET MY GUARD DOWN.

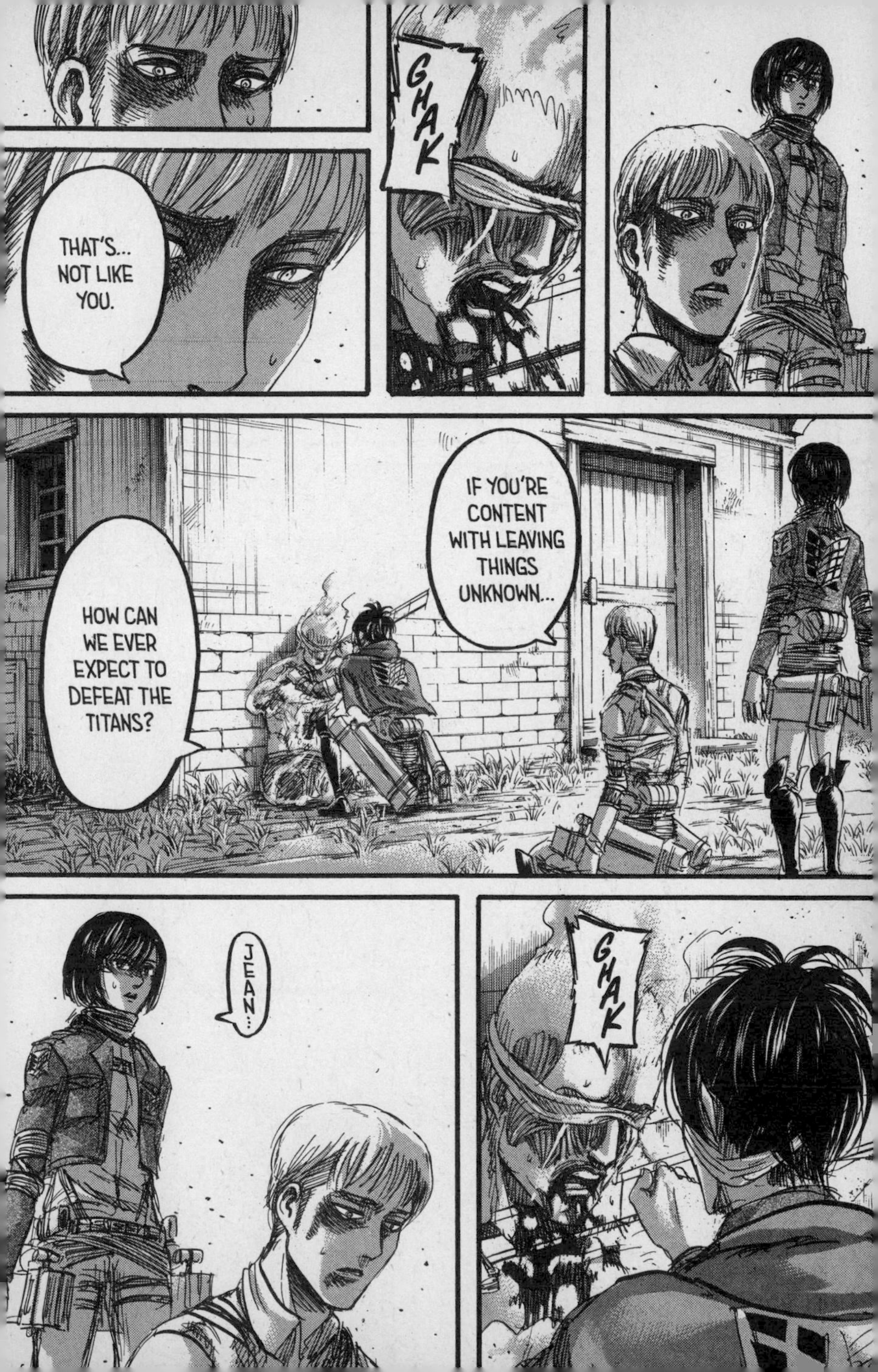
GHAK
THAT'S... NOT LIKE YOU.
IF YOU'RE CONTENT WITH LEAVING THINGS UNKNOWN...
HOW CAN WE EVER EXPECT TO DEFEAT THE TITANS?
GHAK
JEAN...

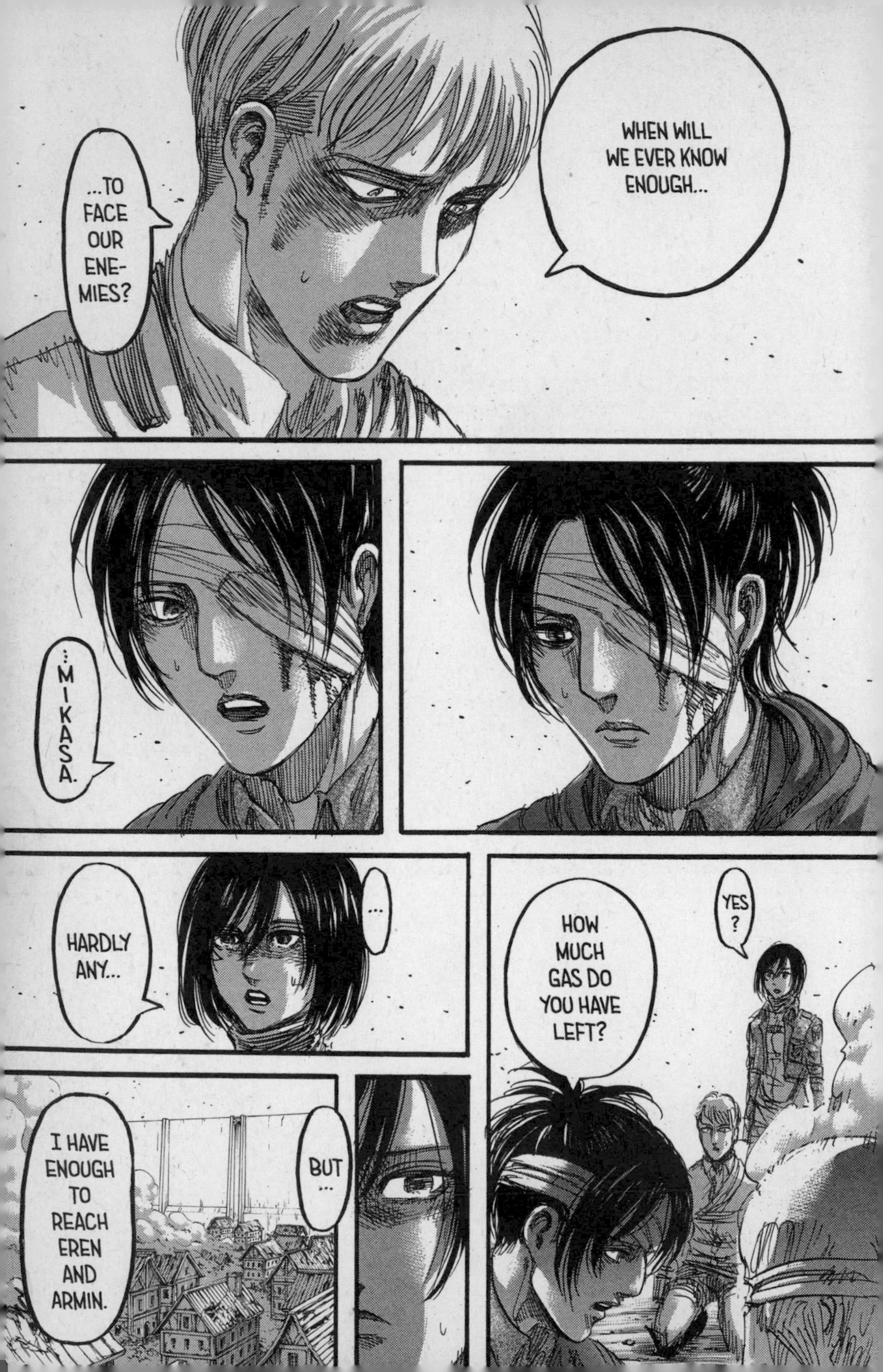
WHEN WILL WE EVER KNOW ENOUGH...
...TO FACE OUR ENEMIES?
...MIKASA.
YES?
HOW MUCH GAS DO YOU HAVE LEFT?
...
HARDLY ANY...
BUT...
I HAVE ENOUGH TO REACH EREN AND ARMIN.

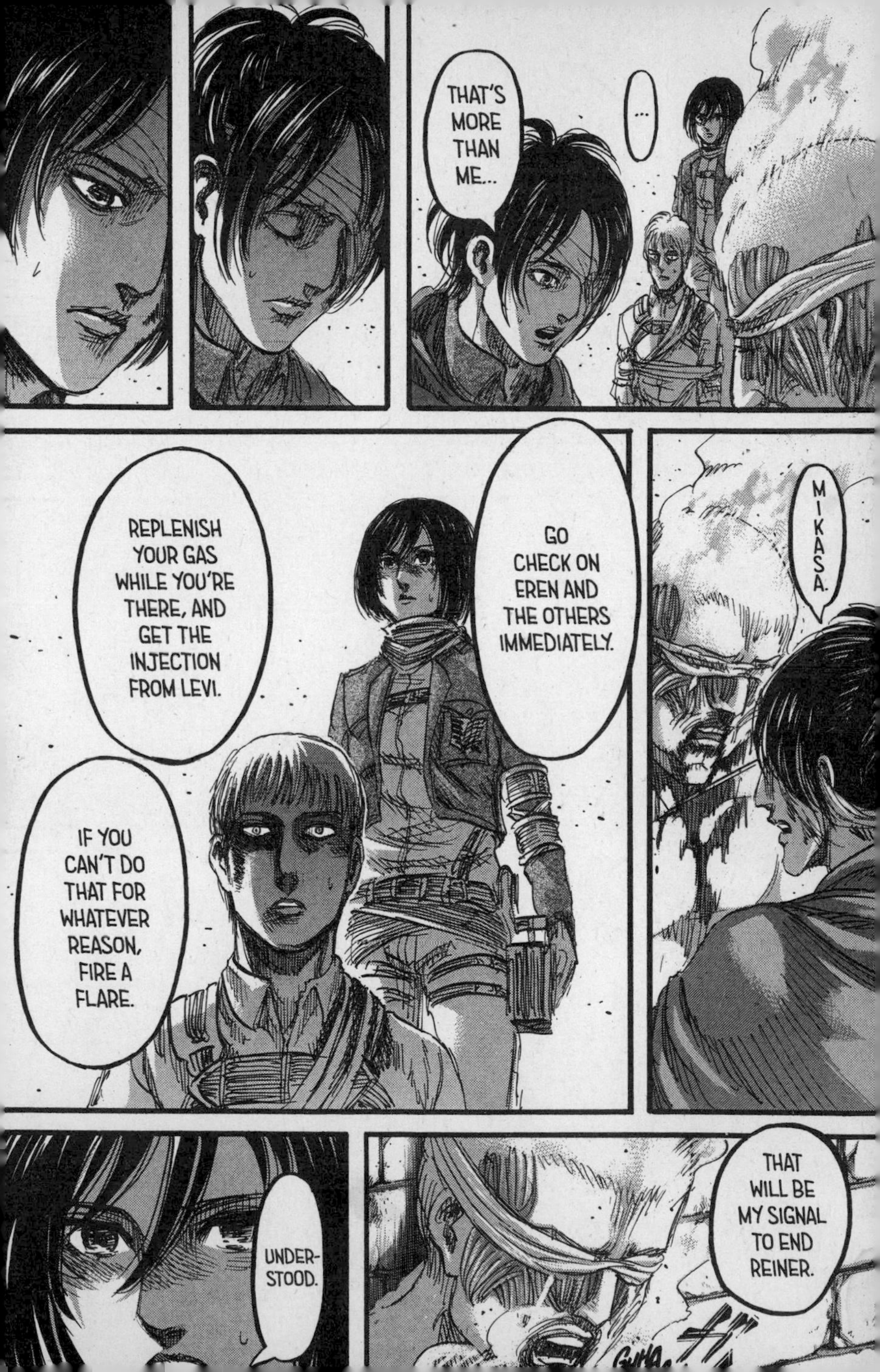
...
THAT'S MORE THAN ME...
MIKASA.
GO CHECK ON EREN AND THE OTHERS IMMEDIATELY.
REPLENISH YOUR GAS WHILE YOU'RE THERE, AND GET THE INJECTION FROM LEVI.
IF YOU CAN'T DO THAT FOR WHATEVER REASON, FIRE A FLARE.
THAT WILL BE MY SIGNAL TO END REINER.
UNDER-STOOD.

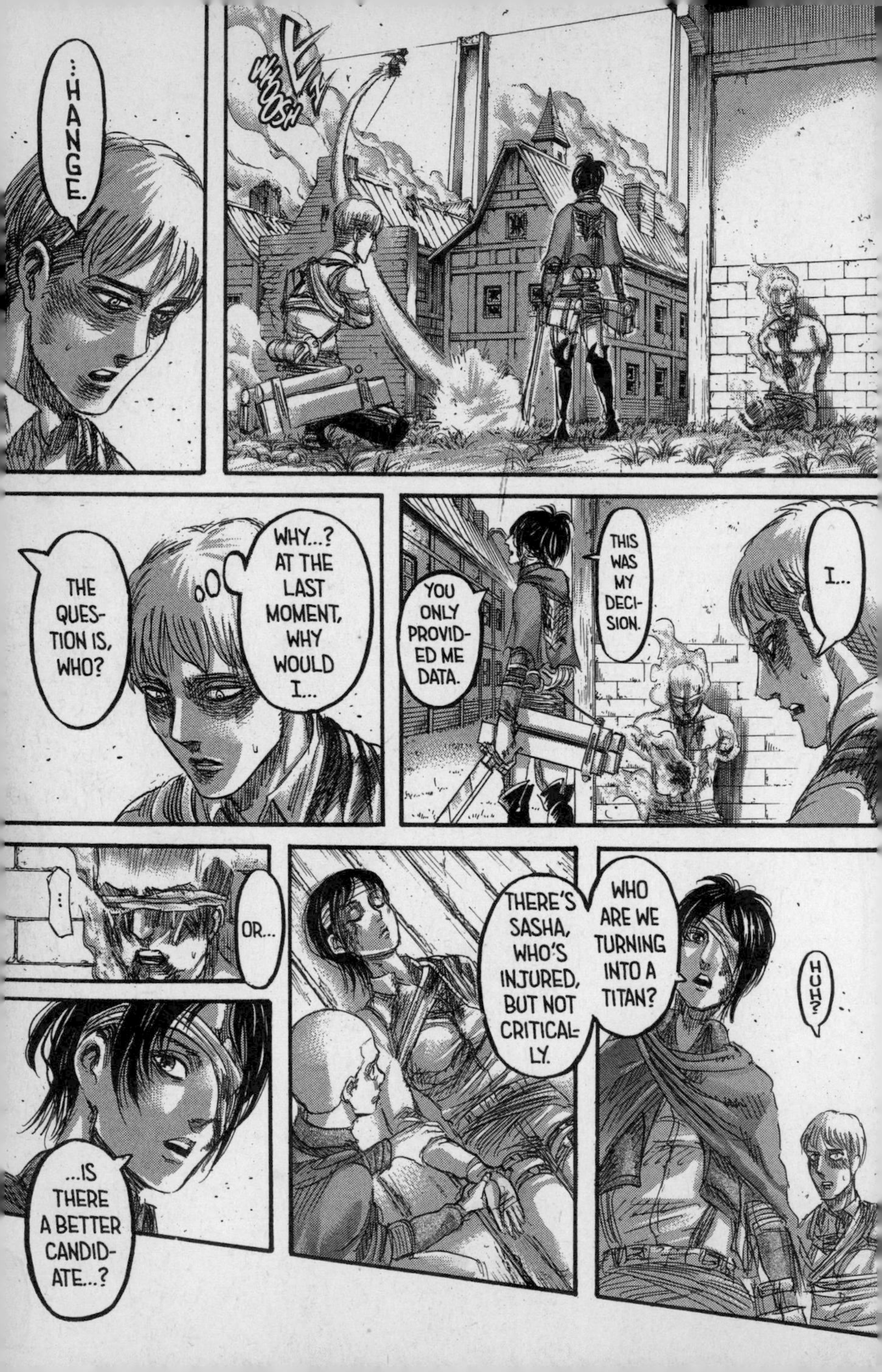
WHOOSH
...HANGE.
I...
THIS WAS MY DECISION.
YOU ONLY PROVIDED ME DATA.
WHY...? AT THE LAST MOMENT, WHY WOULD I...
THE QUESTION IS, WHO?
HUH?
WHO ARE WE TURNING INTO A TITAN?
THERE'S SASHA, WHO'S INJURED, BUT NOT CRITICALLY.
OR...
...
...IS THERE A BETTER CANDIDATE...?

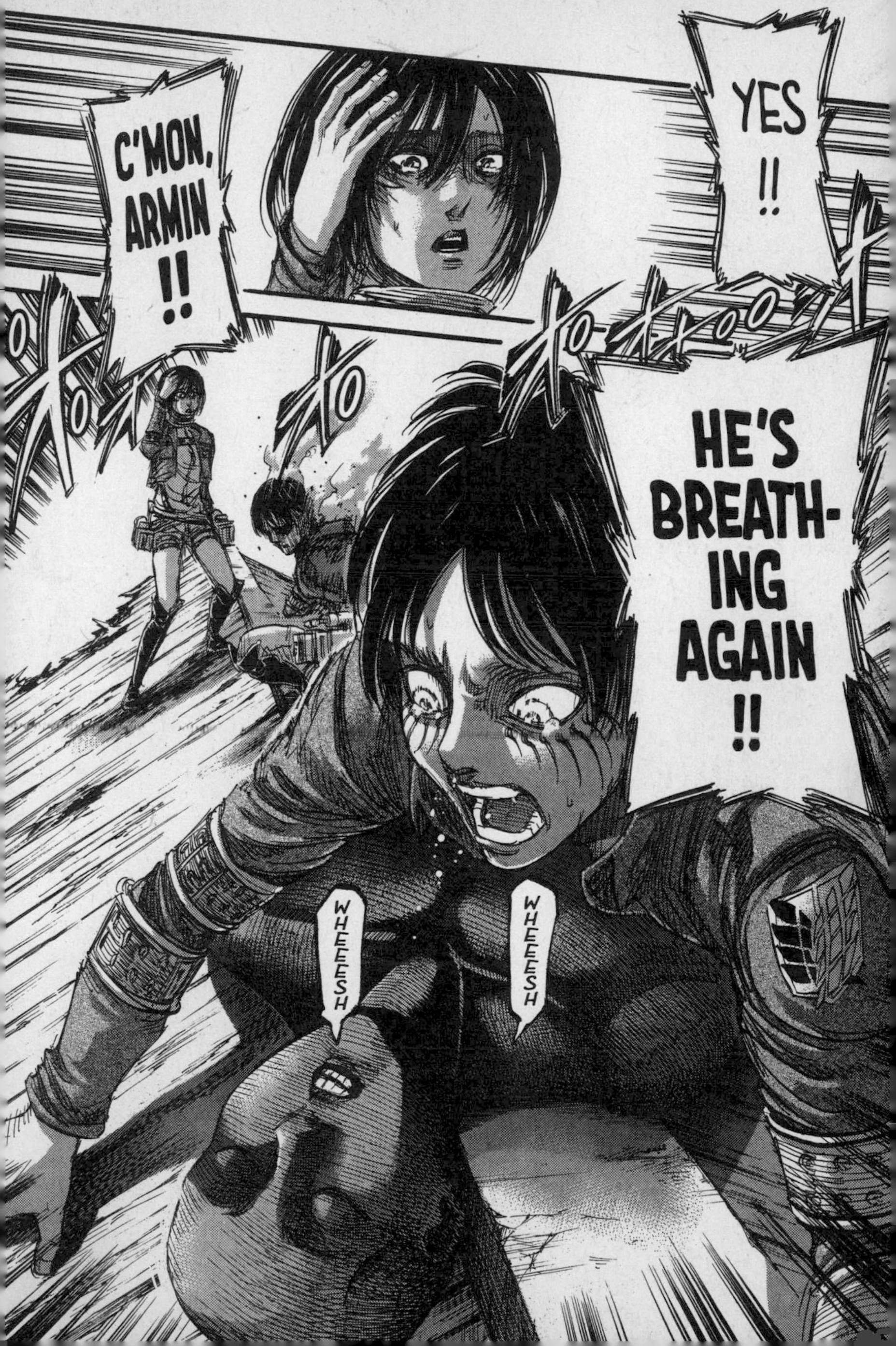
YES !!
C'MON, ARMIN !!
HE'S BREATH-ING AGAIN !!
WHEEEESH
WHEEEESH

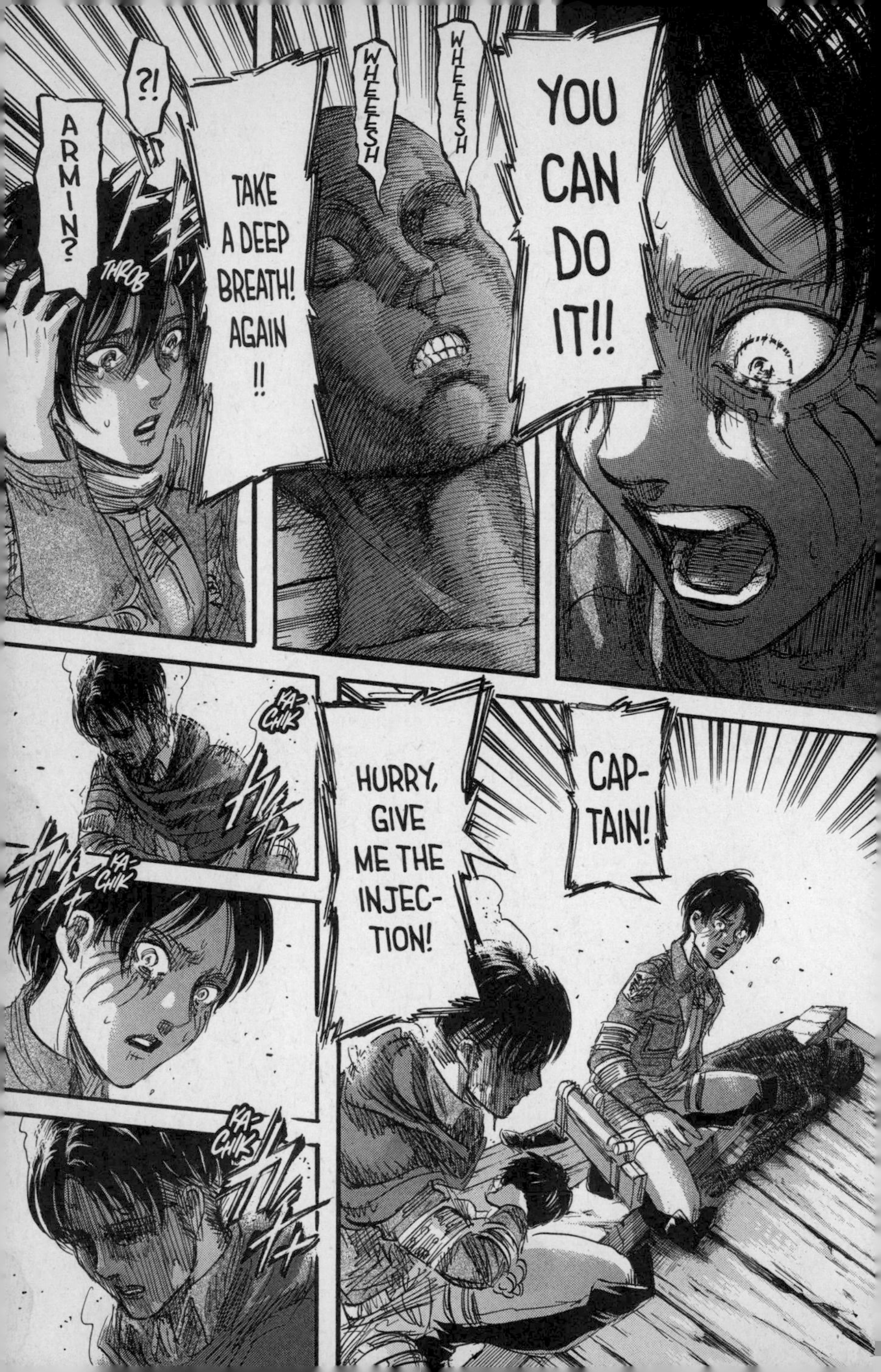
YOU CAN DO IT!!
WHEEEESH
WHEEEESH
TAKE A DEEP BREATH! AGAIN!!
?!
ARMIN?
THROB
CAPTAIN!
HURRY, GIVE ME THE INJECTION!
KA-CHIK
KA-CHIK
KA-CHIK

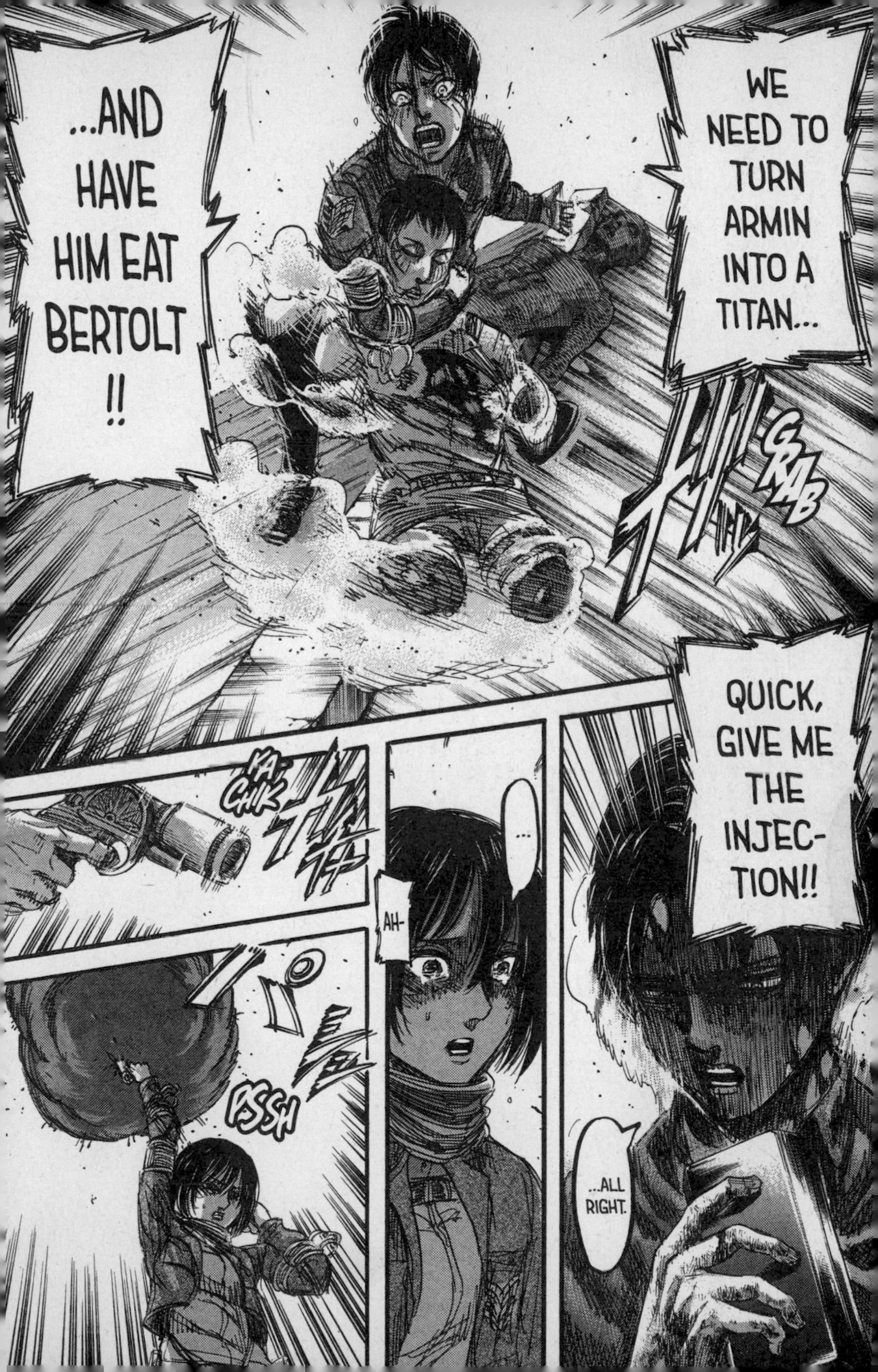
WE NEED TO TURN ARMIN INTO A TITAN...
...AND HAVE HIM EAT BERTOLT!!
GRAB
QUICK, GIVE ME THE INJECTION!!
...ALL RIGHT.
...
AH-
KA-CHIK
PSSH

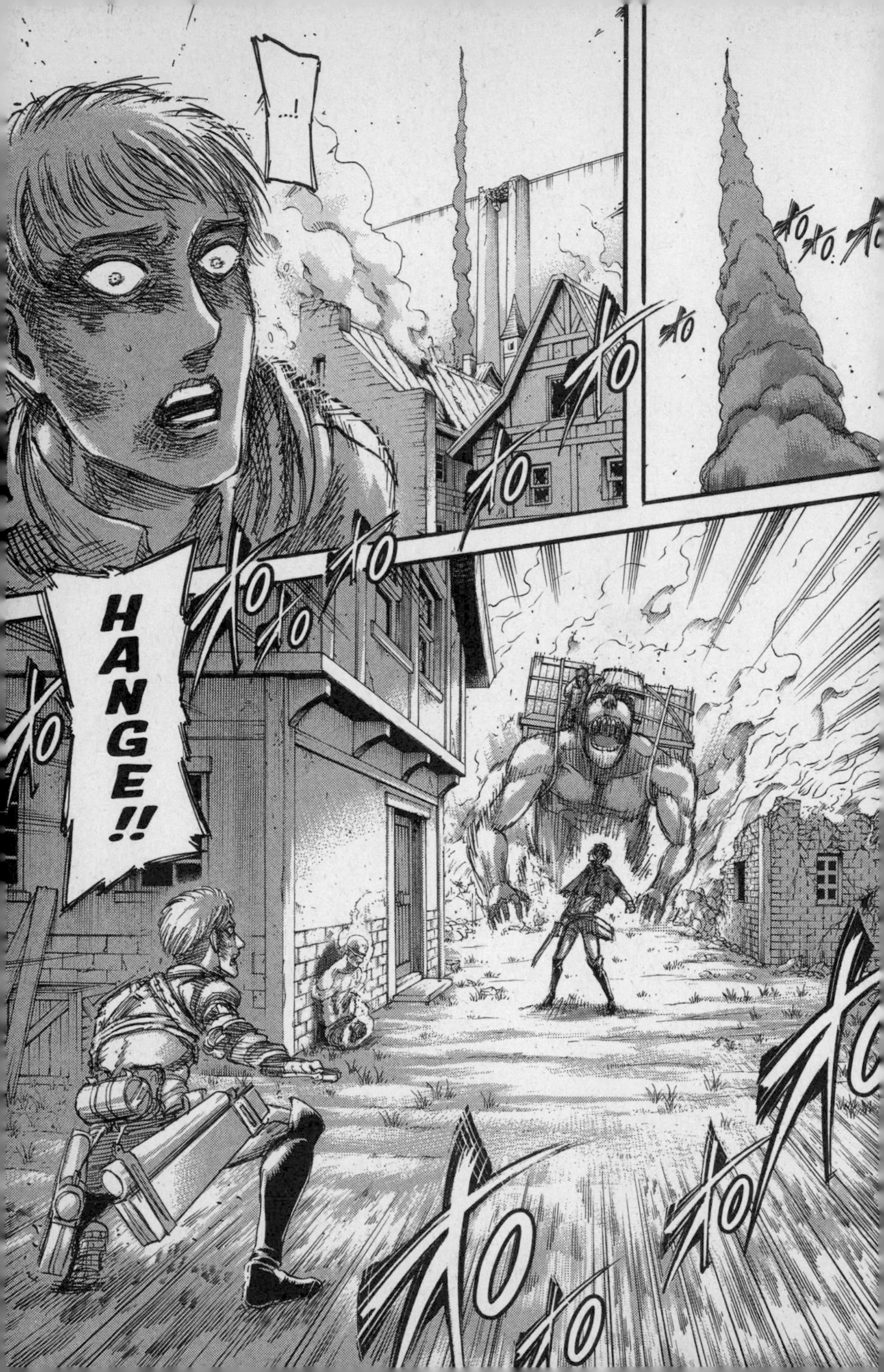
...!
HANGE!!

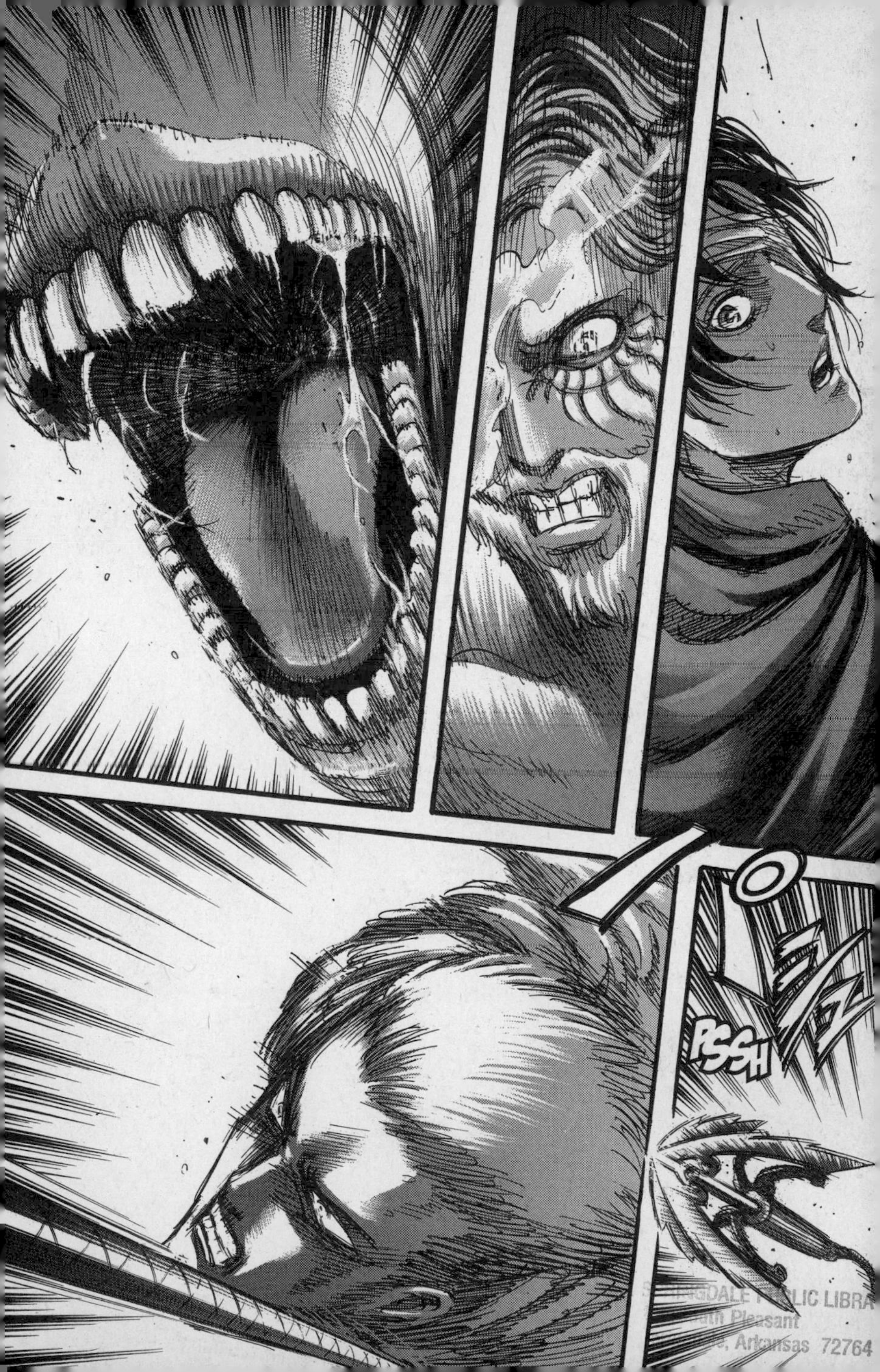
PSSH

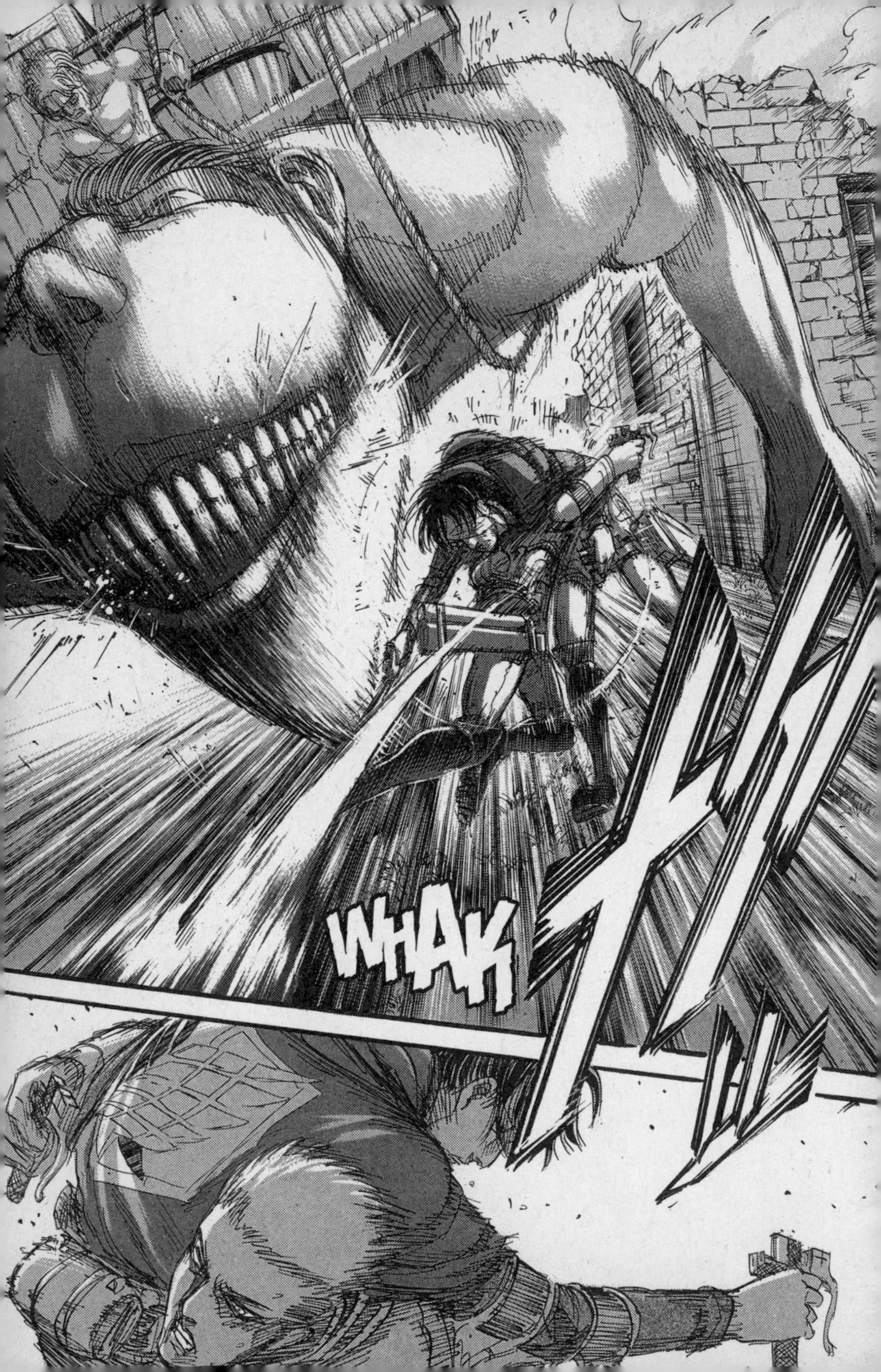
WHAK

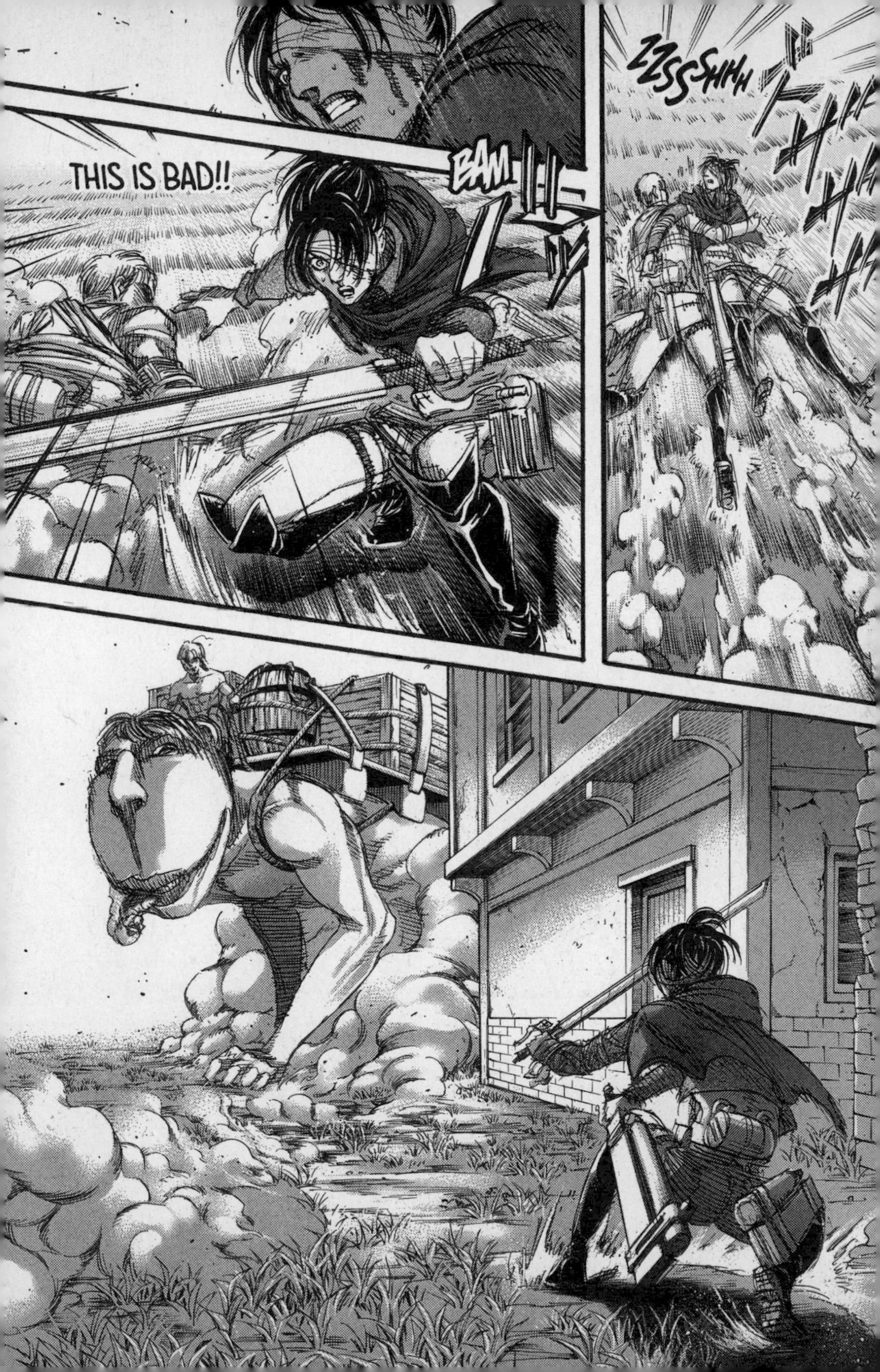
ZZSSSHHH
BAM
THIS IS BAD!!

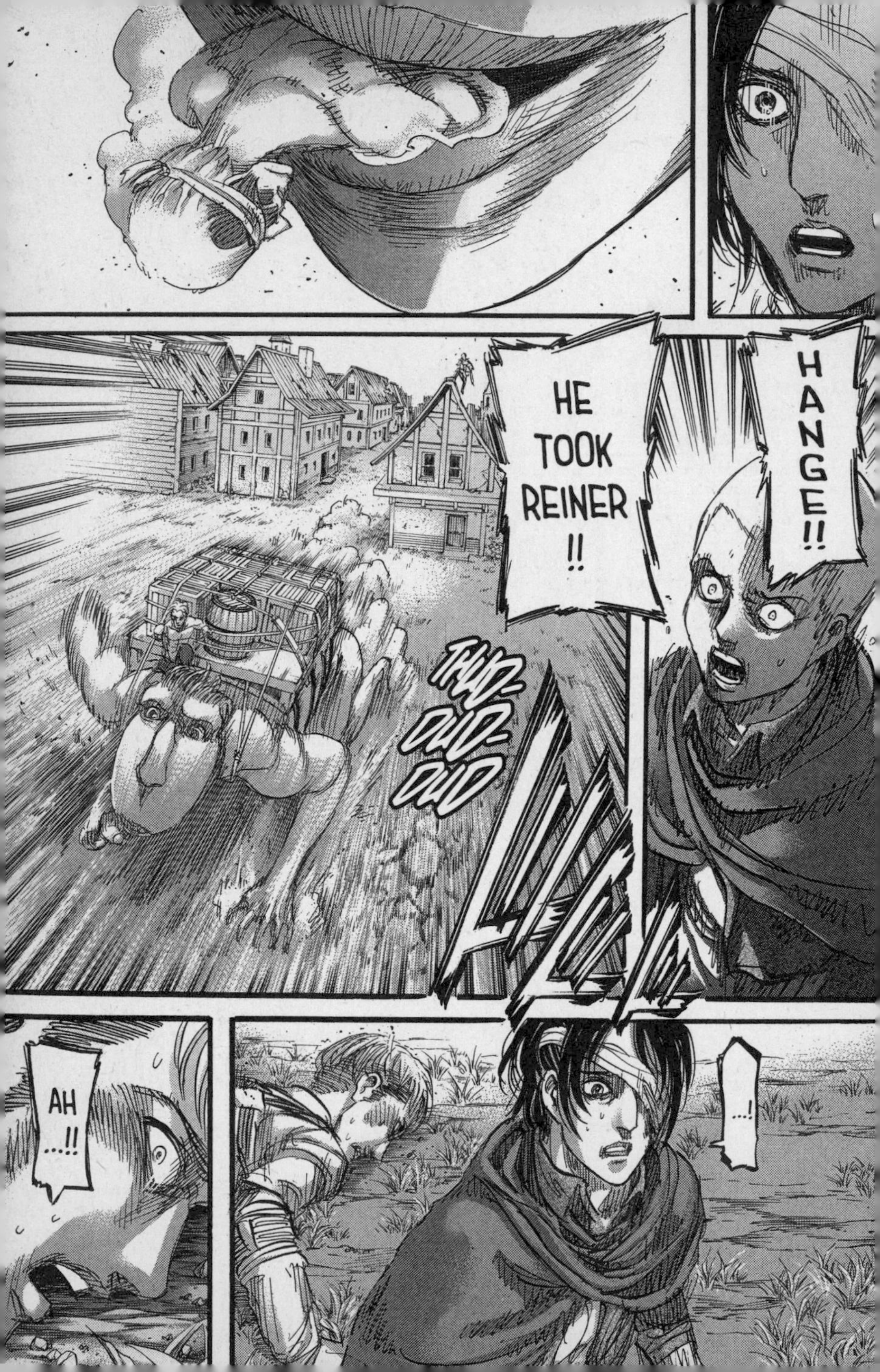
HANGE!!
HE TOOK REINER !!
THUD-DUD-DUD
...!
AH ...!!

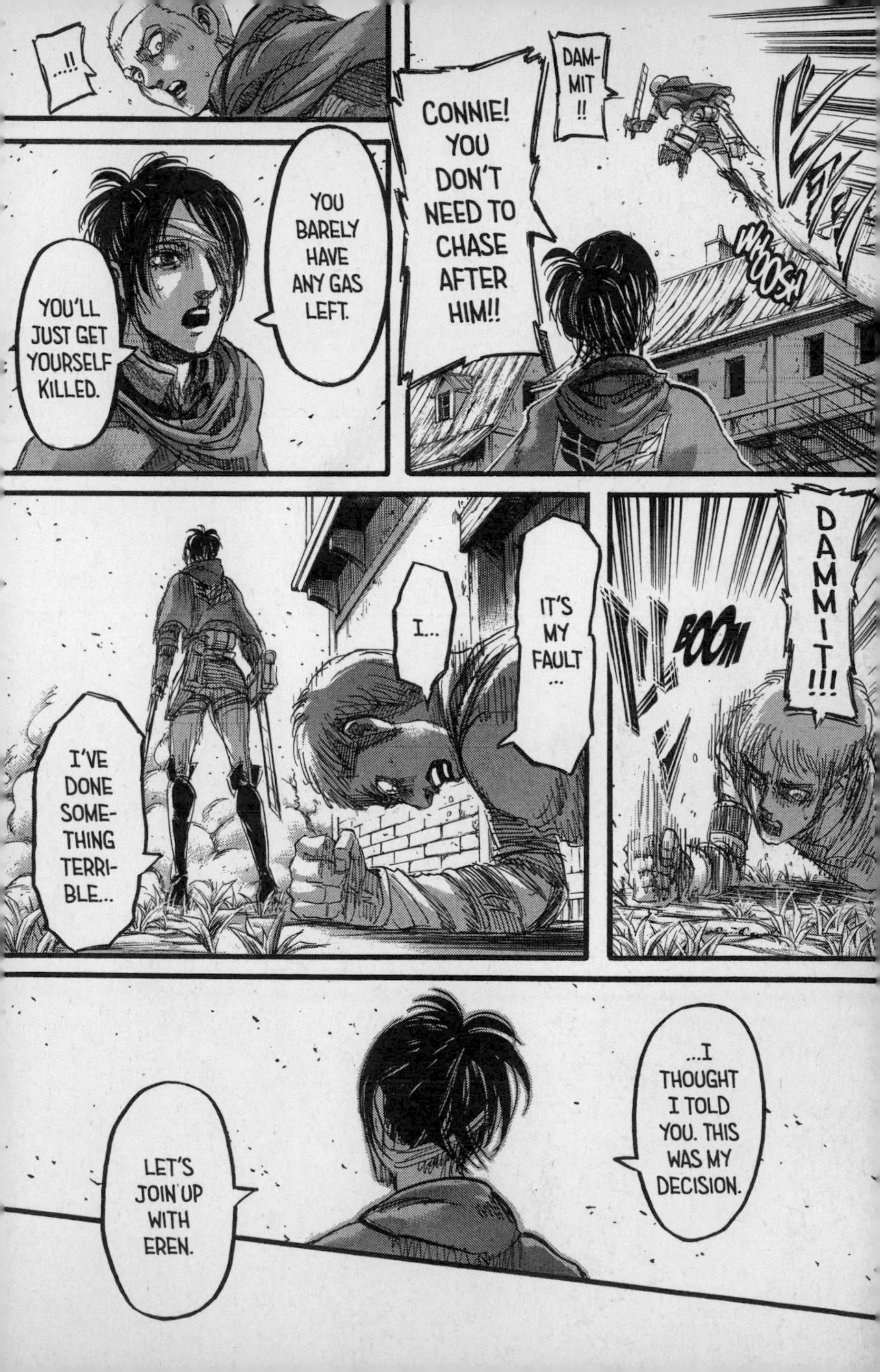
DAM-MIT!!
CONNIE! YOU DON'T NEED TO CHASE AFTER HIM!!
WHOOSH
...!!
YOU BARELY HAVE ANY GAS LEFT.
YOU'LL JUST GET YOURSELF KILLED.
DAMMIT!!!
BOOM
IT'S MY FAULT...
I...
I'VE DONE SOME-THING TERRI-BLE...
...I THOUGHT I TOLD YOU. THIS WAS MY DECISION.
LET'S JOIN UP WITH EREN.

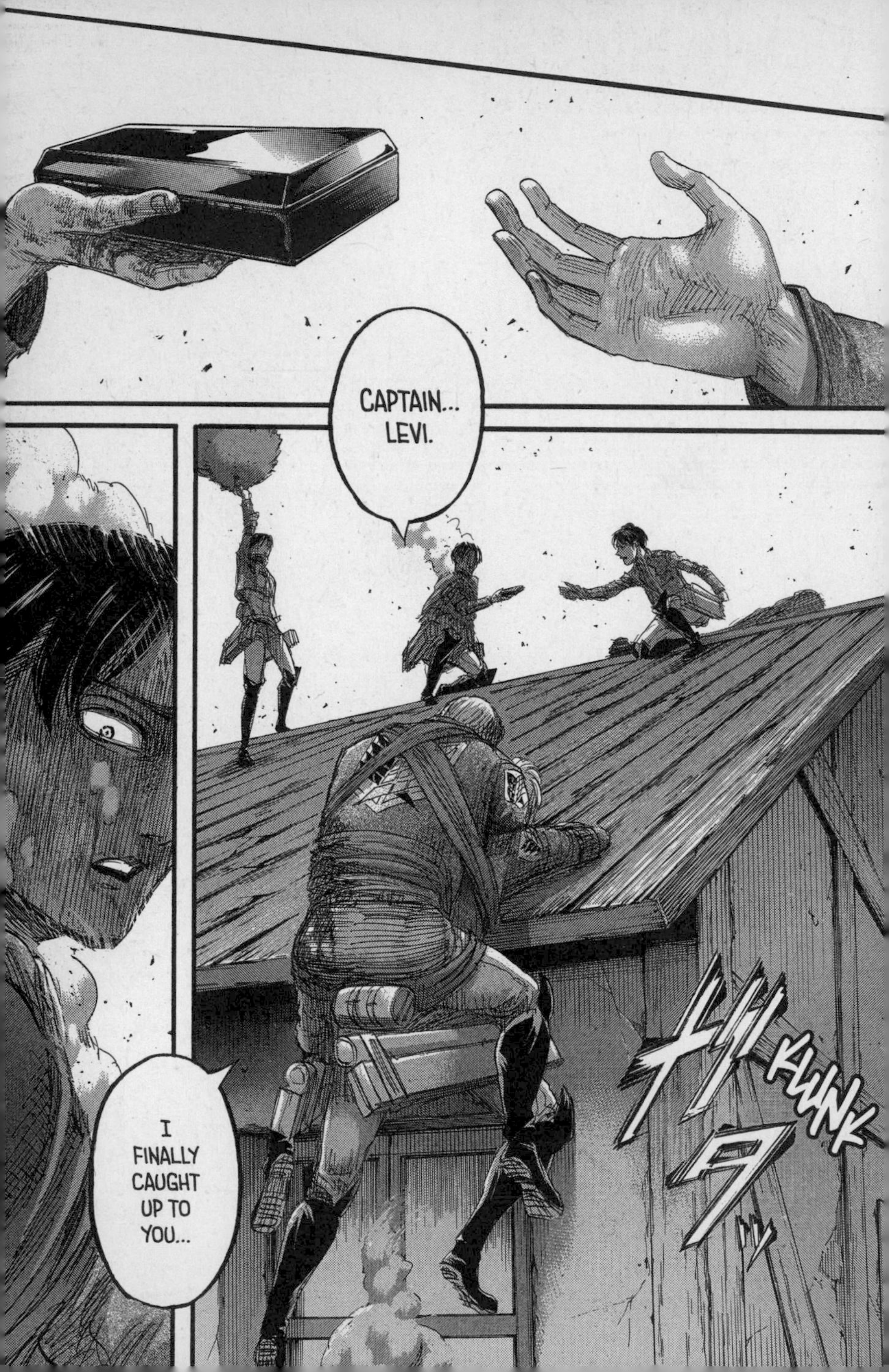
CAPTAIN... LEVI.
KLUNK
I FINALLY CAUGHT UP TO YOU...

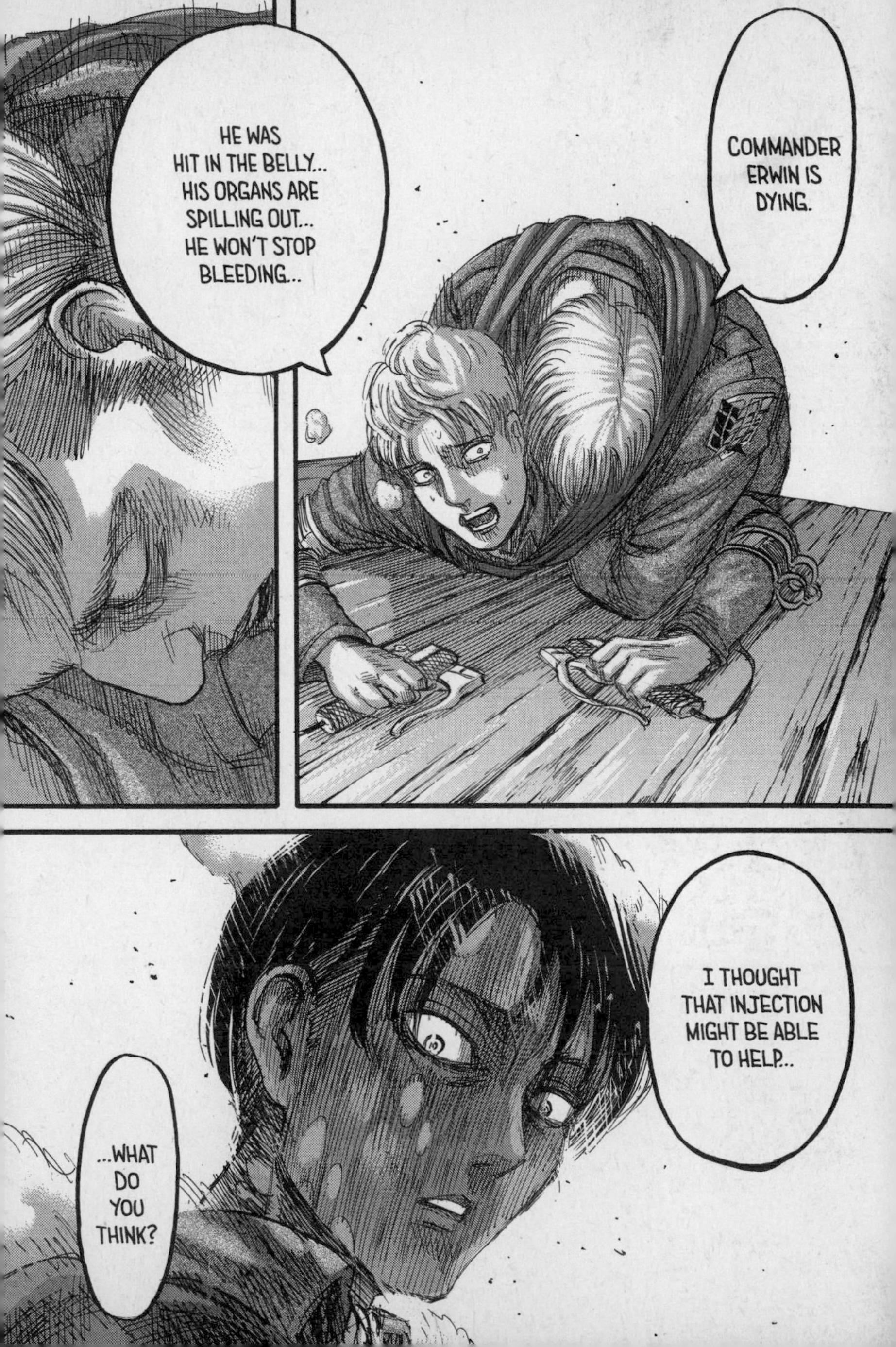
COMMANDER ERWIN IS DYING.
HE WAS HIT IN THE BELLY... HIS ORGANS ARE SPILLING OUT... HE WON'T STOP BLEEDING...
I THOUGHT THAT INJECTION MIGHT BE ABLE TO HELP...
...WHAT DO YOU THINK?

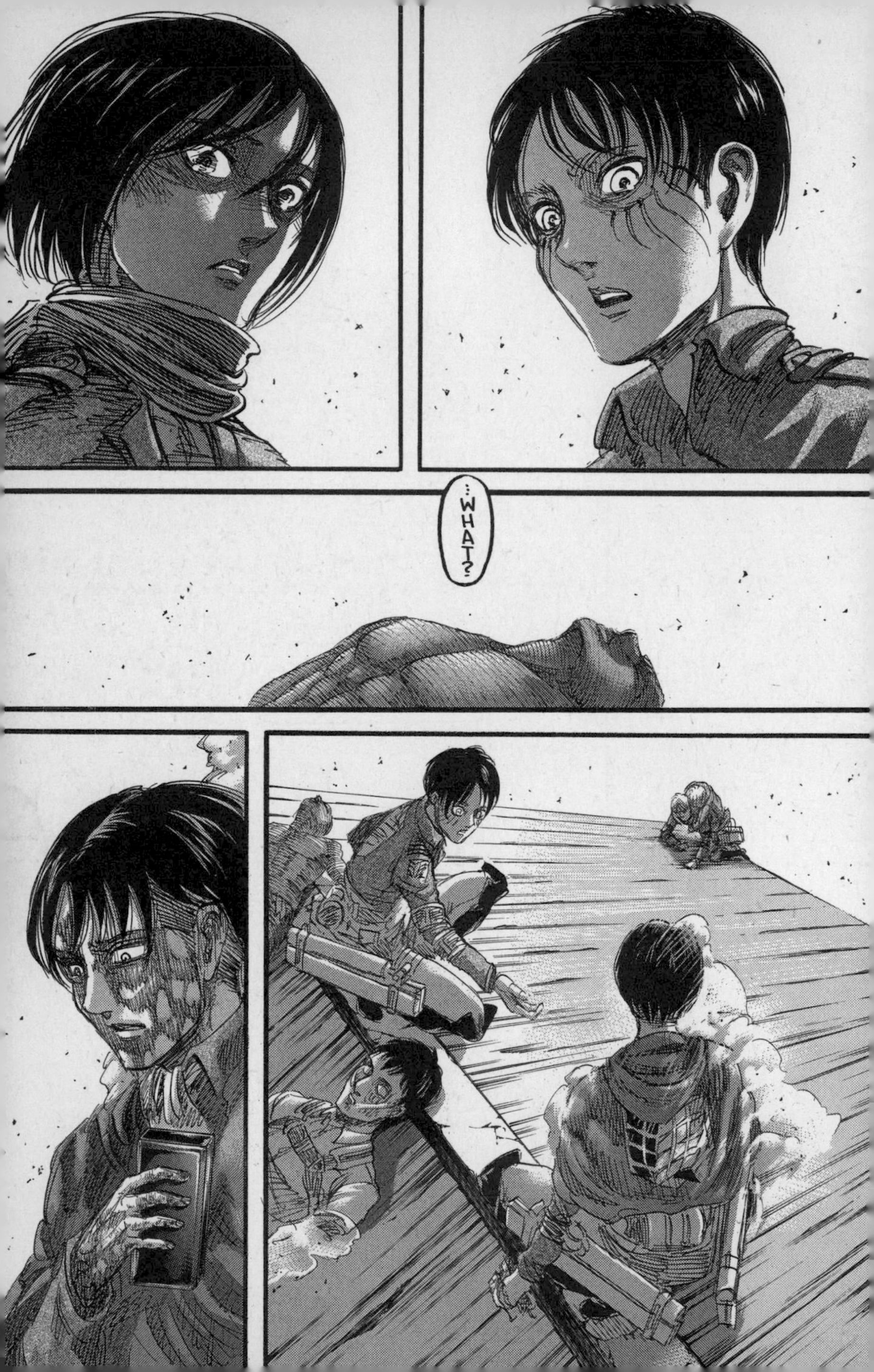
...WHAT?

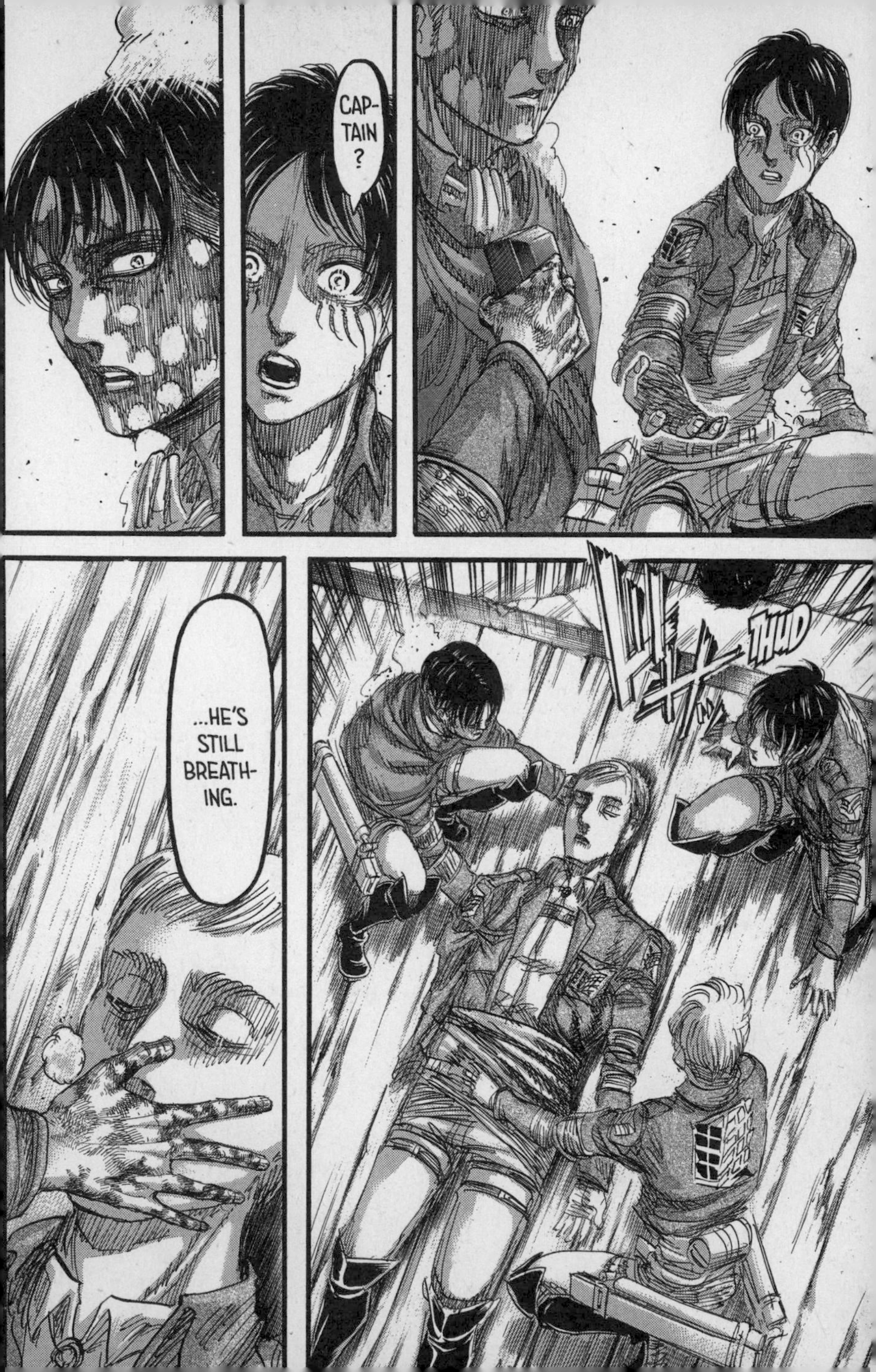
CAP-
TAIN
?
THUD
...HE'S
STILL
BREATH-
ING.

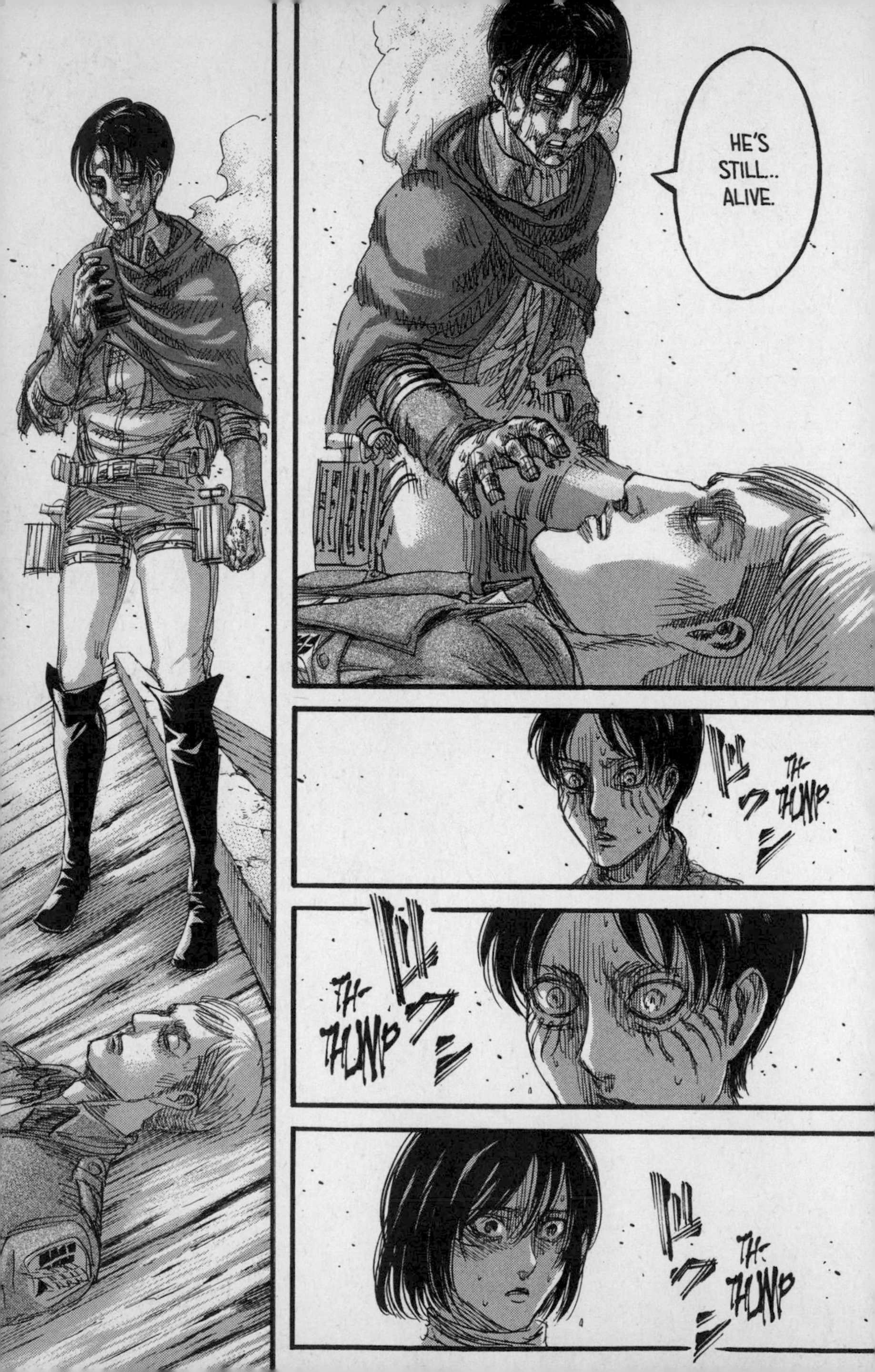
HE'S STILL... ALIVE.
TH-THUMP
TH-THUMP
TH-THUMP

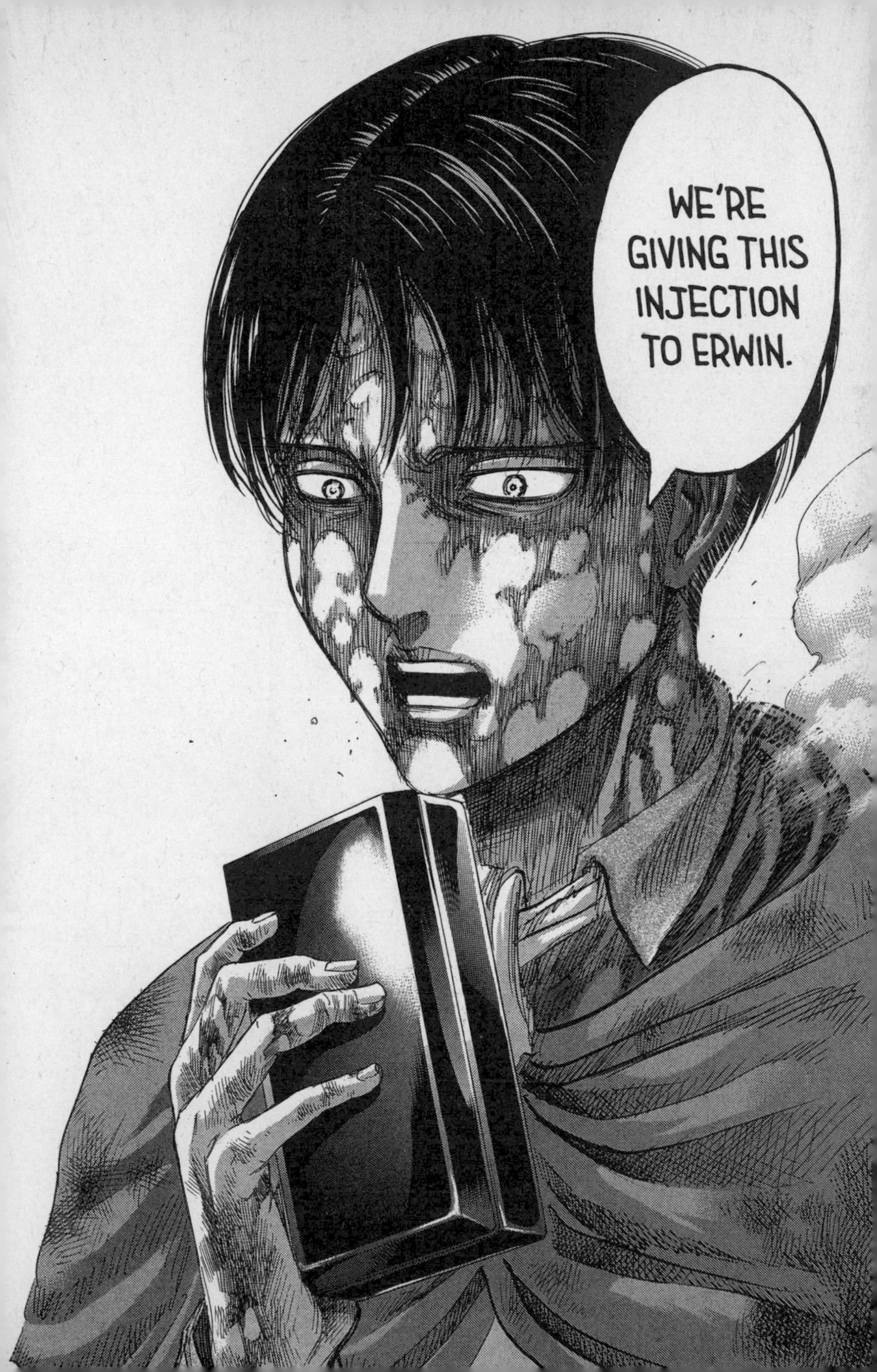
WE'RE GIVING THIS INJECTION TO ERWIN.

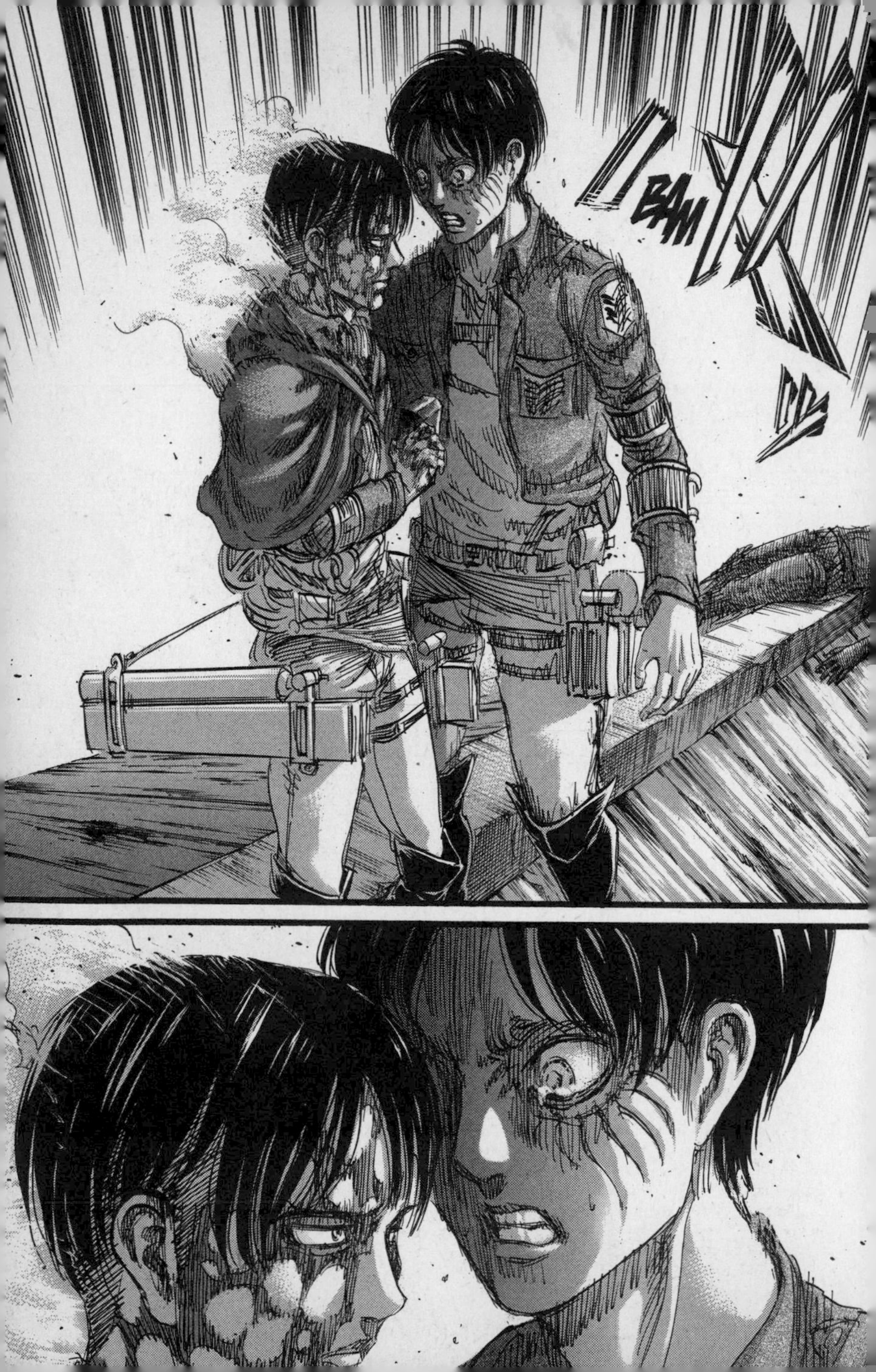
BAM

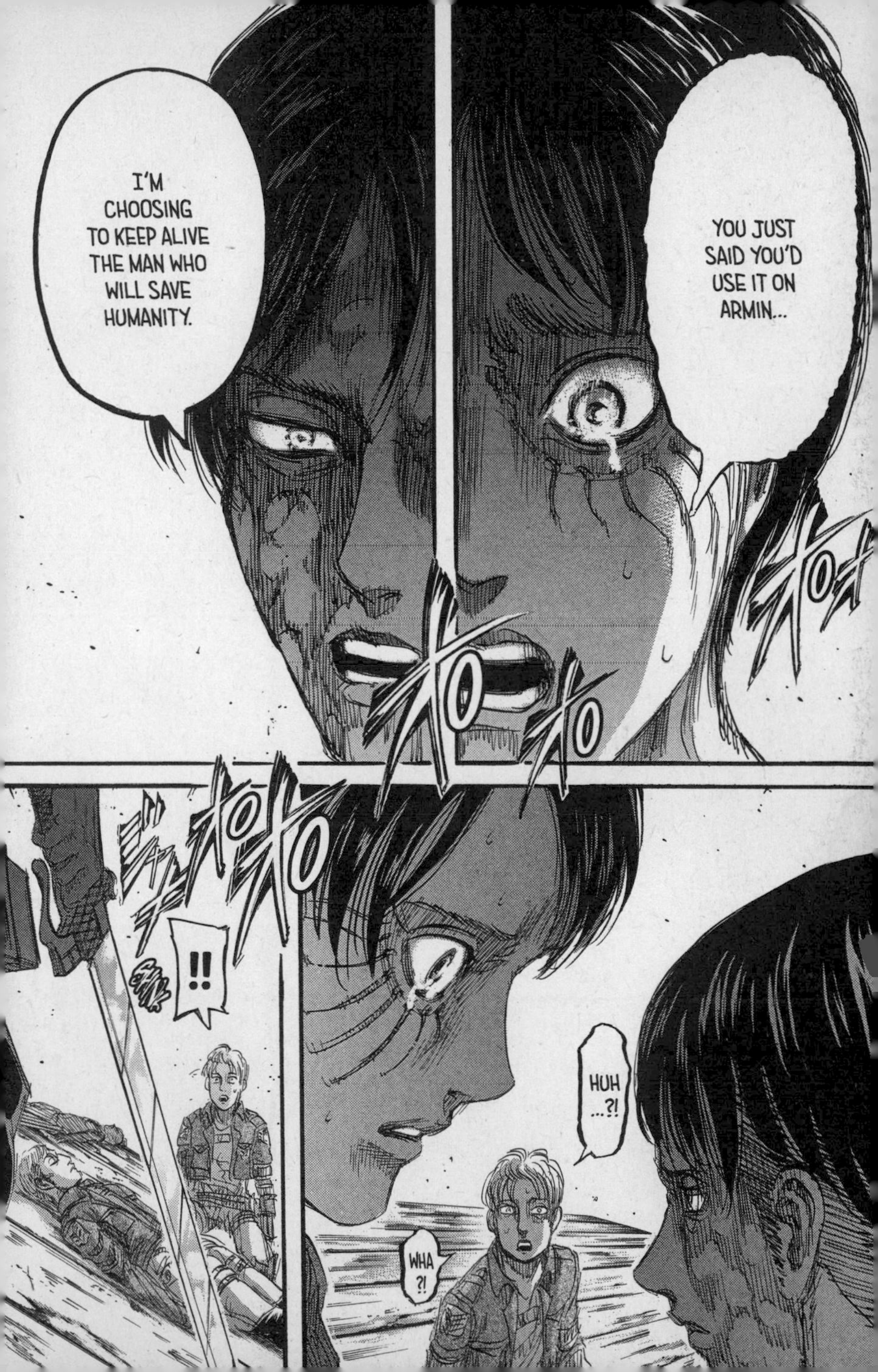
YOU JUST SAID YOU'D USE IT ON ARMIN...
I'M CHOOSING TO KEEP ALIVE THE MAN WHO WILL SAVE HUMANITY.
HUH ...?!
WHA ?!
!!

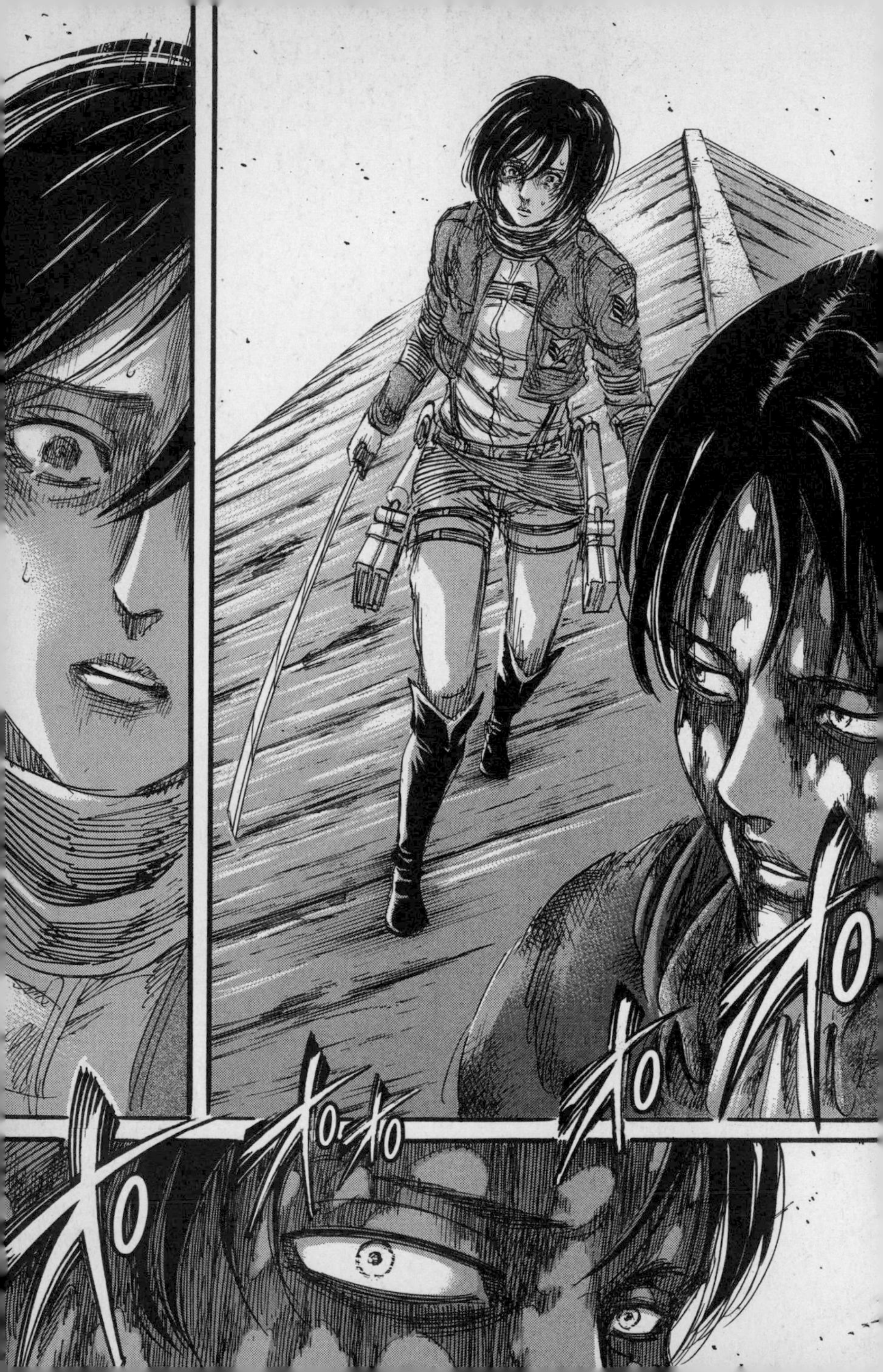

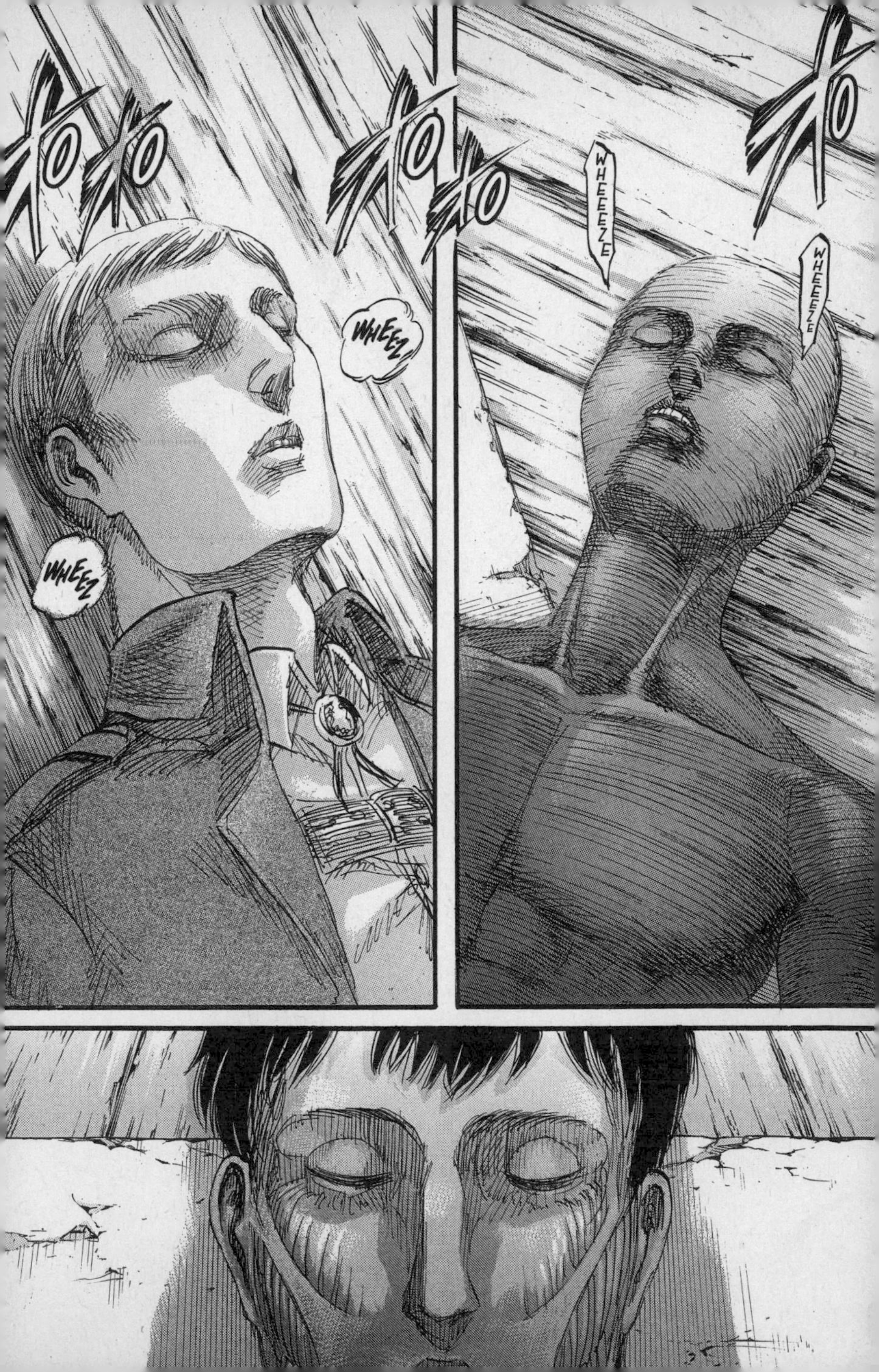
WHEEEZE
WHEEEEZE
WHEEZ
WHEEZ

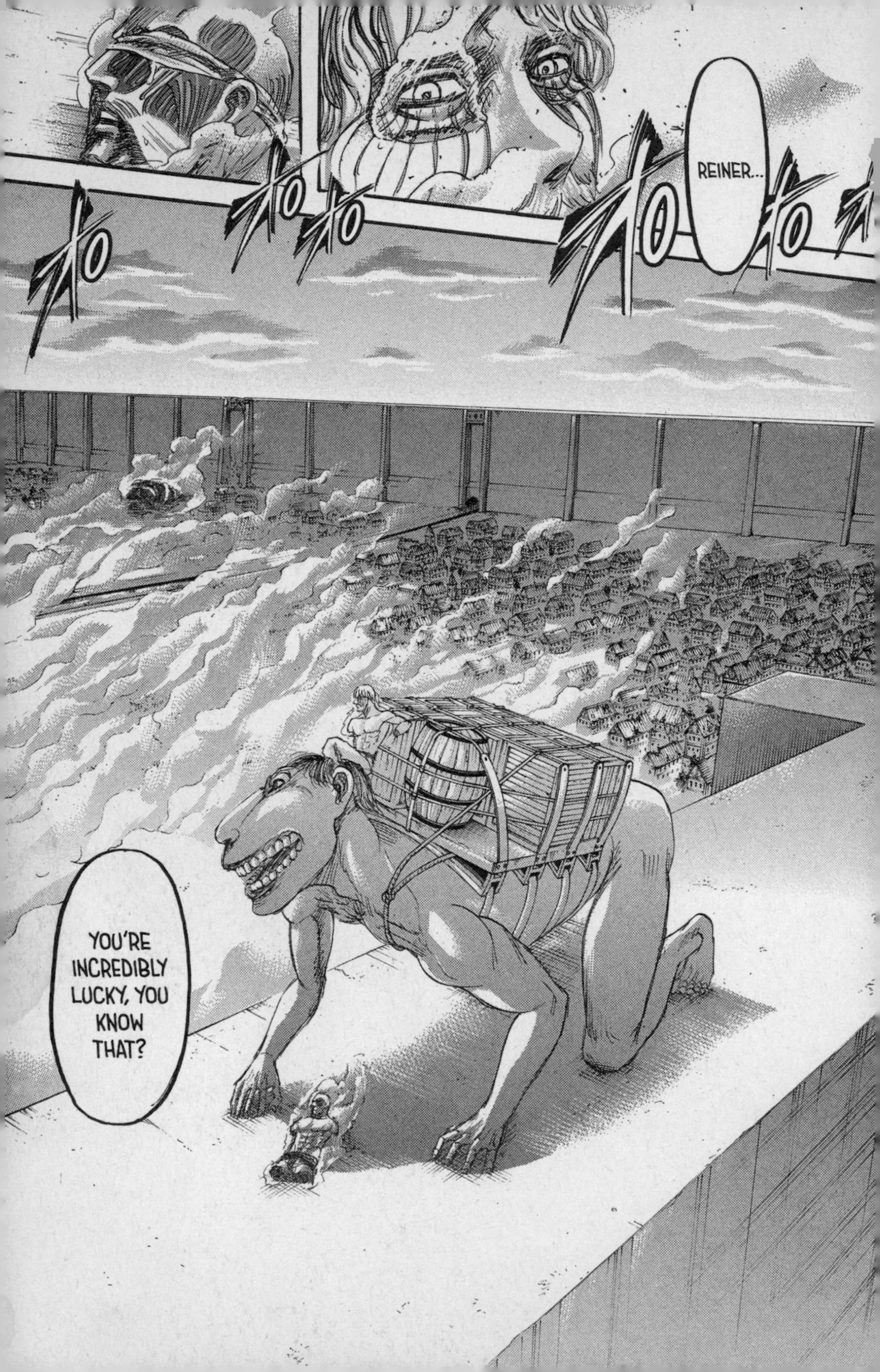
REINER...
YOU'RE INCREDIBLY LUCKY, YOU KNOW THAT?

ATTACK on TITAN

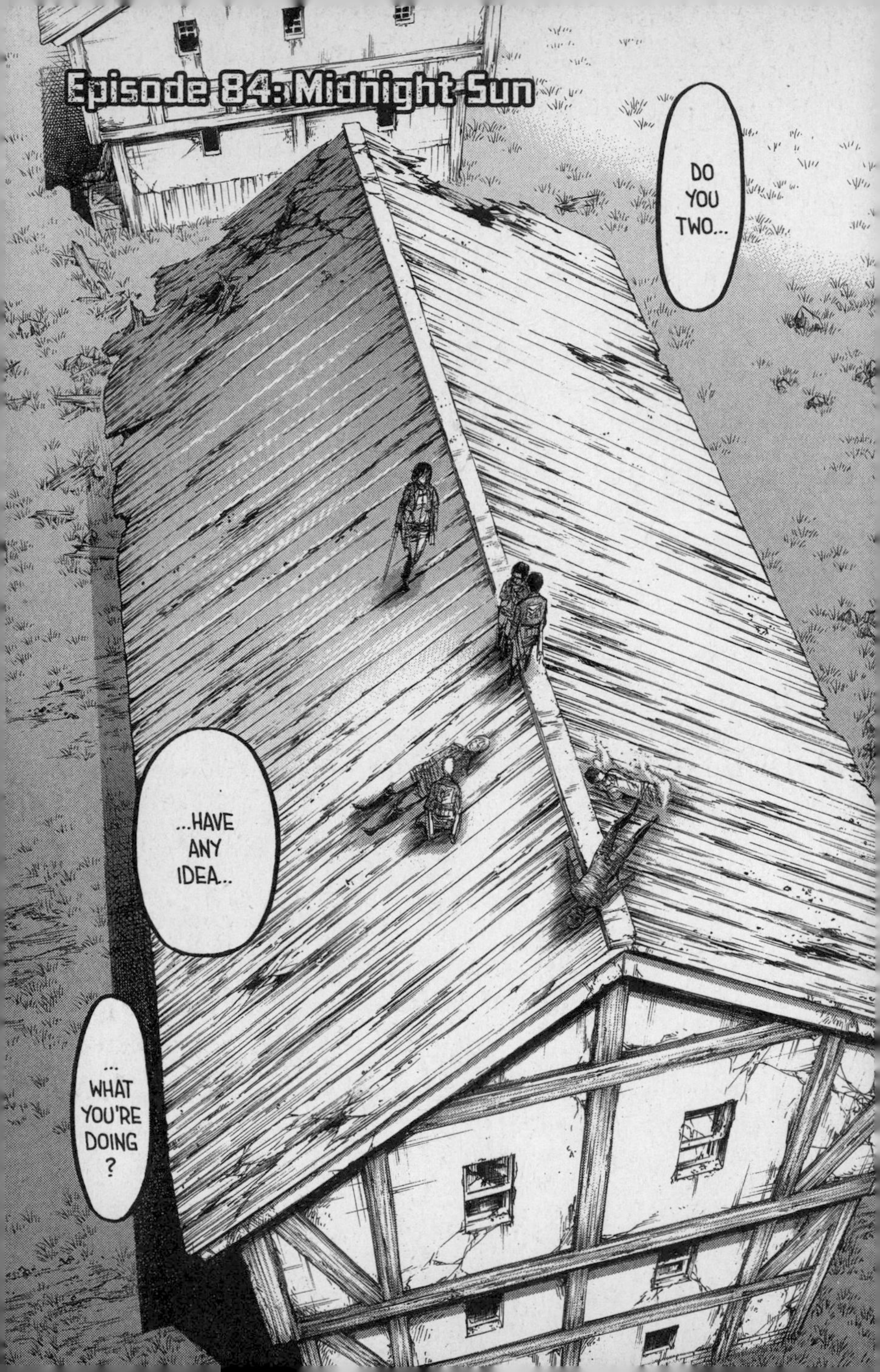
Episode 84: Midnight Sun
DO YOU TWO...
...HAVE ANY IDEA...
... WHAT YOU'RE DOING?

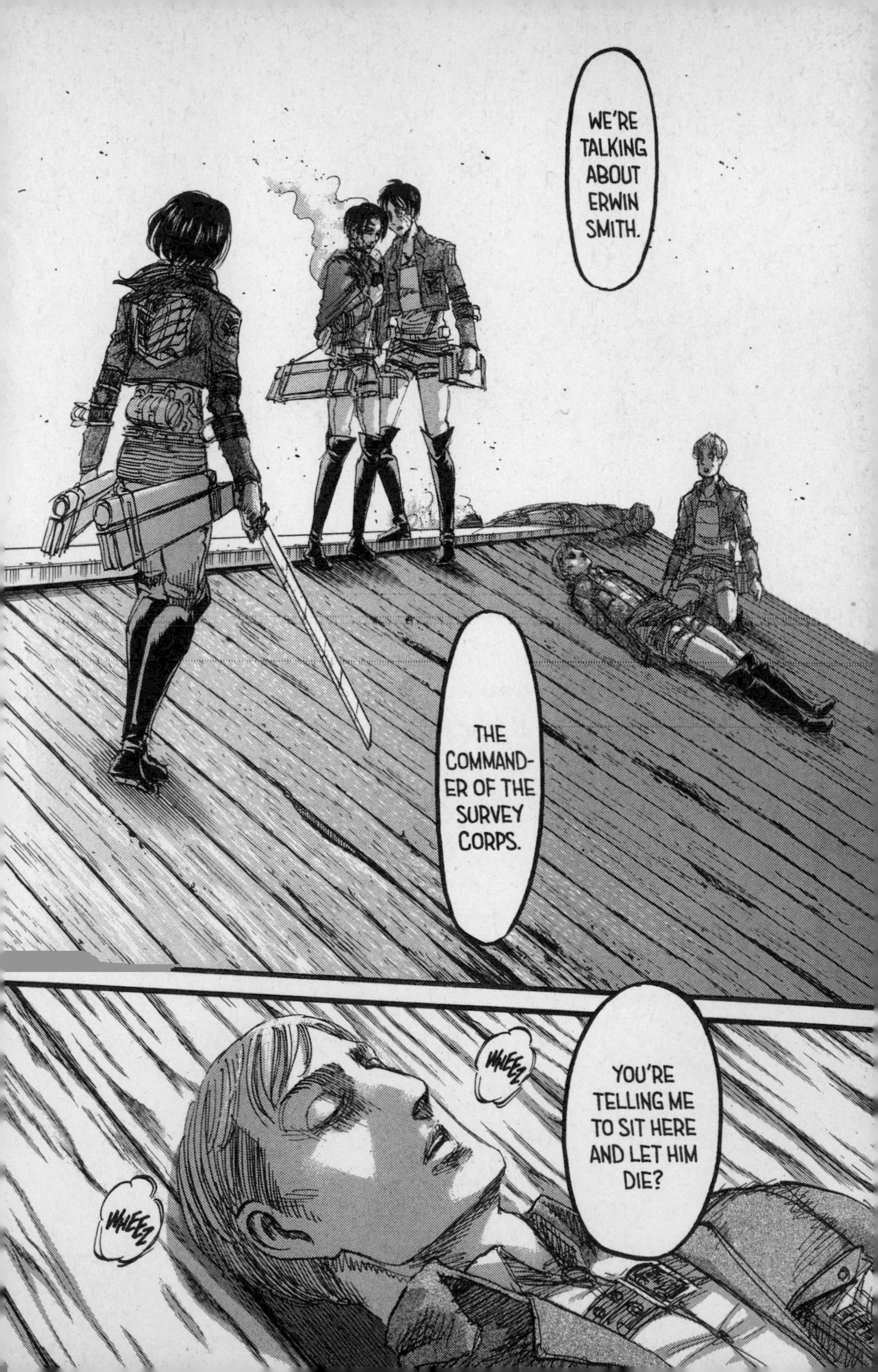
WE'RE TALKING ABOUT ERWIN SMITH.
THE COMMANDER OF THE SURVEY CORPS.
YOU'RE TELLING ME TO SIT HERE AND LET HIM DIE?
WHEEZ
WHEEZ

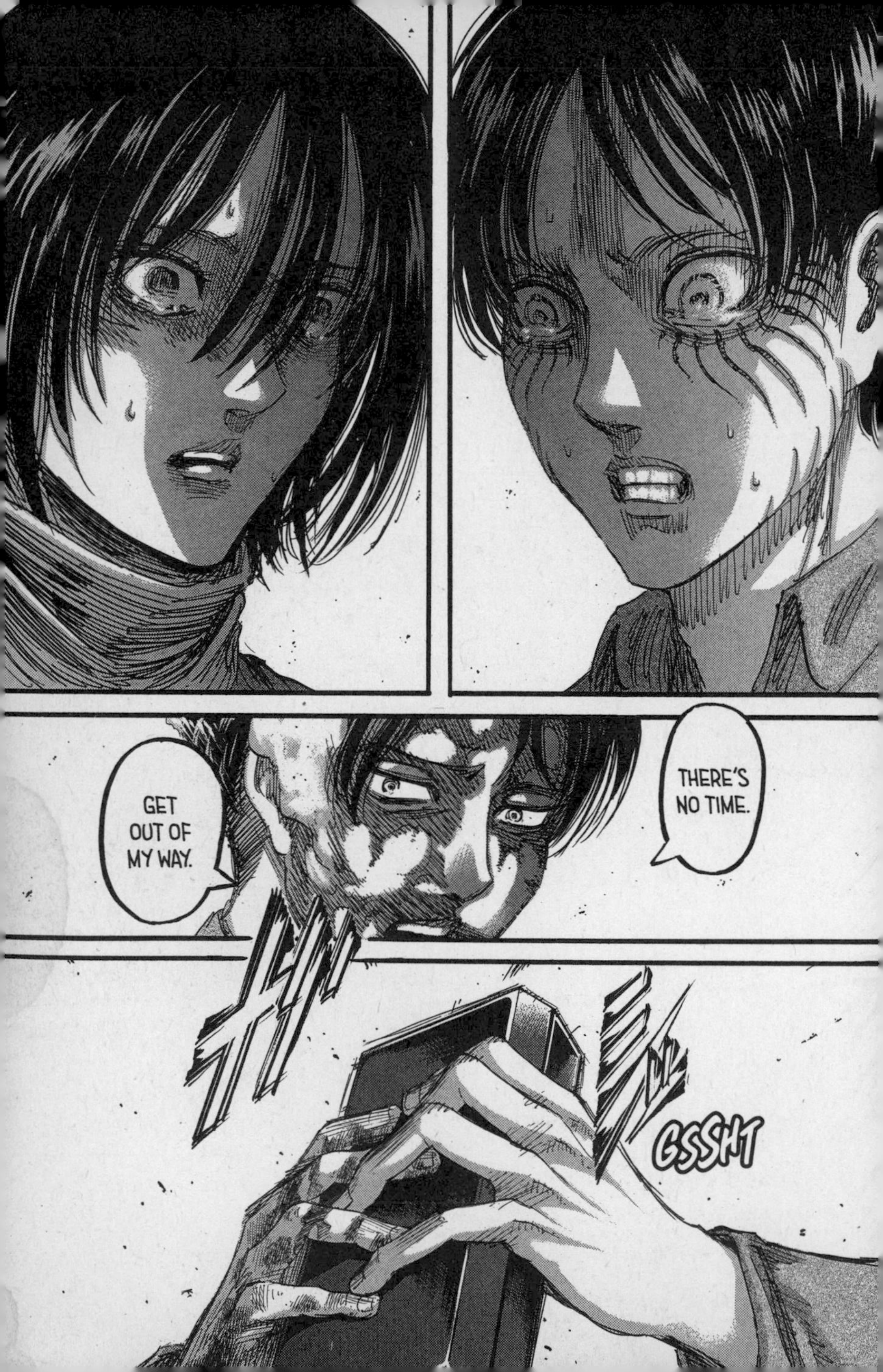
THERE'S NO TIME.
GET OUT OF MY WAY.
GSSHT

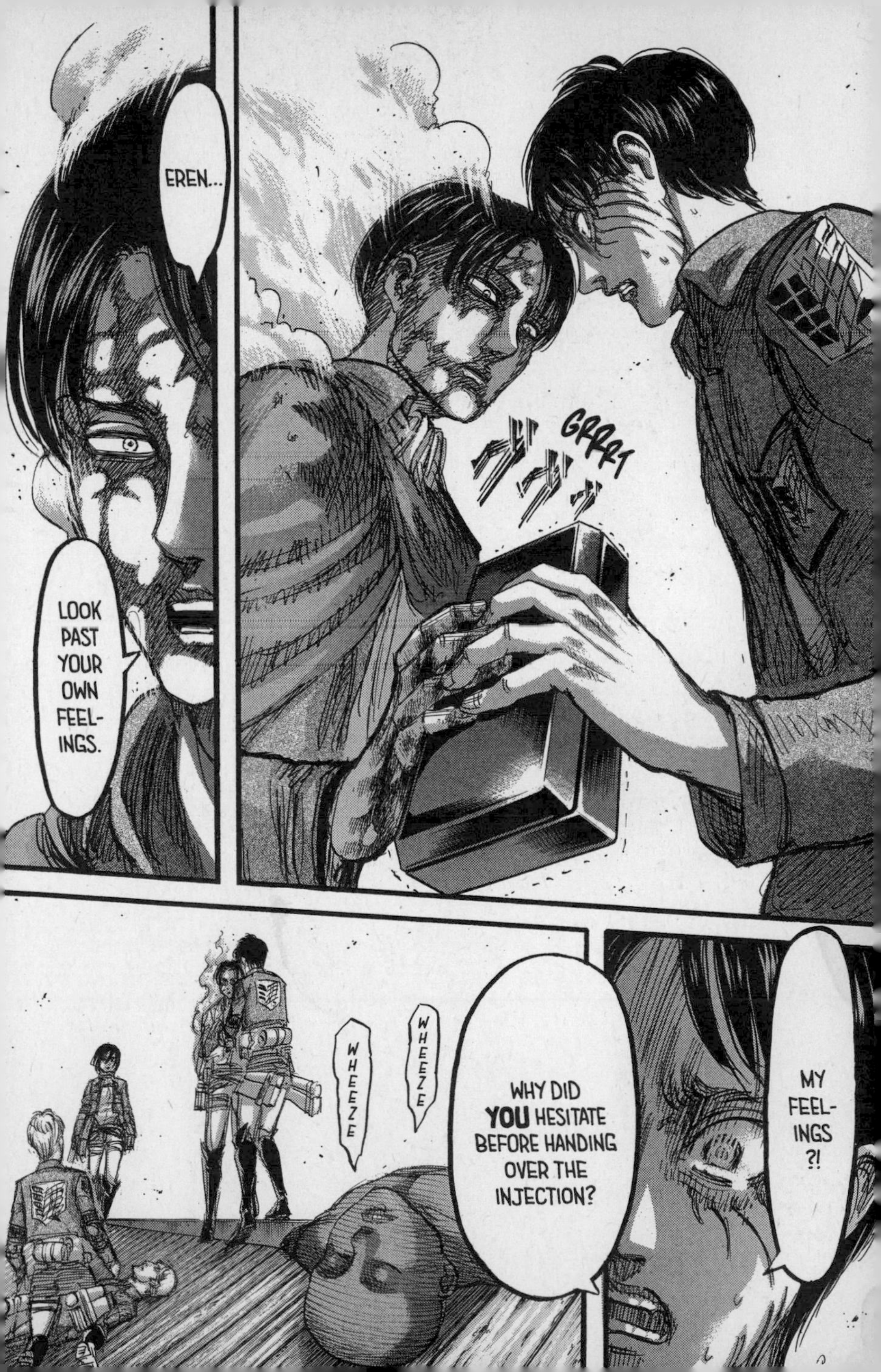
GRRR!
EREN...
LOOK PAST YOUR OWN FEEL- INGS.
MY FEEL- INGS ?!
WHY DID YOU HESITATE BEFORE HANDING OVER THE INJECTION?
WHEEZE
WHEEZE

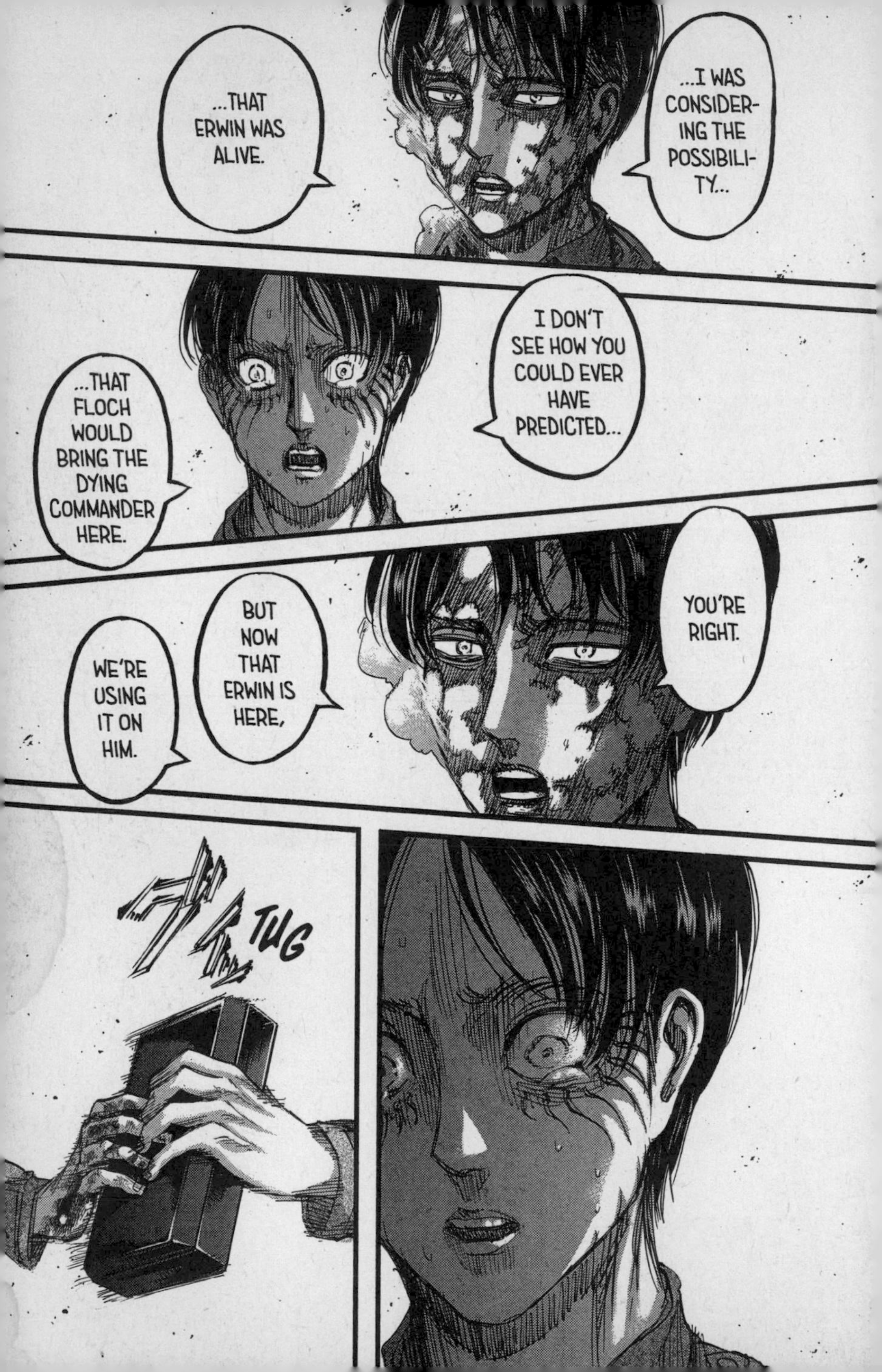
...I WAS CONSIDERING THE POSSIBILITY...
...THAT ERWIN WAS ALIVE.
I DON'T SEE HOW YOU COULD EVER HAVE PREDICTED...
...THAT FLOCH WOULD BRING THE DYING COMMANDER HERE.
YOU'RE RIGHT.
BUT NOW THAT ERWIN IS HERE,
WE'RE USING IT ON HIM.
TUG

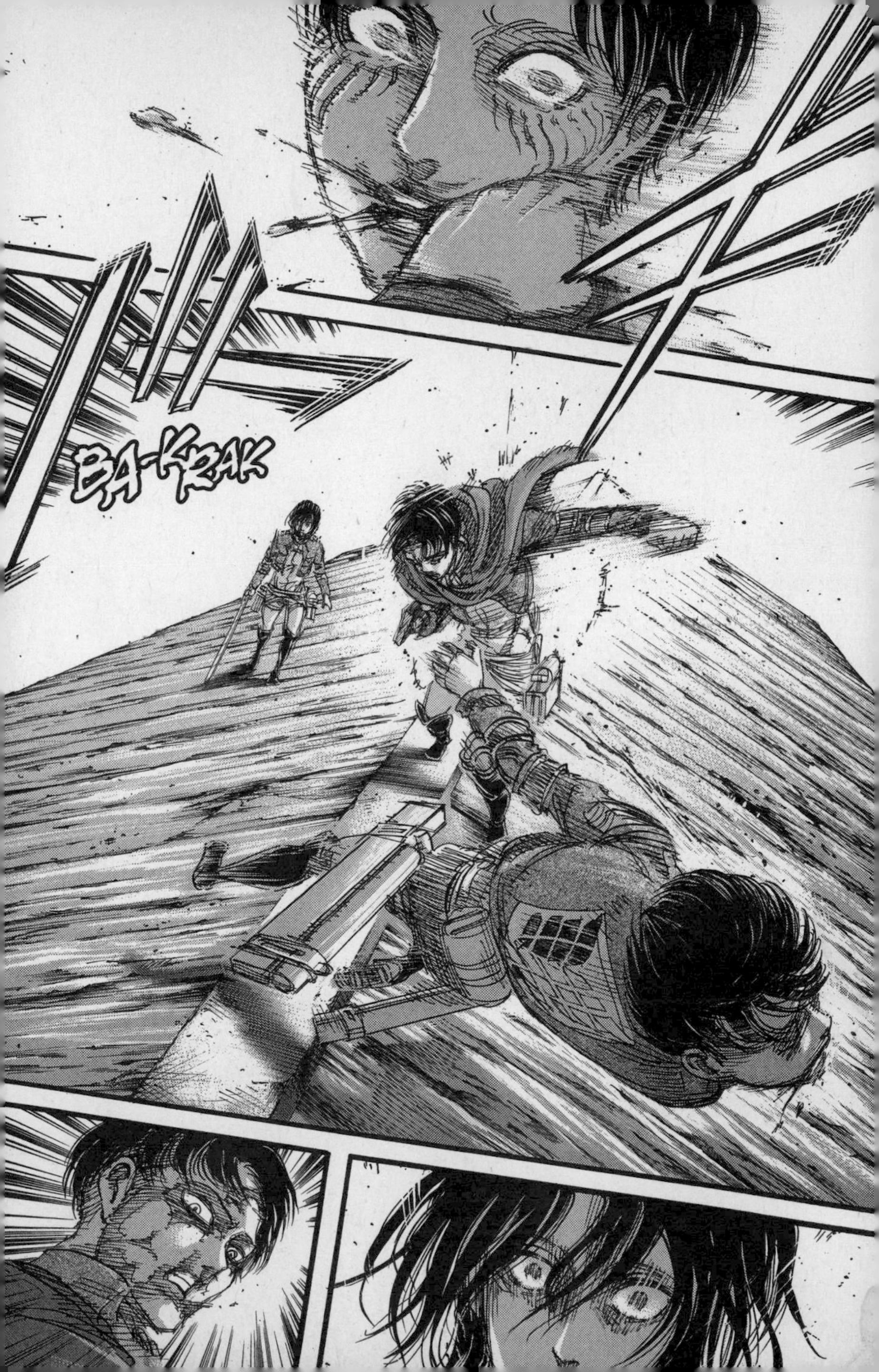
BA-KRAK

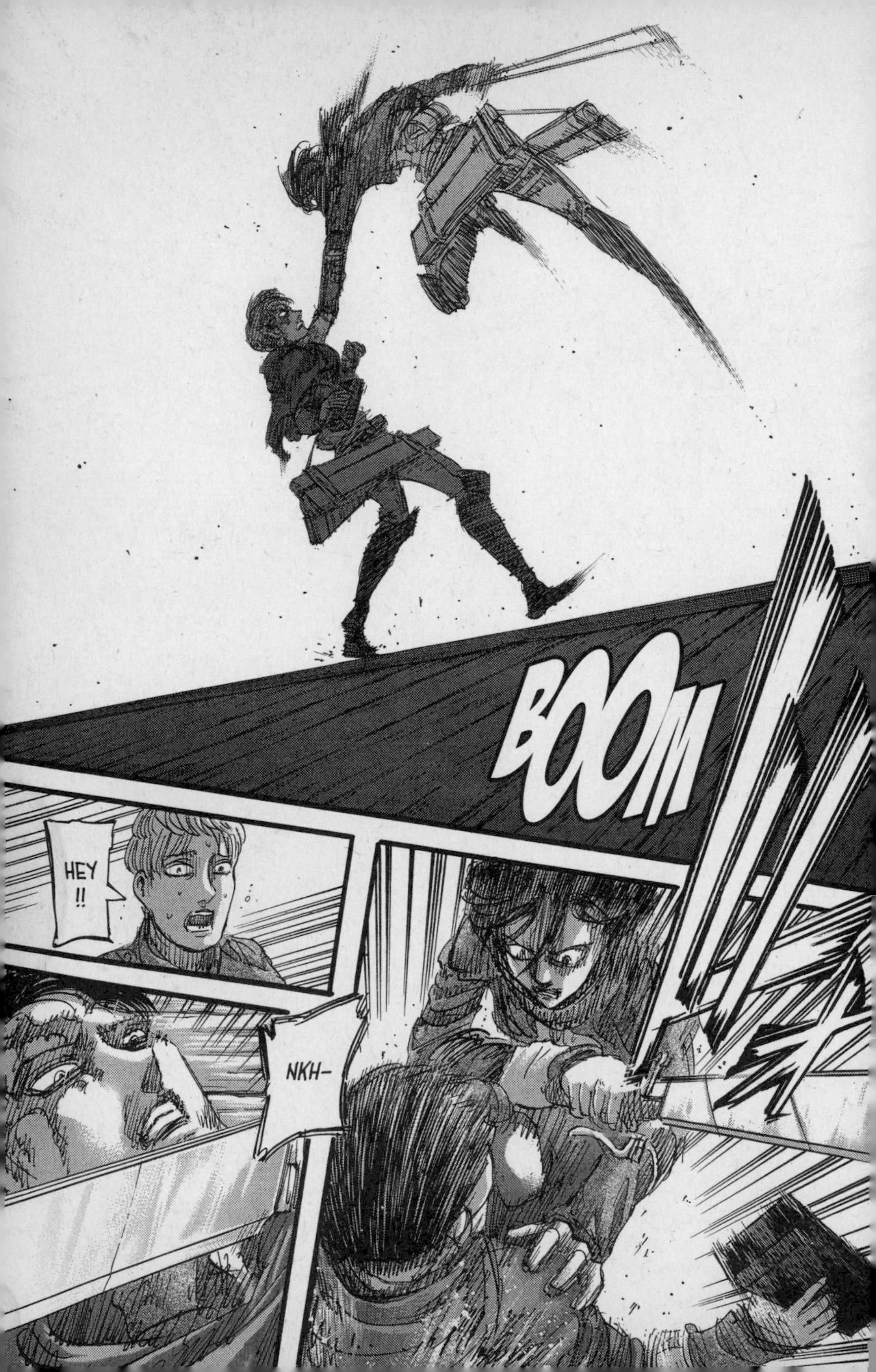
BOOM
HEY !!
NKH-

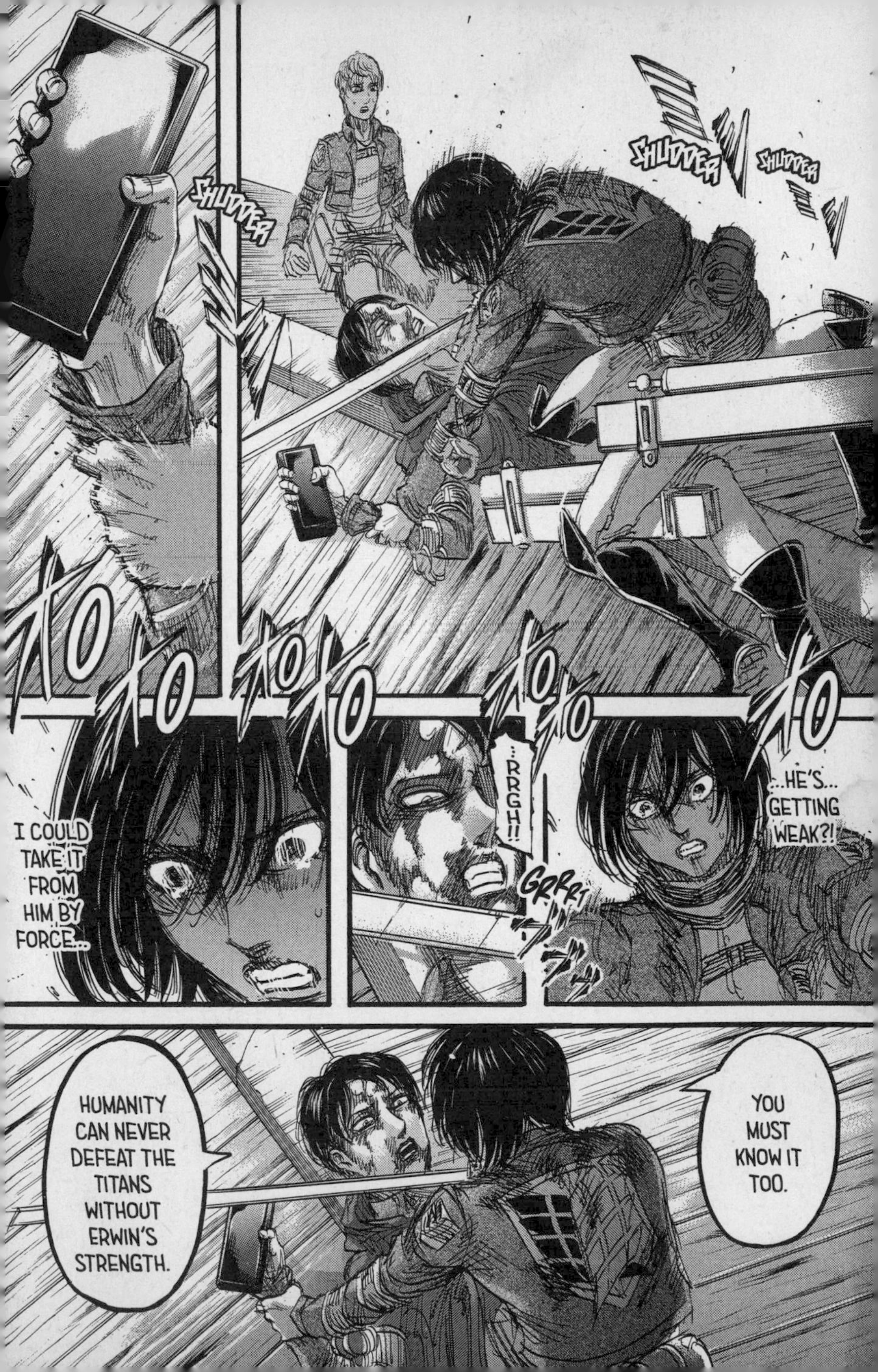
SHUDDER
SHUDDER
SHUDDER
...HE'S... GETTING WEAK?!
...RRGH!!
GRRR
I COULD TAKE IT FROM HIM BY FORCE...
YOU MUST KNOW IT TOO.
HUMANITY CAN NEVER DEFEAT THE TITANS WITHOUT ERWIN'S STRENGTH.

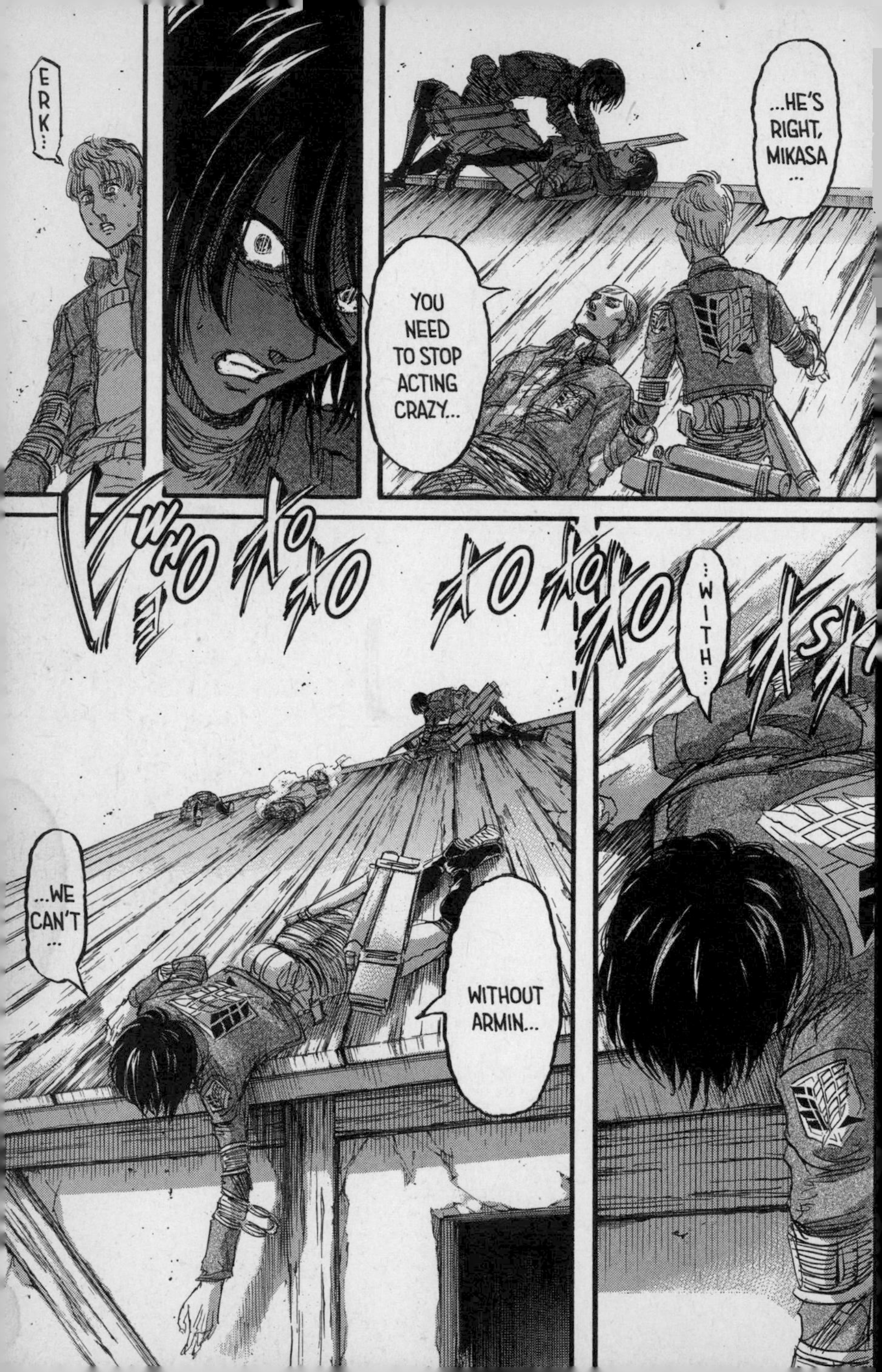
...HE'S RIGHT, MIKASA...
YOU NEED TO STOP ACTING CRAZY...
ERK...
...WITH...
WITHOUT ARMIN...
...WE CAN'T...

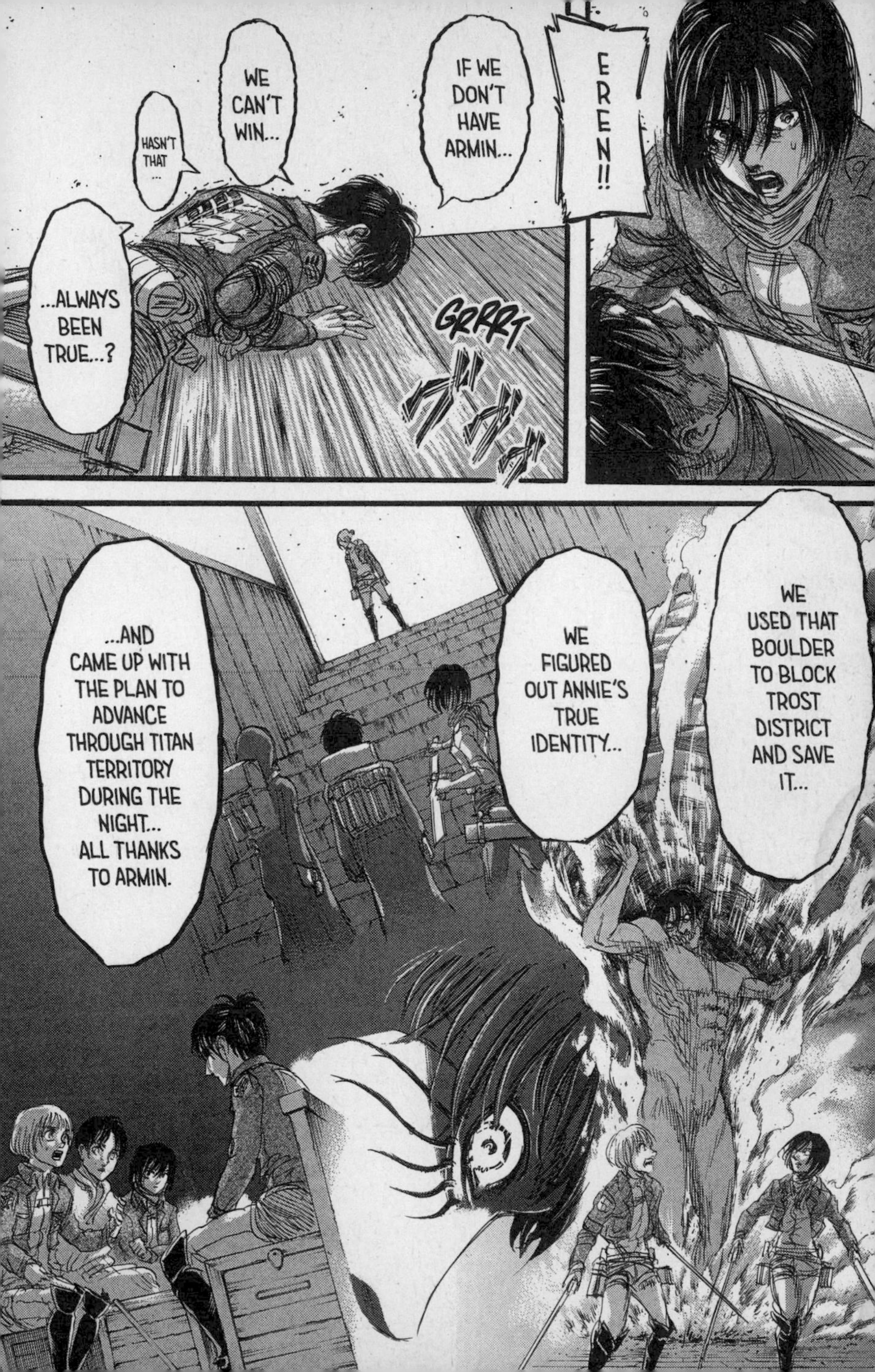
EREN!!
IF WE DON'T HAVE ARMIN...
WE CAN'T WIN...
HASN'T THAT ...
...ALWAYS BEEN TRUE...?
GRRRT
WE USED THAT BOULDER TO BLOCK TROST DISTRICT AND SAVE IT...
WE FIGURED OUT ANNIE'S TRUE IDENTITY...
...AND CAME UP WITH THE PLAN TO ADVANCE THROUGH TITAN TERRITORY DURING THE NIGHT... ALL THANKS TO ARMIN.

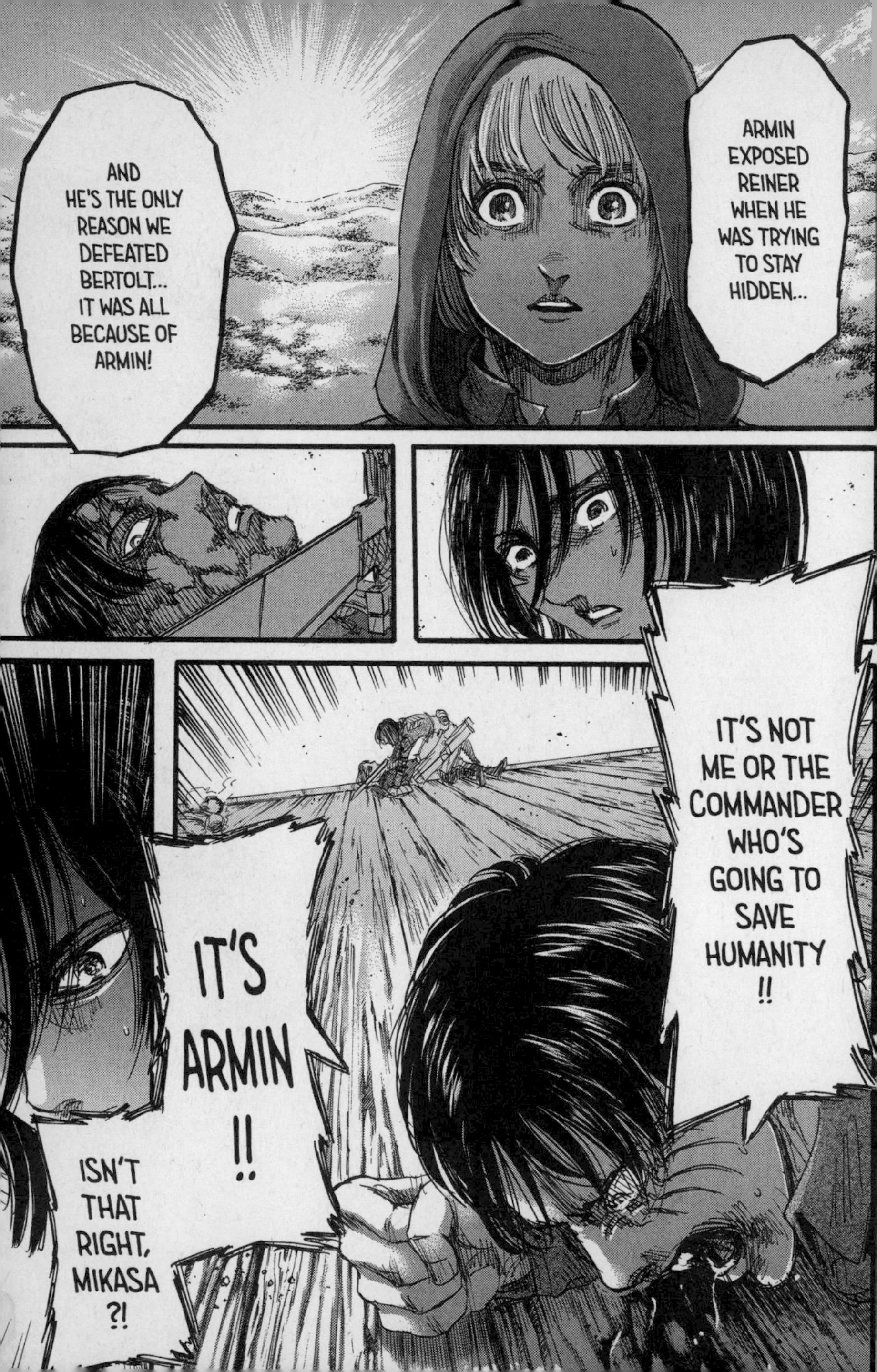
ARMIN EXPOSED REINER WHEN HE WAS TRYING TO STAY HIDDEN...
AND HE'S THE ONLY REASON WE DEFEATED BERTOLT... IT WAS ALL BECAUSE OF ARMIN!
IT'S NOT ME OR THE COMMANDER WHO'S GOING TO SAVE HUMANITY!!
IT'S ARMIN!!
ISN'T THAT RIGHT, MIKASA?!

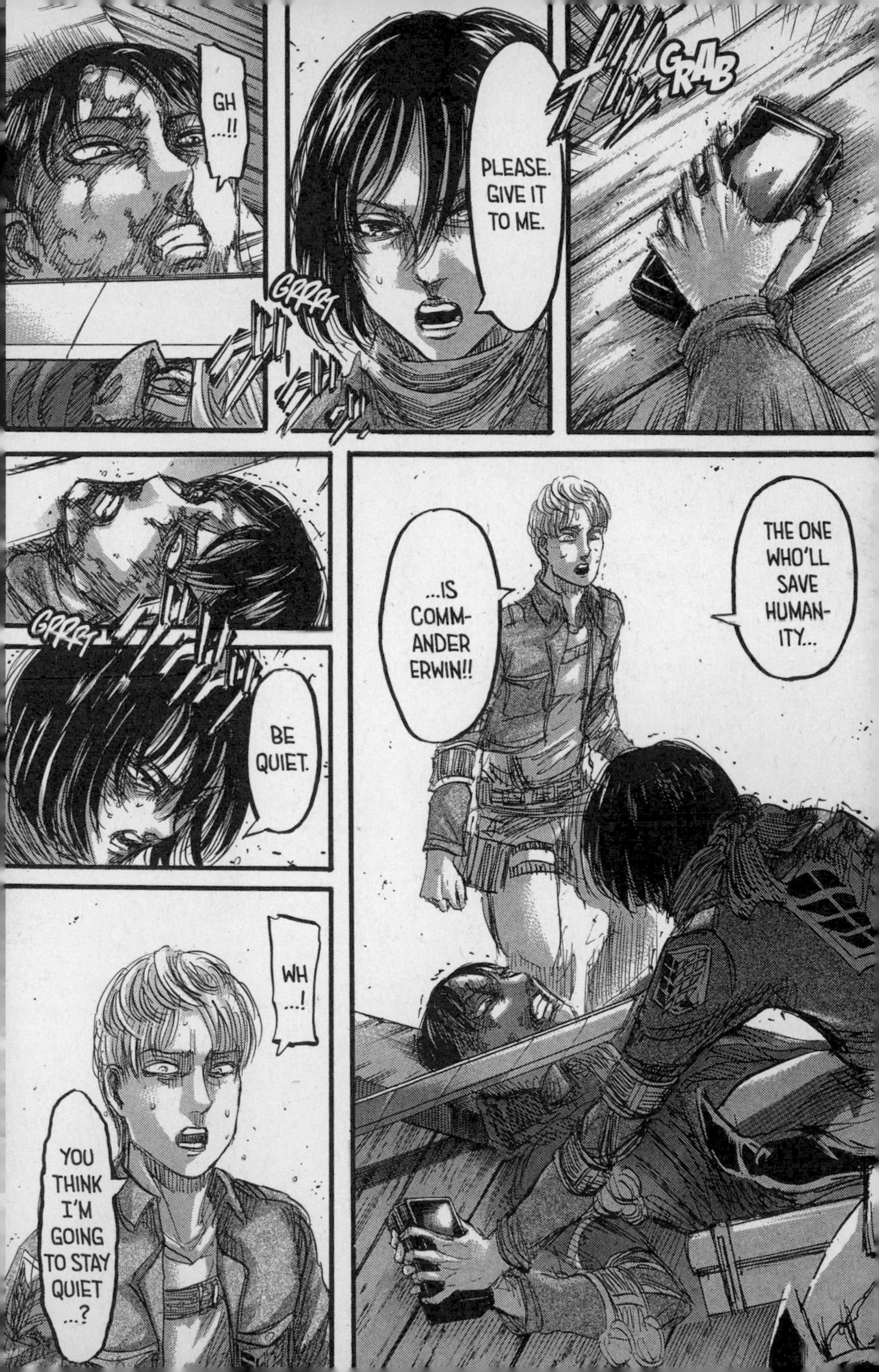
GRAB
PLEASE. GIVE IT TO ME.
GH ...!!
THE ONE WHO'LL SAVE HUMANITY...
...IS COMMANDER ERWIN!!
BE QUIET.
WH ...!
YOU THINK I'M GOING TO STAY QUIET ...?

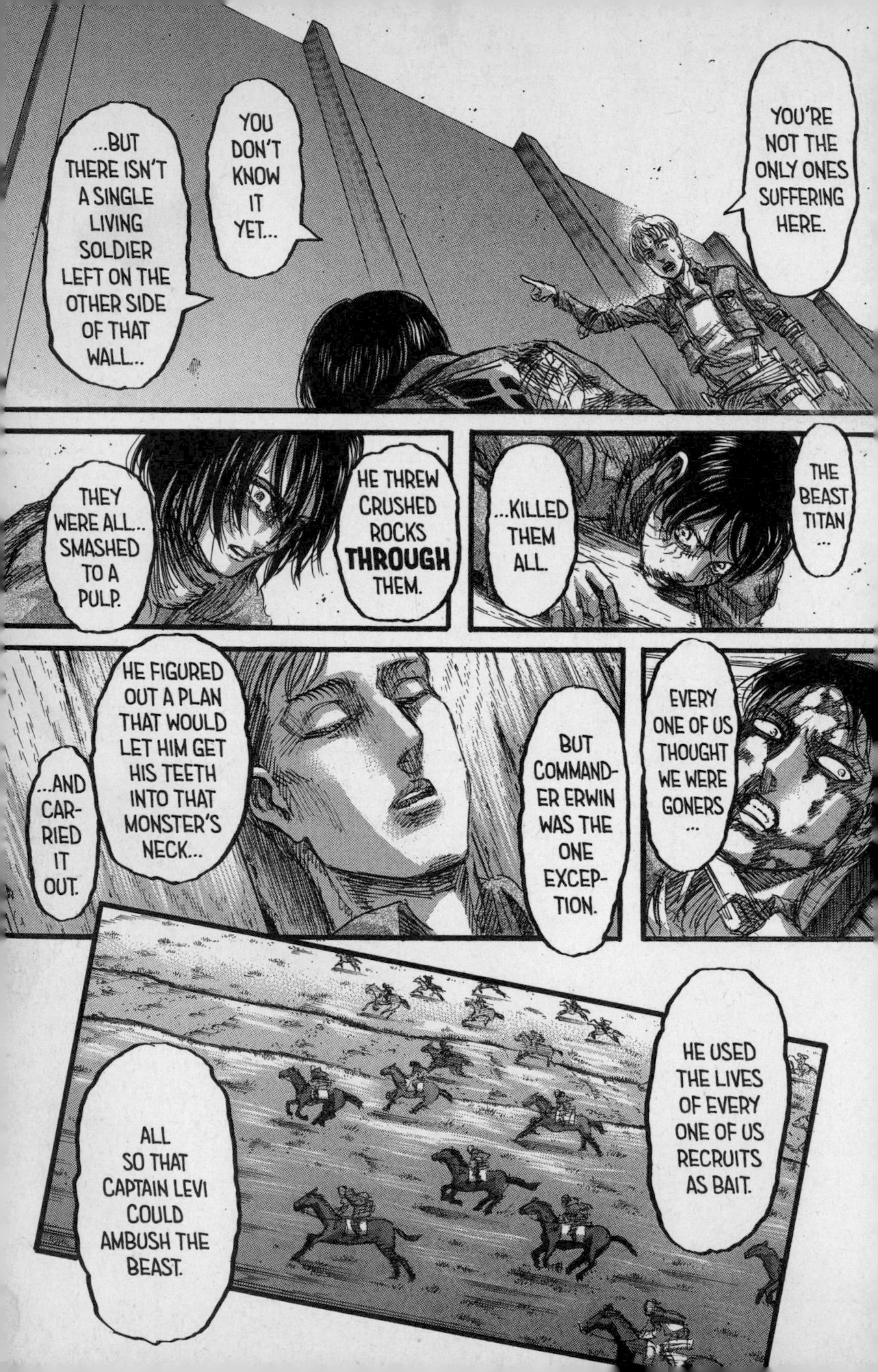
YOU'RE NOT THE ONLY ONES SUFFERING HERE.
YOU DON'T KNOW IT YET...
...BUT THERE ISN'T A SINGLE LIVING SOLDIER LEFT ON THE OTHER SIDE OF THAT WALL...
THE BEAST TITAN...
...KILLED THEM ALL.
HE THREW CRUSHED ROCKS **THROUGH** THEM.
THEY WERE ALL... SMASHED TO A PULP.
EVERY ONE OF US THOUGHT WE WERE GONERS...
BUT COMMANDER ERWIN WAS THE ONE EXCEPTION.
HE FIGURED OUT A PLAN THAT WOULD LET HIM GET HIS TEETH INTO THAT MONSTER'S NECK...
...AND CARRIED IT OUT.
HE USED THE LIVES OF EVERY ONE OF US RECRUITS AS BAIT.
ALL SO THAT CAPTAIN LEVI COULD AMBUSH THE BEAST.

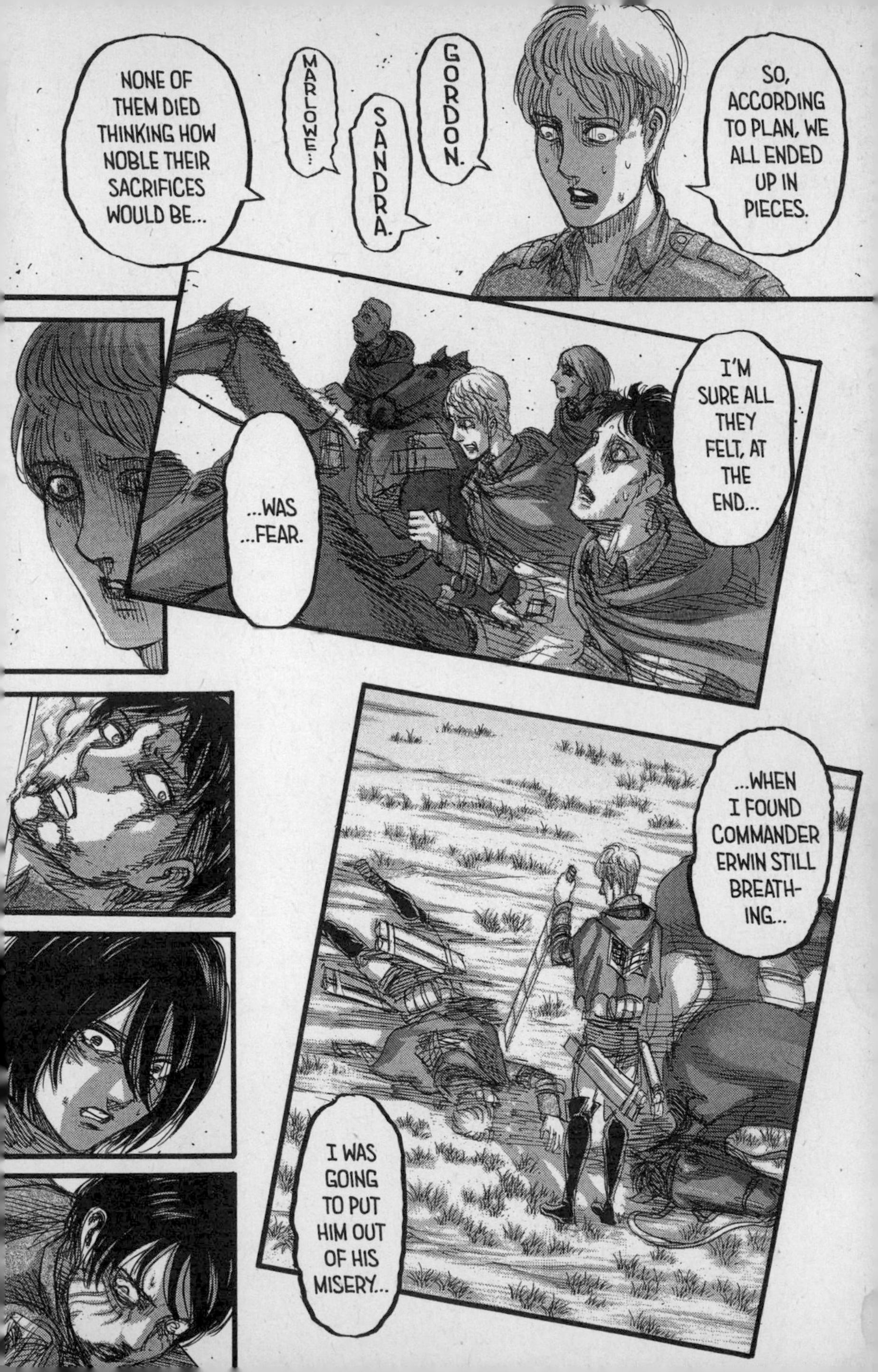
SO, ACCORDING TO PLAN, WE ALL ENDED UP IN PIECES.
GORDON.
SANDRA.
MARLOWE...
NONE OF THEM DIED THINKING HOW NOBLE THEIR SACRIFICES WOULD BE...
I'M SURE ALL THEY FELT, AT THE END...
...WAS ...FEAR.
...WHEN I FOUND COMMANDER ERWIN STILL BREATH-ING...
I WAS GOING TO PUT HIM OUT OF HIS MISERY...

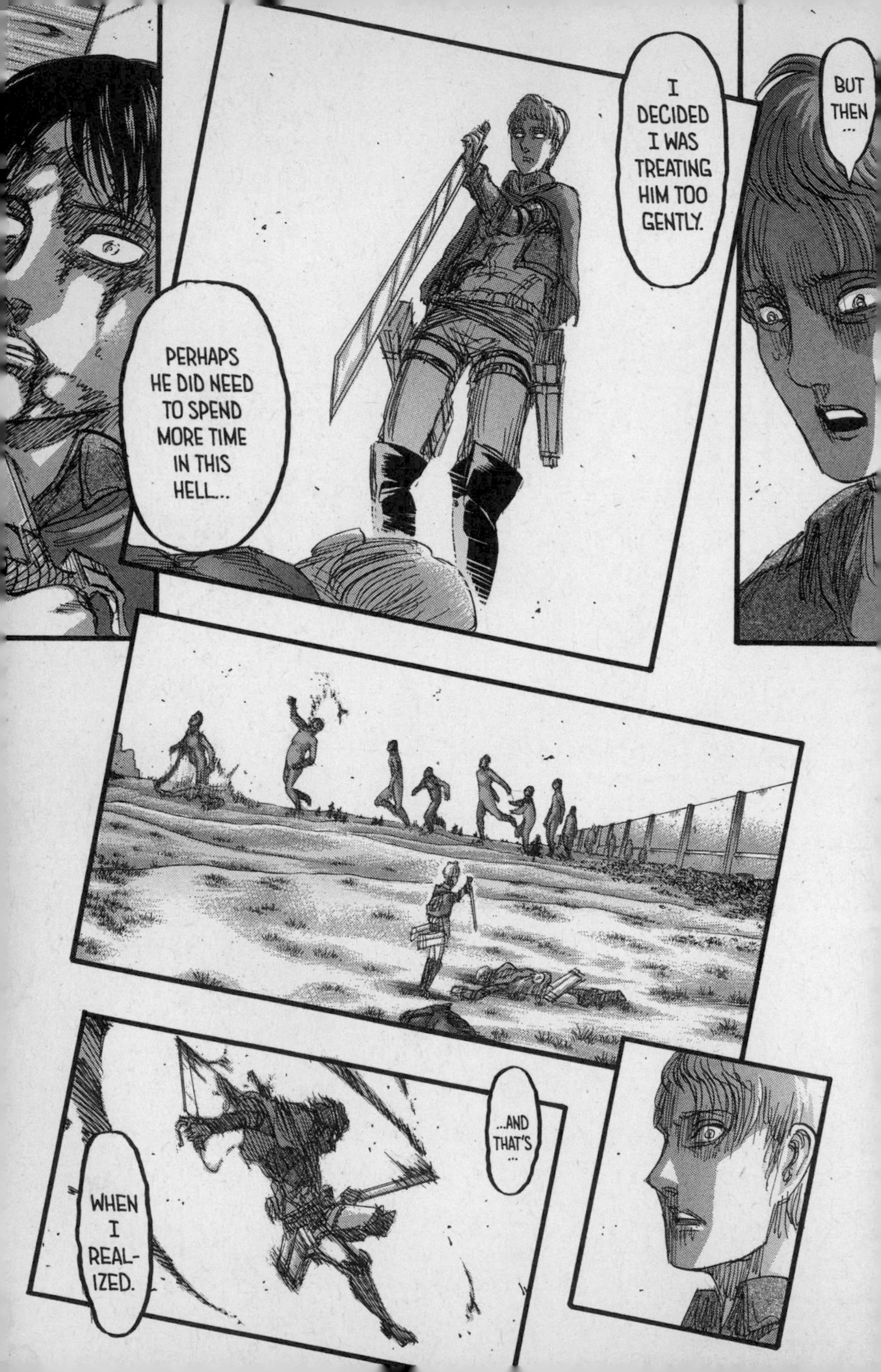
BUT THEN...
I DECIDED I WAS TREATING HIM TOO GENTLY.
PERHAPS HE DID NEED TO SPEND MORE TIME IN THIS HELL...
...AND THAT'S...
WHEN I REALIZED.

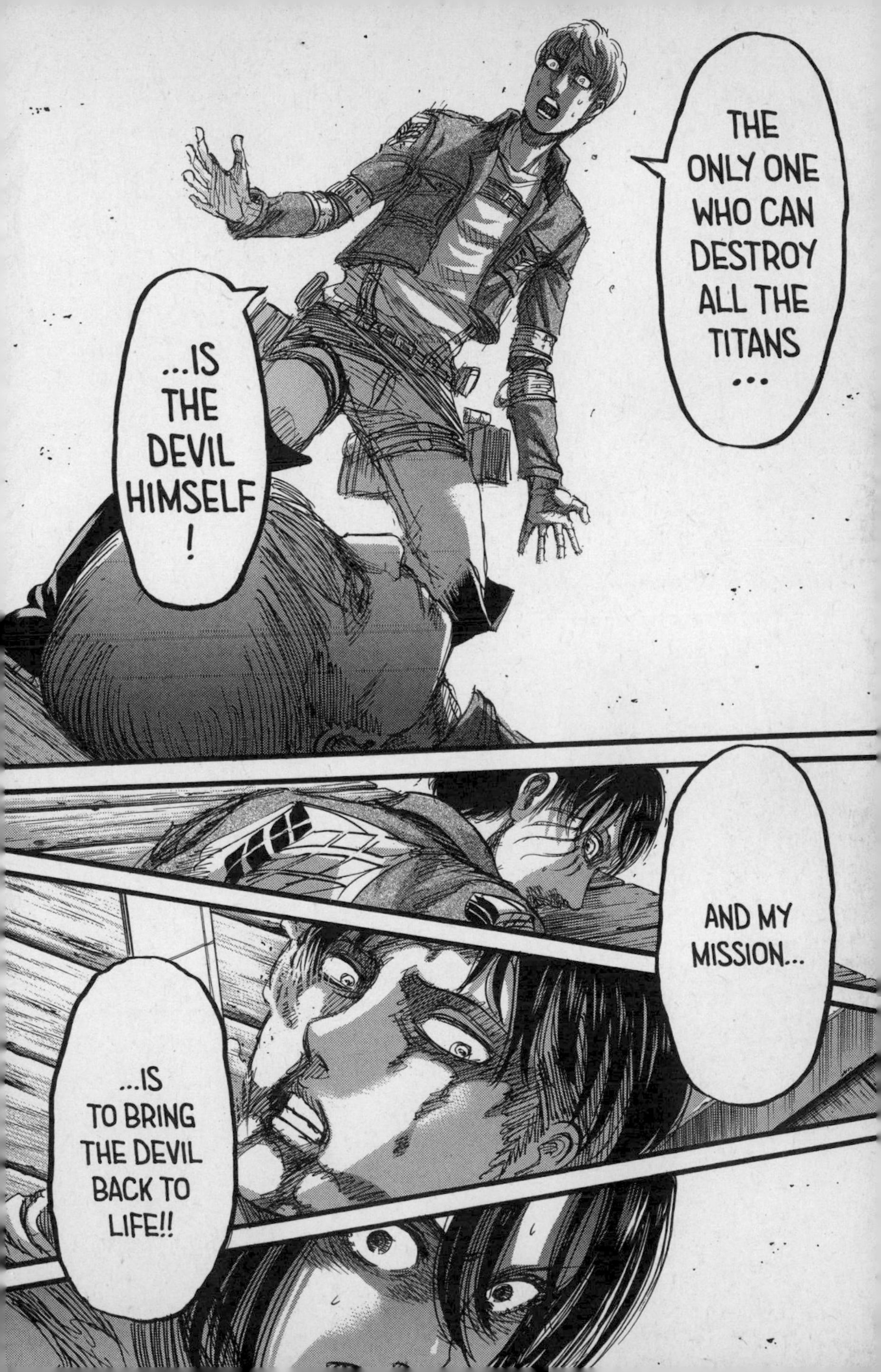
THE ONLY ONE WHO CAN DESTROY ALL THE TITANS ...
...IS THE DEVIL HIMSELF !
AND MY MISSION...
...IS TO BRING THE DEVIL BACK TO LIFE!!

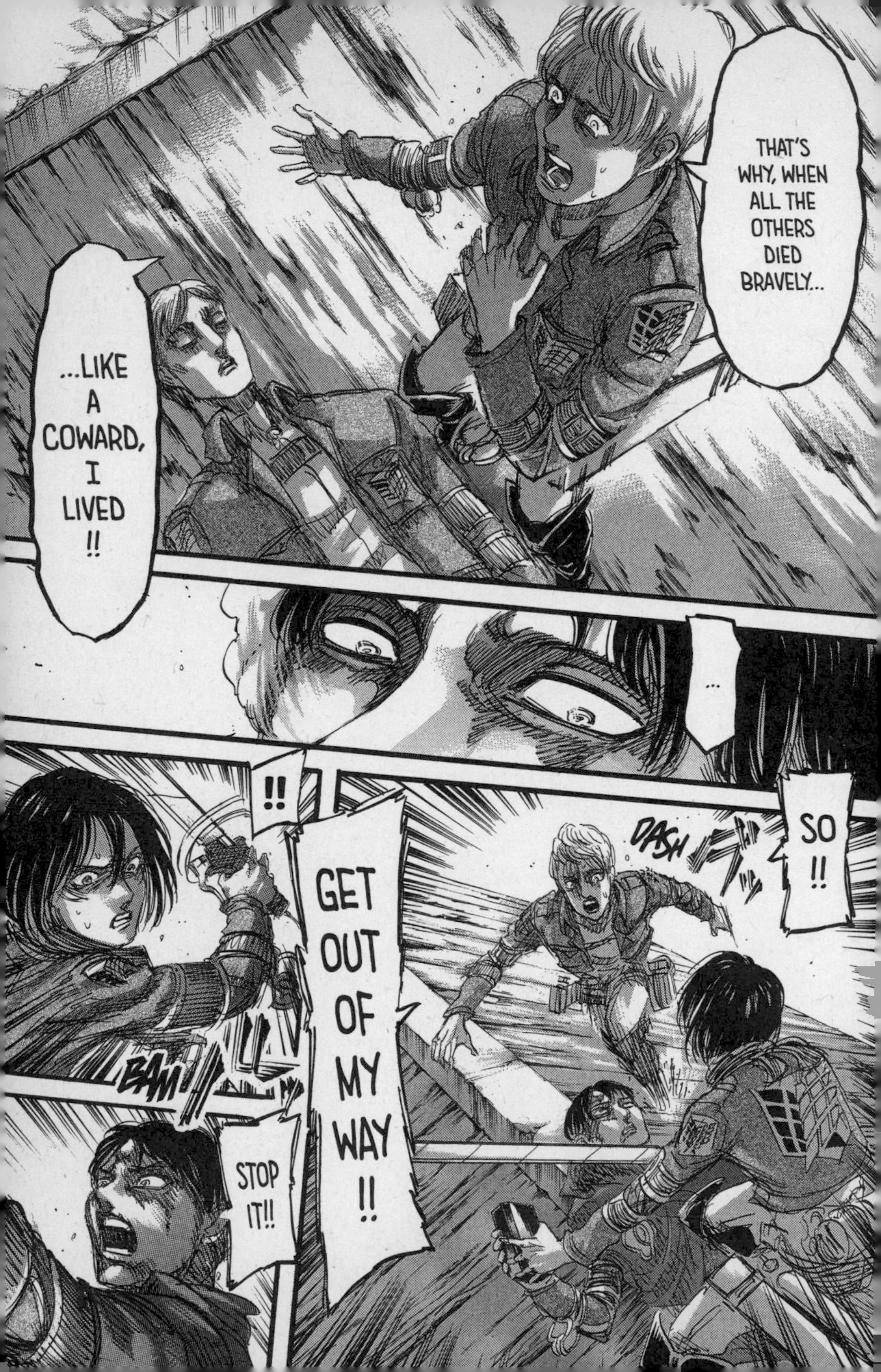
THAT'S WHY, WHEN ALL THE OTHERS DIED BRAVELY...
...LIKE A COWARD, I LIVED !!
...
SO !!
DASH
GET OUT OF MY WAY !!
!!
BAM
STOP IT!!

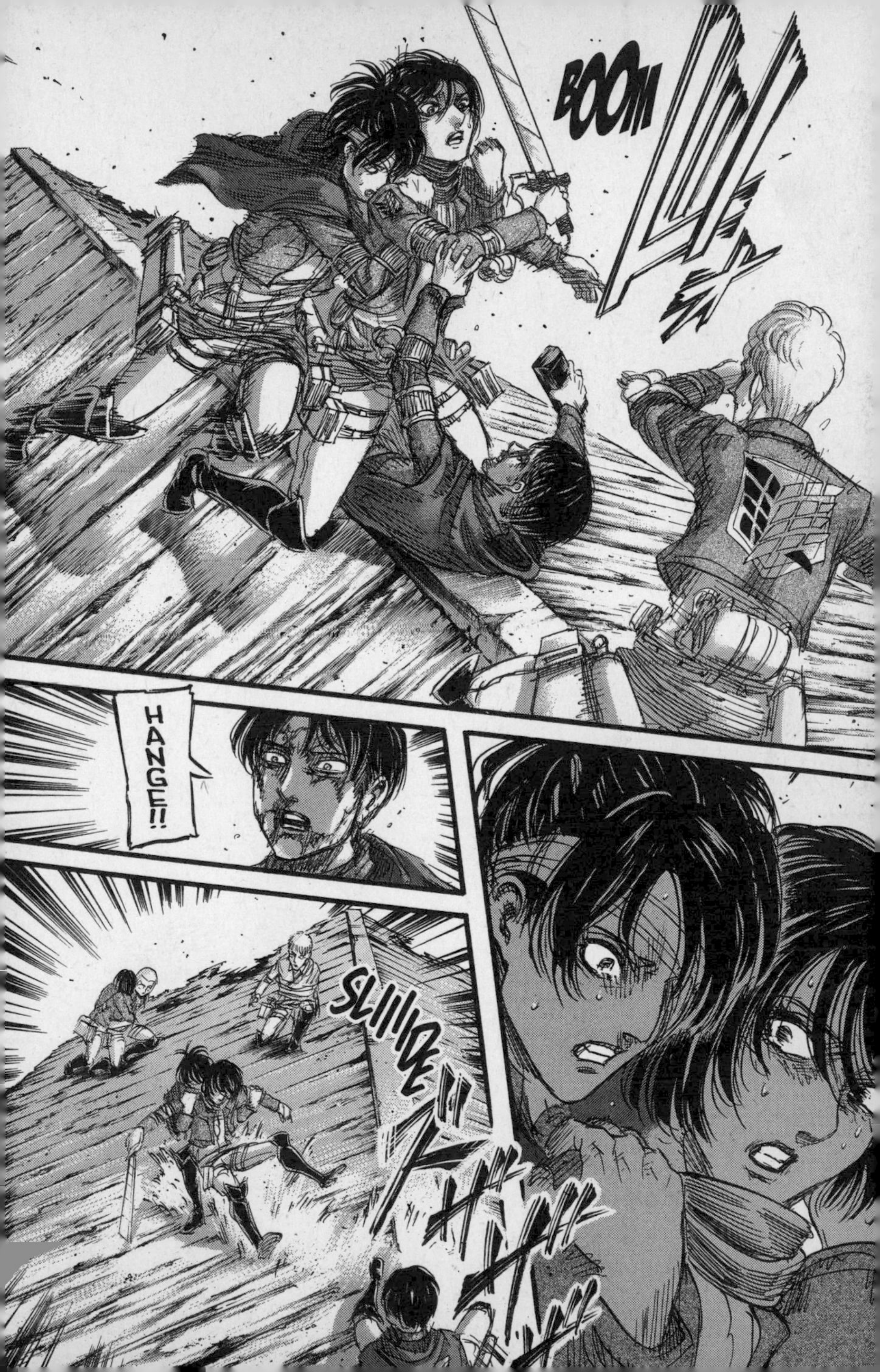
BOOM
HANGE!!
SLIIIDE!!

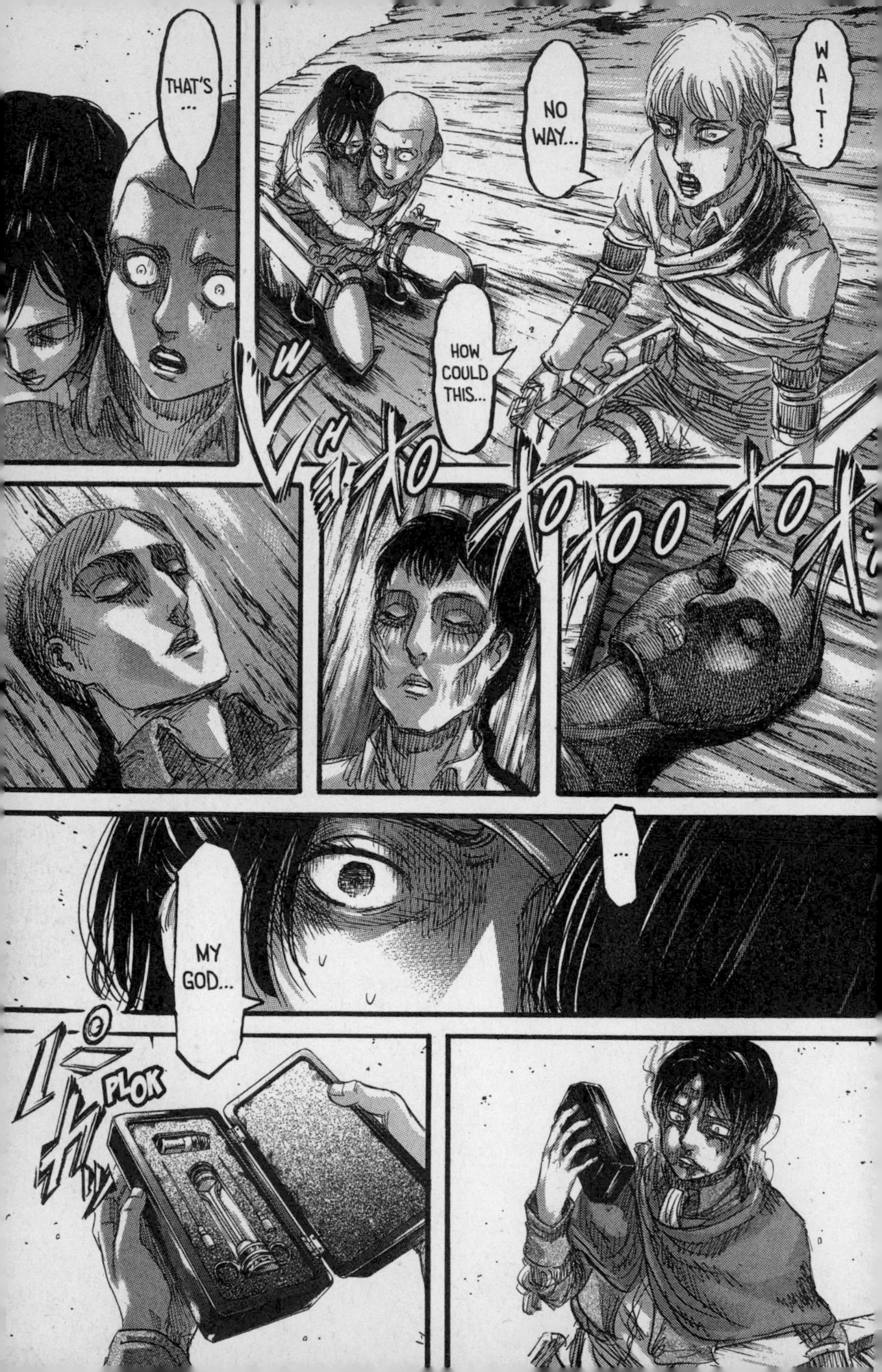
WAIT...
NO WAY...
HOW COULD THIS...
THAT'S...
...
MY GOD...
PLOK

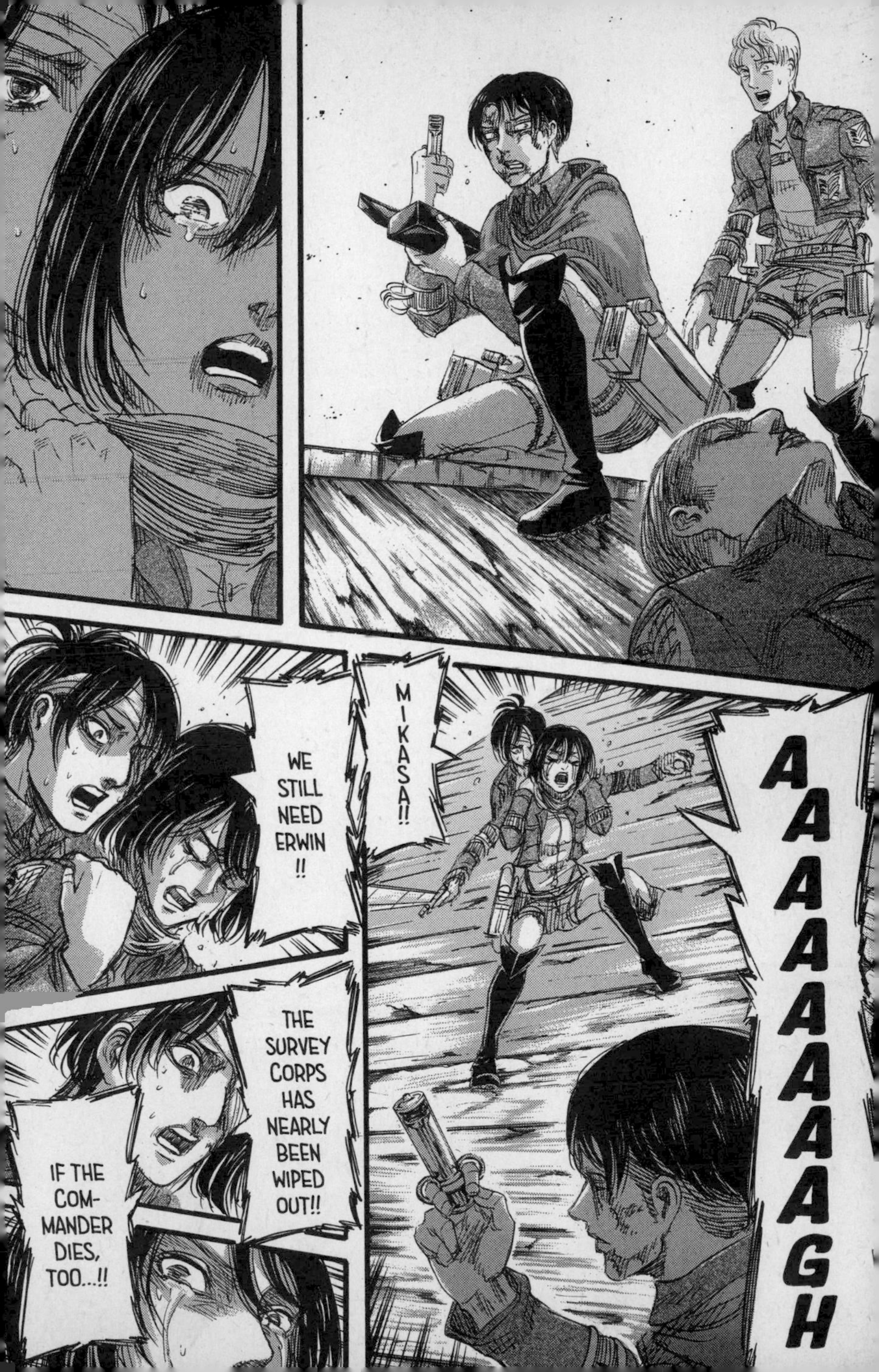
AAAAAAAAGH
MIKASA!!
WE STILL NEED ERWIN !!
THE SURVEY CORPS HAS NEARLY BEEN WIPED OUT!!
IF THE COM-MANDER DIES, TOO...!!

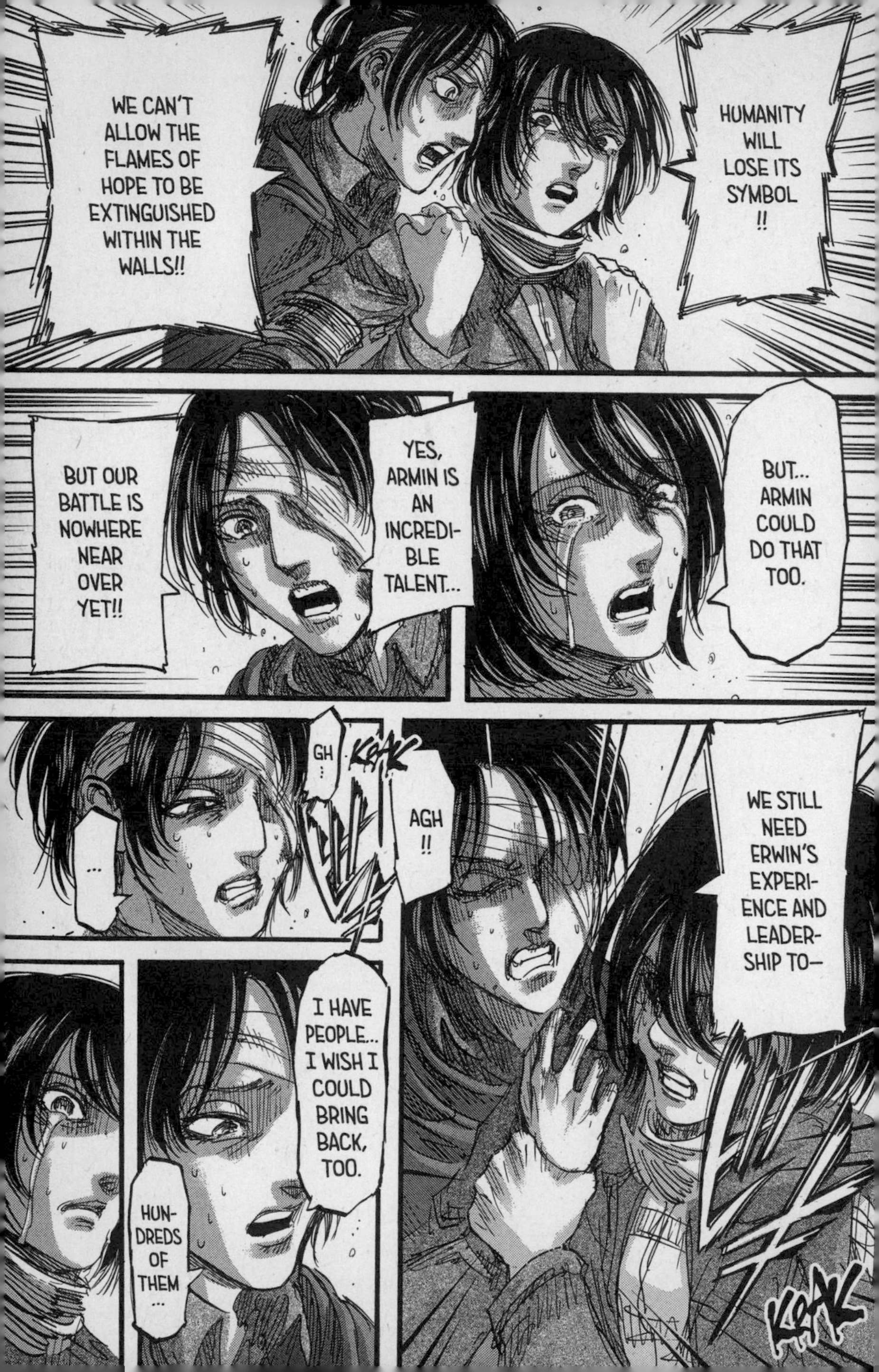
HUMANITY WILL LOSE ITS SYMBOL !!
WE CAN'T ALLOW THE FLAMES OF HOPE TO BE EXTINGUISHED WITHIN THE WALLS!!
BUT... ARMIN COULD DO THAT TOO.
YES, ARMIN IS AN INCREDI-BLE TALENT...
BUT OUR BATTLE IS NOWHERE NEAR OVER YET!!
WE STILL NEED ERWIN'S EXPERI-ENCE AND LEADER-SHIP TO—
AGH !!
KRAK
GH ...
KRAK
...
I HAVE PEOPLE... I WISH I COULD BRING BACK, TOO.
HUN-DREDS OF THEM ...

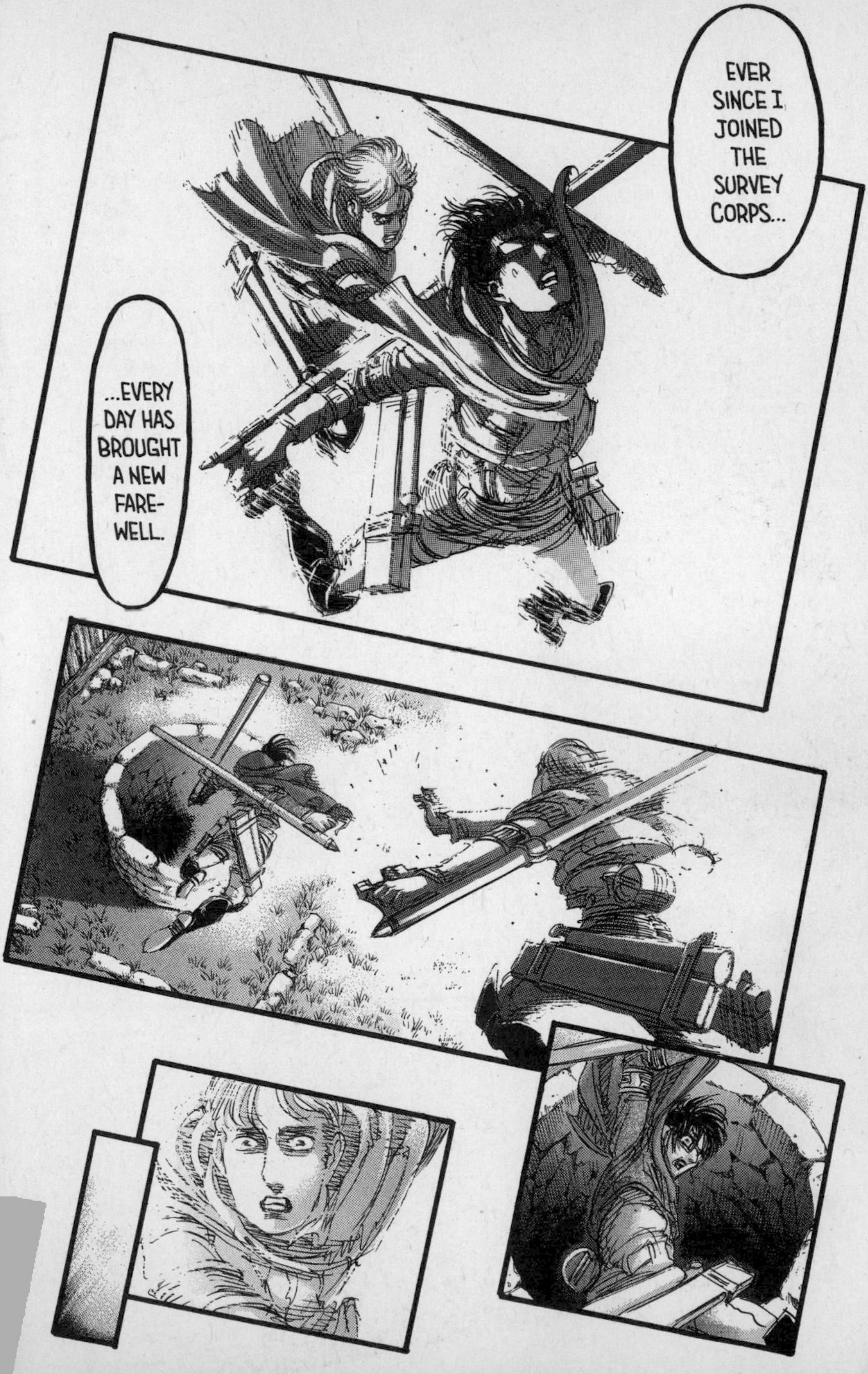
EVER SINCE I JOINED THE SURVEY CORPS...
...EVERY DAY HAS BROUGHT A NEW FARE-WELL.

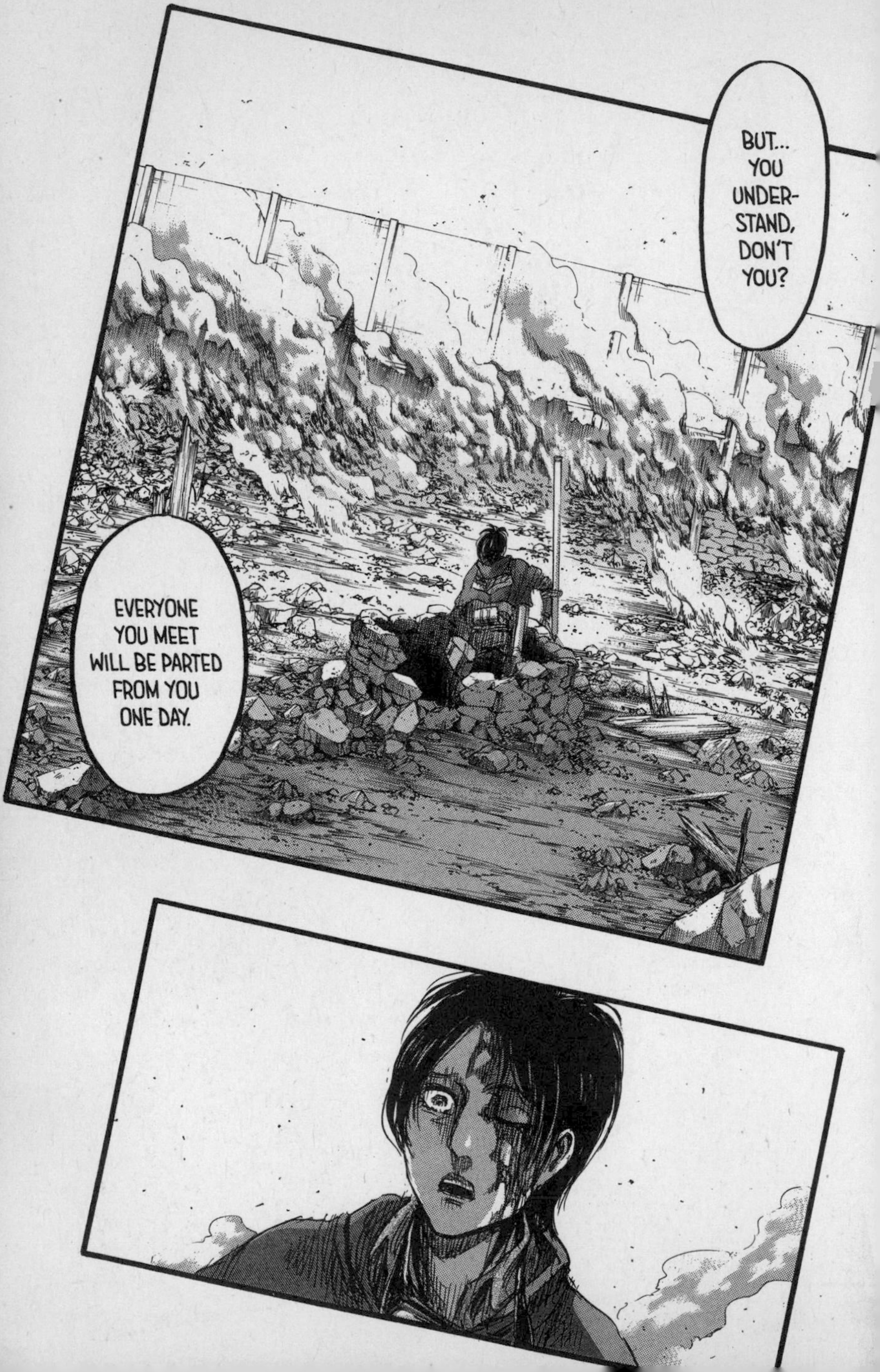
BUT... YOU UNDER-STAND, DON'T YOU?
EVERYONE YOU MEET WILL BE PARTED FROM YOU ONE DAY.

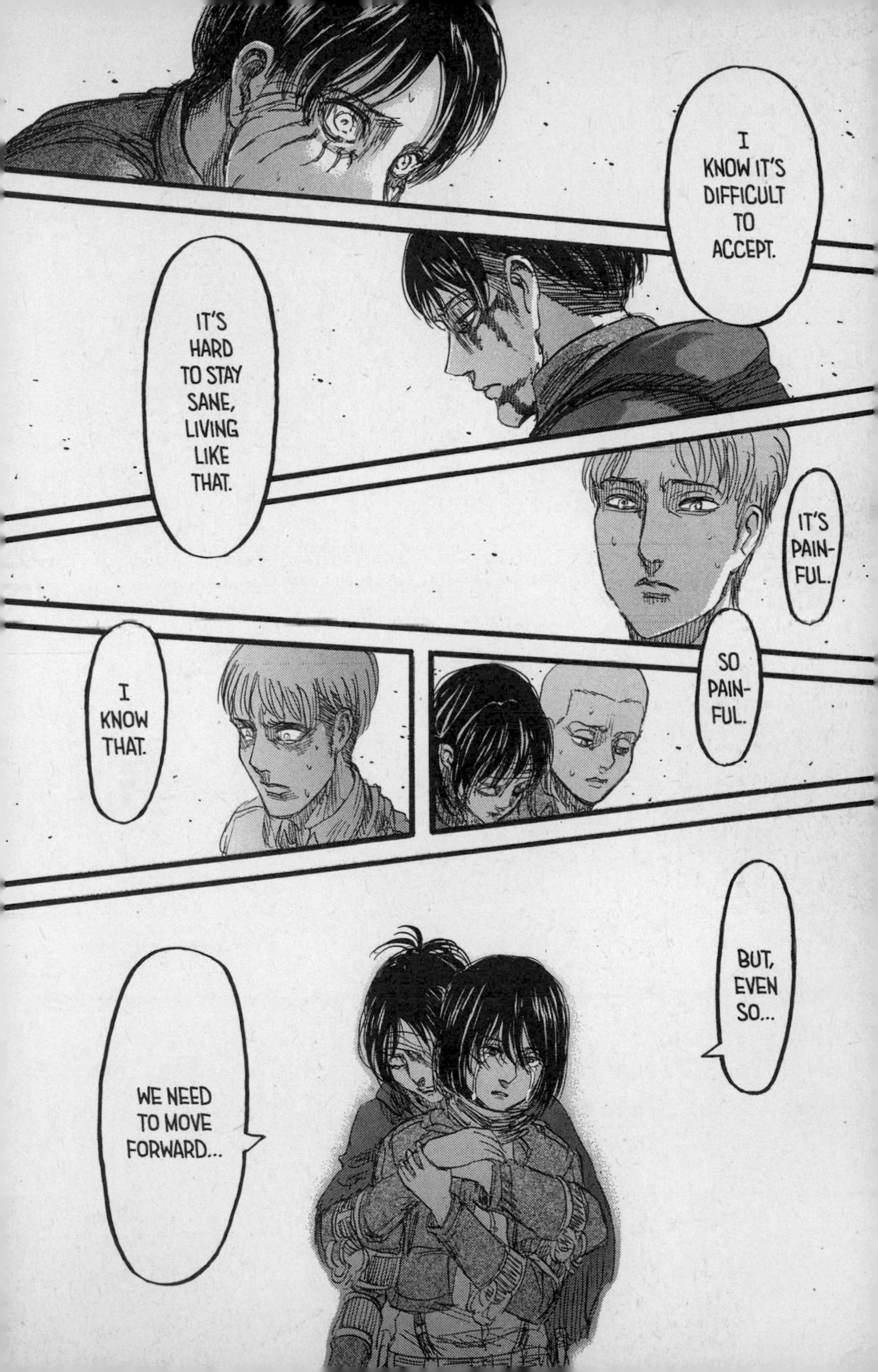
I KNOW IT'S DIFFICULT TO ACCEPT.
IT'S HARD TO STAY SANE, LIVING LIKE THAT.
IT'S PAIN-FUL.
SO PAIN-FUL.
I KNOW THAT.
BUT, EVEN SO...
WE NEED TO MOVE FORWARD...

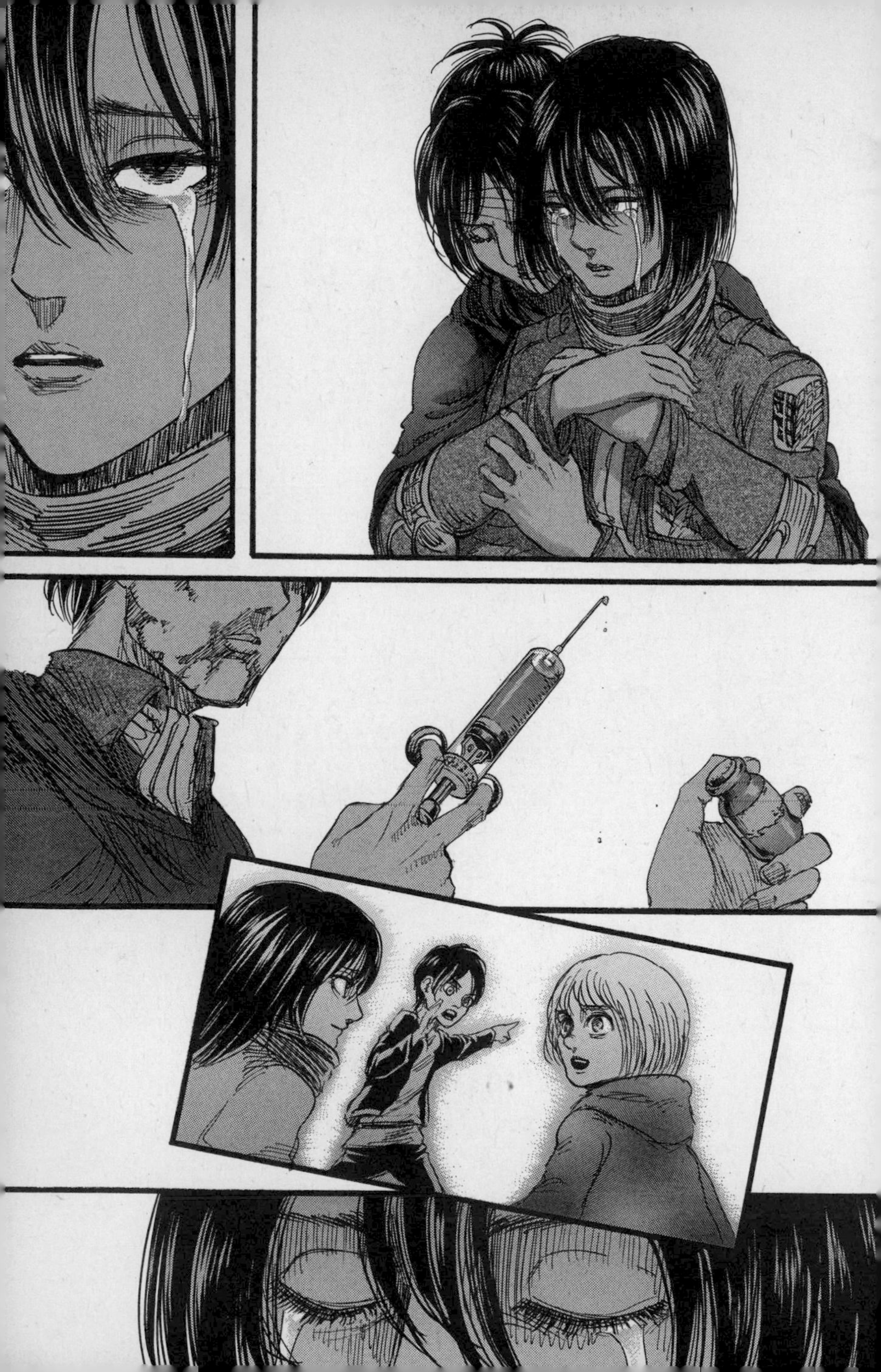

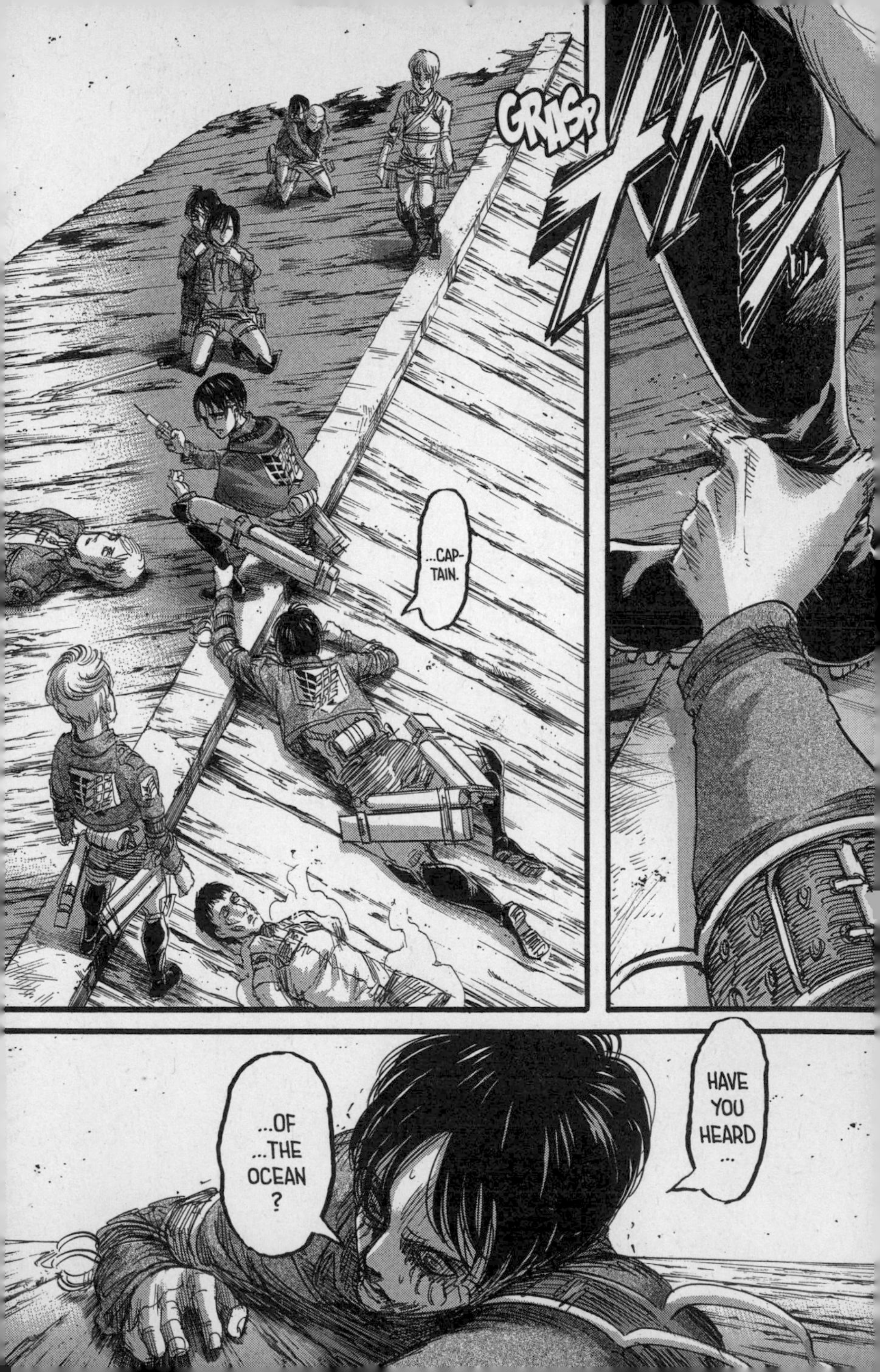
GRASP
...CAP-TAIN.
HAVE YOU HEARD ...
...OF ...THE OCEAN ?

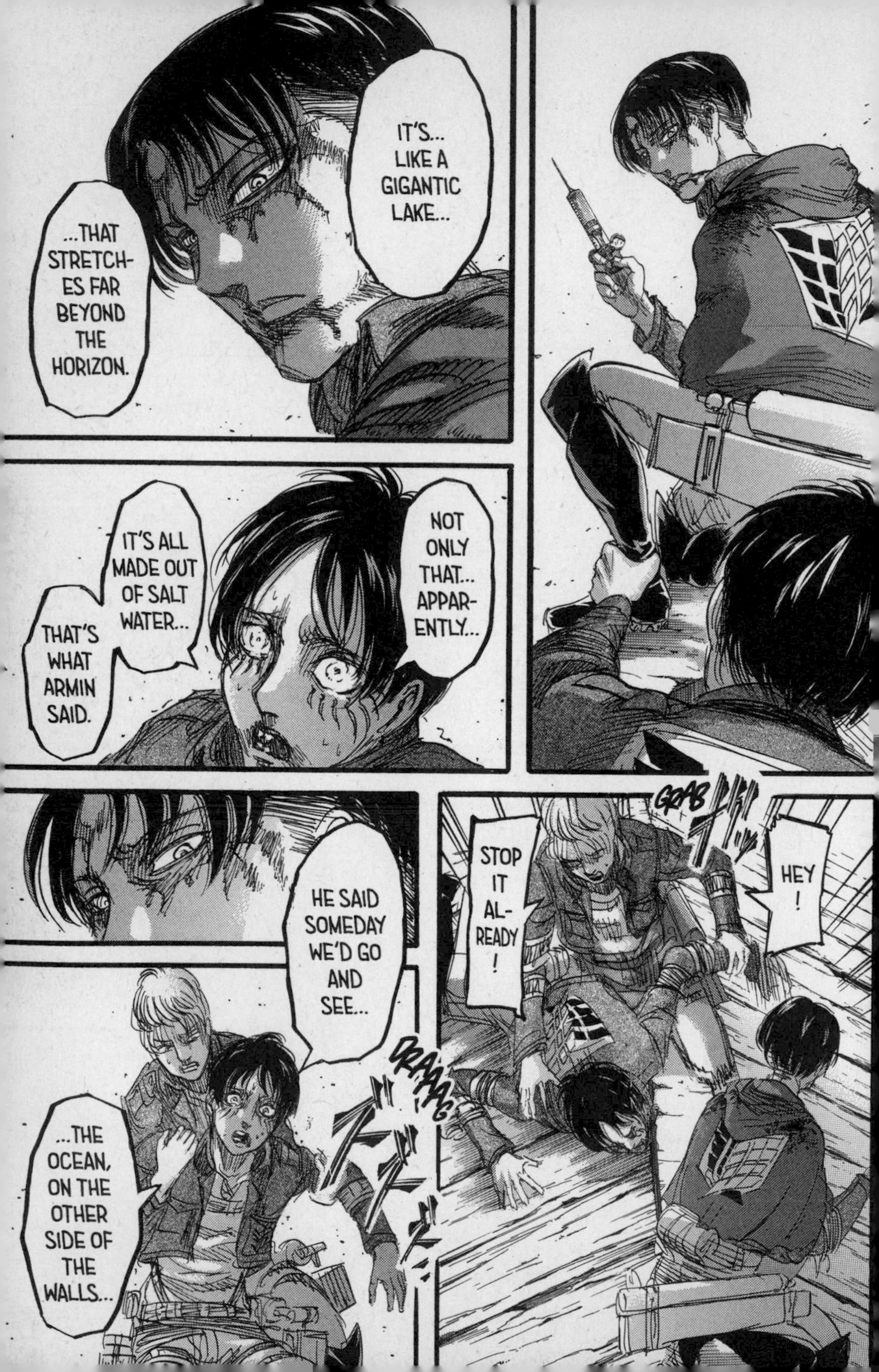
IT'S... LIKE A GIGANTIC LAKE...
...THAT STRETCHES FAR BEYOND THE HORIZON.
NOT ONLY THAT... APPARENTLY...
IT'S ALL MADE OUT OF SALT WATER...
THAT'S WHAT ARMIN SAID.
GRAB
HEY!
STOP IT AL-READY!
HE SAID SOMEDAY WE'D GO AND SEE...
DRAAAAG
...THE OCEAN, ON THE OTHER SIDE OF THE WALLS...

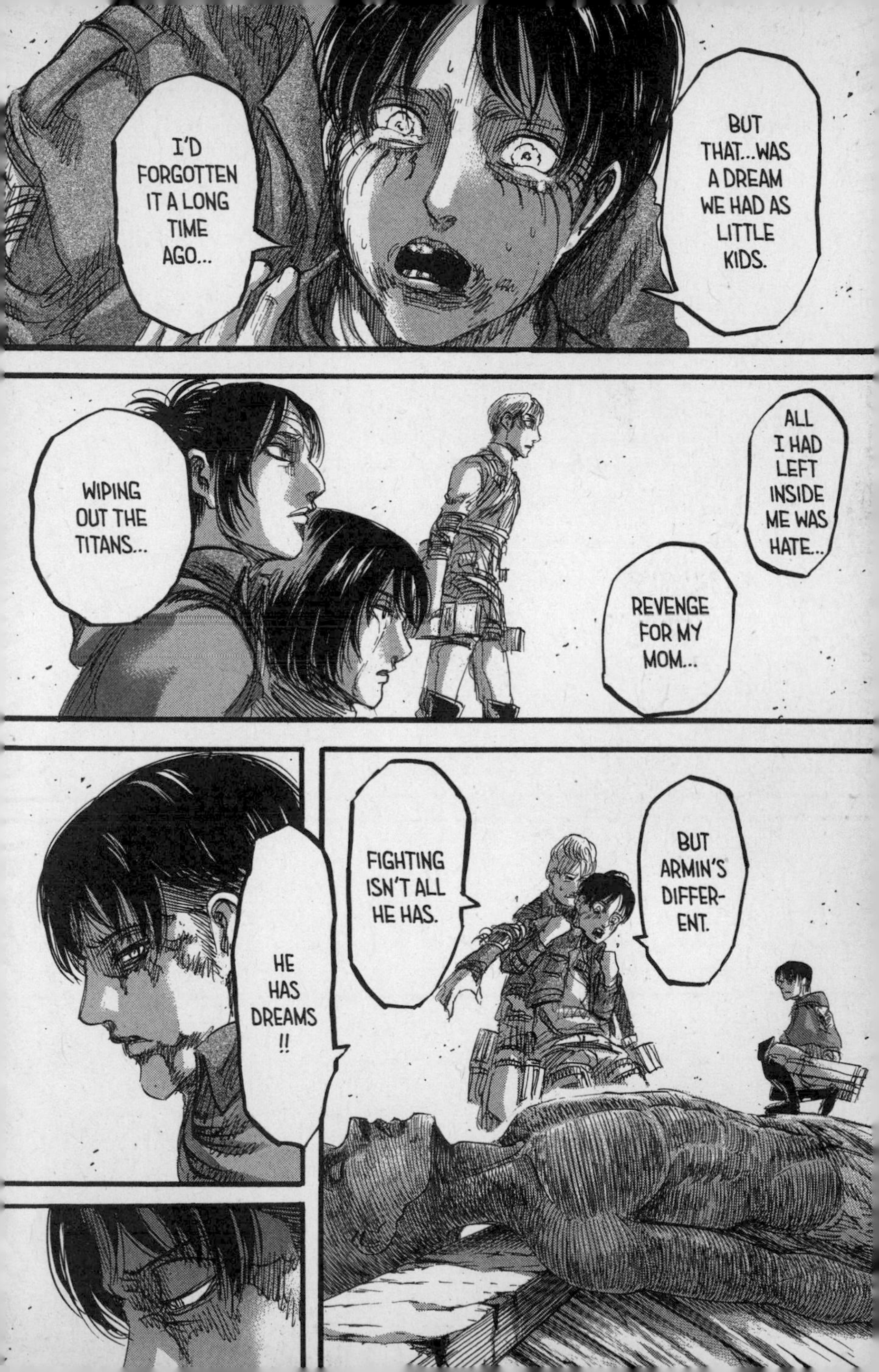
BUT THAT...WAS A DREAM WE HAD AS LITTLE KIDS.
I'D FORGOTTEN IT A LONG TIME AGO...
ALL I HAD LEFT INSIDE ME WAS HATE...
REVENGE FOR MY MOM...
WIPING OUT THE TITANS...
BUT ARMIN'S DIFFER-ENT.
FIGHTING ISN'T ALL HE HAS.
HE HAS DREAMS!!

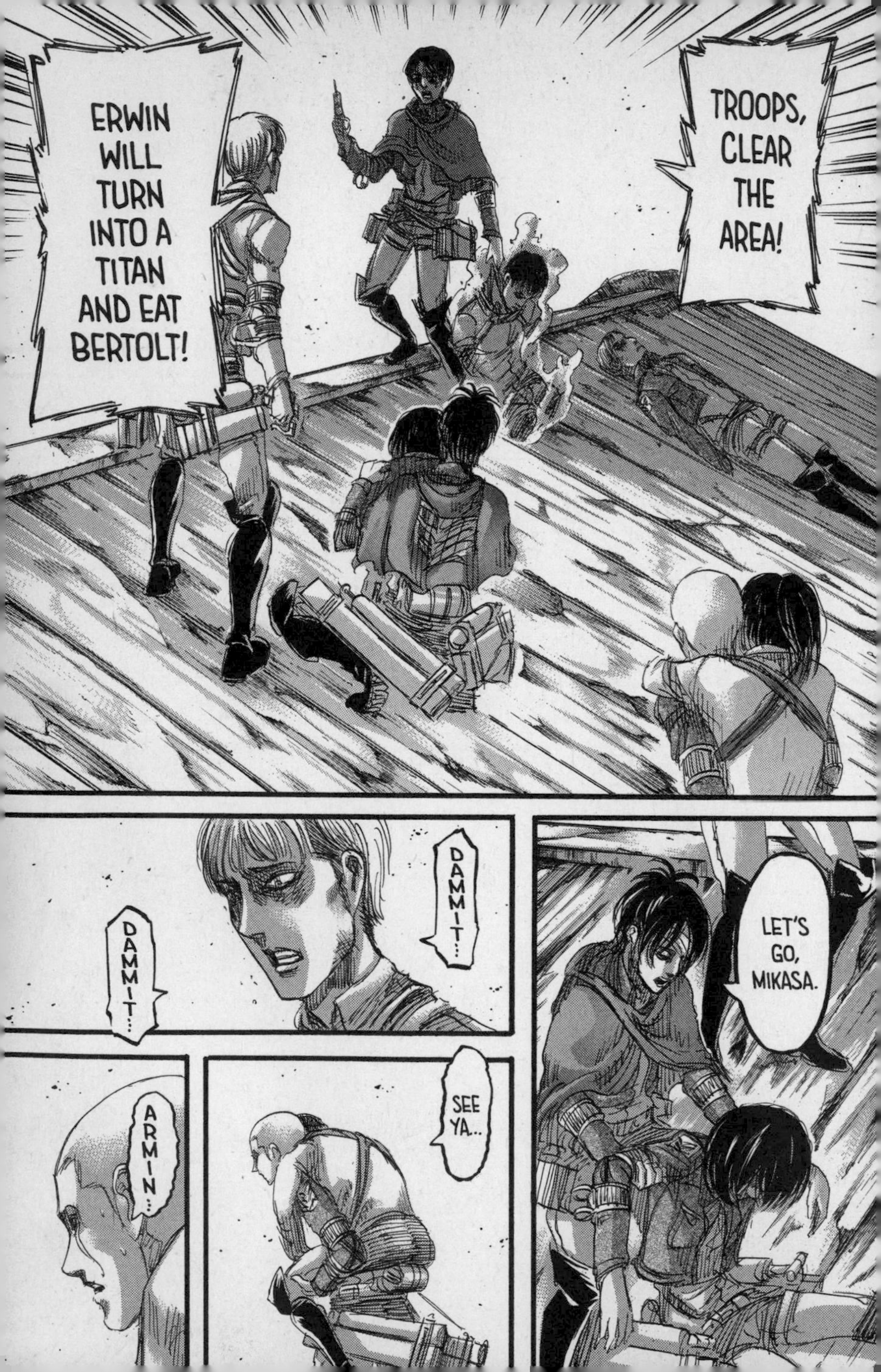
TROOPS, CLEAR THE AREA!
ERWIN WILL TURN INTO A TITAN AND EAT BERTOLT!
LET'S GO, MIKASA.
DAMMIT...
DAMMIT...
SEE YA...
ARMIN...

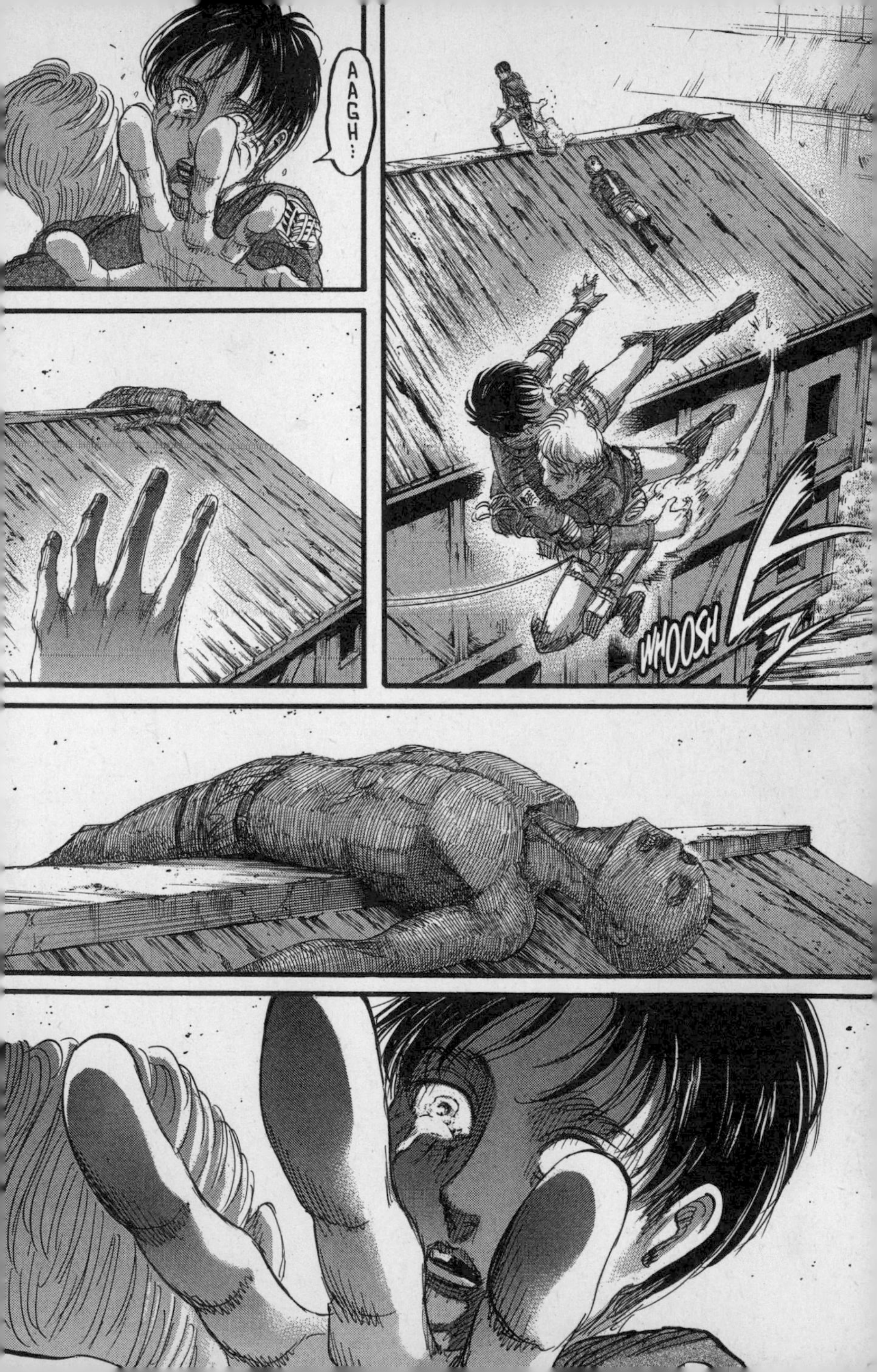
AAGH...
WHOOSH

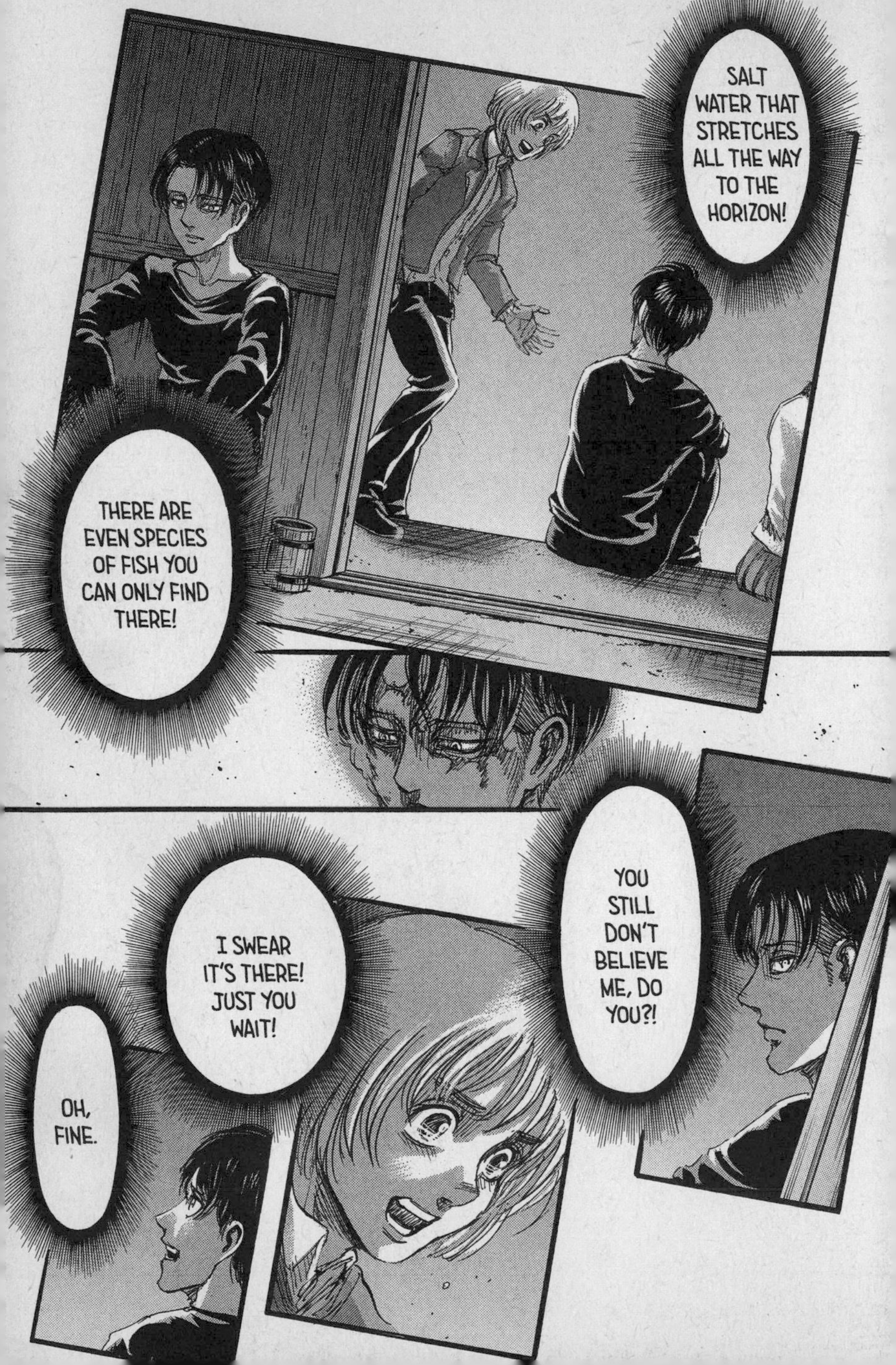
SALT WATER THAT STRETCHES ALL THE WAY TO THE HORIZON!
THERE ARE EVEN SPECIES OF FISH YOU CAN ONLY FIND THERE!
YOU STILL DON'T BELIEVE ME, DO YOU?!
I SWEAR IT'S THERE! JUST YOU WAIT!
OH, FINE.

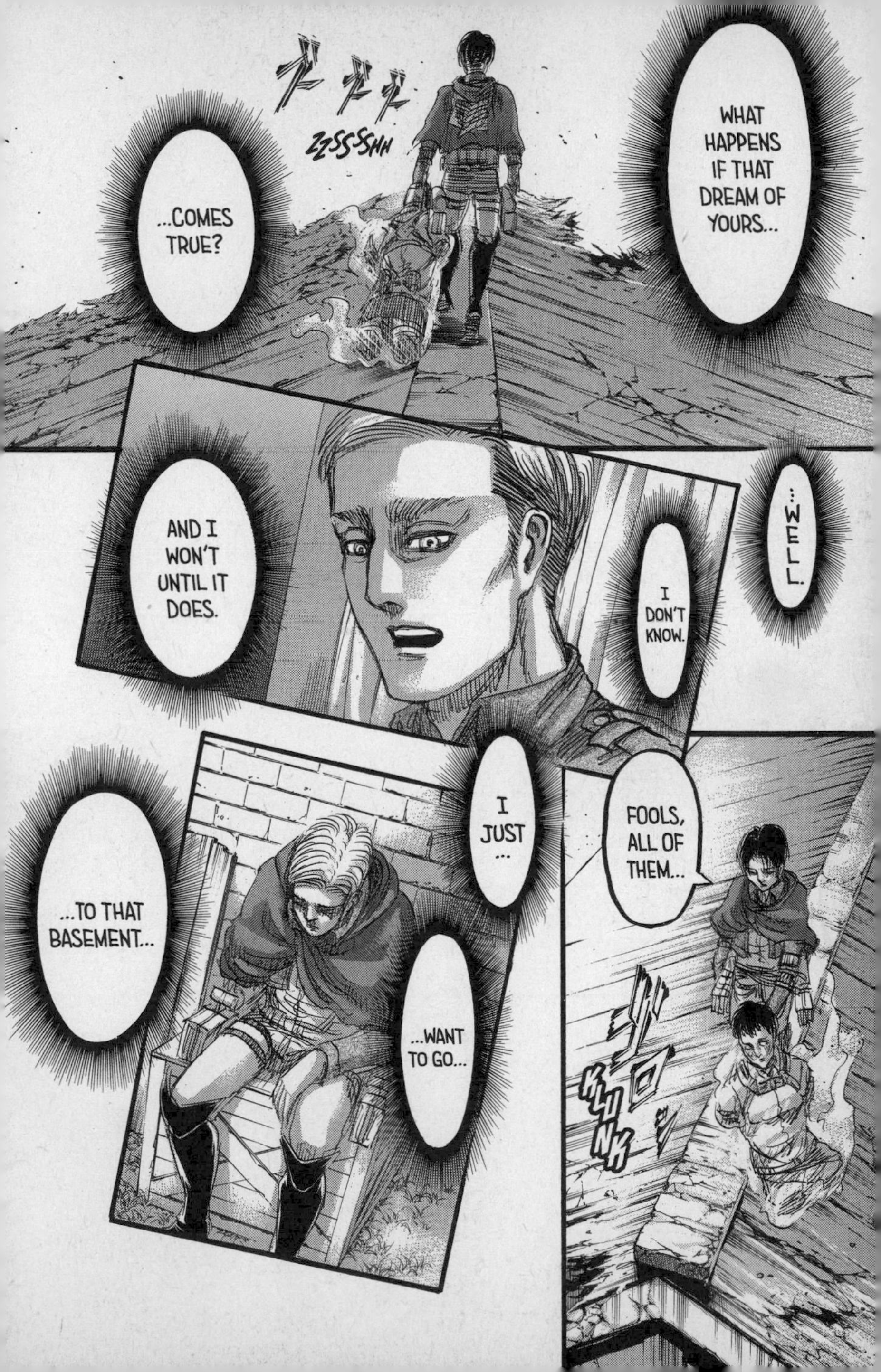
WHAT HAPPENS IF THAT DREAM OF YOURS...
ZZSS-SSHH
...COMES TRUE?
...WELL.
I DON'T KNOW.
AND I WON'T UNTIL IT DOES.
FOOLS, ALL OF THEM...
KLUNK
I JUST ...
...WANT TO GO...
...TO THAT BASEMENT...

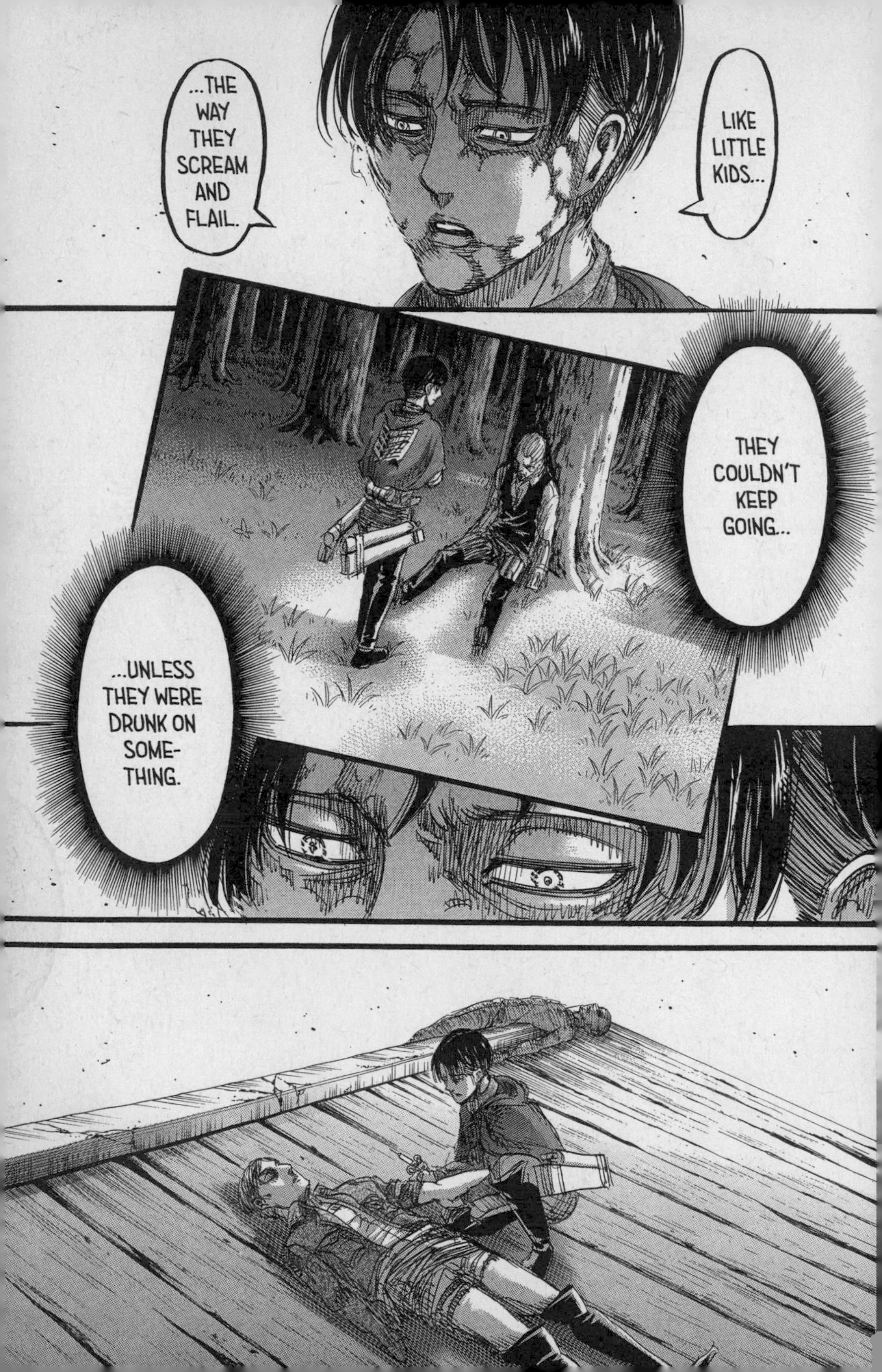
LIKE LITTLE KIDS...
...THE WAY THEY SCREAM AND FLAIL.
THEY COULDN'T KEEP GOING...
...UNLESS THEY WERE DRUNK ON SOME-THING.

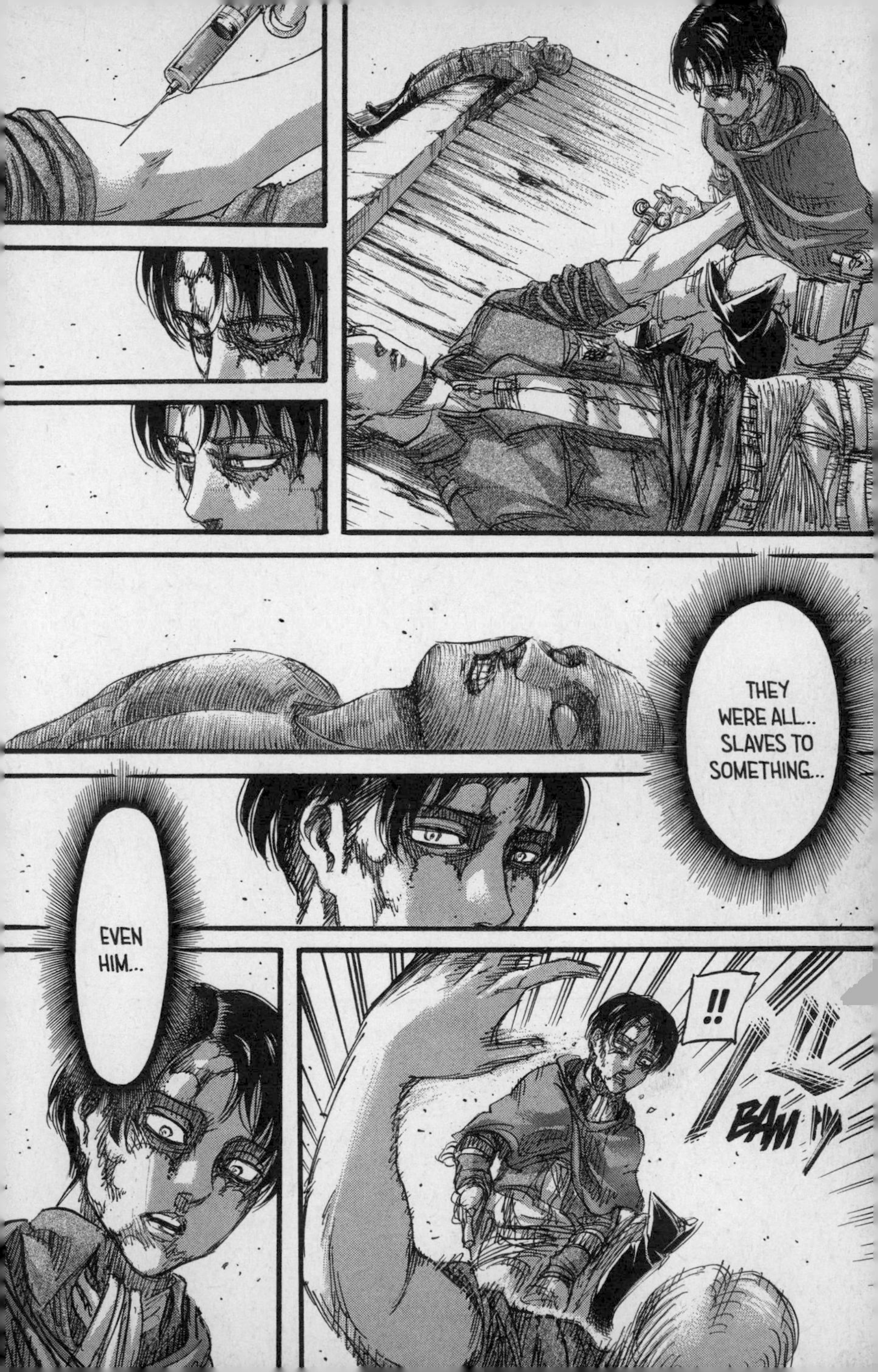
THEY WERE ALL... SLAVES TO SOMETHING...
EVEN HIM...
!!
BAM

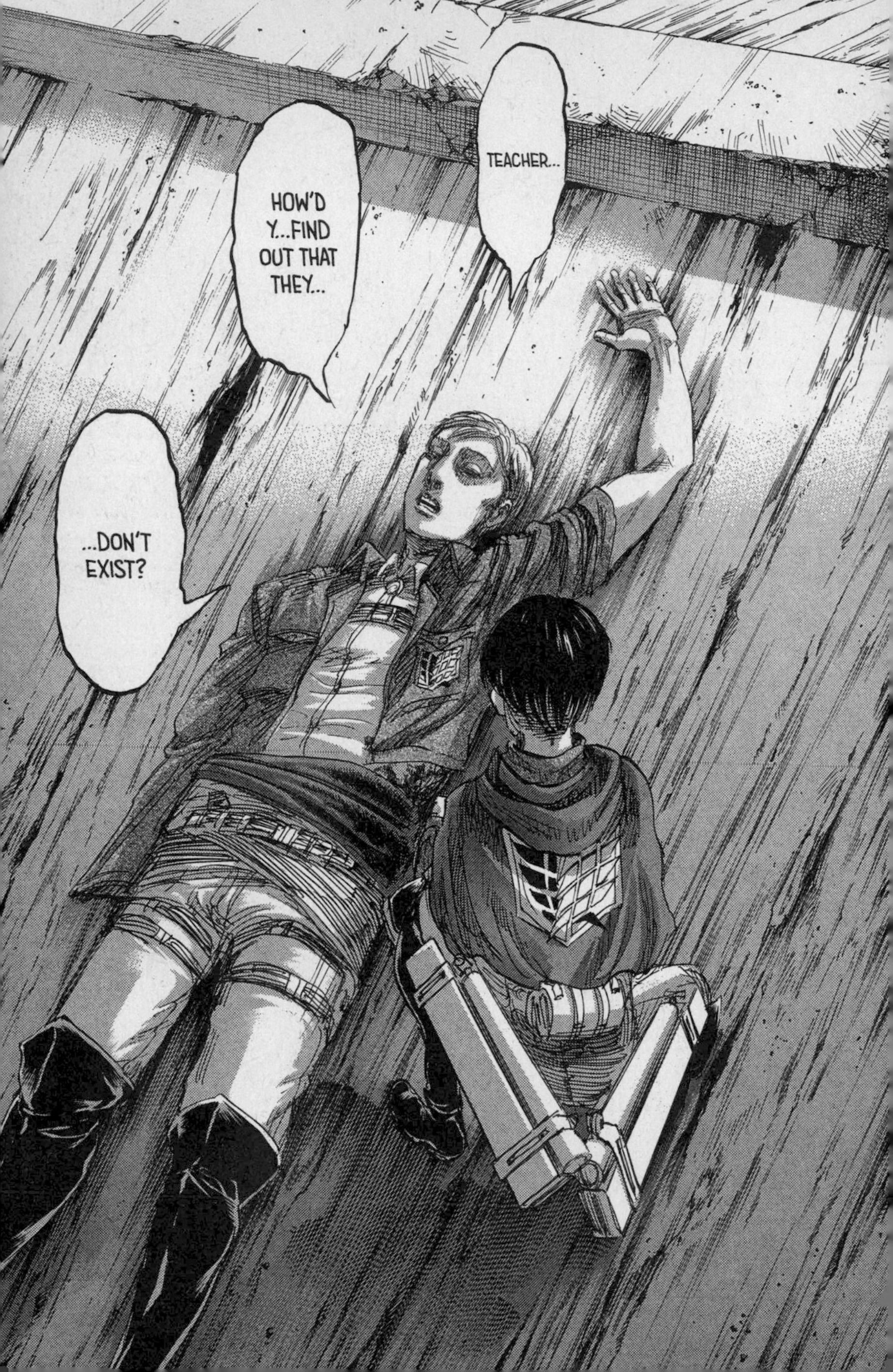
TEACHER...
HOW'D Y...FIND OUT THAT THEY...
...DON'T EXIST?

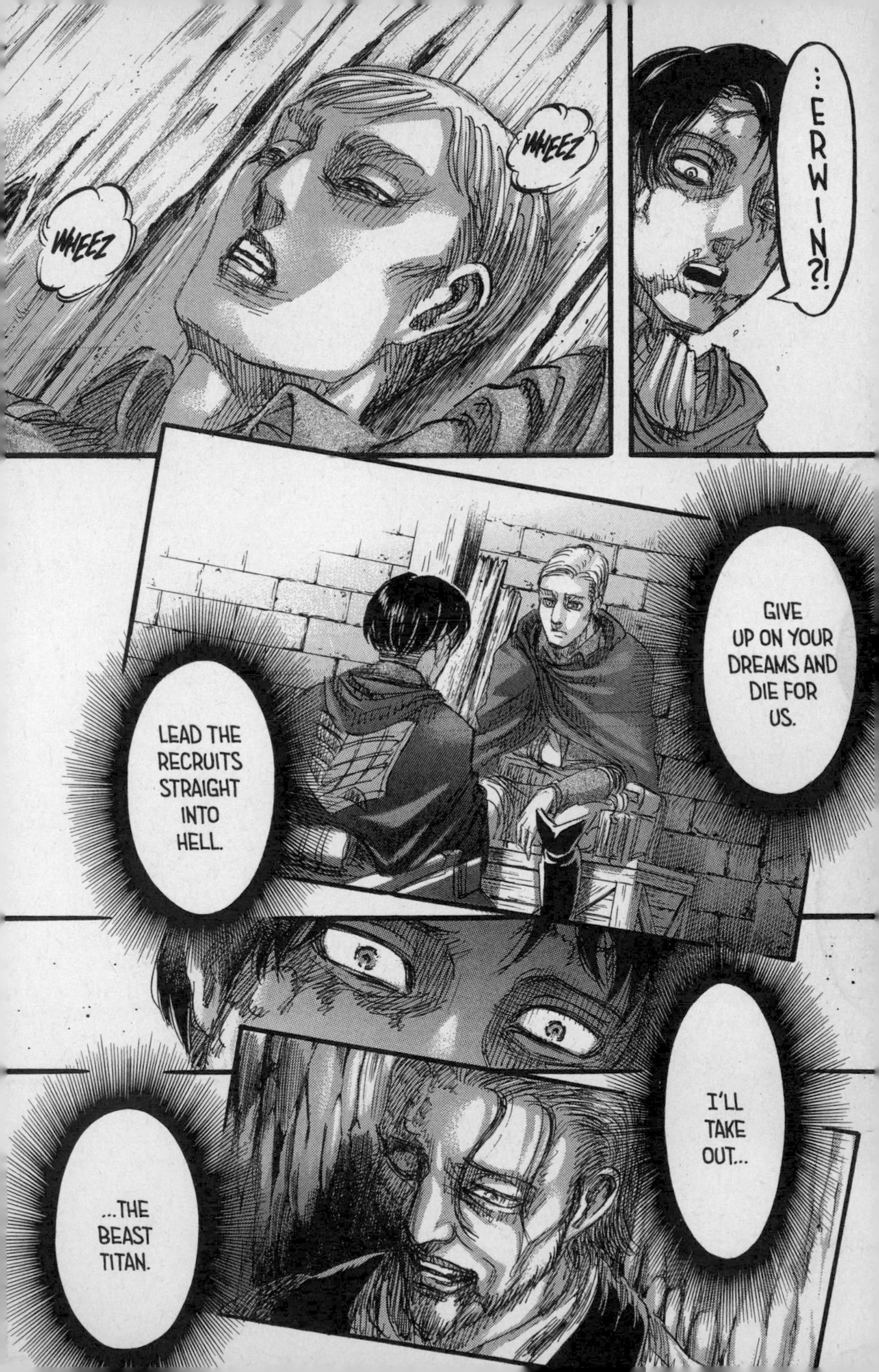
...ERWIN?!
WHEEZ
WHEEZ
GIVE UP ON YOUR DREAMS AND DIE FOR US.
LEAD THE RECRUITS STRAIGHT INTO HELL.
I'LL TAKE OUT...
...THE BEAST TITAN.

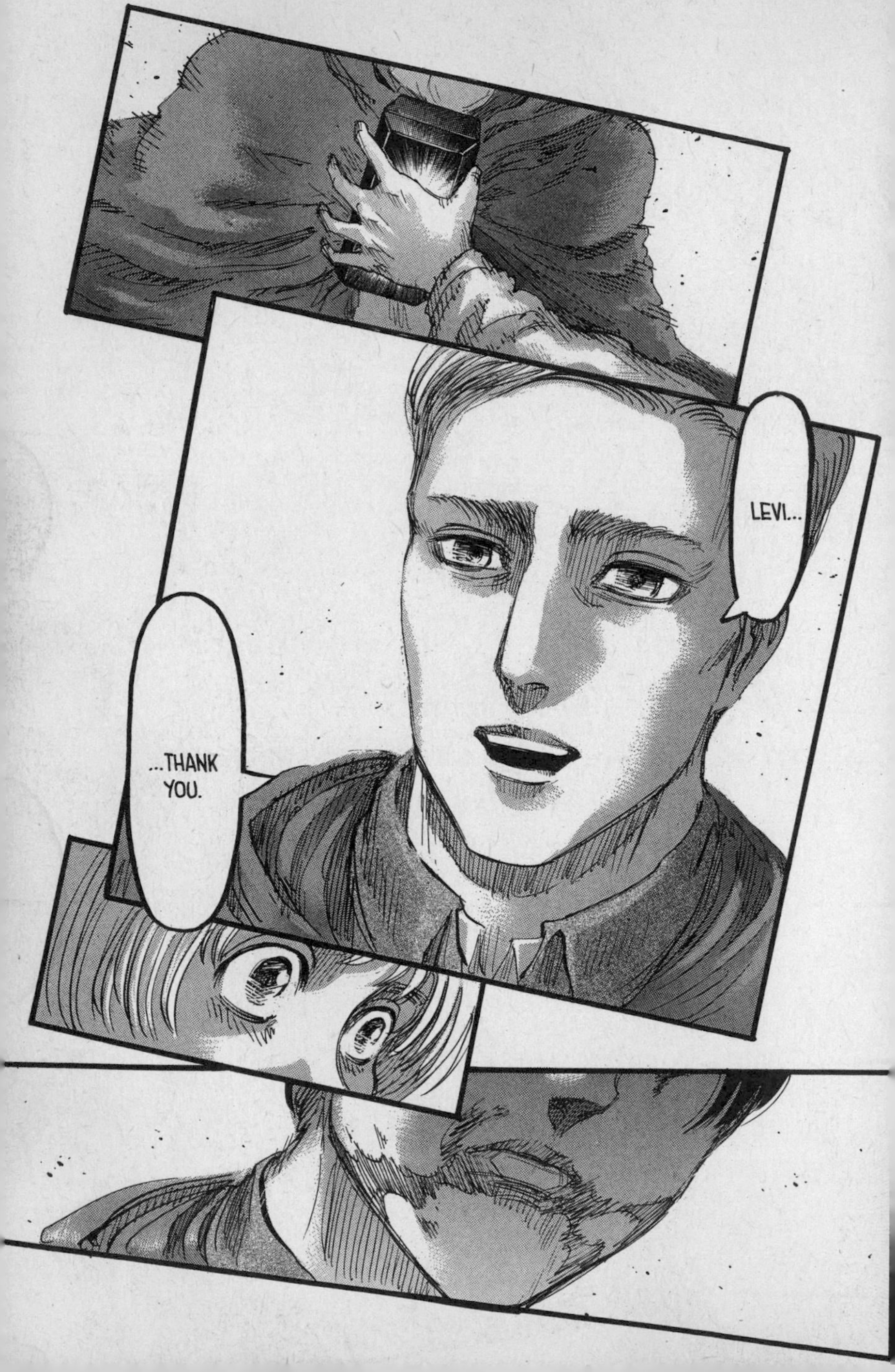
LEVI...
...THANK YOU.

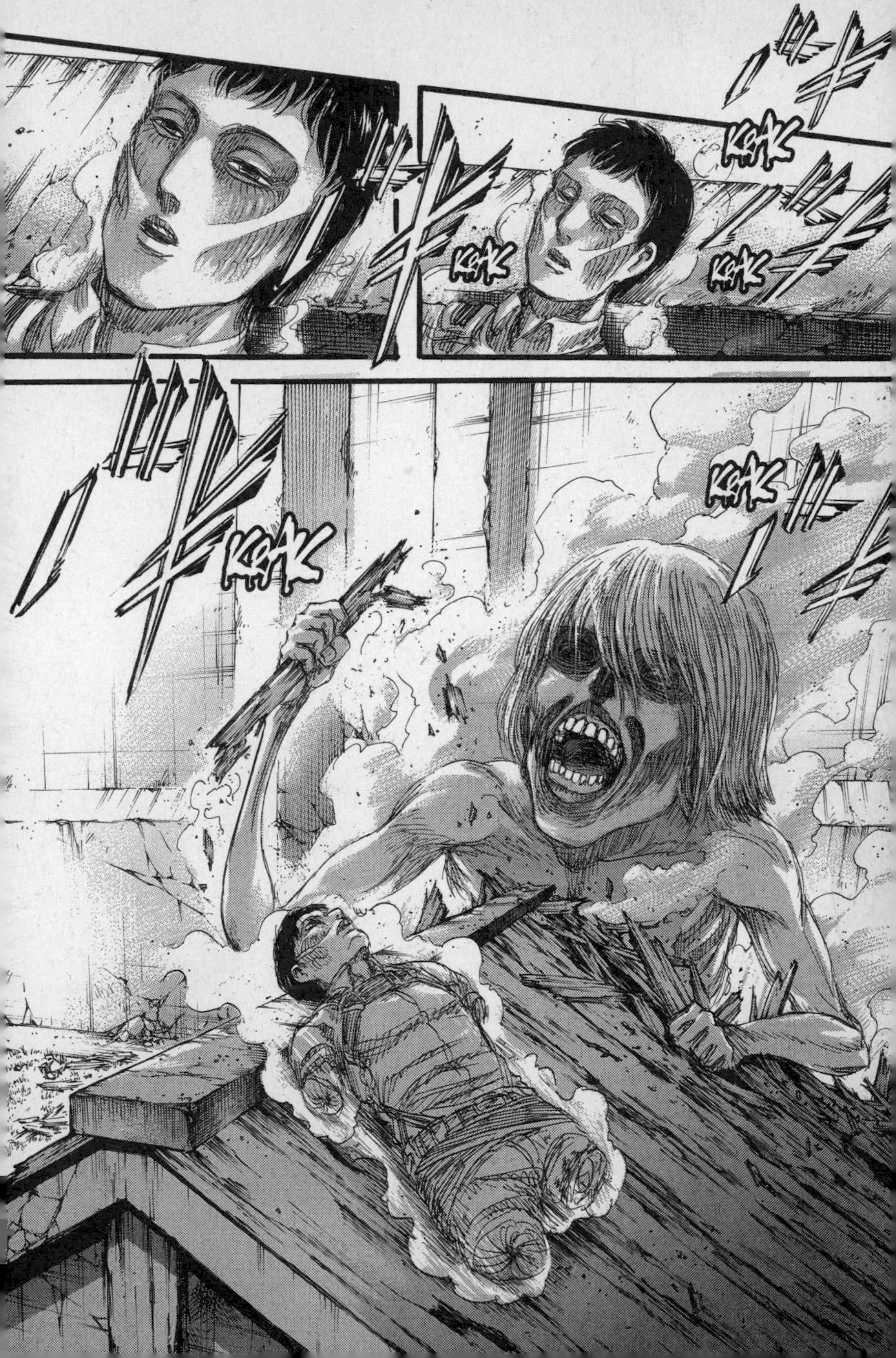
KRAK
KRAK
KRAK
KRAK
KRAK

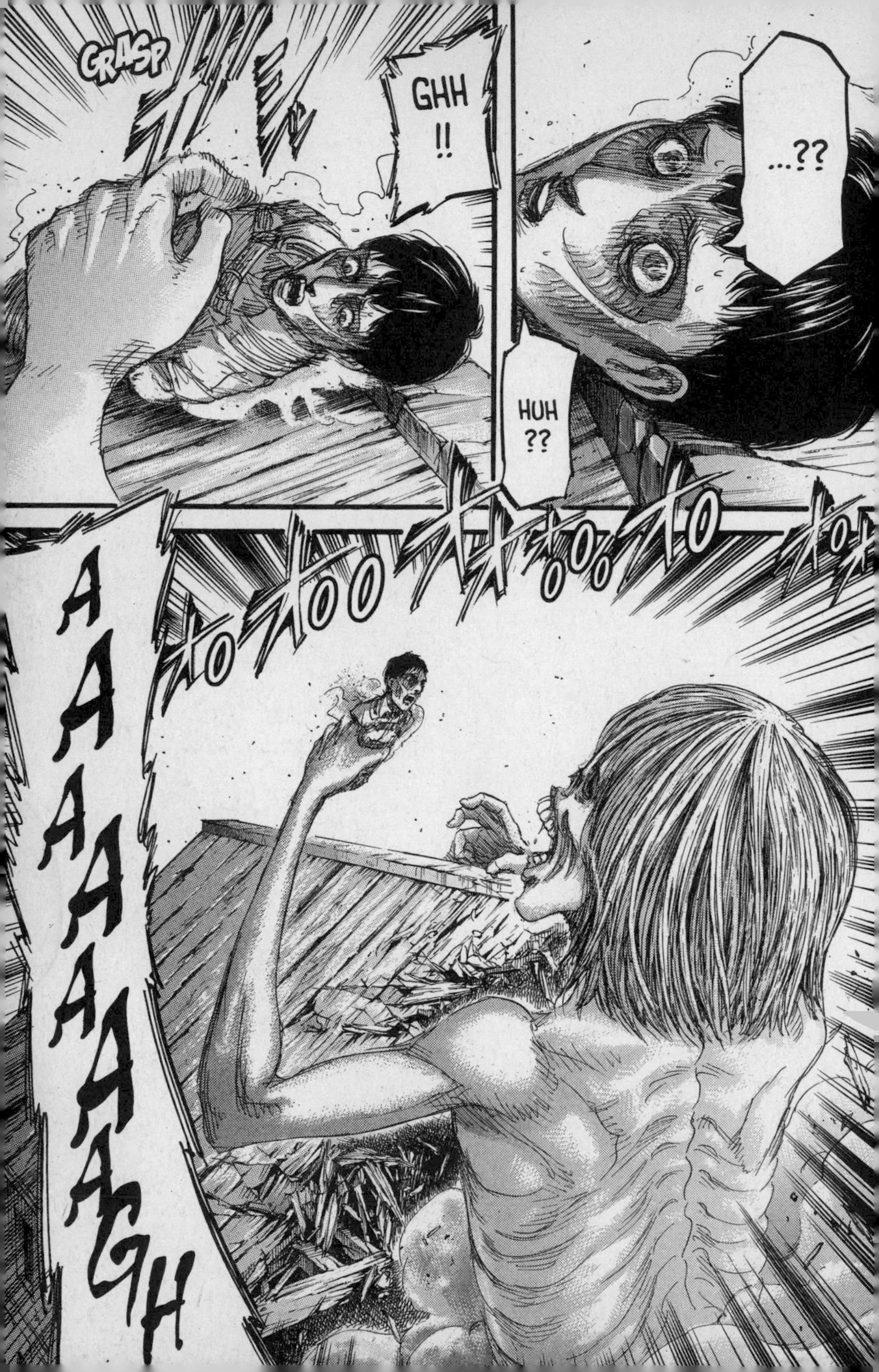
...??
HUH ??
GRASP
GHH !!
AAAAAAAAGH

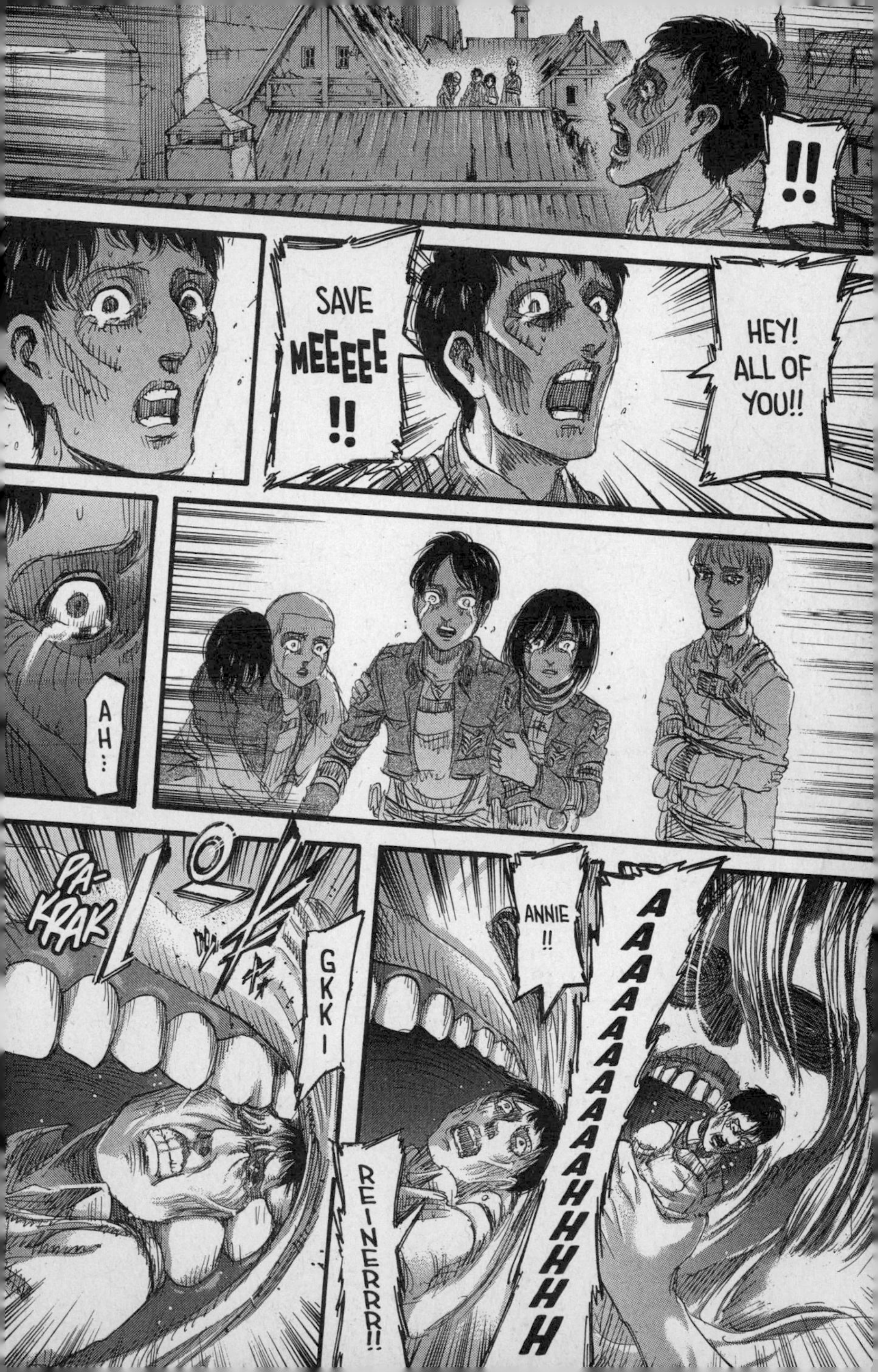
!!
HEY! ALL OF YOU!!
SAVE MEEEEE !!
AH...
AAAAAAAAAAAHHHHHH
ANNIE !!
REINERRR!!
GKKI
PA-KRAK

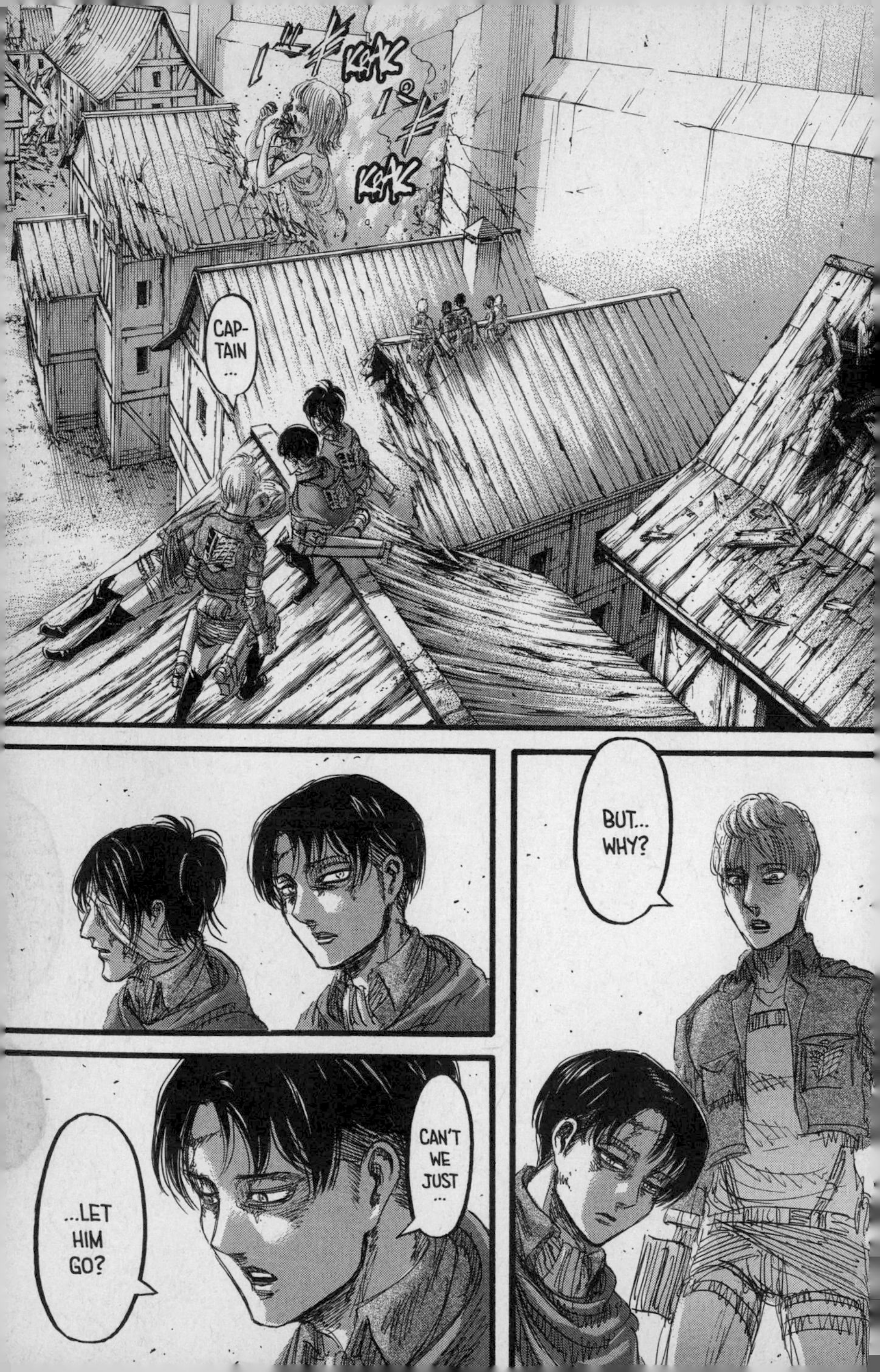
KRAK
KRAK
CAP-TAIN ...
BUT... WHY?
CAN'T WE JUST ...
...LET HIM GO?

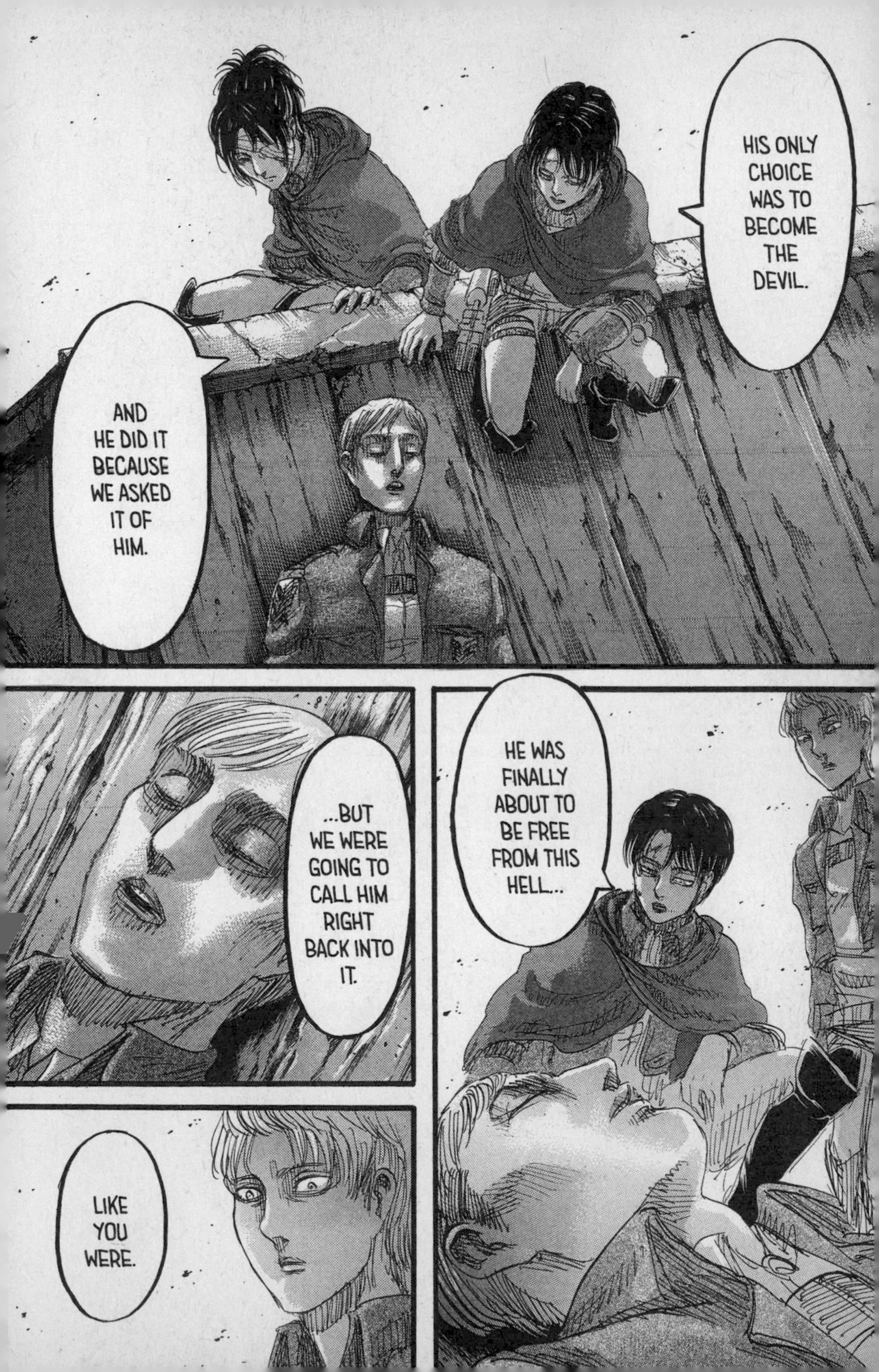
HIS ONLY CHOICE WAS TO BECOME THE DEVIL.
AND HE DID IT BECAUSE WE ASKED IT OF HIM.
HE WAS FINALLY ABOUT TO BE FREE FROM THIS HELL...
...BUT WE WERE GOING TO CALL HIM RIGHT BACK INTO IT.
LIKE YOU WERE.

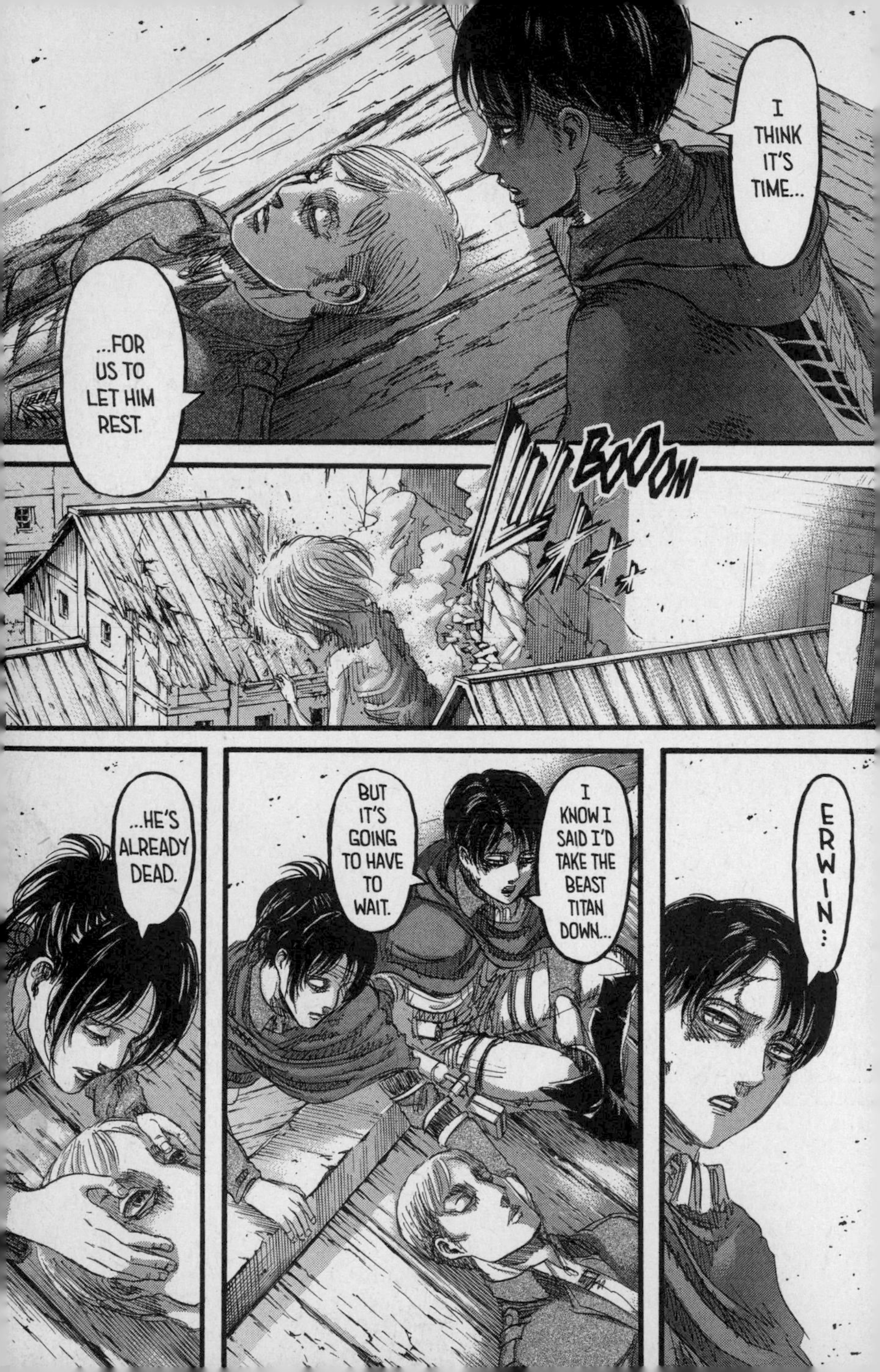
I THINK IT'S TIME...
...FOR US TO LET HIM REST.
BOOOM
ERWIN...
I KNOW I SAID I'D TAKE THE BEAST TITAN DOWN...
BUT IT'S GOING TO HAVE TO WAIT.
...HE'S ALREADY DEAD.

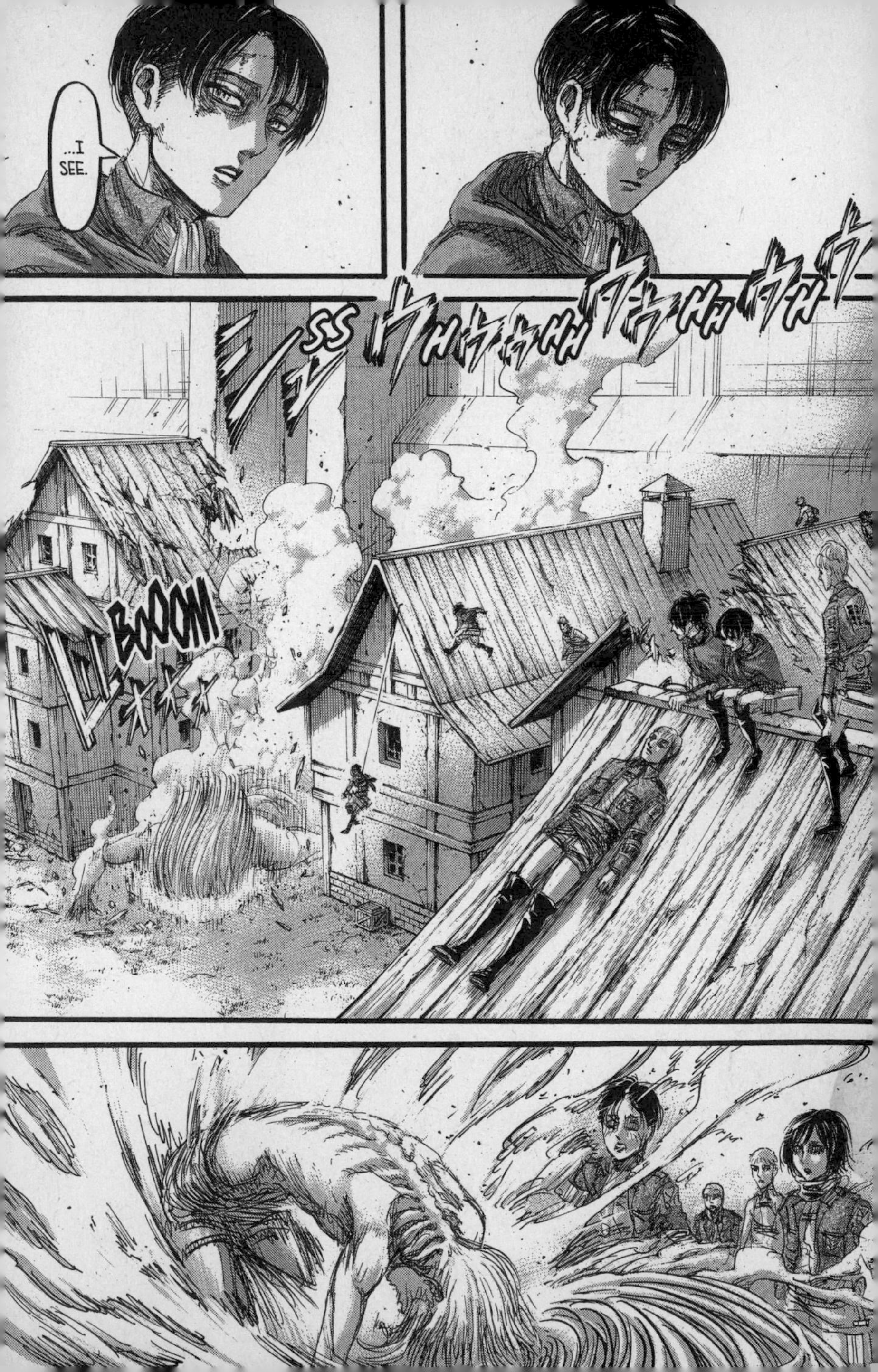
...I SEE.
SS
BOOOM

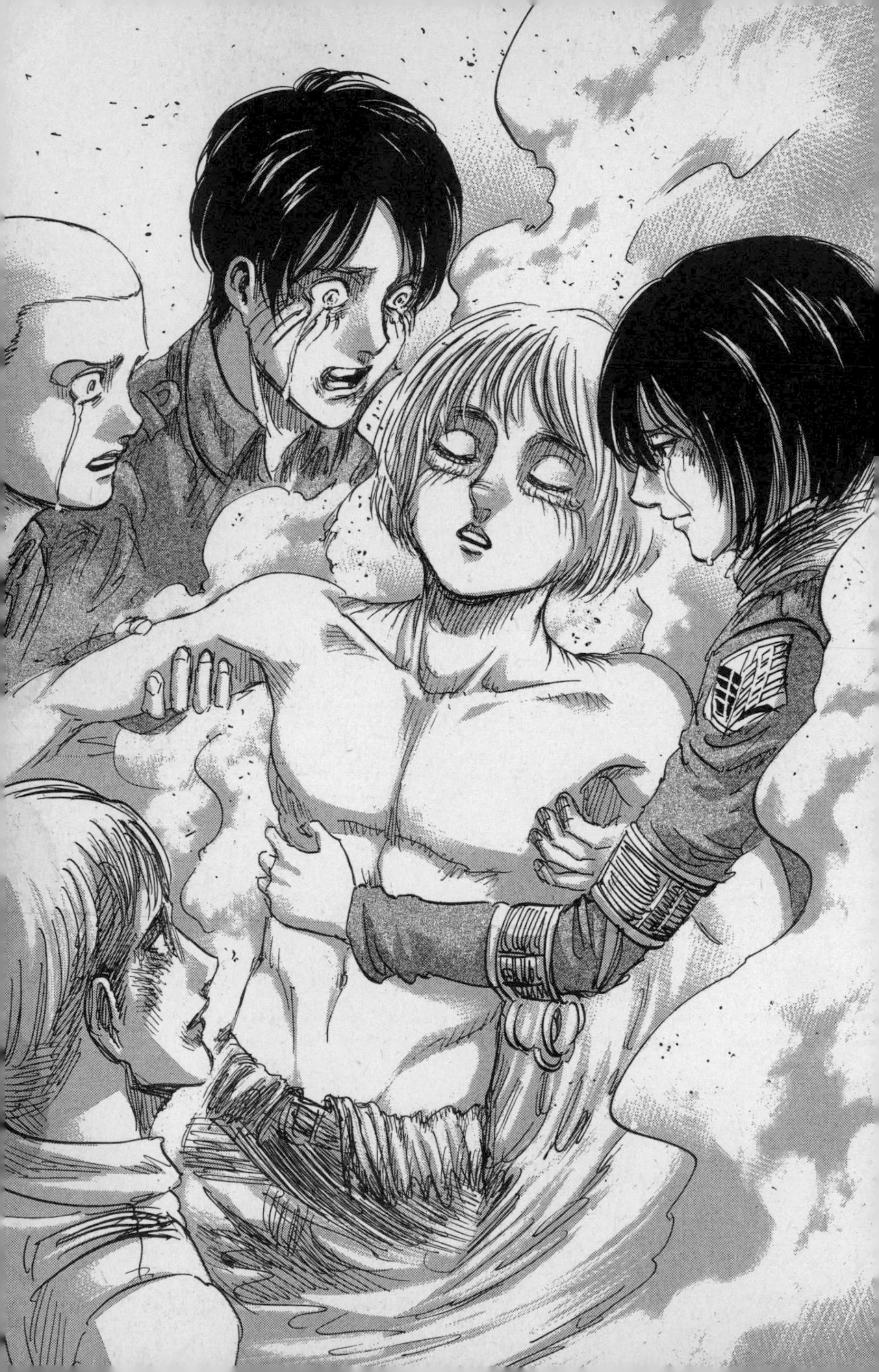

ATTACK on TITAN

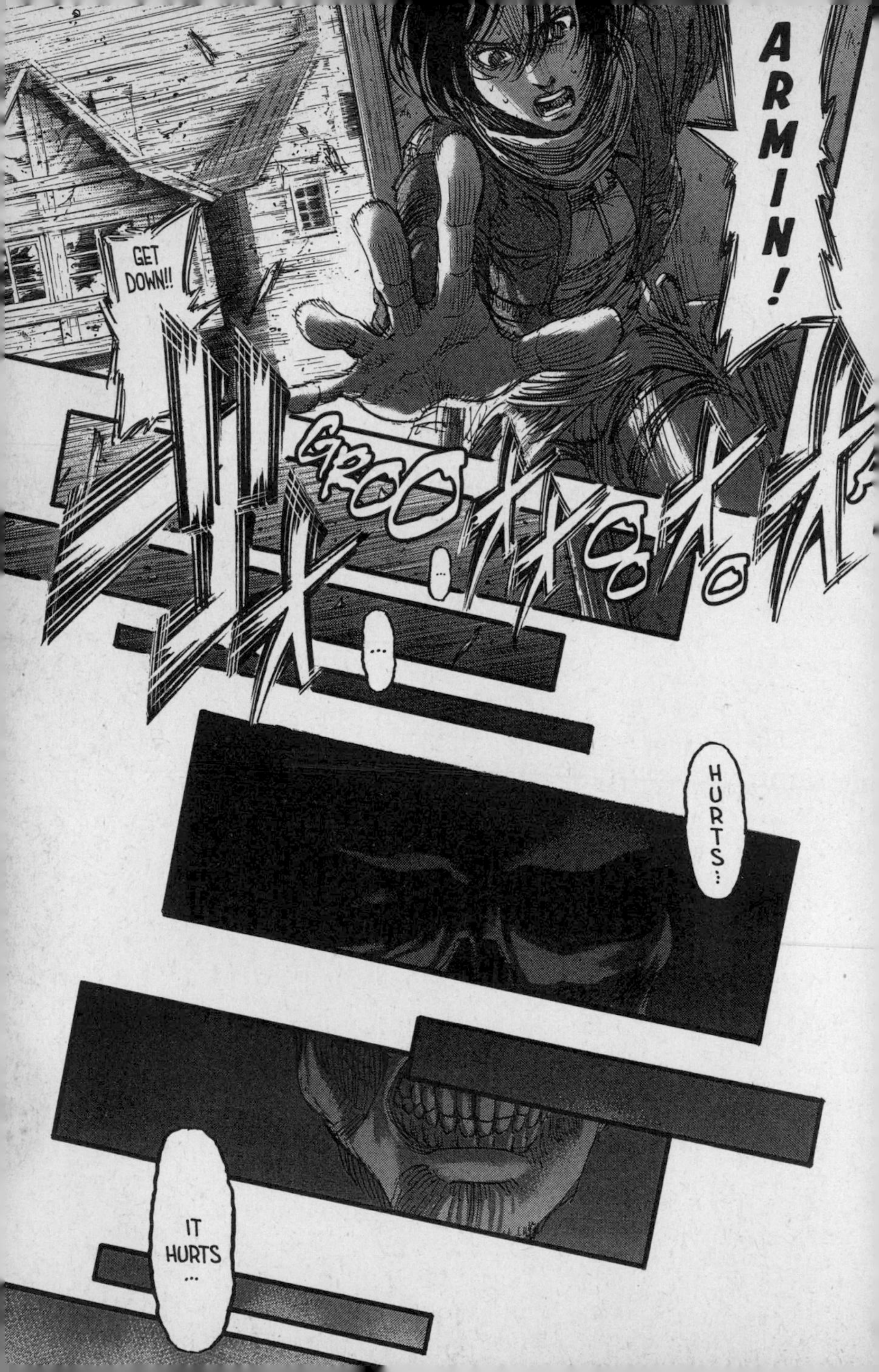
ARMIN!
GET DOWN!!
GROOOOOOO
...
...
HURTS...
IT HURTS...

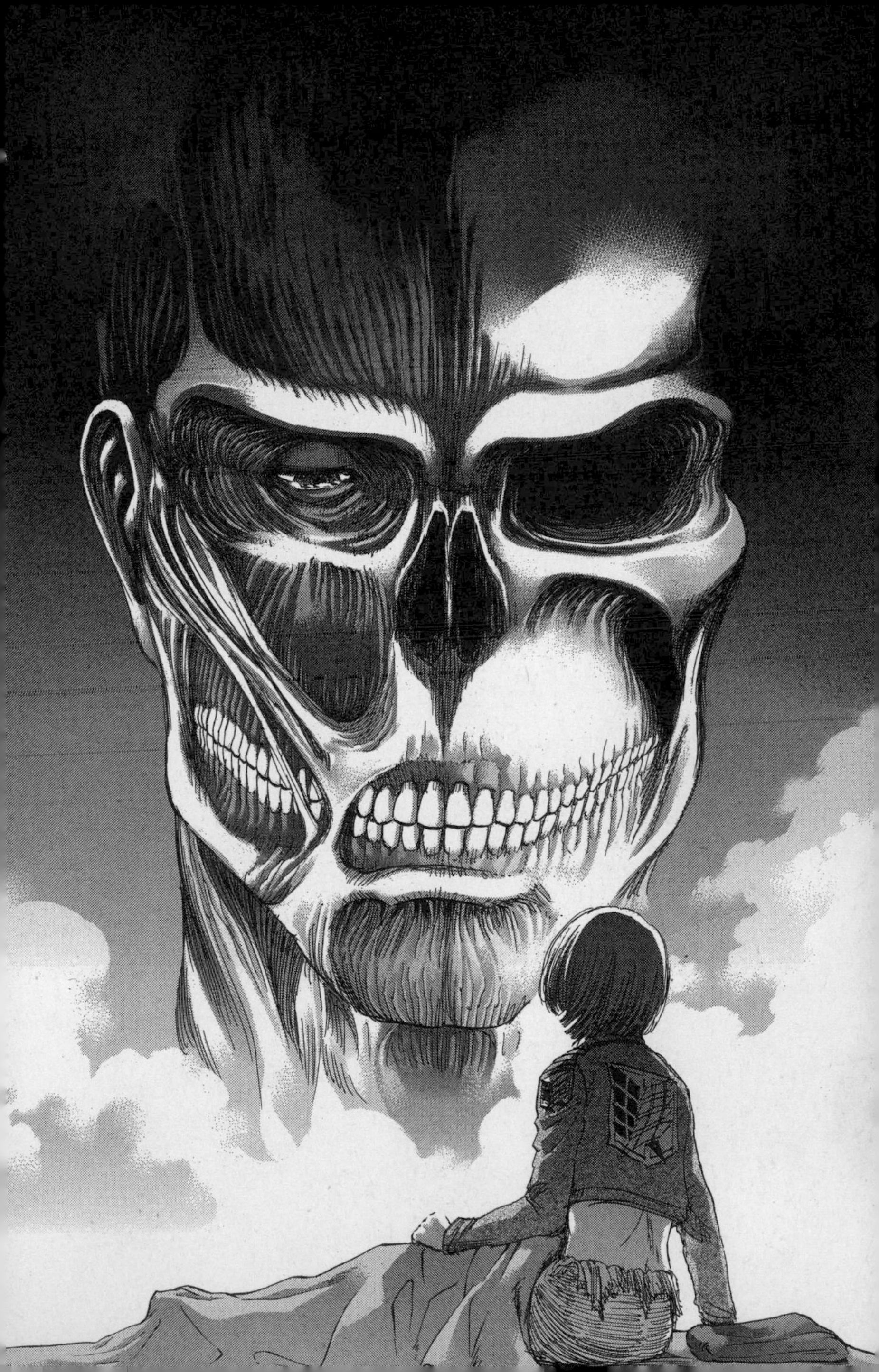

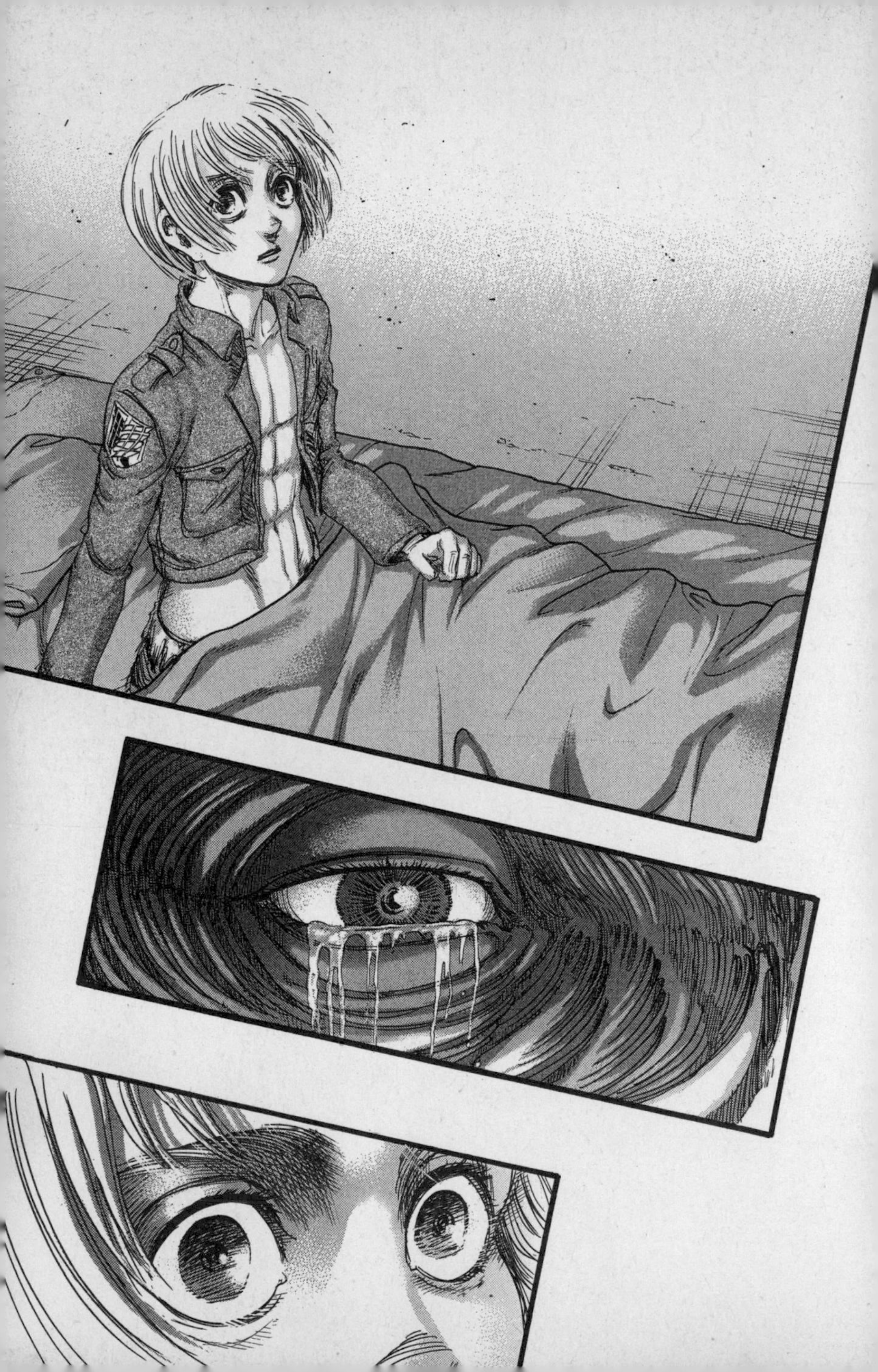

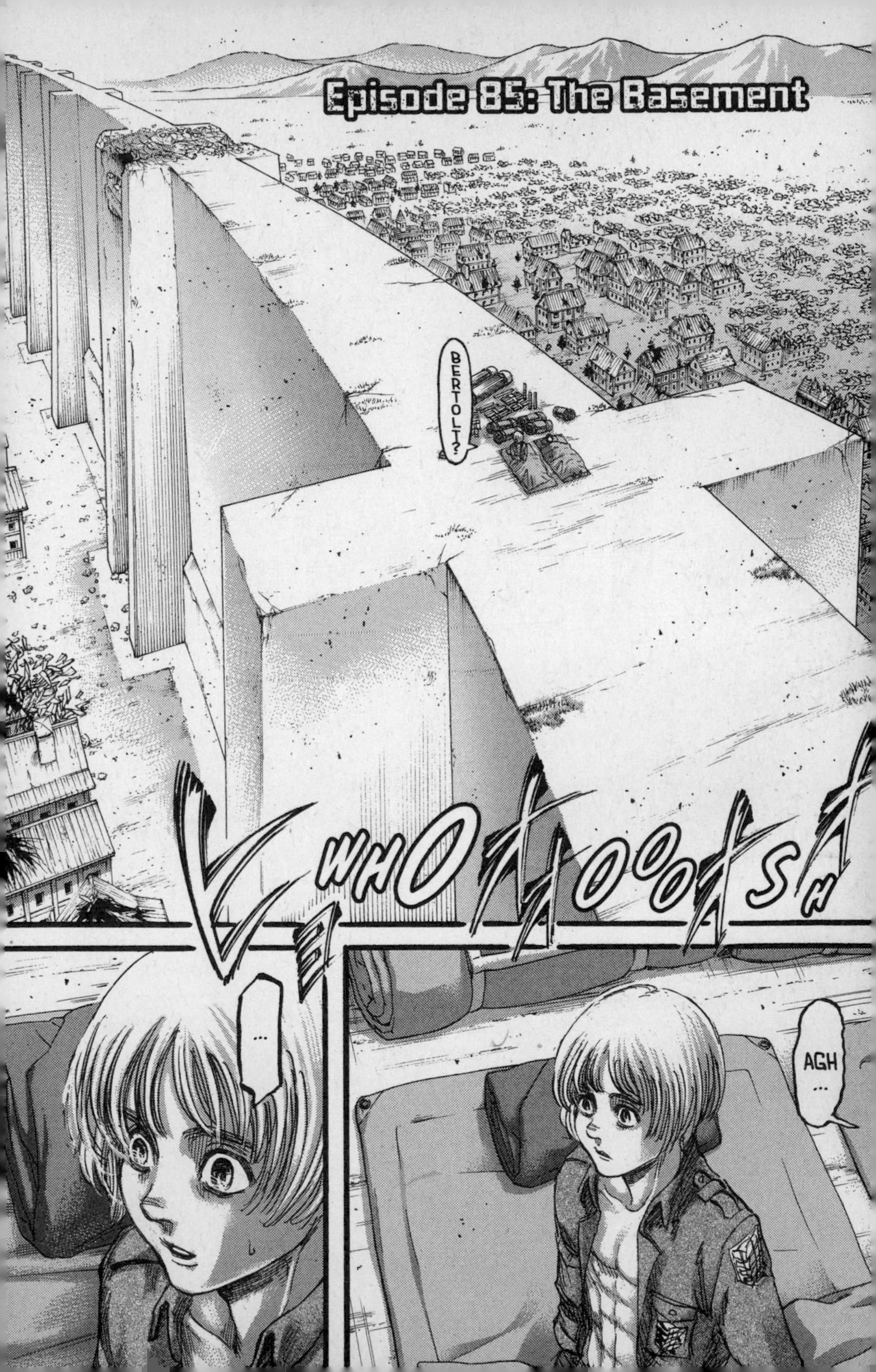
Episode 85: The Basement
BERTOLT?
WHOOOOSH
AGH ...
...

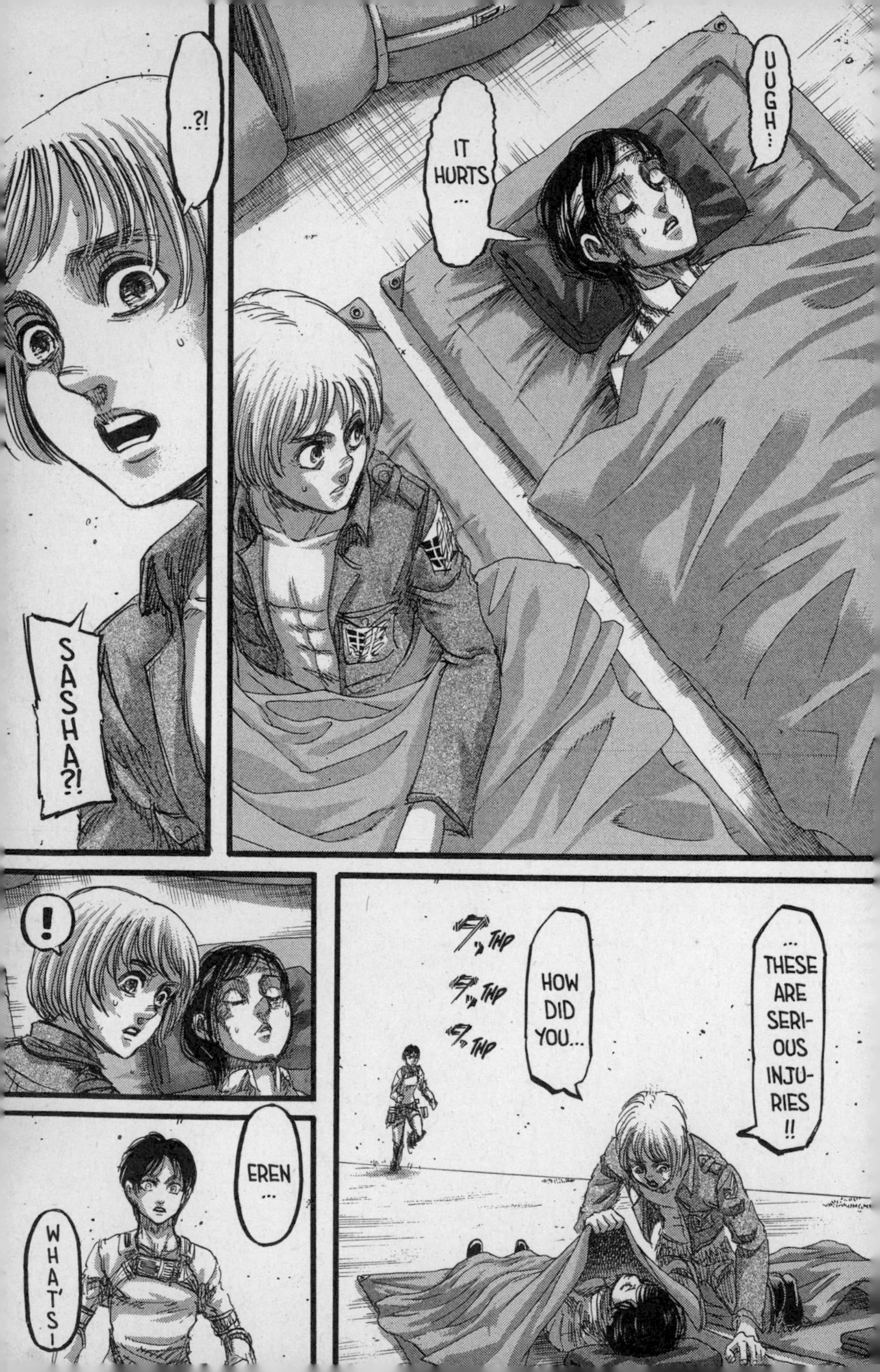
UUGH...
IT HURTS...
..?!
SASHA?!
...THESE ARE SERIOUS INJURIES!!
HOW DID YOU...
THD
THD
THD
!
EREN...
WHAT'S

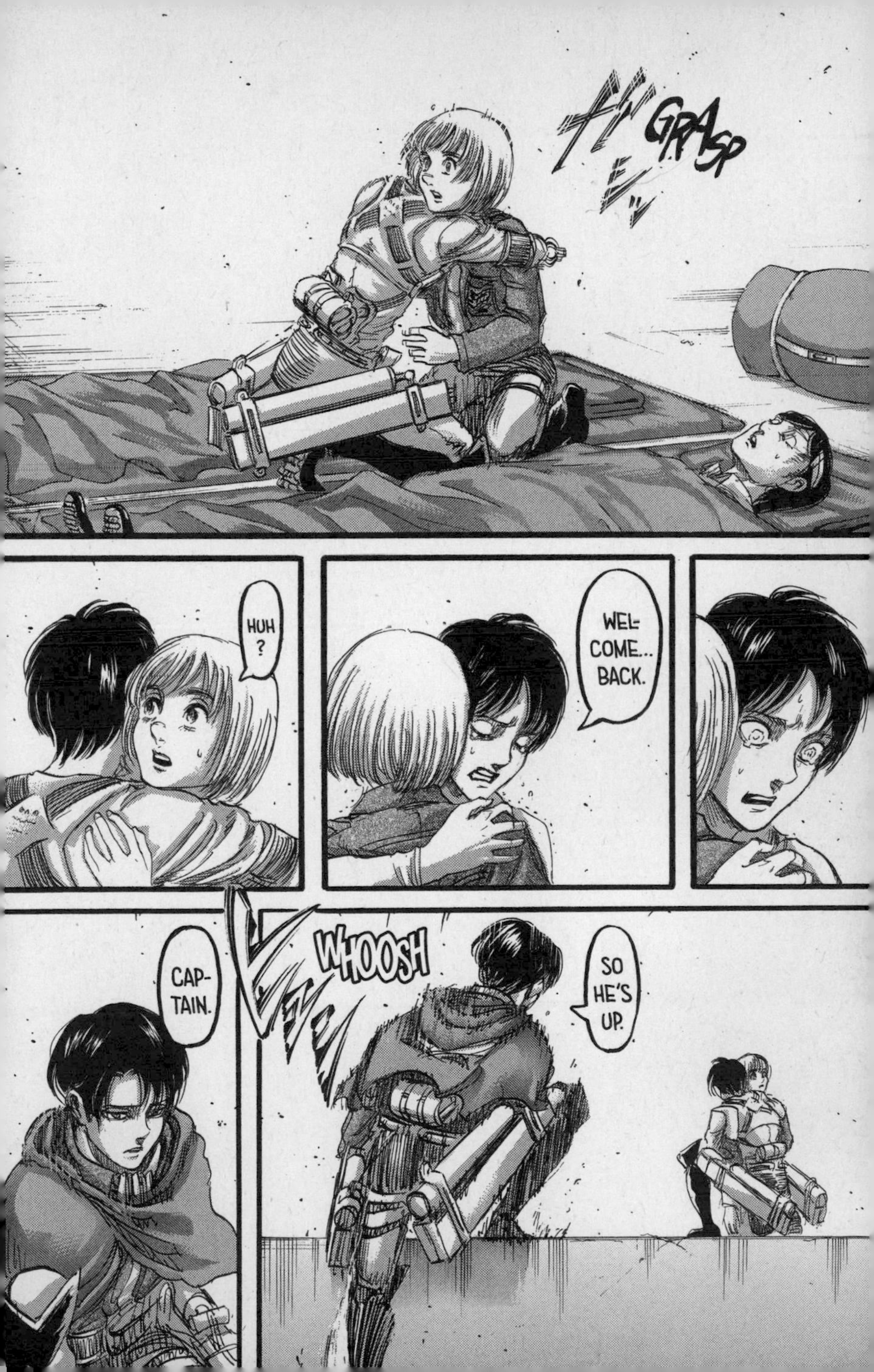
GRASP
WEL-COME... BACK.
HUH?
WHOOSH
SO HE'S UP.
CAP-TAIN.

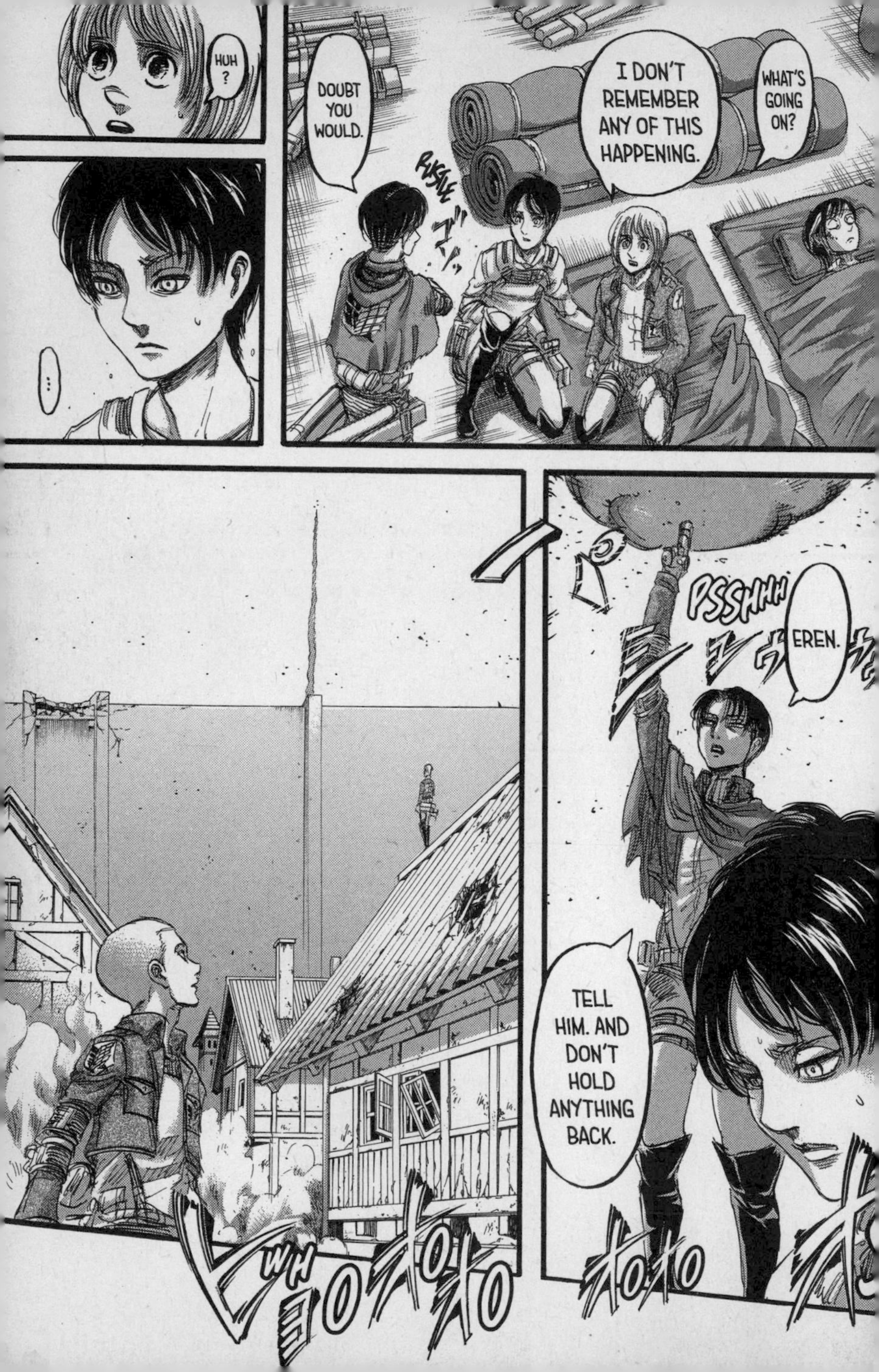
WHAT'S GOING ON?
I DON'T REMEMBER ANY OF THIS HAPPENING.
DOUBT YOU WOULD.
RUSTLE
HUH?
...
PSSHHH
EREN.
TELL HIM. AND DON'T HOLD ANYTHING BACK.

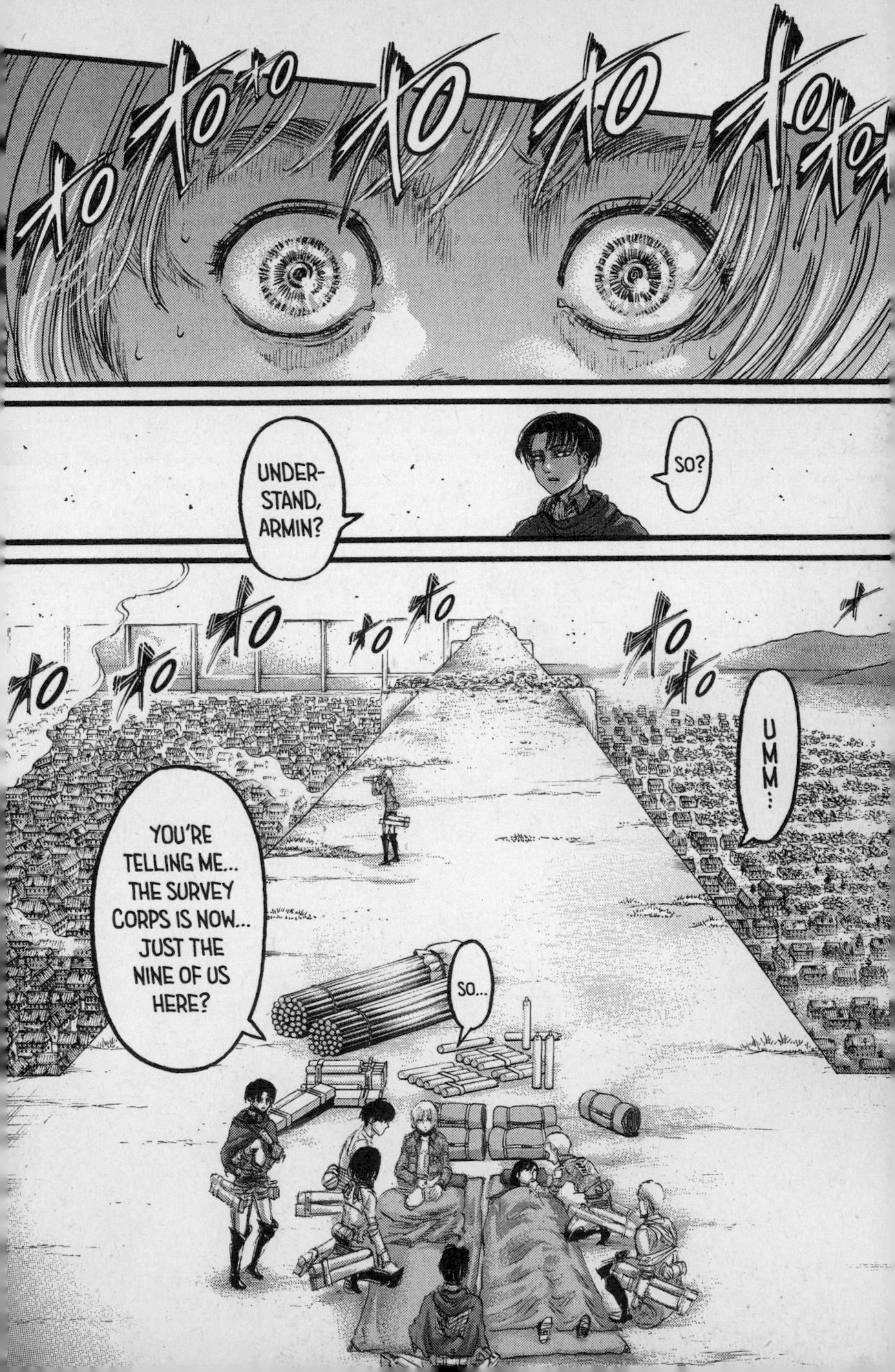
オロオロ
SO?
UNDER-STAND, ARMIN?
オロ
UMM...
SO...
YOU'RE TELLING ME... THE SURVEY CORPS IS NOW... JUST THE NINE OF US HERE?

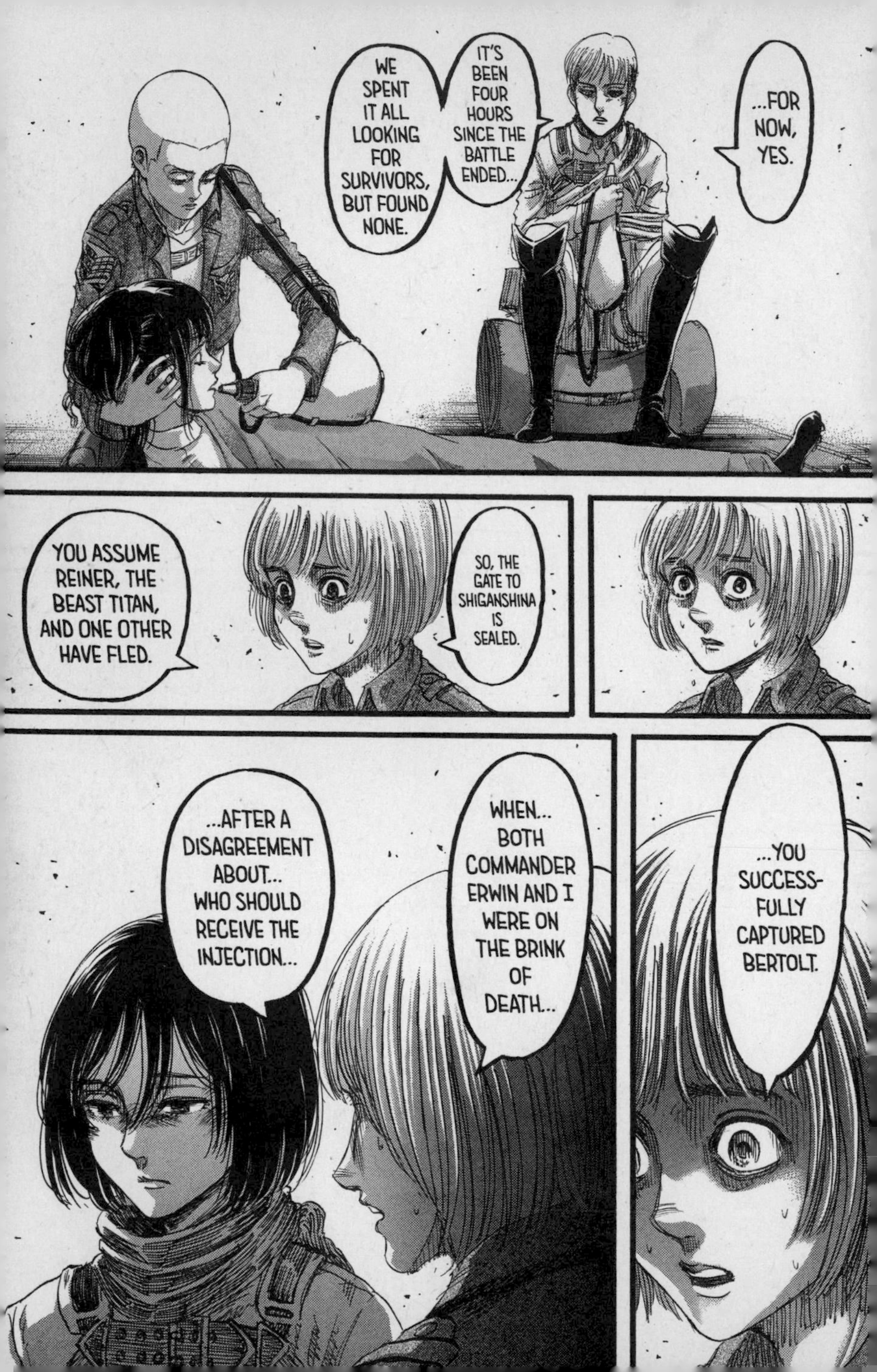
...FOR NOW, YES.
IT'S BEEN FOUR HOURS SINCE THE BATTLE ENDED...
WE SPENT IT ALL LOOKING FOR SURVIVORS, BUT FOUND NONE.
SO, THE GATE TO SHIGANSHINA IS SEALED.
YOU ASSUME REINER, THE BEAST TITAN, AND ONE OTHER HAVE FLED.
...YOU SUCCESS-FULLY CAPTURED BERTOLT.
WHEN... BOTH COMMANDER ERWIN AND I WERE ON THE BRINK OF DEATH...
...AFTER A DISAGREEMENT ABOUT... WHO SHOULD RECEIVE THE INJECTION...

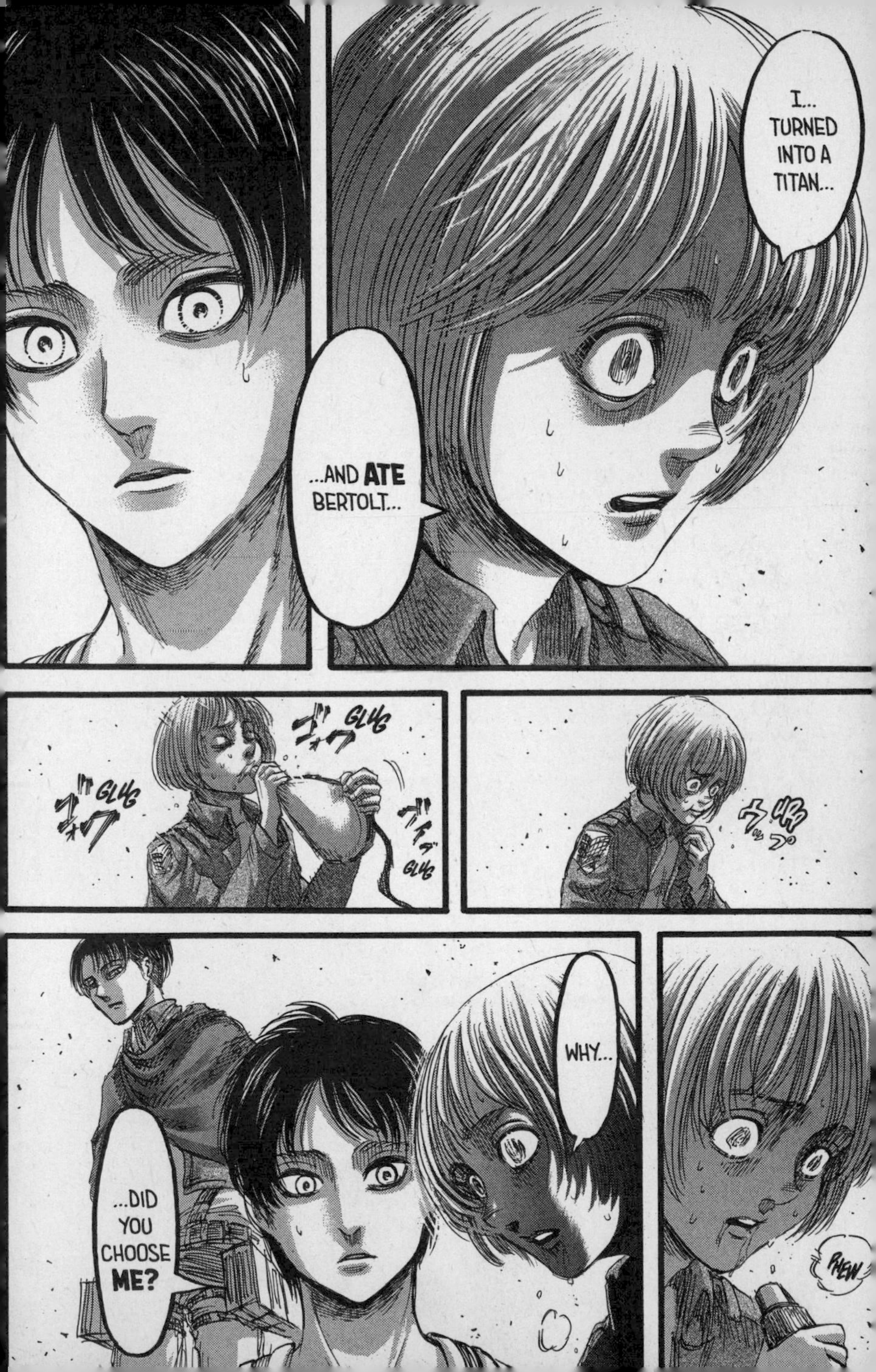
I... TURNED INTO A TITAN...
...AND **ATE** BERTOLT...
ウップ
GLUG
GLUG
GLUG
WHY...
...DID YOU CHOOSE **ME?**
PHEW

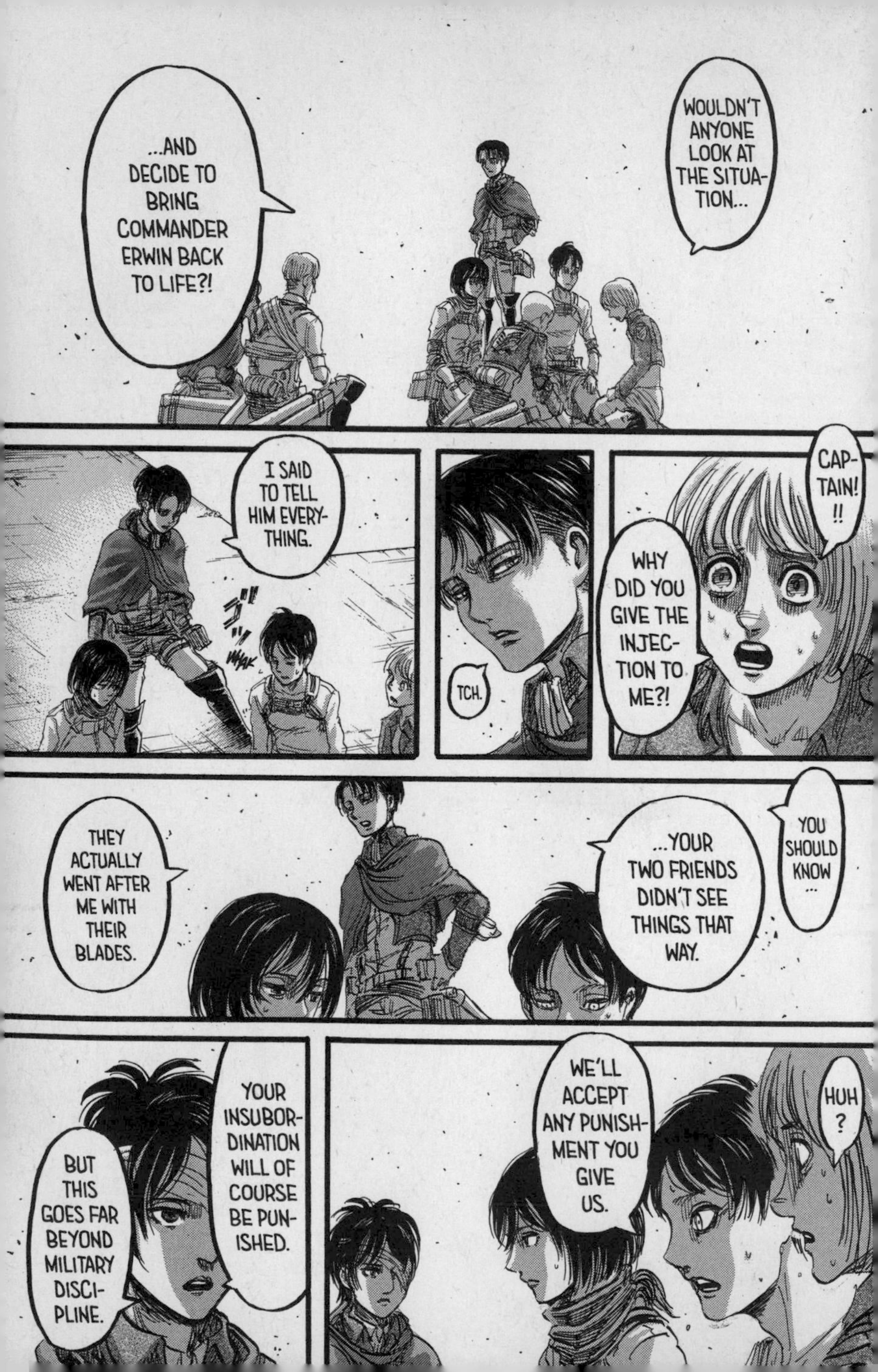
WOULDN'T ANYONE LOOK AT THE SITUATION...
...AND DECIDE TO BRING COMMANDER ERWIN BACK TO LIFE?!
CAPTAIN!!!
WHY DID YOU GIVE THE INJECTION TO ME?!
TCH.
I SAID TO TELL HIM EVERYTHING.
WHAK
YOU SHOULD KNOW...
...YOUR TWO FRIENDS DIDN'T SEE THINGS THAT WAY.
THEY ACTUALLY WENT AFTER ME WITH THEIR BLADES.
HUH?
WE'LL ACCEPT ANY PUNISHMENT YOU GIVE US.
YOUR INSUBORDINATION WILL OF COURSE BE PUNISHED.
BUT THIS GOES FAR BEYOND MILITARY DISCIPLINE.

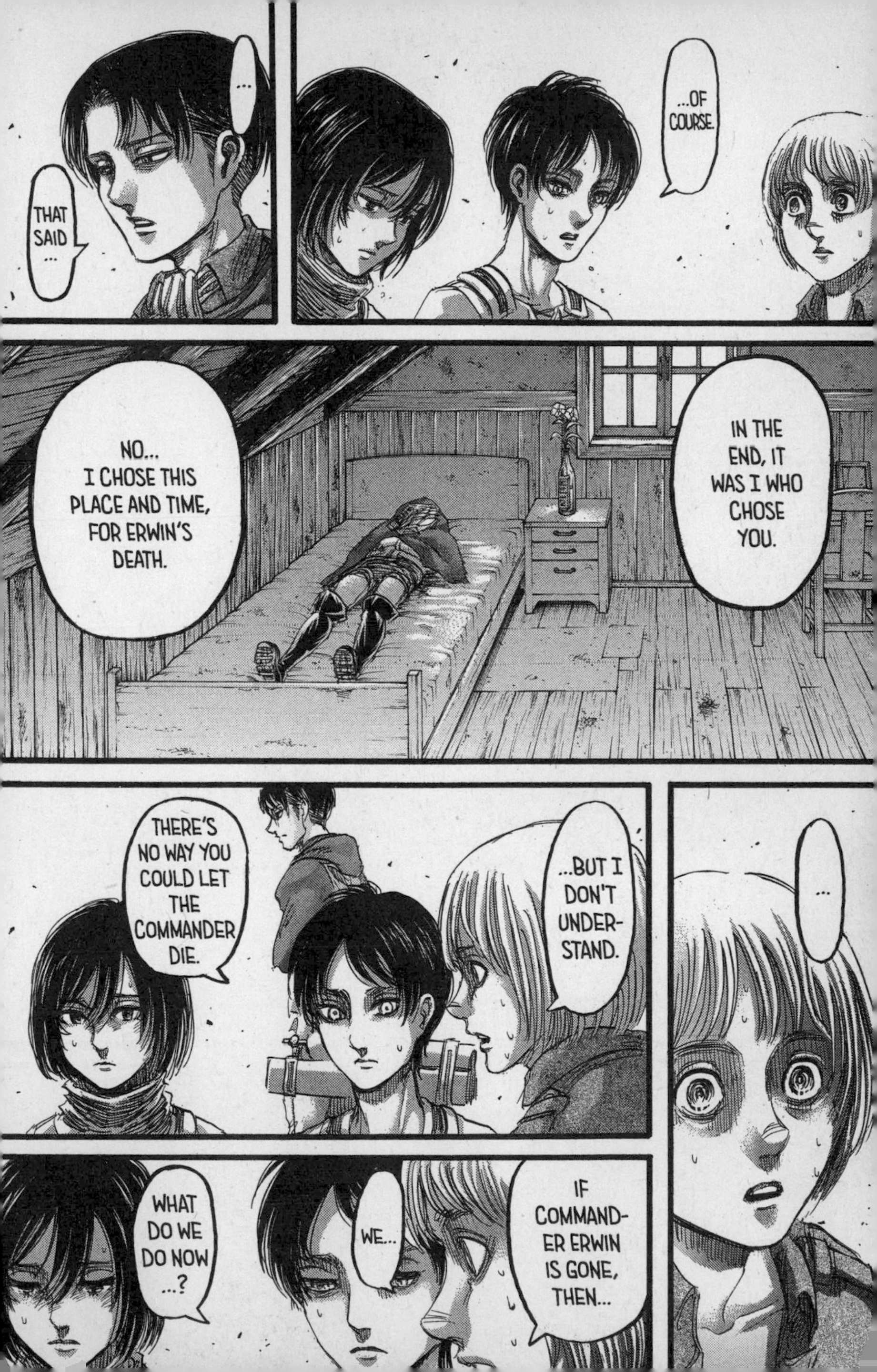
...OF COURSE.
...
THAT SAID ...
IN THE END, IT WAS I WHO CHOSE YOU.
NO... I CHOSE THIS PLACE AND TIME, FOR ERWIN'S DEATH.
...
...BUT I DON'T UNDER-STAND.
THERE'S NO WAY YOU COULD LET THE COMMANDER DIE.
IF COMMAND-ER ERWIN IS GONE, THEN...
WE...
WHAT DO WE DO NOW ...?

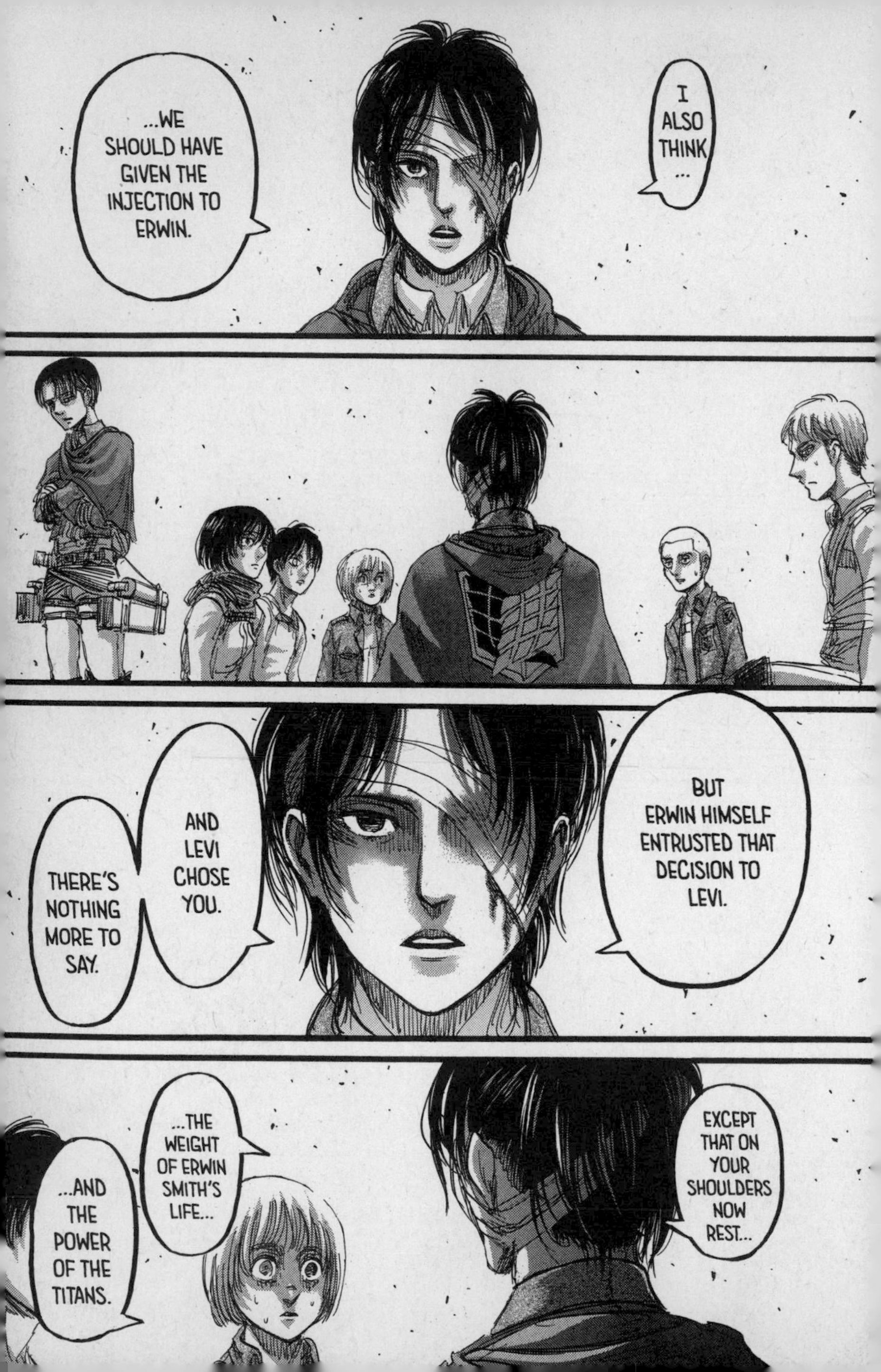
I ALSO THINK...
...WE SHOULD HAVE GIVEN THE INJECTION TO ERWIN.
BUT ERWIN HIMSELF ENTRUSTED THAT DECISION TO LEVI.
AND LEVI CHOSE YOU.
THERE'S NOTHING MORE TO SAY.
EXCEPT THAT ON YOUR SHOULDERS NOW REST...
...THE WEIGHT OF ERWIN SMITH'S LIFE...
...AND THE POWER OF THE TITANS.

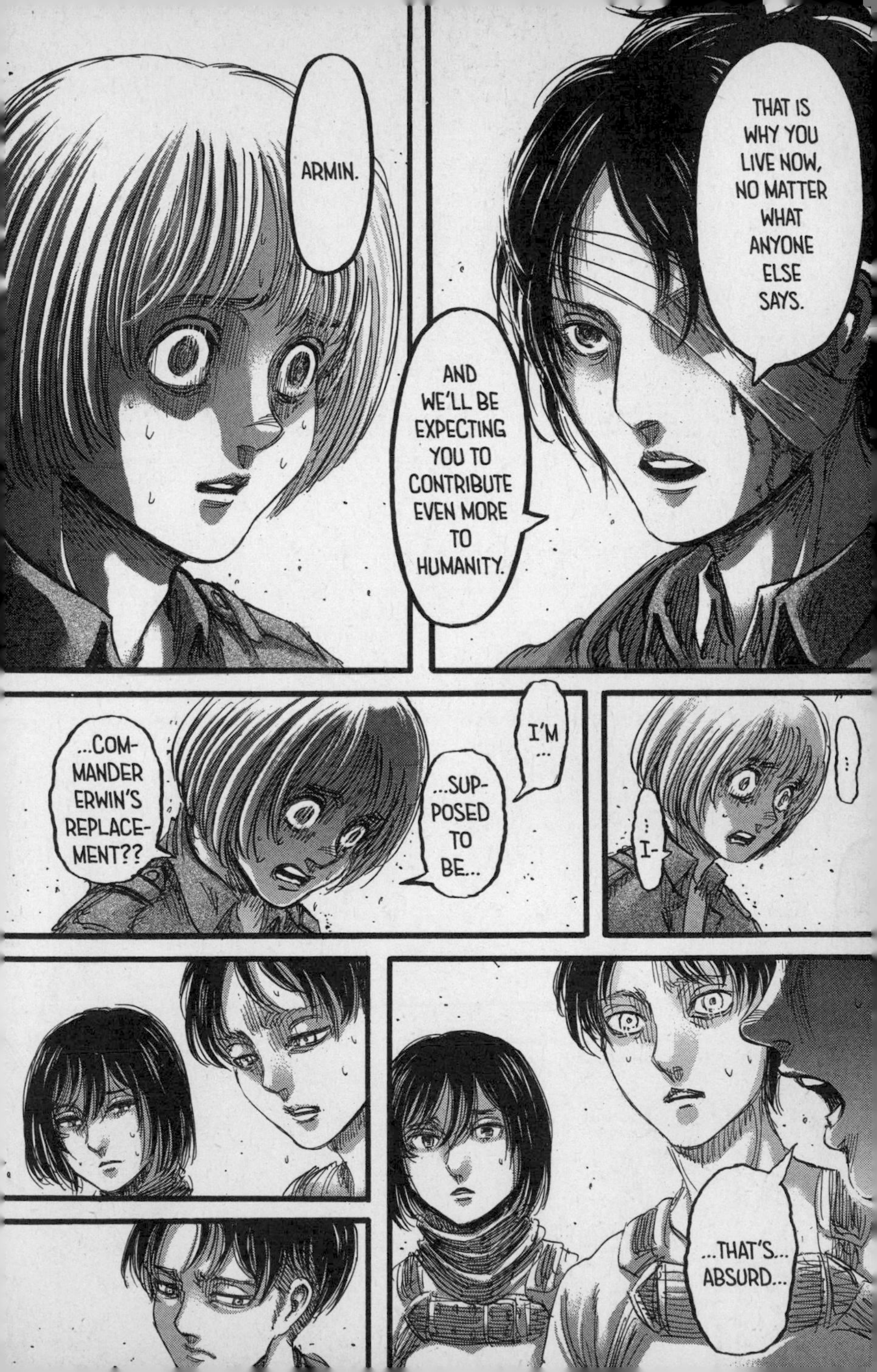
THAT IS WHY YOU LIVE NOW, NO MATTER WHAT ANYONE ELSE SAYS.
AND WE'LL BE EXPECTING YOU TO CONTRIBUTE EVEN MORE TO HUMANITY.
ARMIN.
...
... I-
I'M ...
...SUP-POSED TO BE...
...COM-MANDER ERWIN'S REPLACE-MENT??
...THAT'S... ABSURD...

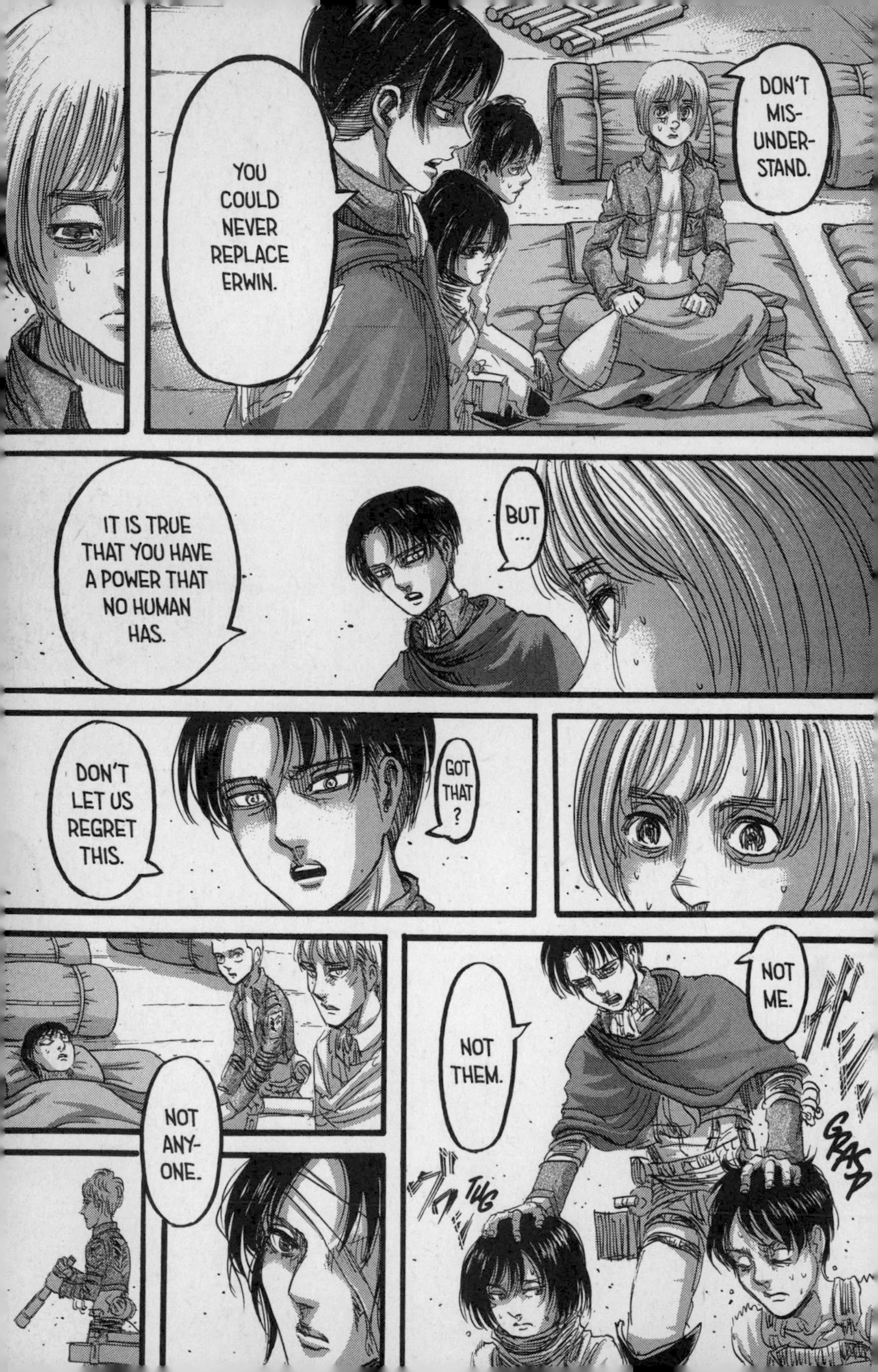
DON'T MIS-UNDER-STAND.
YOU COULD NEVER REPLACE ERWIN.
BUT ...
IT IS TRUE THAT YOU HAVE A POWER THAT NO HUMAN HAS.
GOT THAT?
DON'T LET US REGRET THIS.
NOT ME.
GRASP
NOT THEM.
TUG
NOT ANY-ONE.

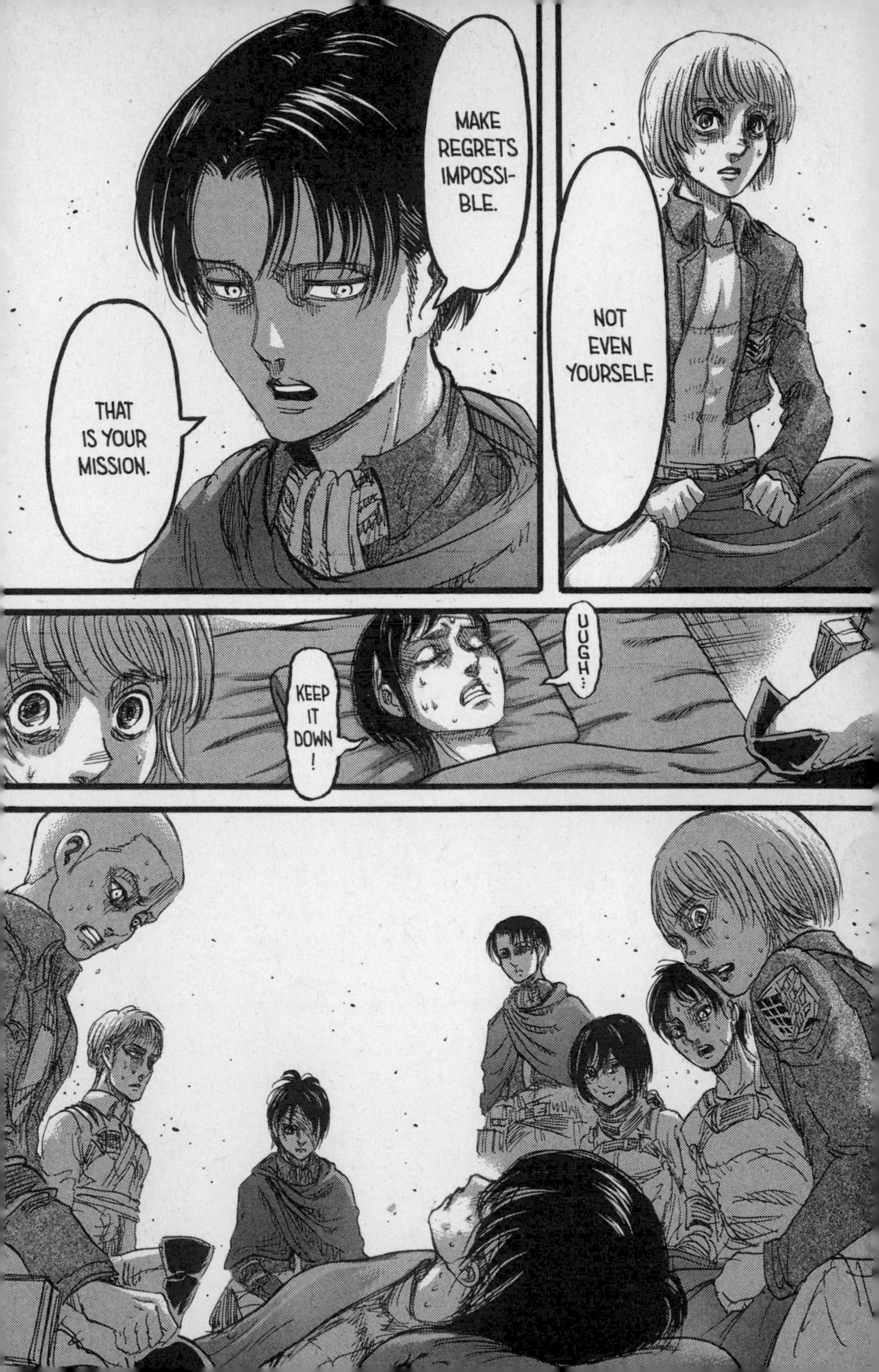
NOT EVEN YOURSELF.
MAKE REGRETS IMPOSSI-BLE.
THAT IS YOUR MISSION.
UUGH...
KEEP IT DOWN!

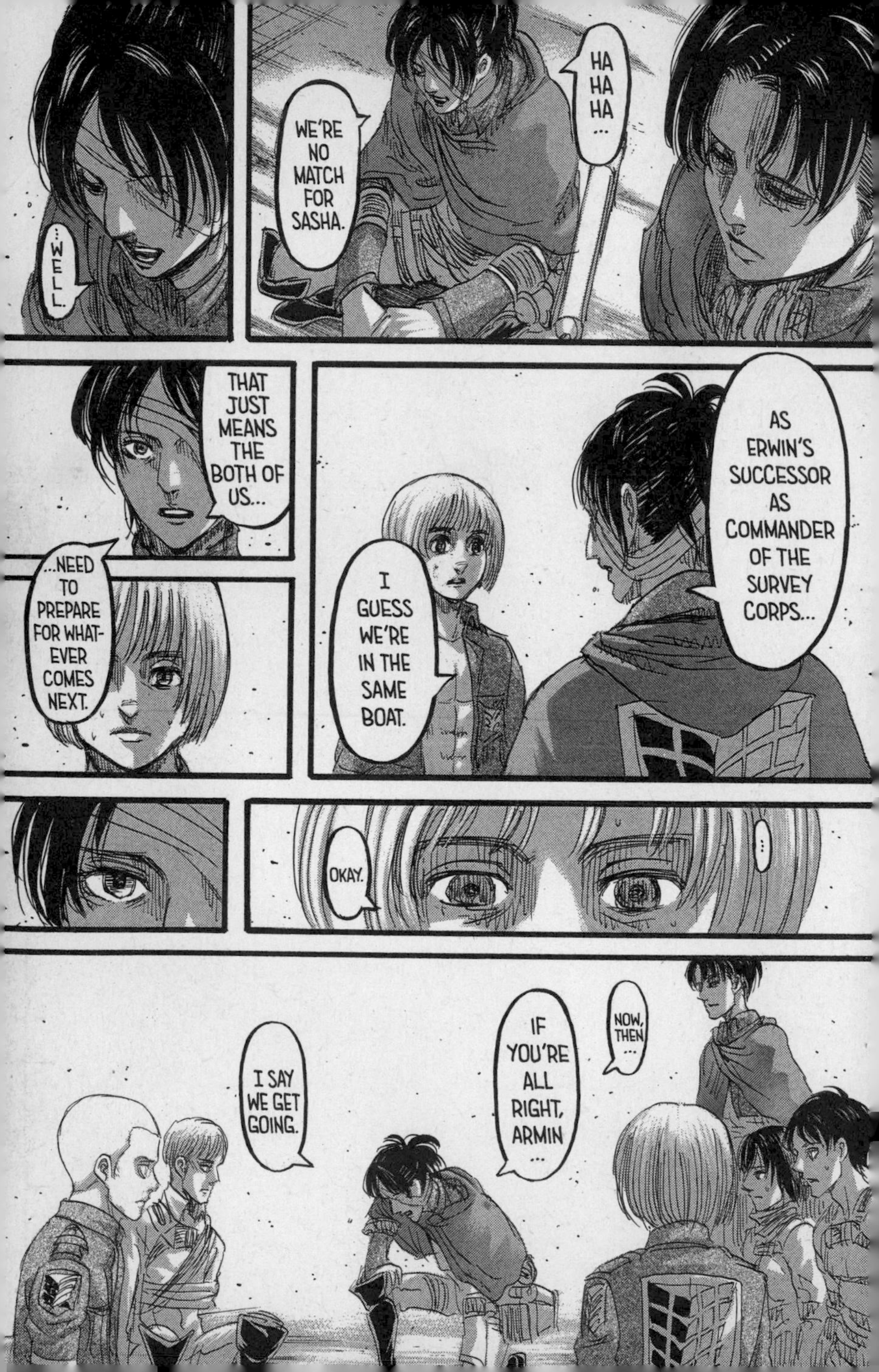
HA HA HA ...
WE'RE NO MATCH FOR SASHA.
...WELL.
AS ERWIN'S SUCCESSOR AS COMMANDER OF THE SURVEY CORPS...
I GUESS WE'RE IN THE SAME BOAT.
THAT JUST MEANS THE BOTH OF US...
...NEED TO PREPARE FOR WHAT-EVER COMES NEXT.
...
OKAY.
NOW, THEN...
IF YOU'RE ALL RIGHT, ARMIN...
I SAY WE GET GOING.

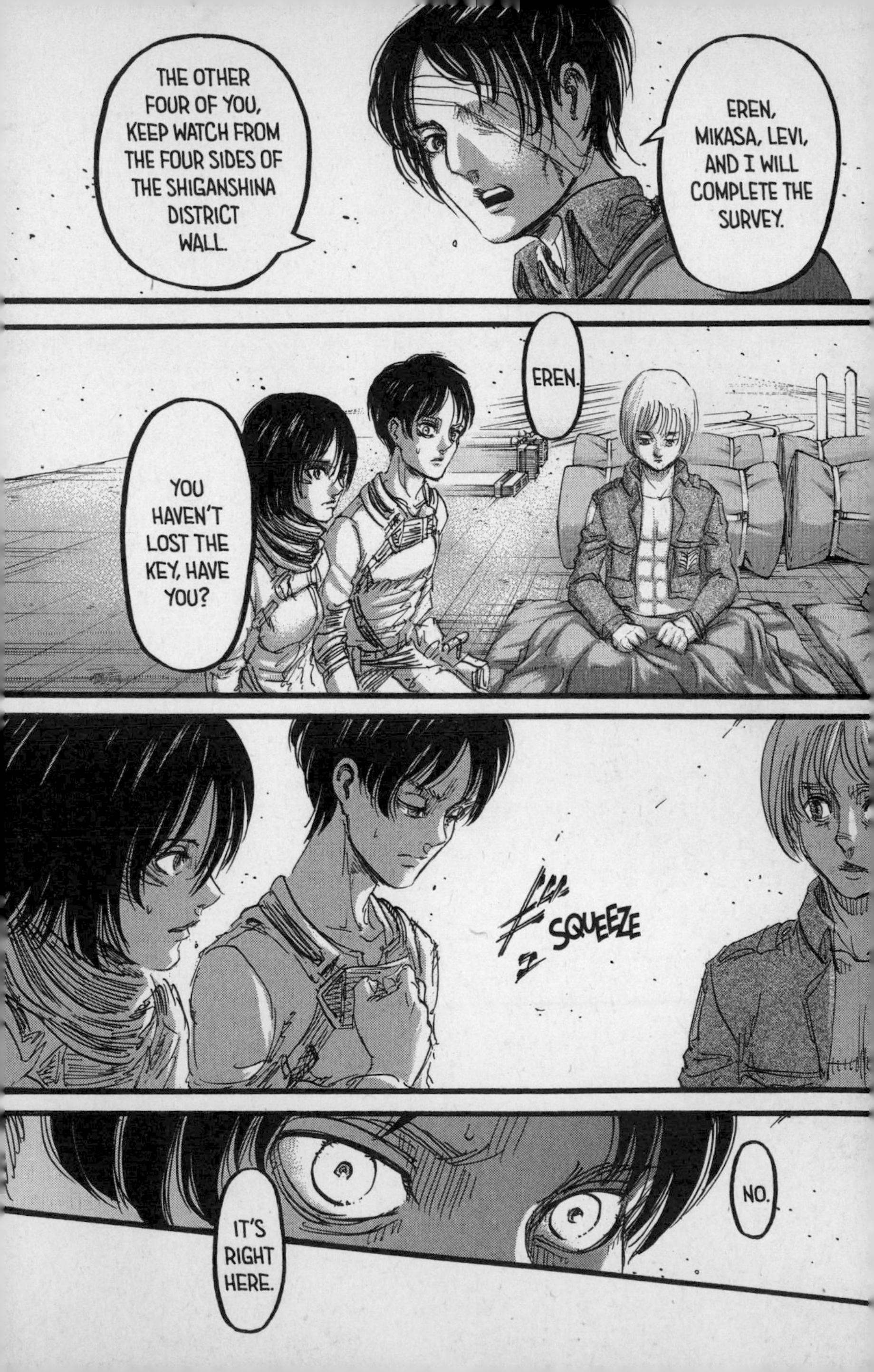
EREN, MIKASA, LEVI, AND I WILL COMPLETE THE SURVEY.
THE OTHER FOUR OF YOU, KEEP WATCH FROM THE FOUR SIDES OF THE SHIGANSHINA DISTRICT WALL.
EREN.
YOU HAVEN'T LOST THE KEY, HAVE YOU?
SQUEEZE
NO.
IT'S RIGHT HERE.

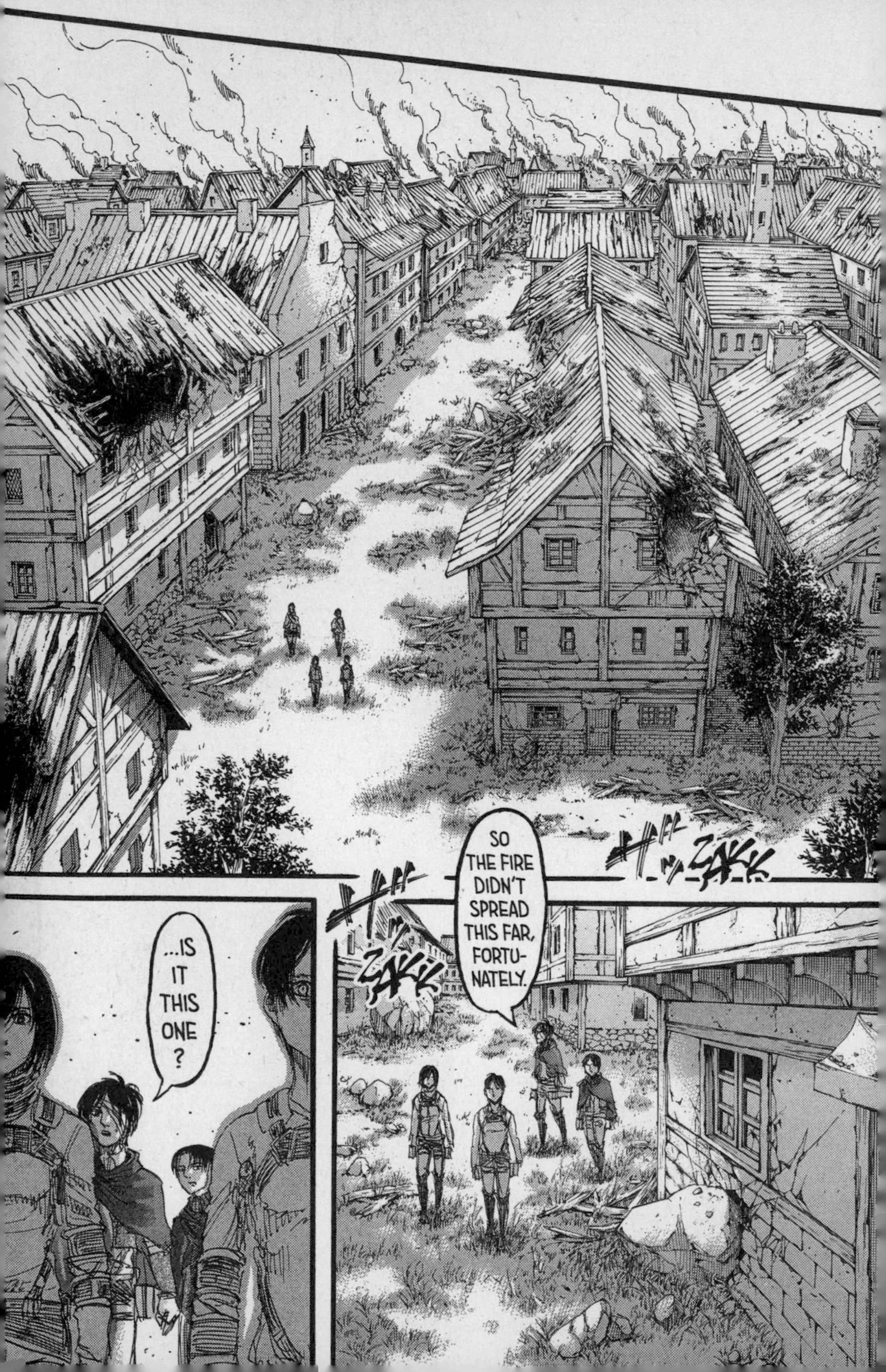
ZAK
ZAK
SO THE FIRE DIDN'T SPREAD THIS FAR, FORTU-NATELY.
...IS IT THIS ONE?

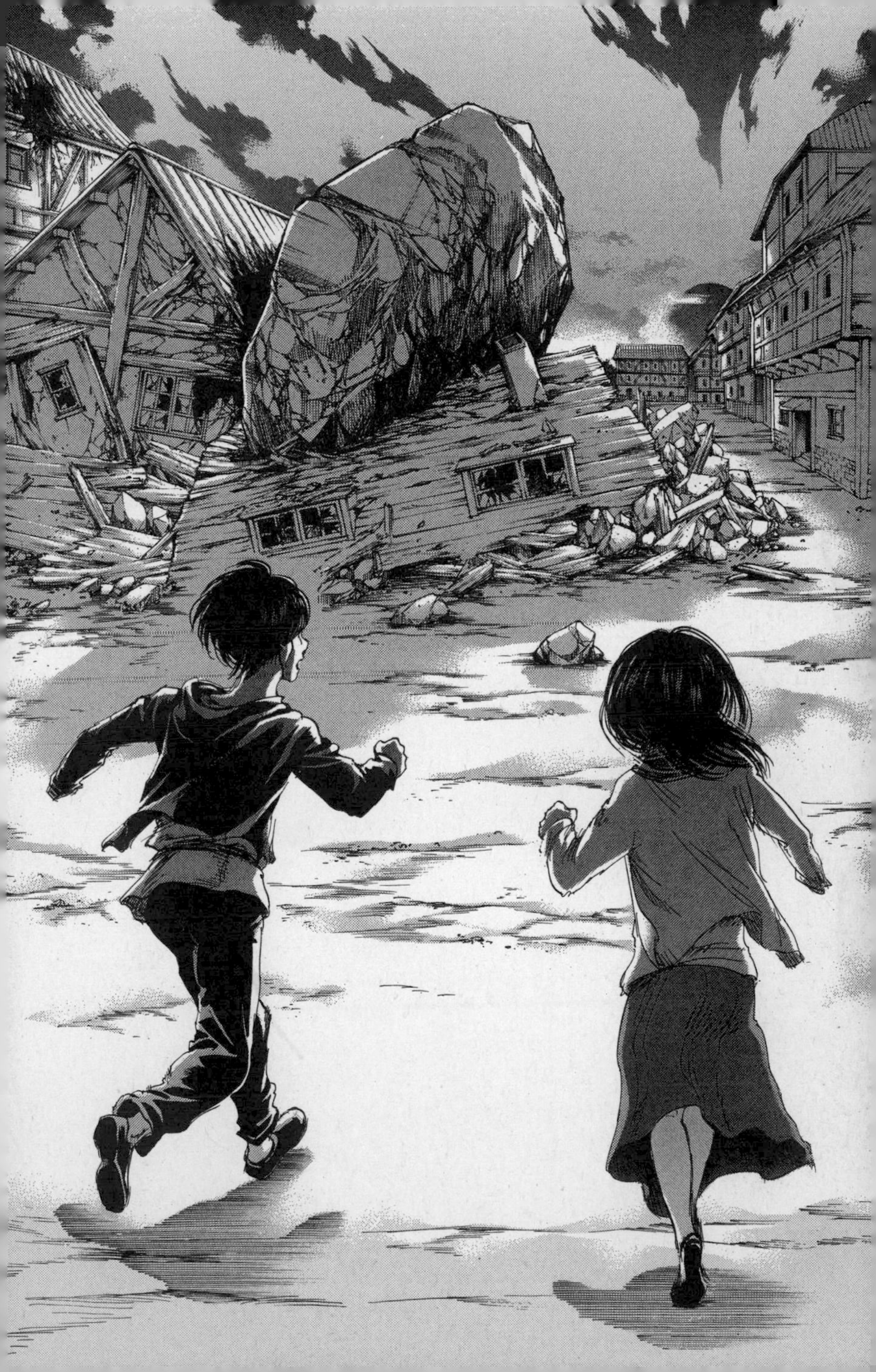

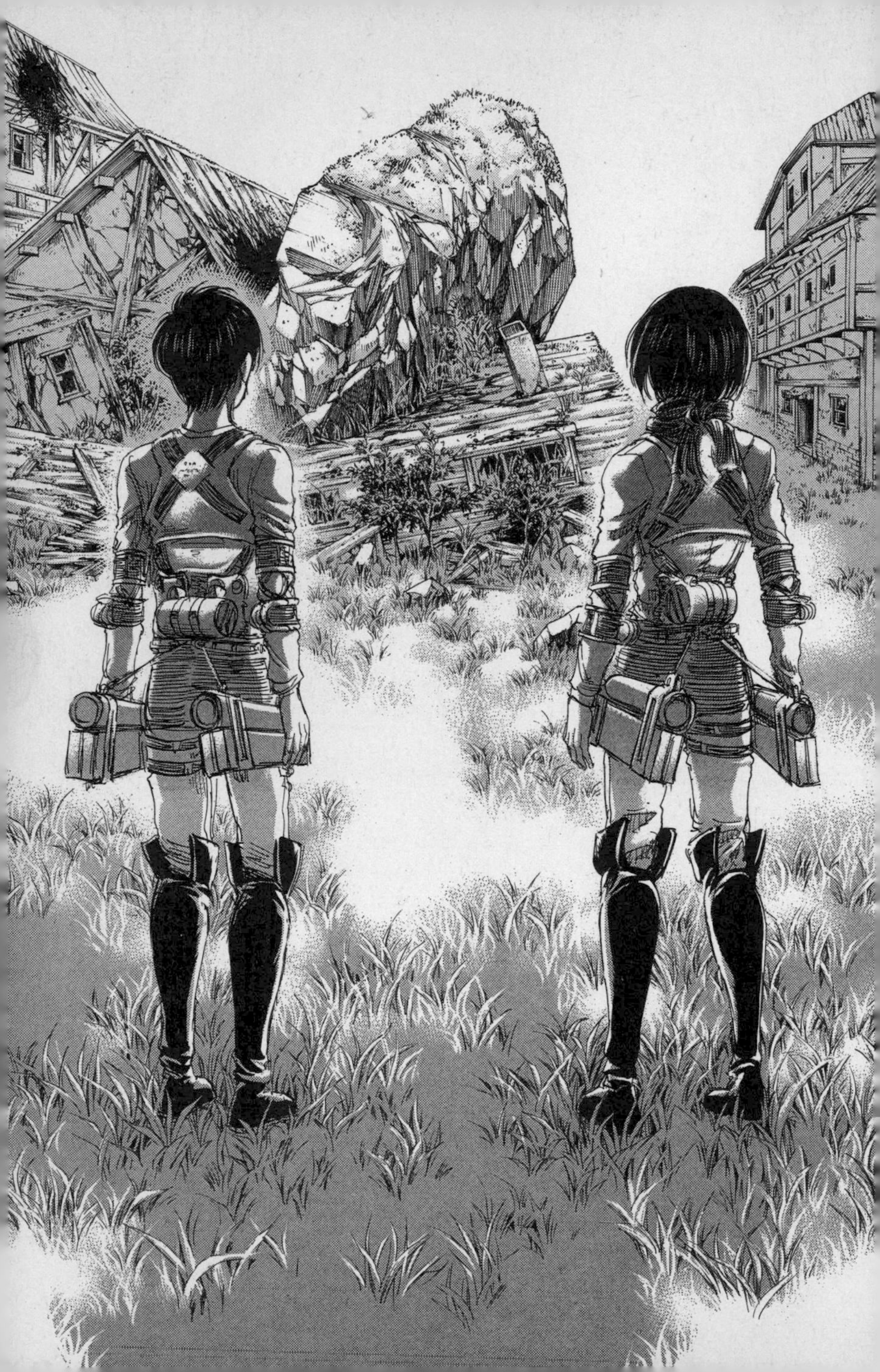

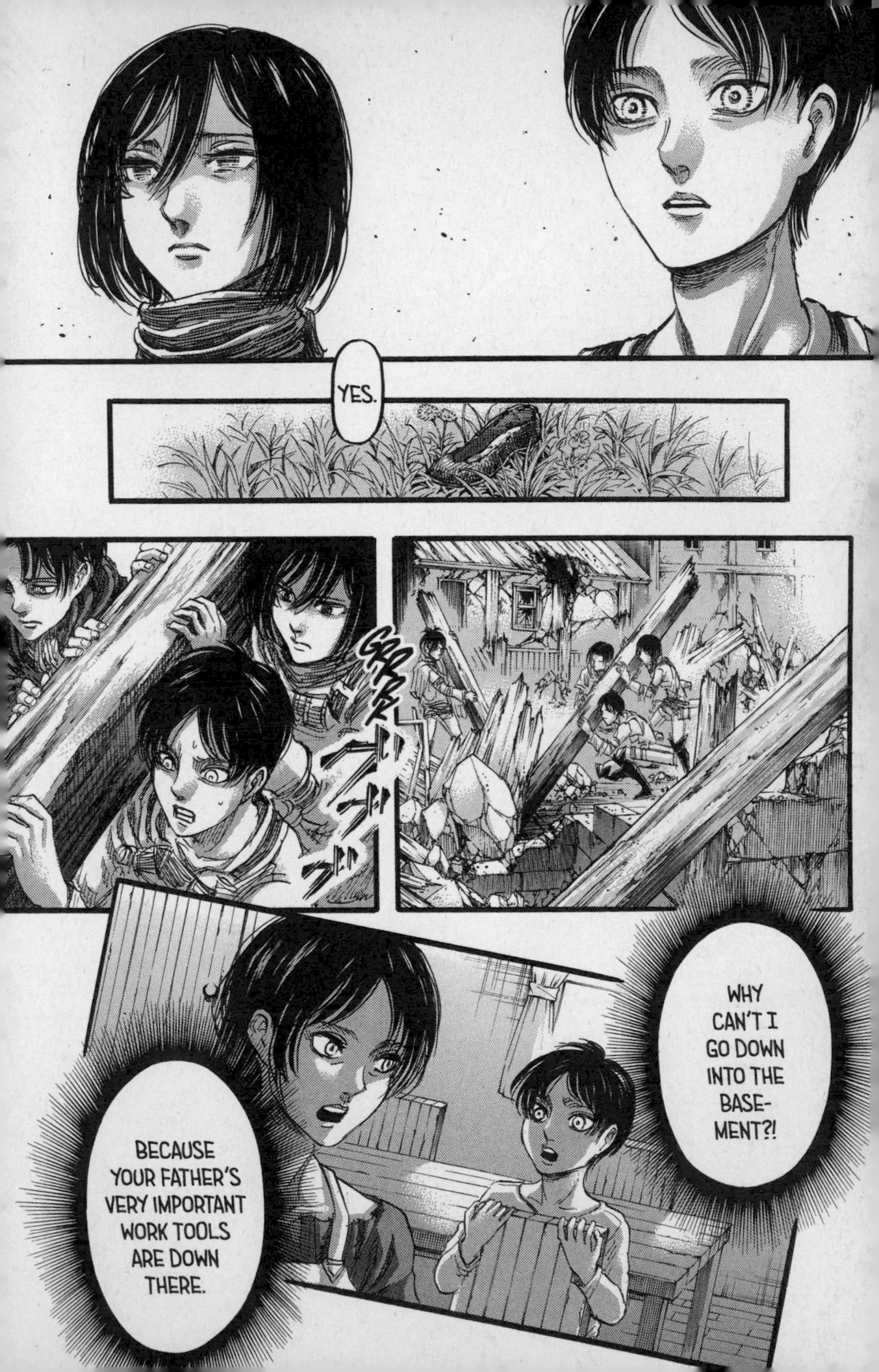
YES.
WHY CAN'T I GO DOWN INTO THE BASEMENT?!
BECAUSE YOUR FATHER'S VERY IMPORTANT WORK TOOLS ARE DOWN THERE.

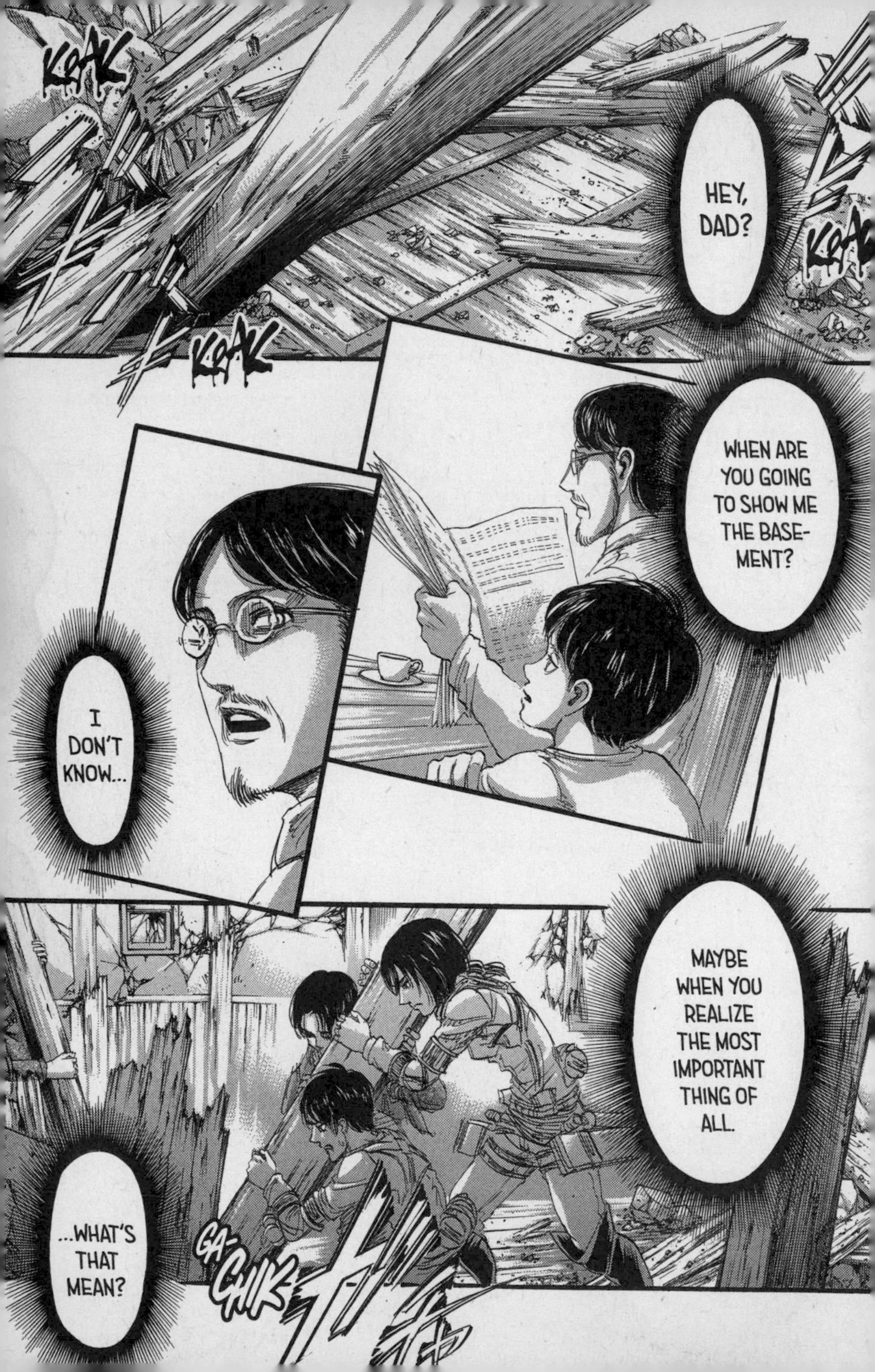
HEY, DAD?
KRAK
KRAK
KRAK
WHEN ARE YOU GOING TO SHOW ME THE BASE-MENT?
I DON'T KNOW...
MAYBE WHEN YOU REALIZE THE MOST IMPORTANT THING OF ALL.
GA-CHIK
...WHAT'S THAT MEAN?

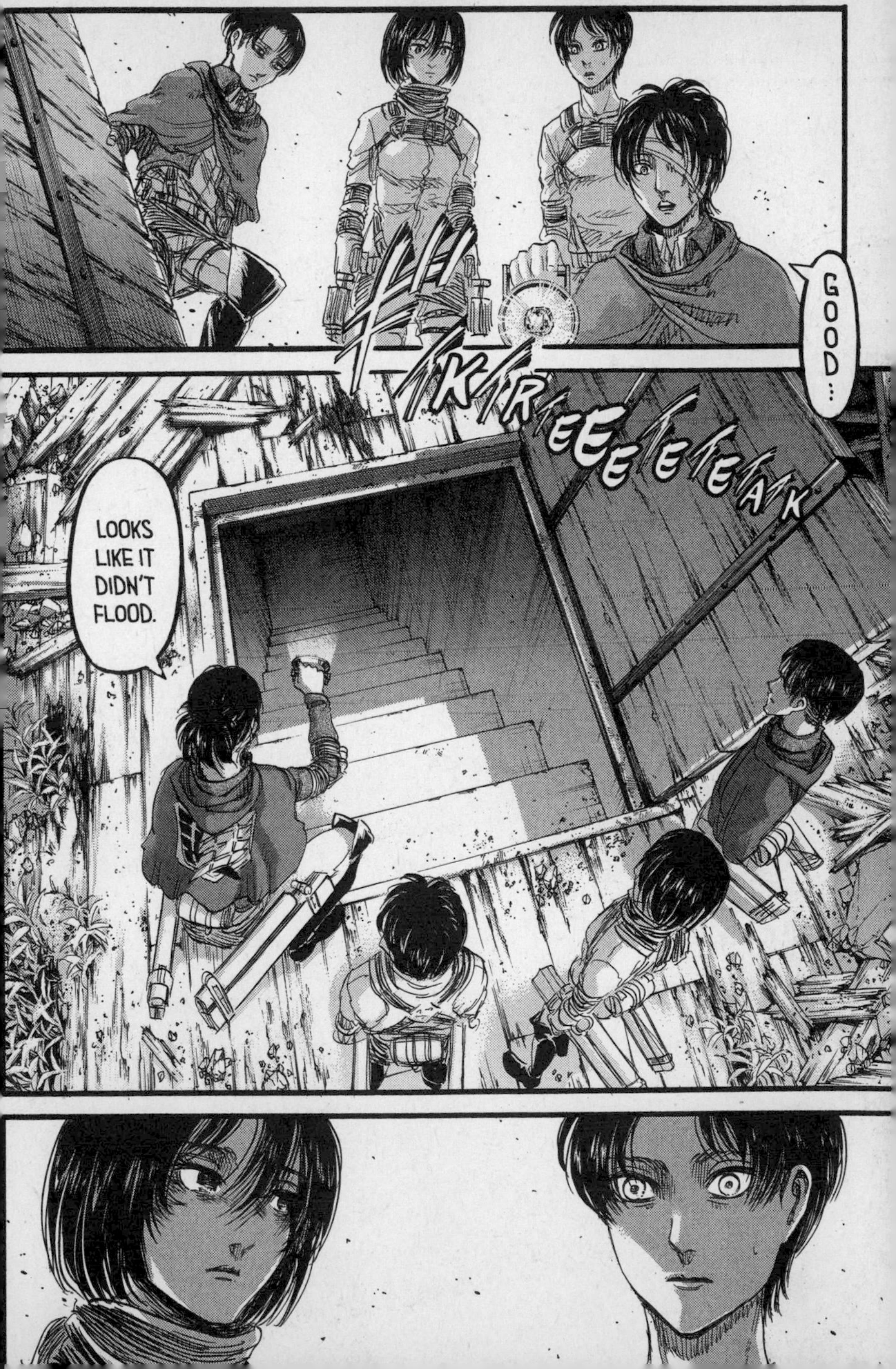
GOOD...
KKREEEEEAK
LOOKS LIKE IT DIDN'T FLOOD.

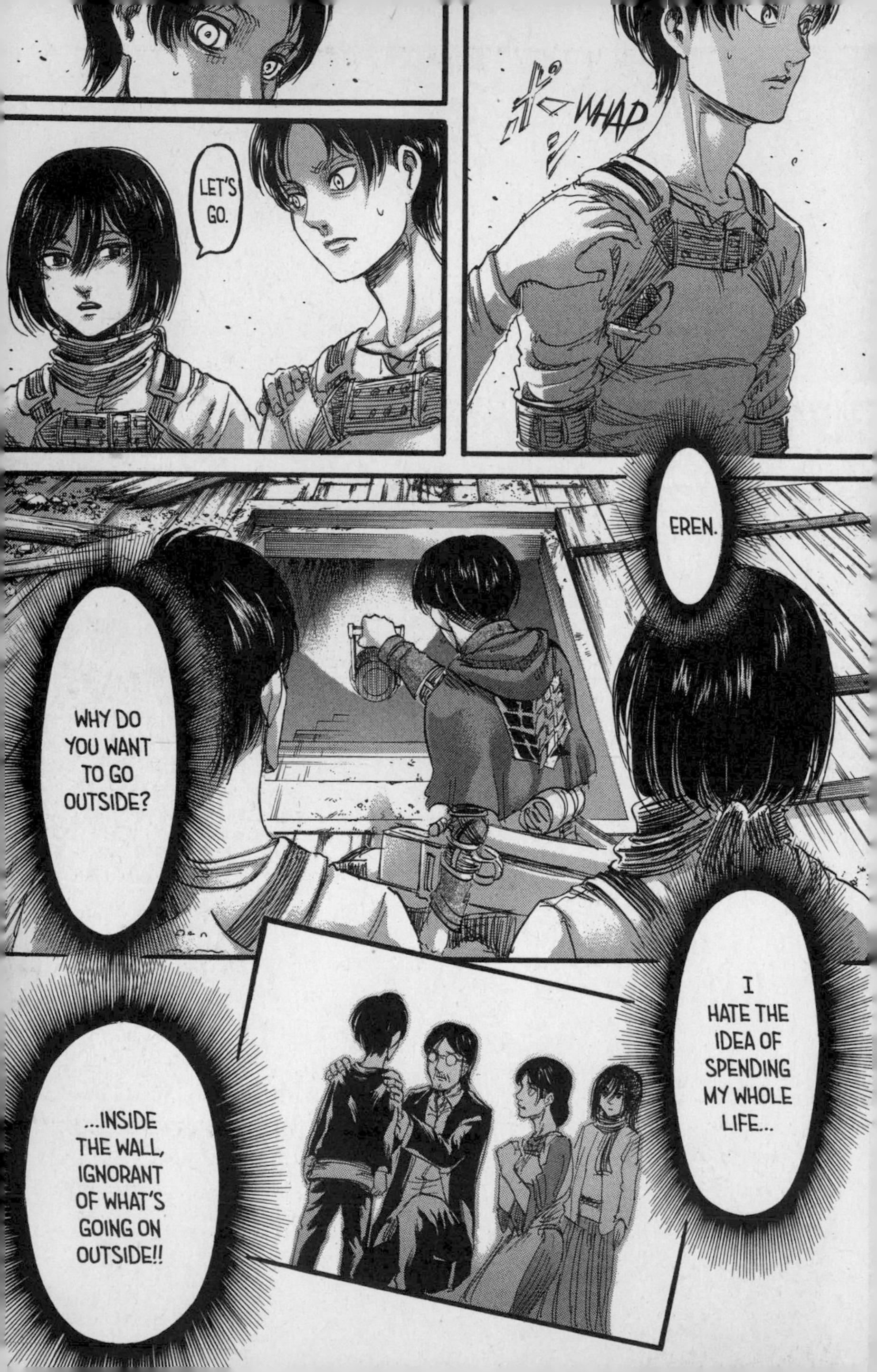
WHAP
LET'S GO.
EREN.
WHY DO YOU WANT TO GO OUTSIDE?
I HATE THE IDEA OF SPENDING MY WHOLE LIFE...
...INSIDE THE WALL, IGNORANT OF WHAT'S GOING ON OUTSIDE!!

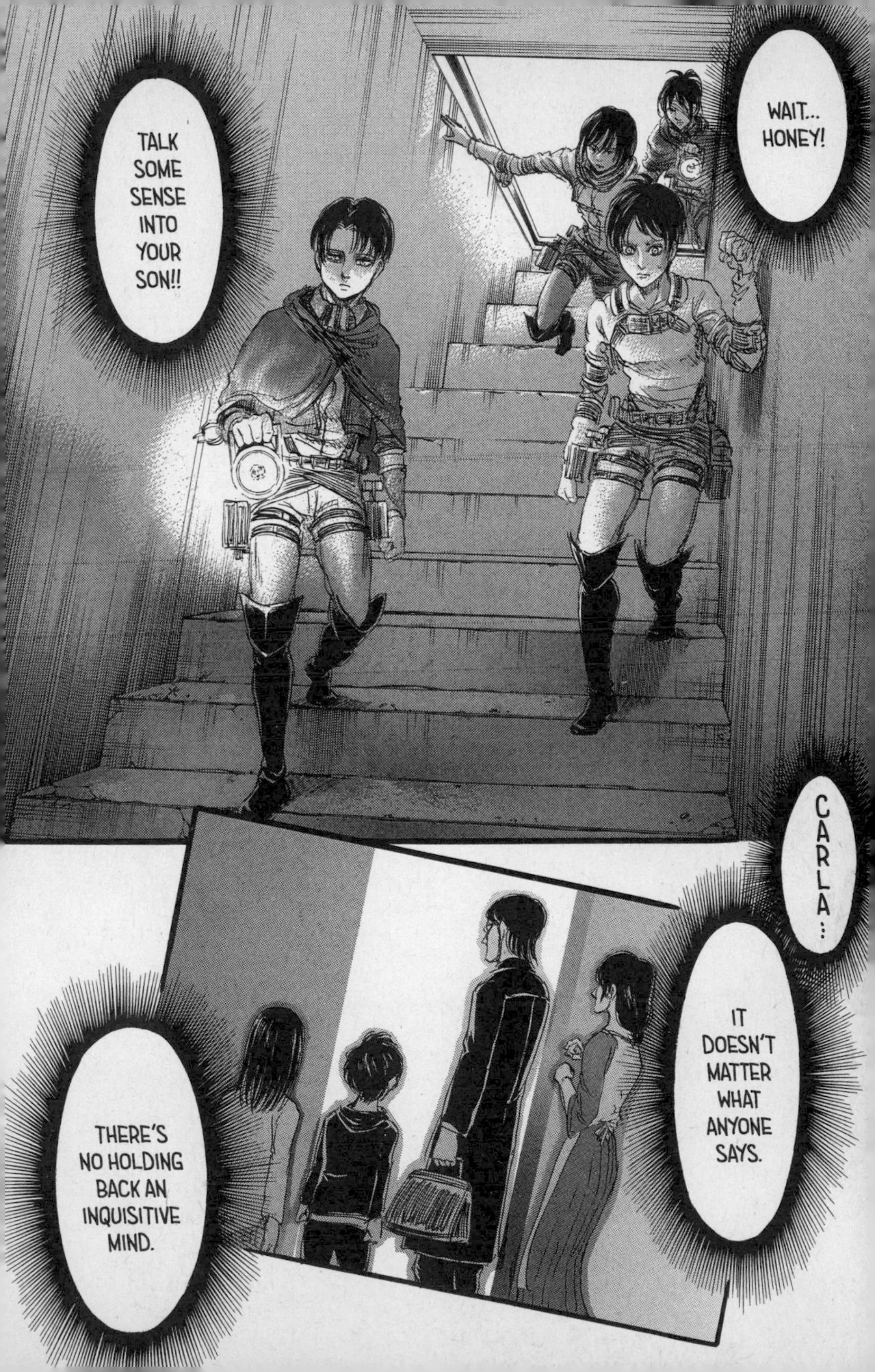
WAIT... HONEY!
TALK SOME SENSE INTO YOUR SON!!
CARLA...
IT DOESN'T MATTER WHAT ANYONE SAYS.
THERE'S NO HOLDING BACK AN INQUISITIVE MIND.

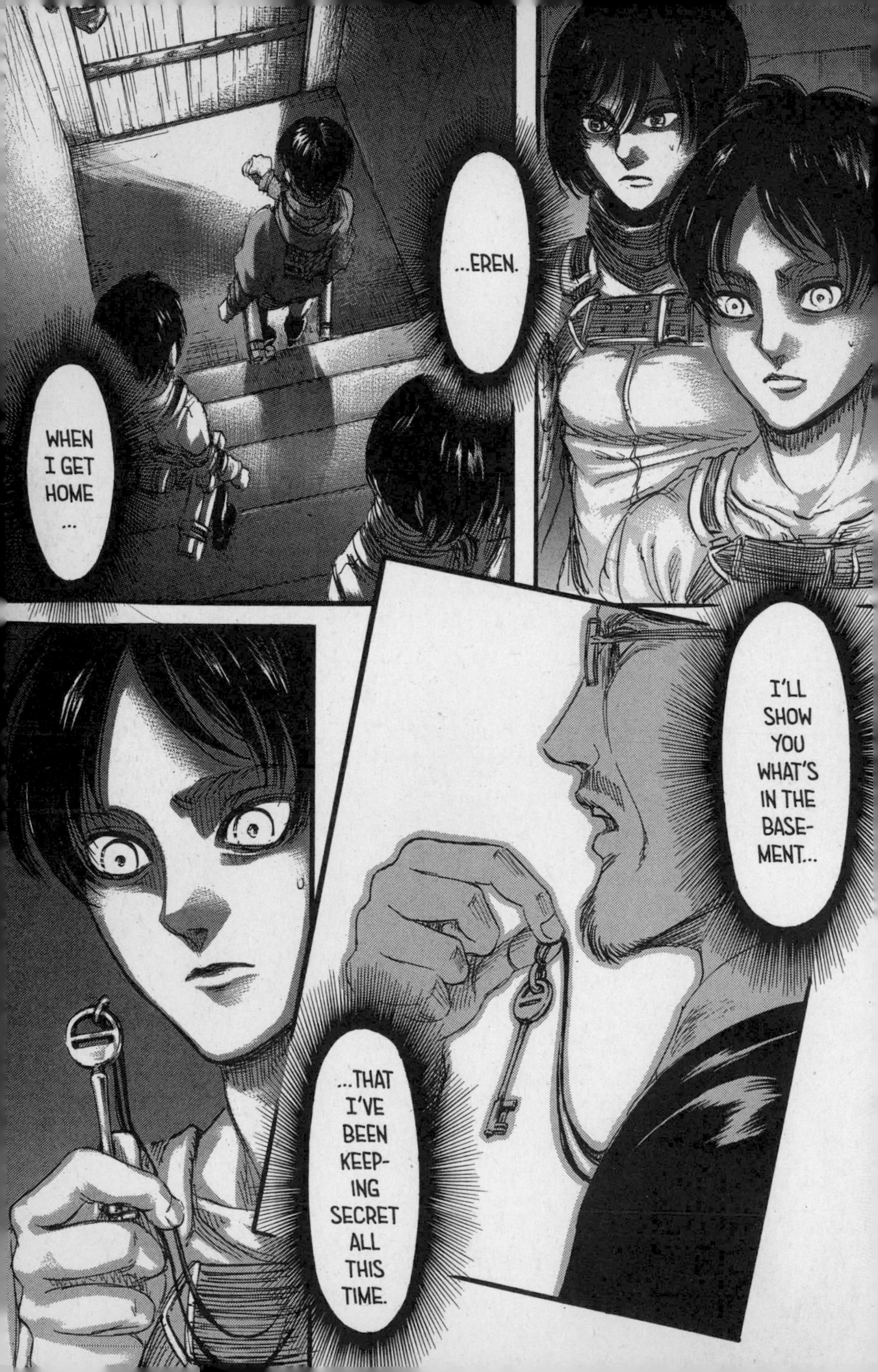
...EREN.
WHEN I GET HOME ...
I'LL SHOW YOU WHAT'S IN THE BASEMENT...
...THAT I'VE BEEN KEEPING SECRET ALL THIS TIME.

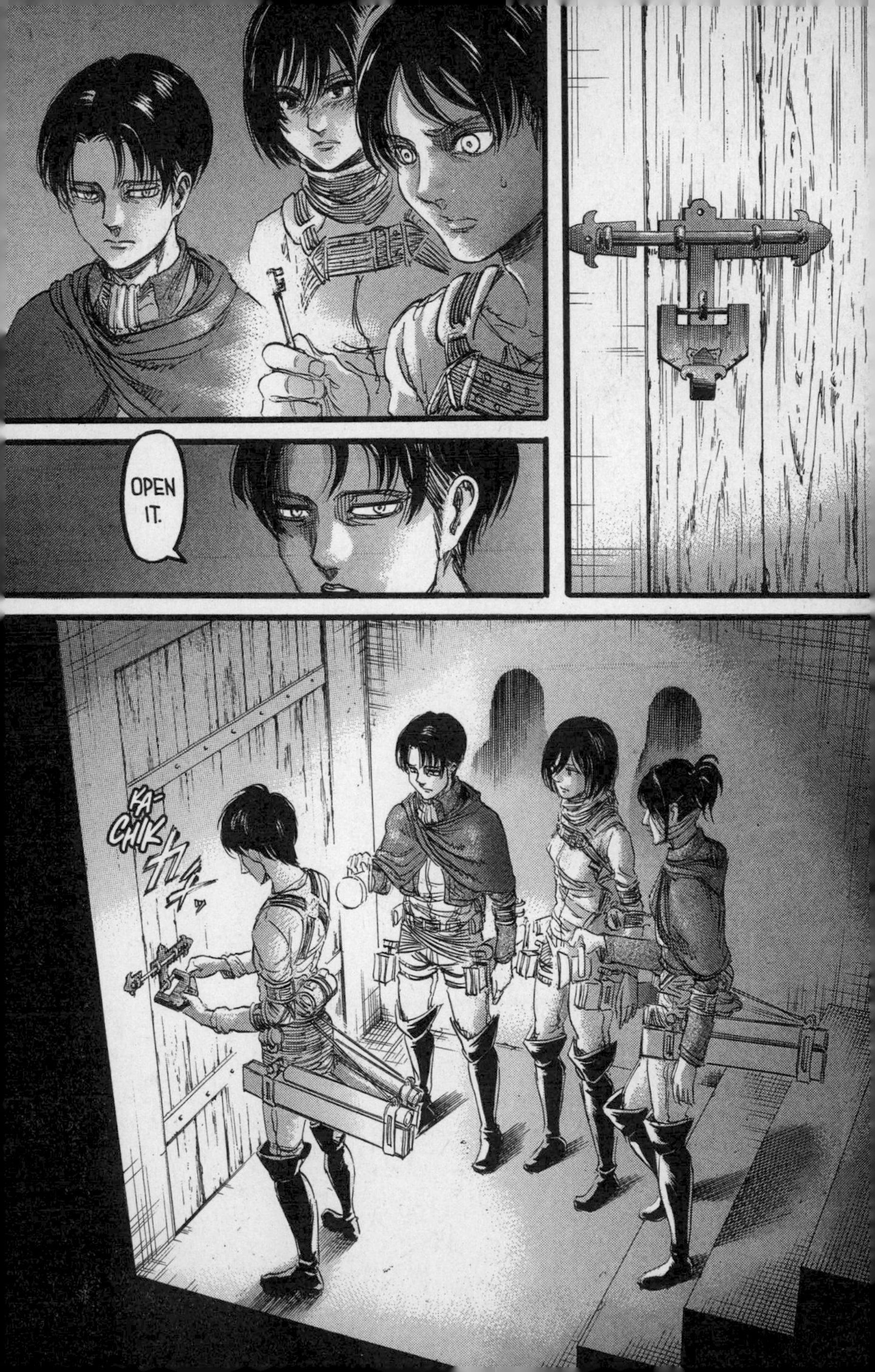
OPEN IT.
KA-CHIK

AH!!

?

HURRY UP.

EREN ?

WHAT'S WRONG ?

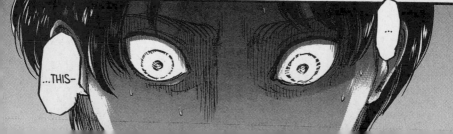

...

...THIS—

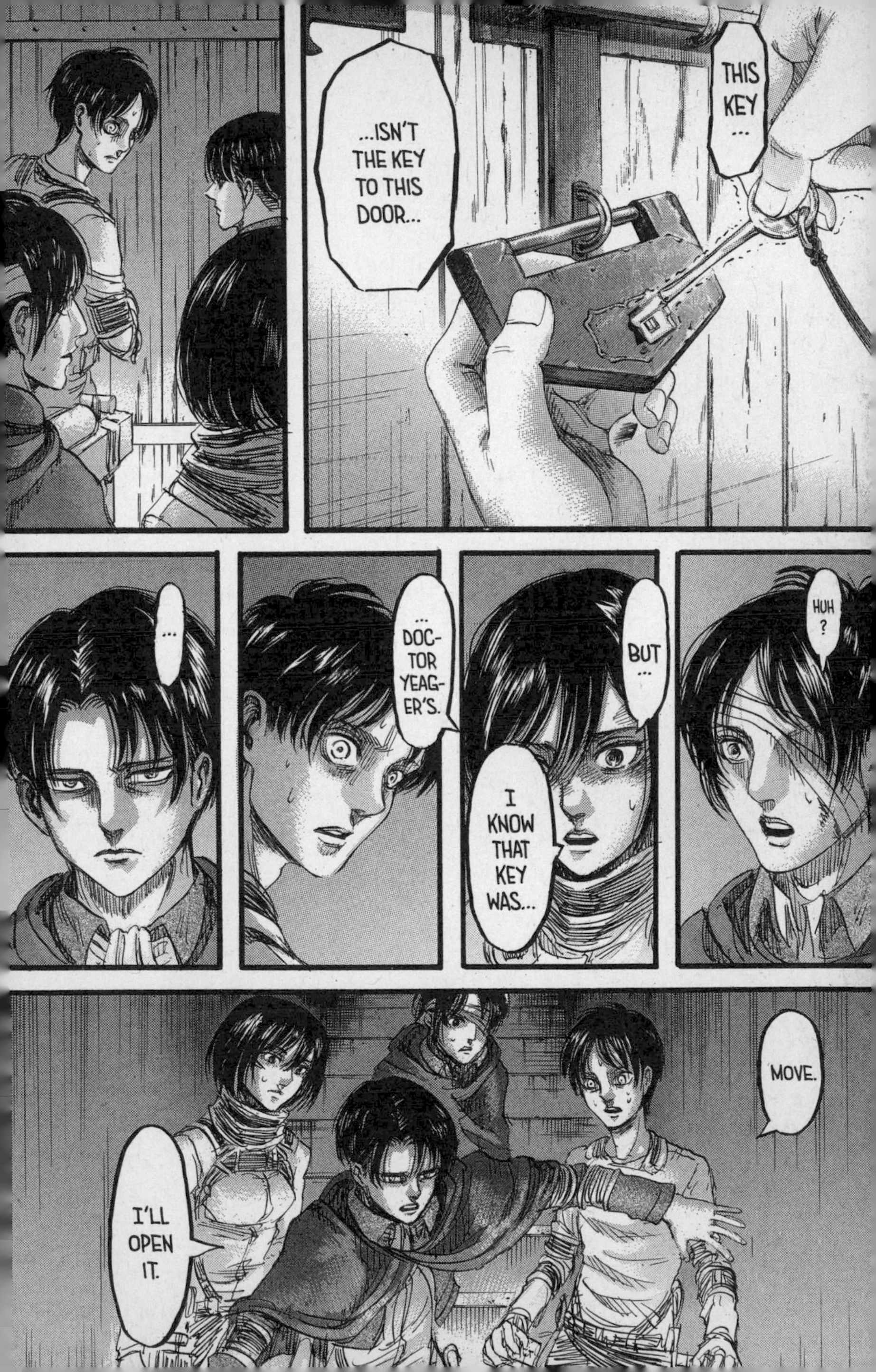
THIS KEY ...
...ISN'T THE KEY TO THIS DOOR...
HUH ?
BUT ...
I KNOW THAT KEY WAS...
... DOCTOR YEAGER'S.
...
MOVE.
I'LL OPEN IT.

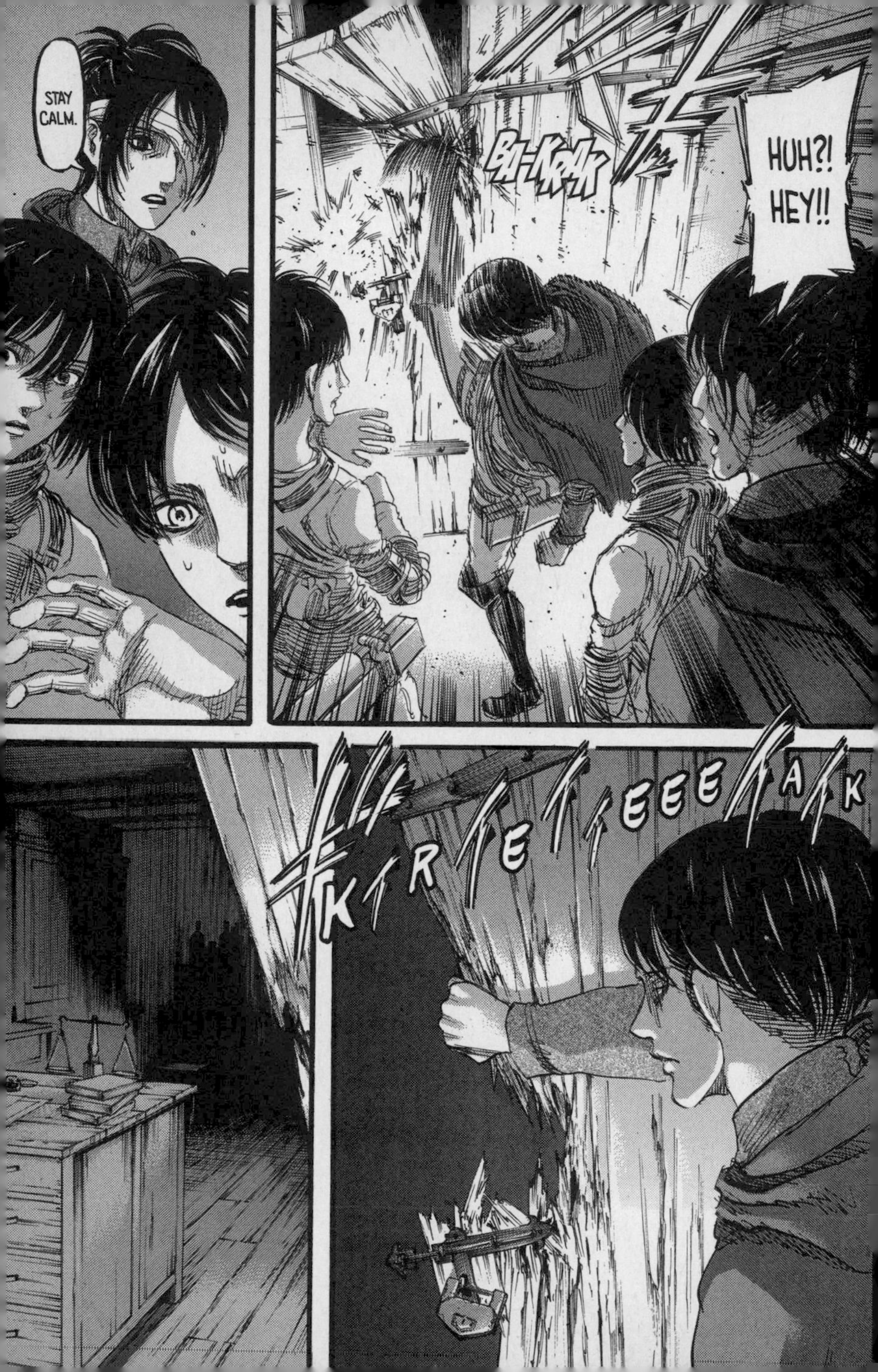
HUH?! HEY!!
BA-KRAK
STAY CALM.
KREEEEAK

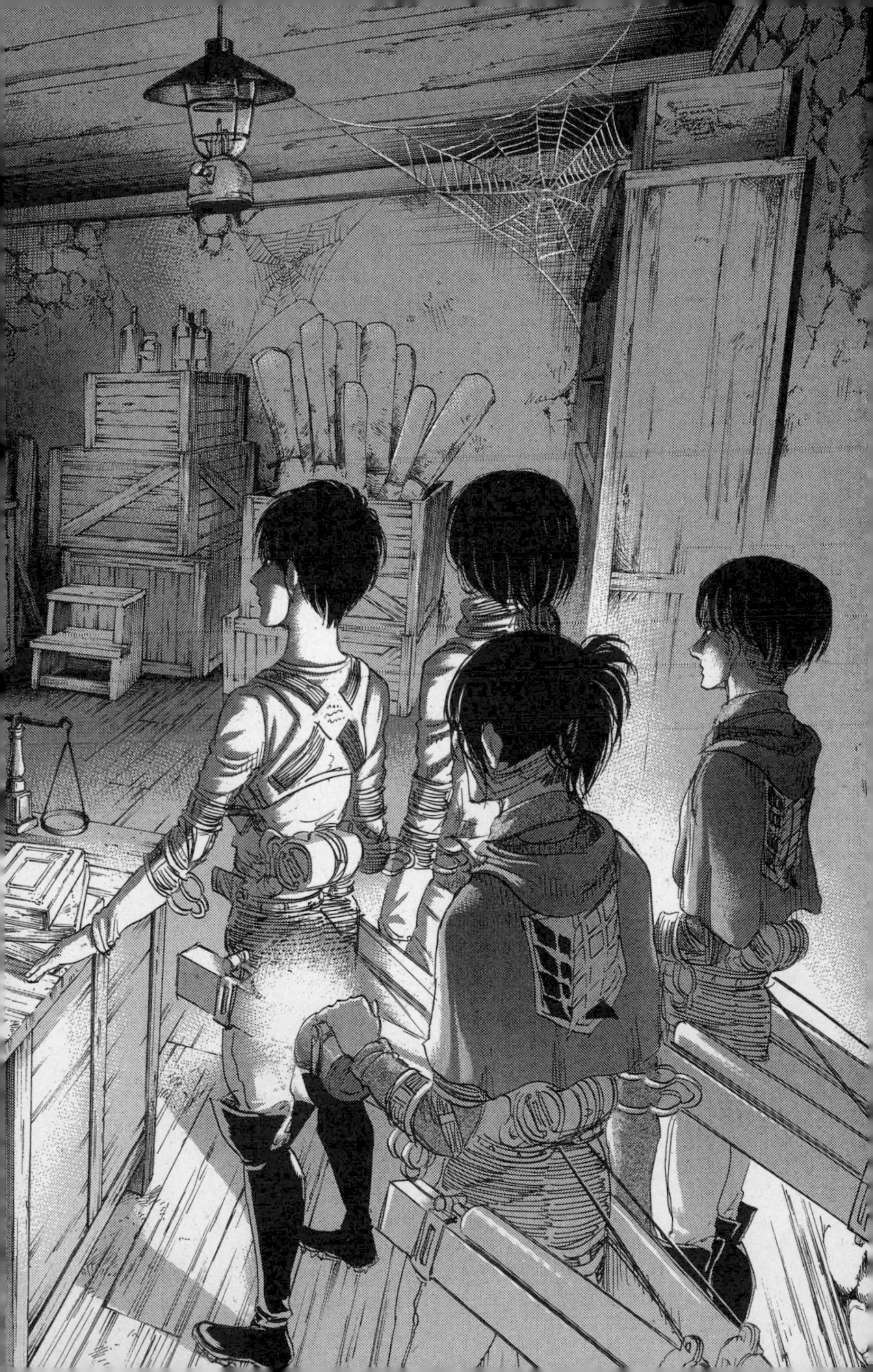

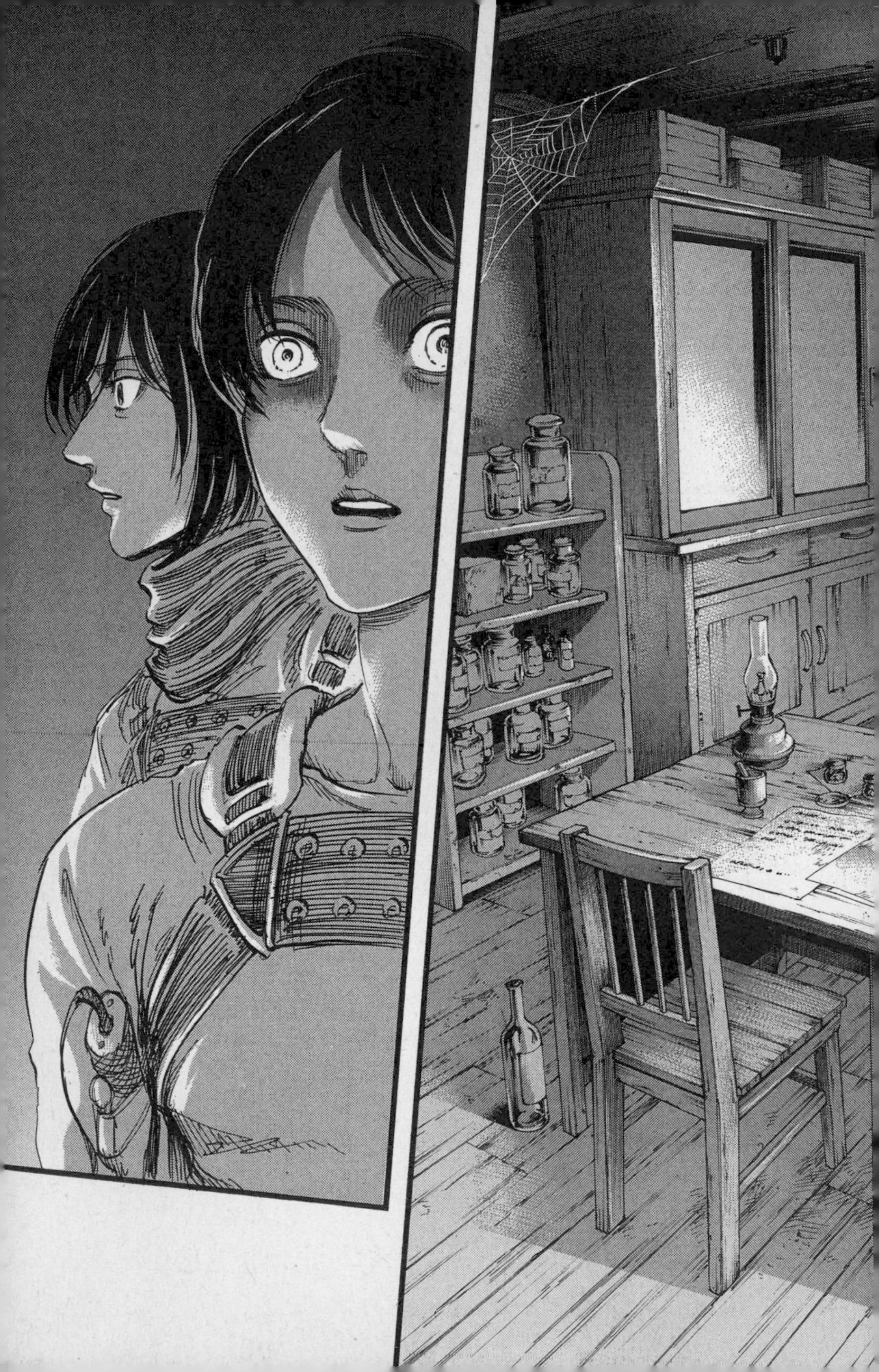

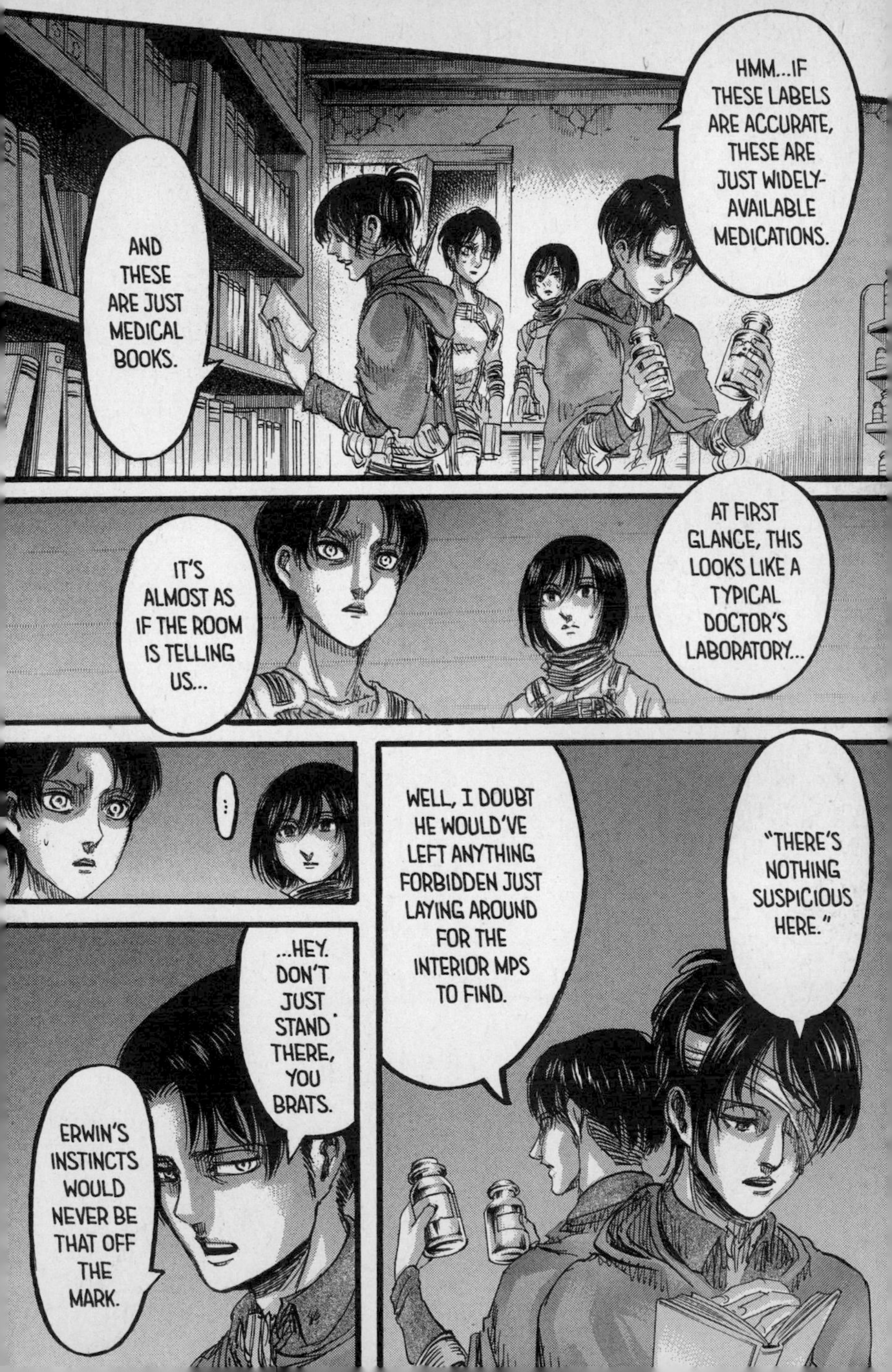
HMM...IF THESE LABELS ARE ACCURATE, THESE ARE JUST WIDELY-AVAILABLE MEDICATIONS.
AND THESE ARE JUST MEDICAL BOOKS.
AT FIRST GLANCE, THIS LOOKS LIKE A TYPICAL DOCTOR'S LABORATORY...
IT'S ALMOST AS IF THE ROOM IS TELLING US...
"THERE'S NOTHING SUSPICIOUS HERE."
WELL, I DOUBT HE WOULD'VE LEFT ANYTHING FORBIDDEN JUST LAYING AROUND FOR THE INTERIOR MPS TO FIND.
...
...HEY. DON'T JUST STAND THERE, YOU BRATS.
ERWIN'S INSTINCTS WOULD NEVER BE THAT OFF THE MARK.

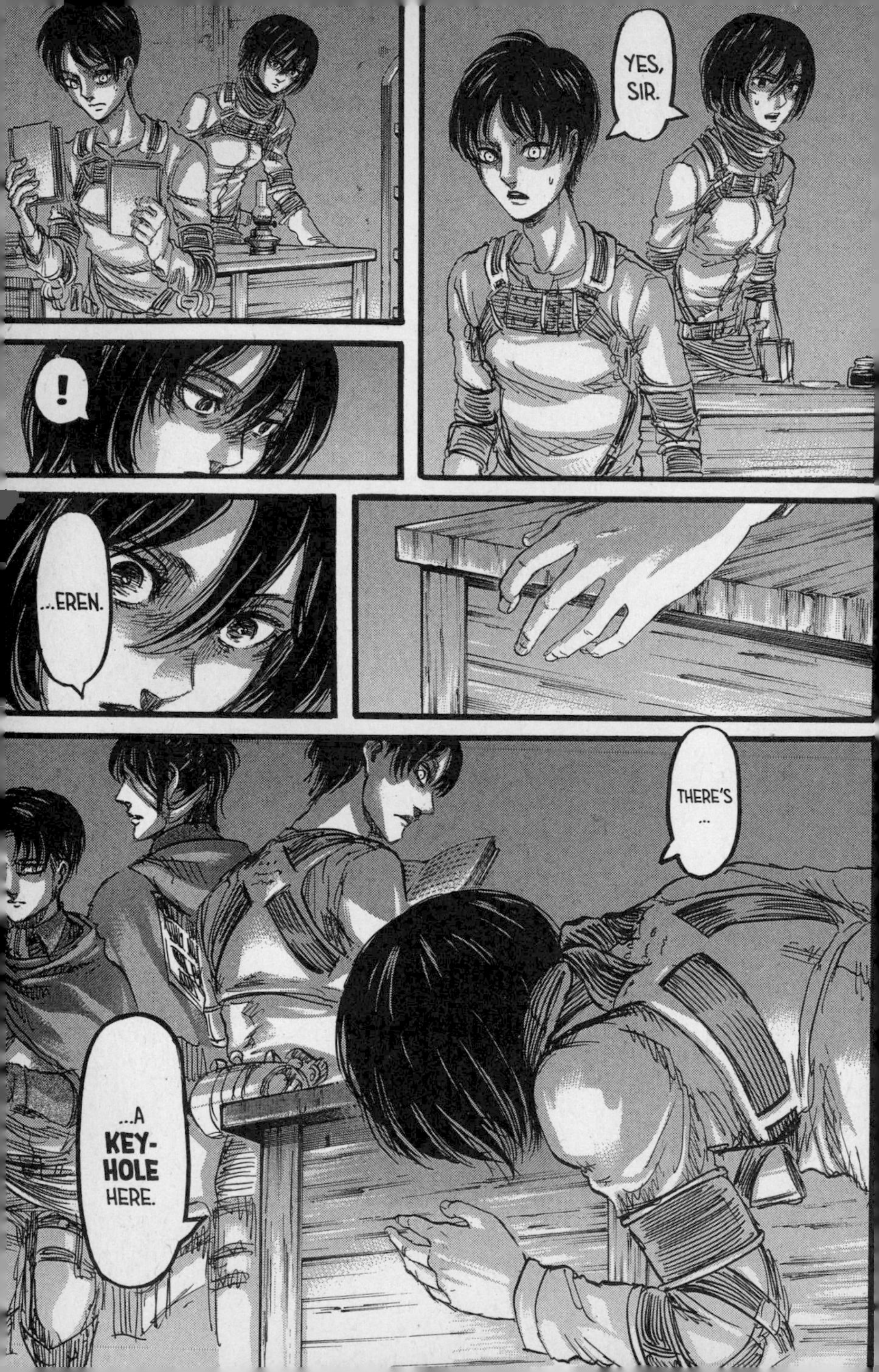
YES, SIR.
!
...EREN.
THERE'S ...
...A KEY-HOLE HERE.

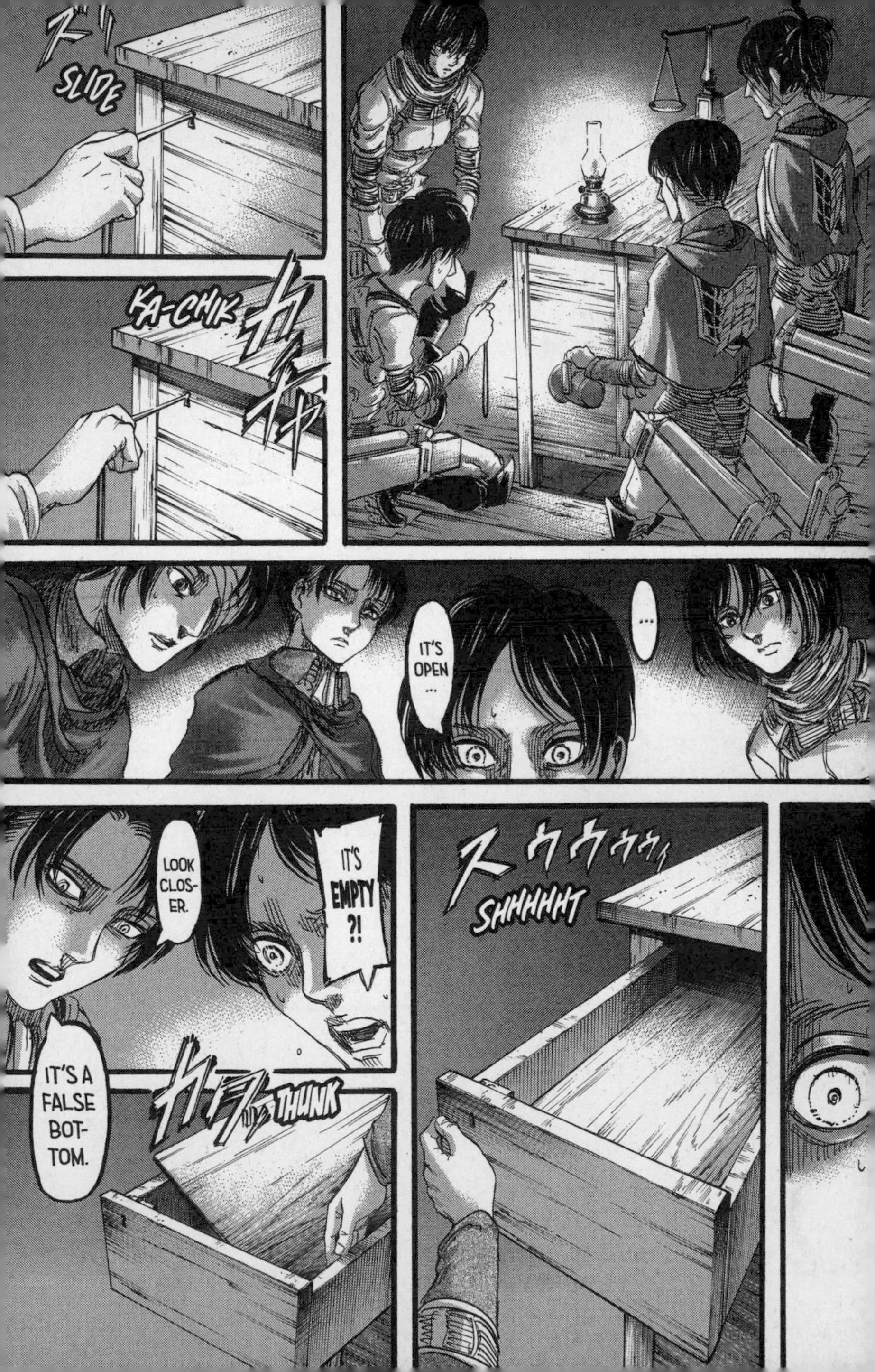

SLIDE
KA-CHIK
...
IT'S OPEN ...
SHHHHHT
IT'S EMPTY?!
LOOK CLOSER.
IT'S A FALSE BOTTOM.
THUNK

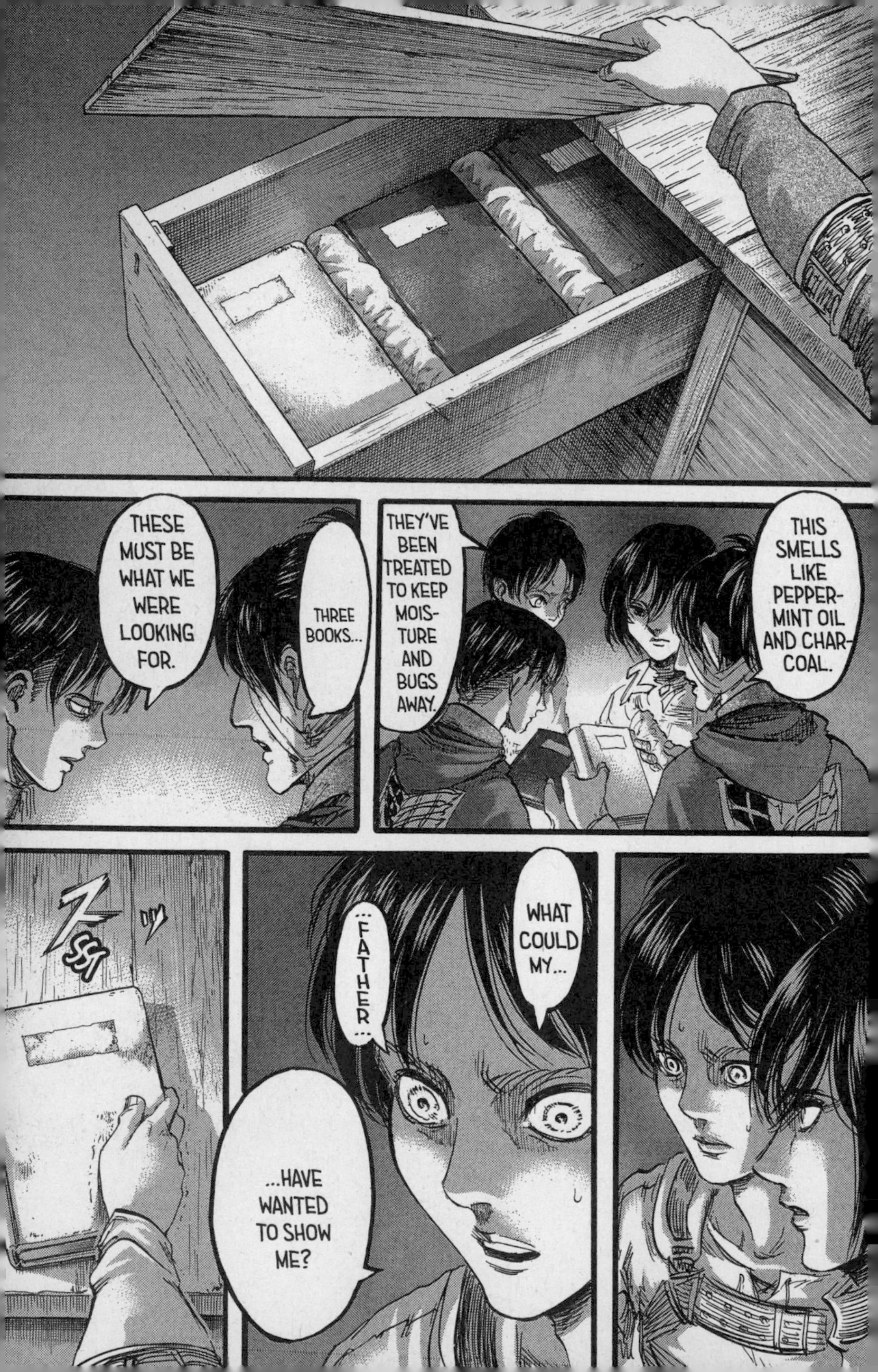
THIS SMELLS LIKE PEPPERMINT OIL AND CHARCOAL.
THEY'VE BEEN TREATED TO KEEP MOIS-TURE AND BUGS AWAY.
THREE BOOKS...
THESE MUST BE WHAT WE WERE LOOKING FOR.
WHAT COULD MY...
...FATHER...
...HAVE WANTED TO SHOW ME?
スッ

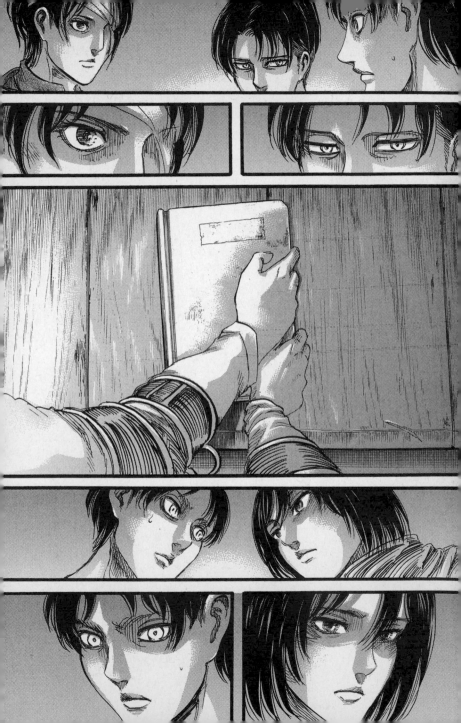

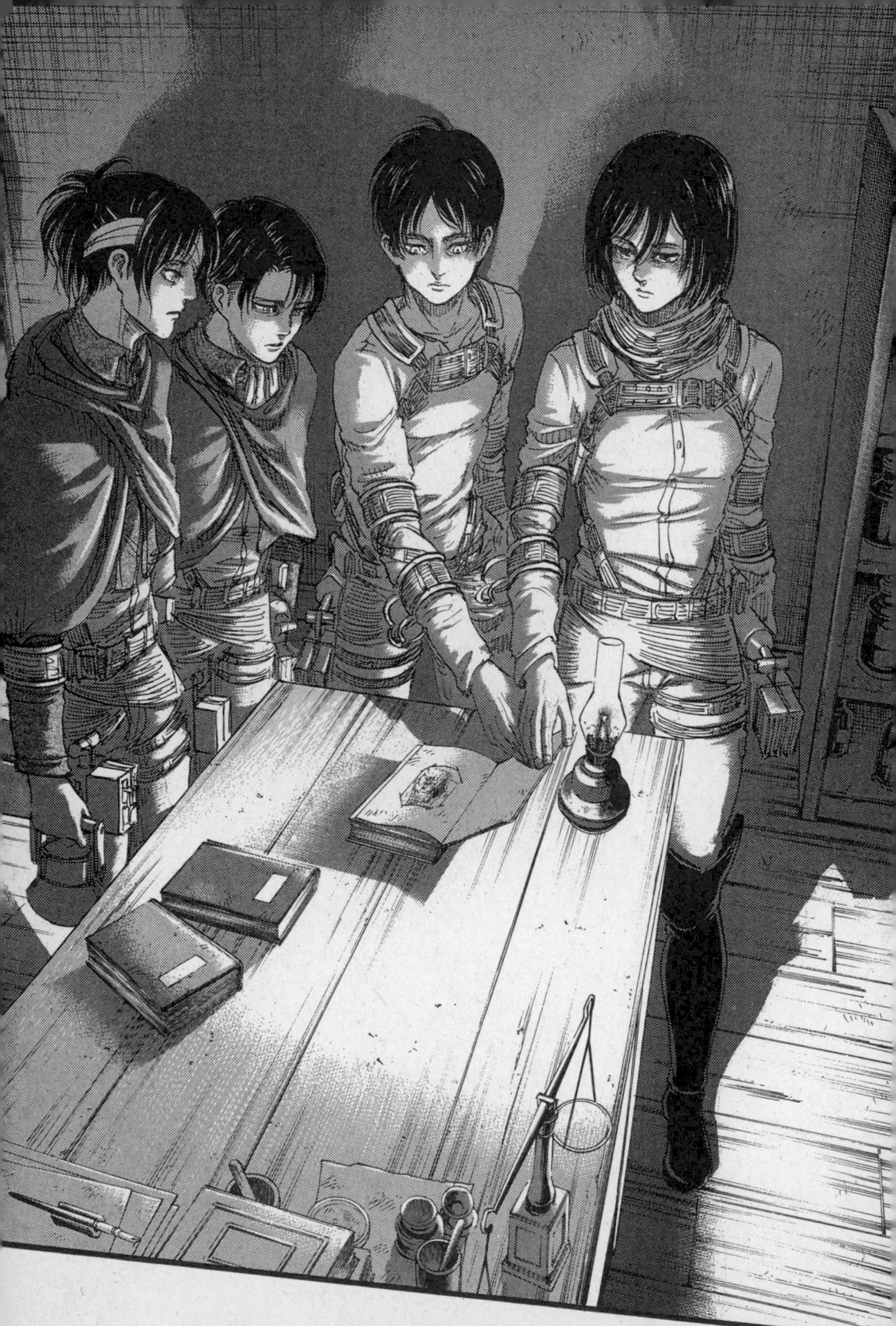

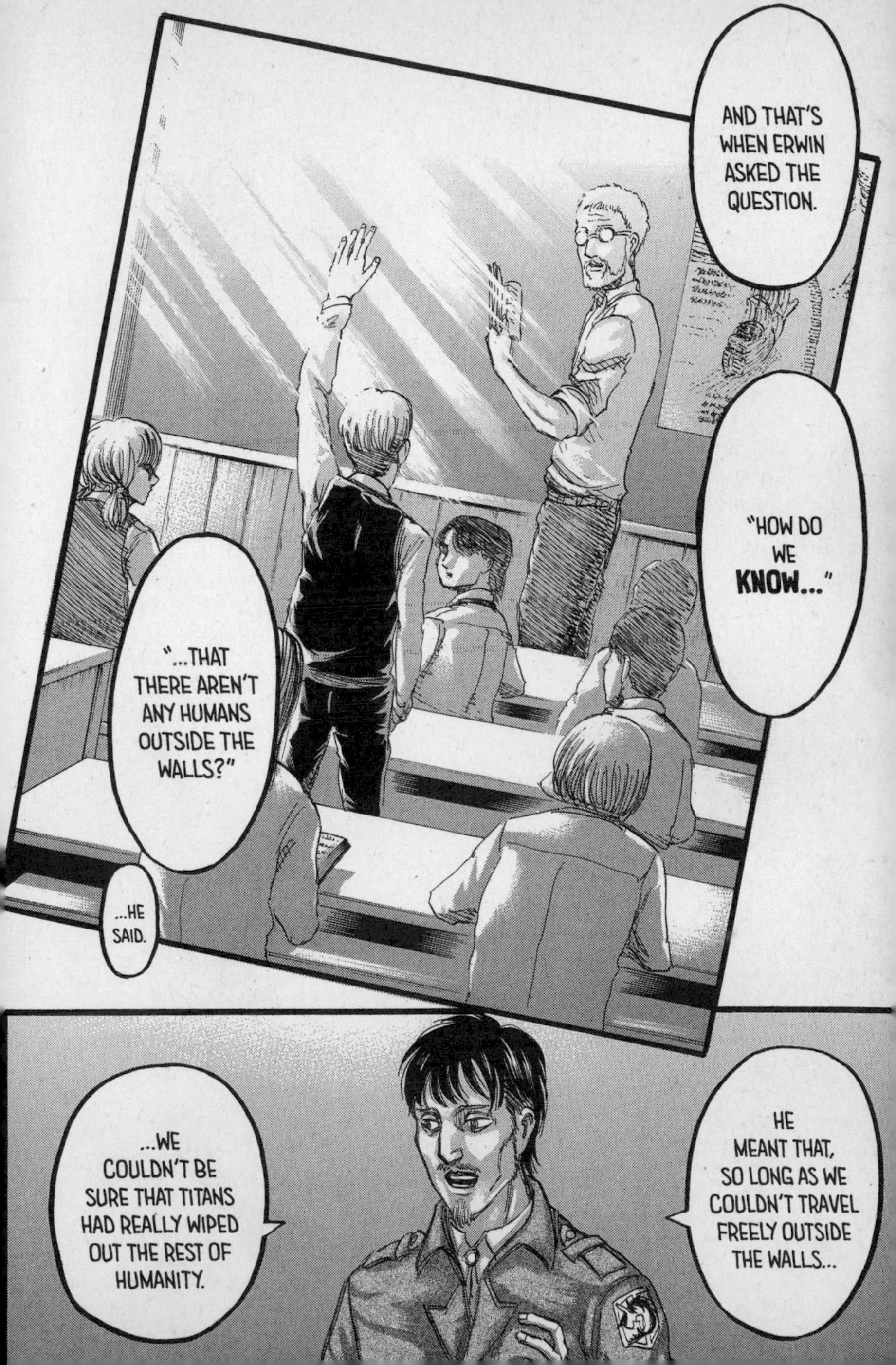
AND THAT'S WHEN ERWIN ASKED THE QUESTION.
"HOW DO WE **KNOW...**"
"...THAT THERE AREN'T ANY HUMANS OUTSIDE THE WALLS?"
...HE SAID.
HE MEANT THAT, SO LONG AS WE COULDN'T TRAVEL FREELY OUTSIDE THE WALLS...
...WE COULDN'T BE SURE THAT TITANS HAD REALLY WIPED OUT THE REST OF HUMANITY.

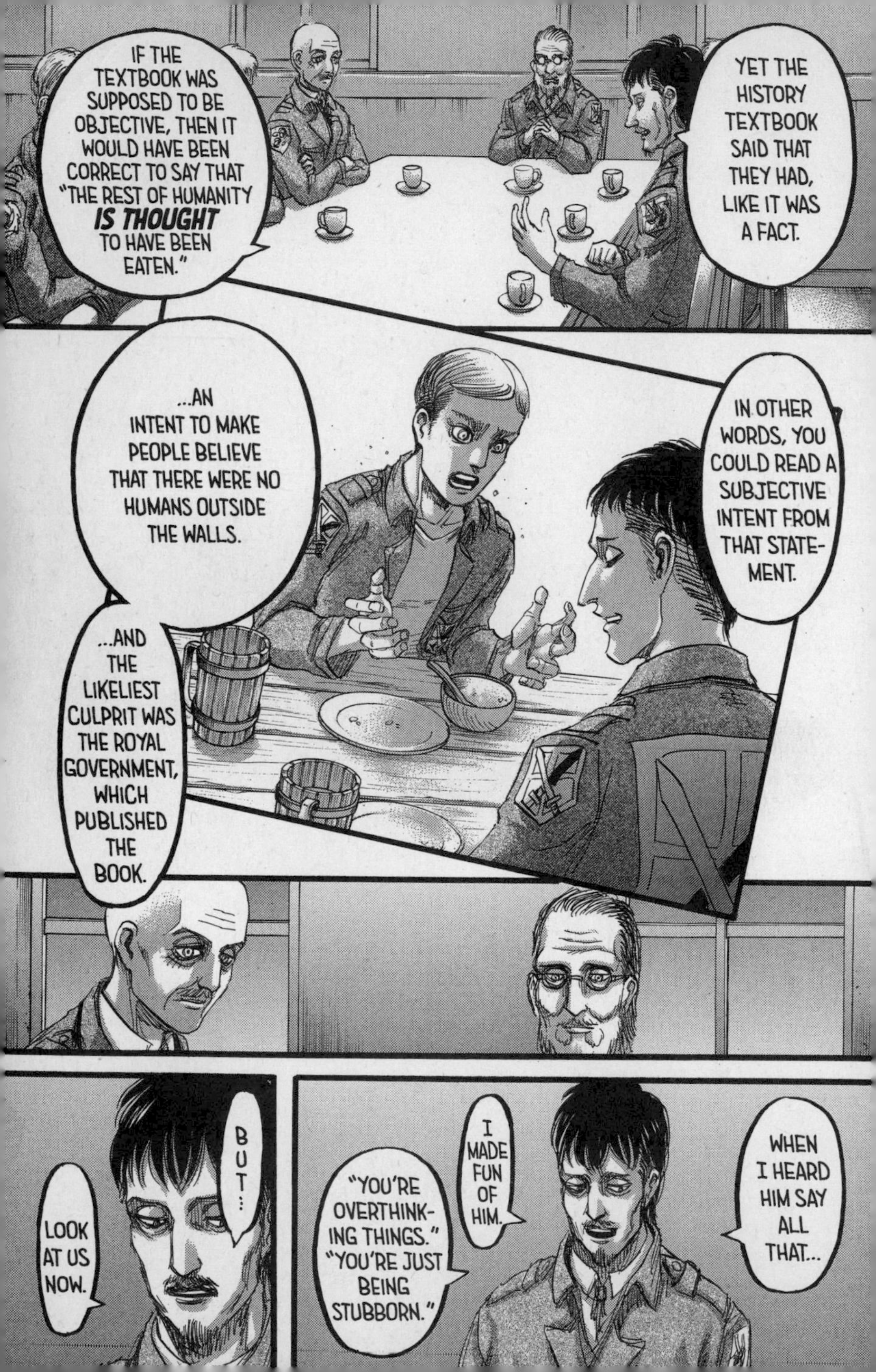
YET THE HISTORY TEXTBOOK SAID THAT THEY HAD, LIKE IT WAS A FACT.
IF THE TEXTBOOK WAS SUPPOSED TO BE OBJECTIVE, THEN IT WOULD HAVE BEEN CORRECT TO SAY THAT "THE REST OF HUMANITY ***IS THOUGHT*** TO HAVE BEEN EATEN."
IN OTHER WORDS, YOU COULD READ A SUBJECTIVE INTENT FROM THAT STATE-MENT.
...AN INTENT TO MAKE PEOPLE BELIEVE THAT THERE WERE NO HUMANS OUTSIDE THE WALLS.
...AND THE LIKELIEST CULPRIT WAS THE ROYAL GOVERNMENT, WHICH PUBLISHED THE BOOK.
WHEN I HEARD HIM SAY ALL THAT...
I MADE FUN OF HIM.
"YOU'RE OVERTHINK-ING THINGS." "YOU'RE JUST BEING STUBBORN."
BUT...
LOOK AT US NOW.

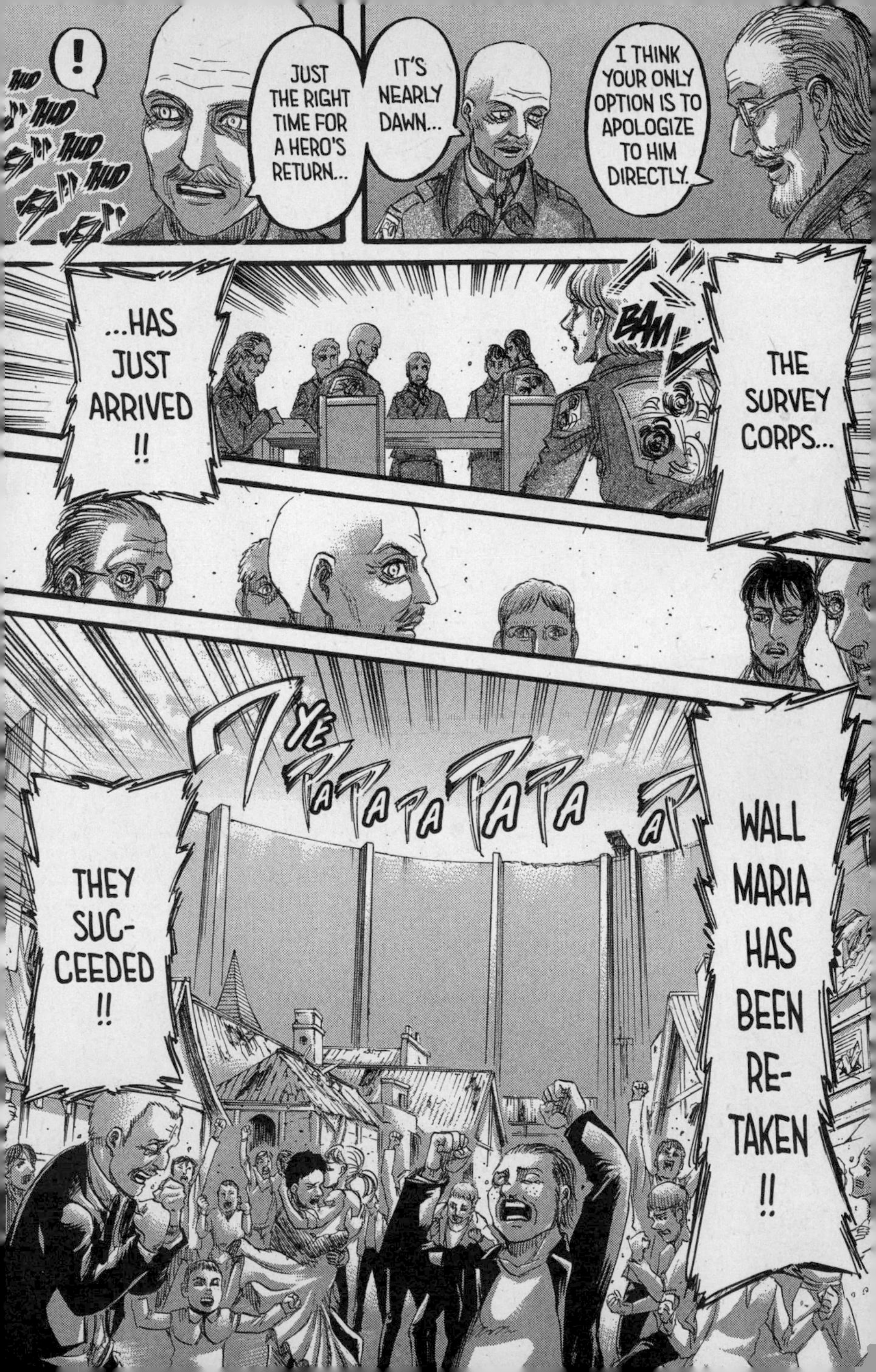
I THINK YOUR ONLY OPTION IS TO APOLOGIZE TO HIM DIRECTLY.
IT'S NEARLY DAWN...
JUST THE RIGHT TIME FOR A HERO'S RETURN...
!
THUD THUD THUD THUD
THE SURVEY CORPS...
BAM
...HAS JUST ARRIVED !!
WALL MARIA HAS BEEN RE-TAKEN !!
THEY SUC-CEEDED !!

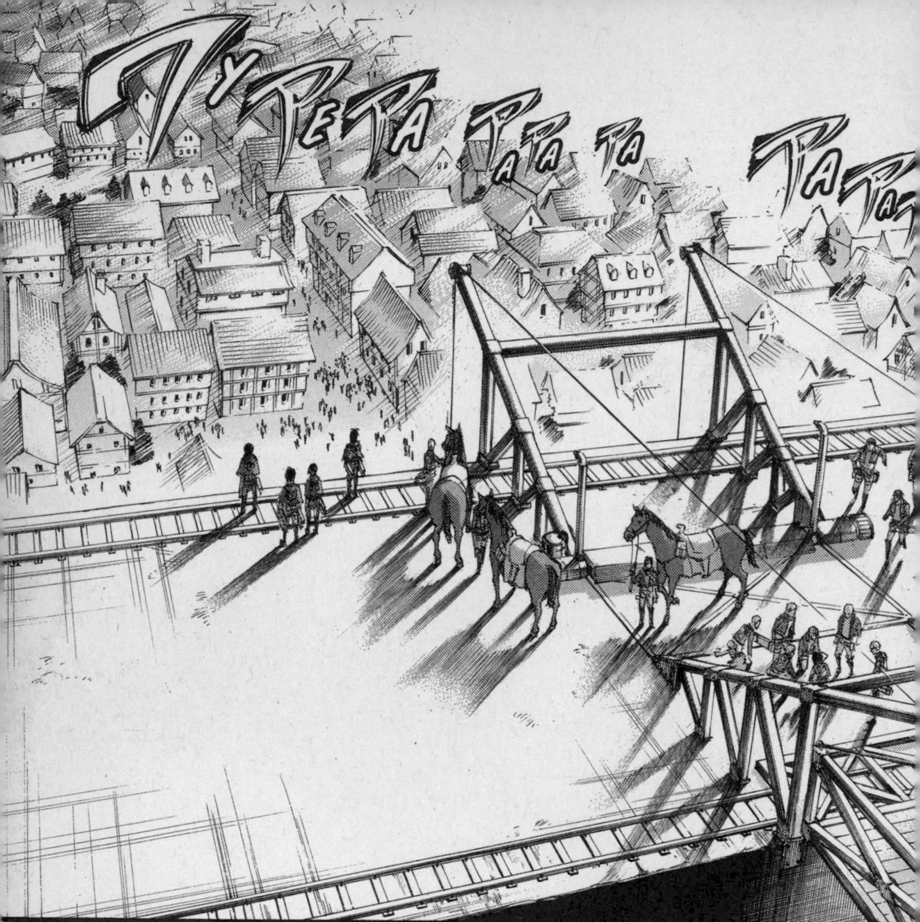
PETA PATA TA
PATA

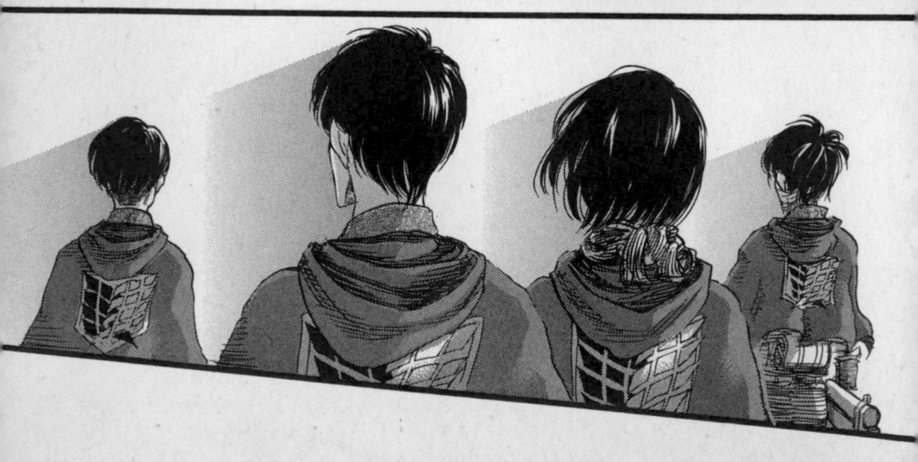

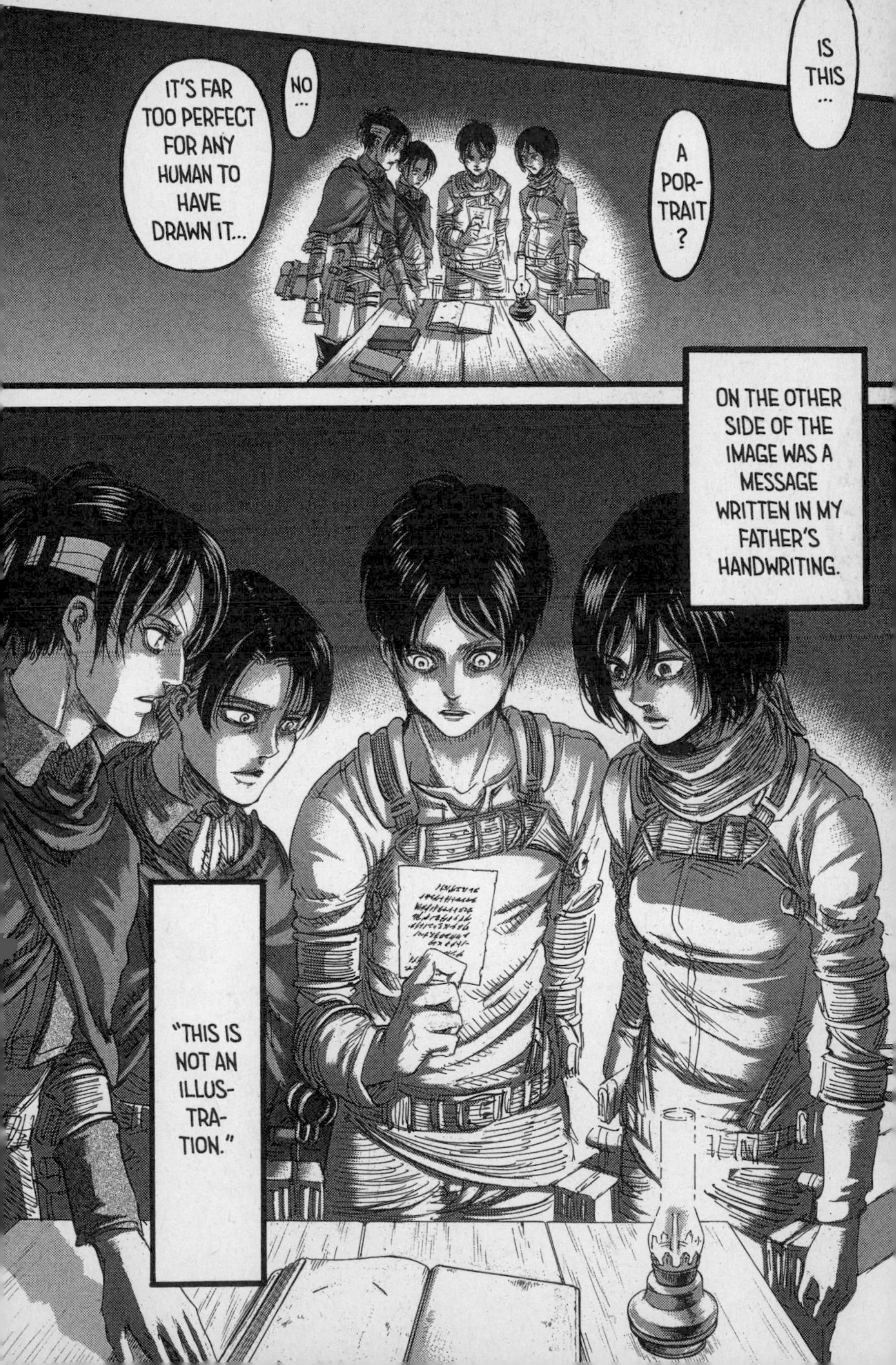
IS THIS ...
A POR-TRAIT?
NO ...
IT'S FAR TOO PERFECT FOR ANY HUMAN TO HAVE DRAWN IT...
ON THE OTHER SIDE OF THE IMAGE WAS A MESSAGE WRITTEN IN MY FATHER'S HANDWRITING.
"THIS IS NOT AN ILLUS-TRA-TION."

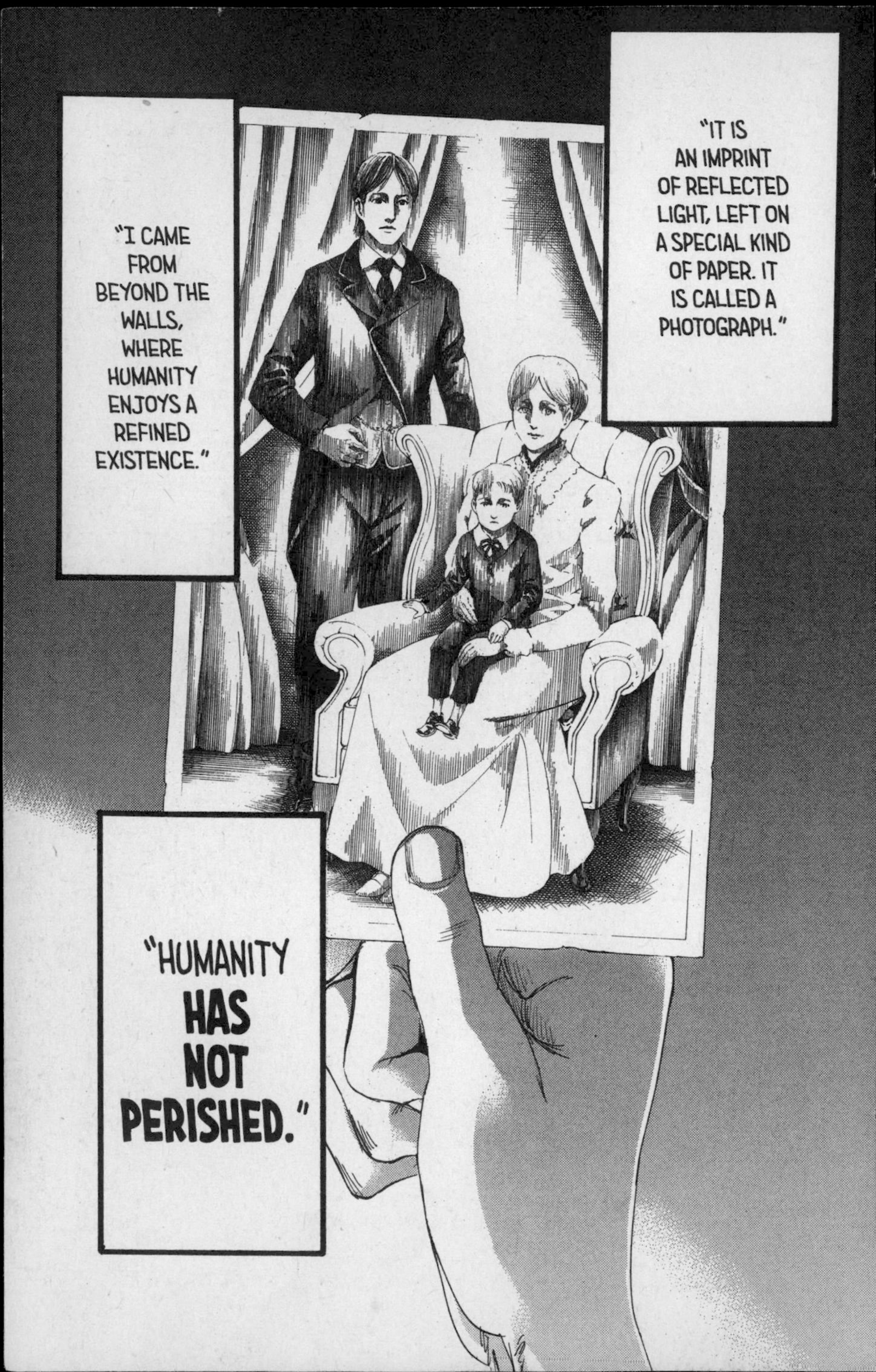
"IT IS AN IMPRINT OF REFLECTED LIGHT, LEFT ON A SPECIAL KIND OF PAPER. IT IS CALLED A PHOTOGRAPH."
"I CAME FROM BEYOND THE WALLS, WHERE HUMANITY ENJOYS A REFINED EXISTENCE."
"HUMANITY HAS NOT PERISHED."

ATTACK on TITAN

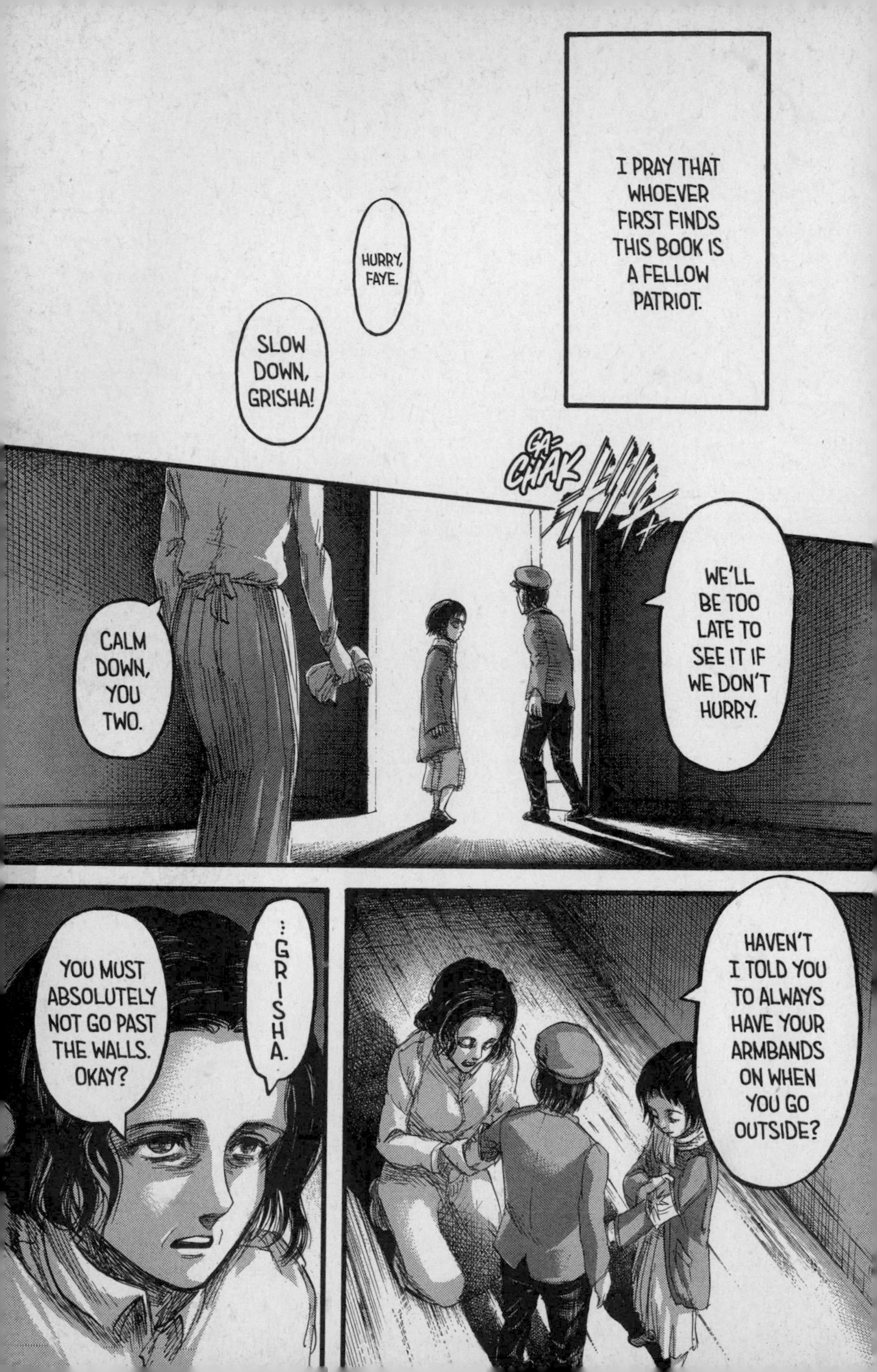
I PRAY THAT WHOEVER FIRST FINDS THIS BOOK IS A FELLOW PATRIOT.
HURRY, FAYE.
SLOW DOWN, GRISHA!
GA-CHAK
WE'LL BE TOO LATE TO SEE IT IF WE DON'T HURRY.
CALM DOWN, YOU TWO.
HAVEN'T I TOLD YOU TO ALWAYS HAVE YOUR ARMBANDS ON WHEN YOU GO OUTSIDE?
...GRISHA.
YOU MUST ABSOLUTELY NOT GO PAST THE WALLS. OKAY?

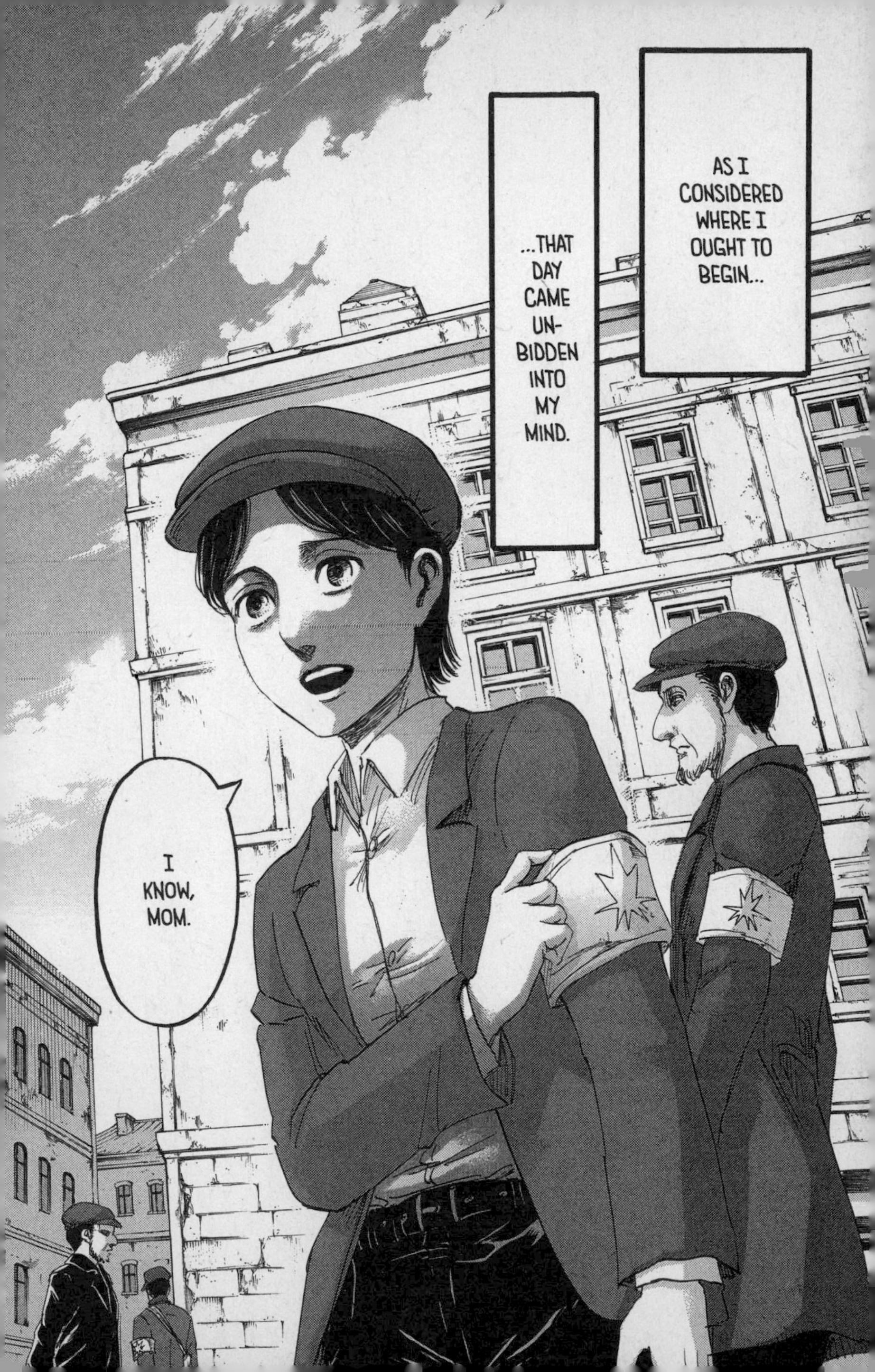
AS I CONSIDERED WHERE I OUGHT TO BEGIN...
...THAT DAY CAME UN-BIDDEN INTO MY MIND.
I KNOW, MOM.

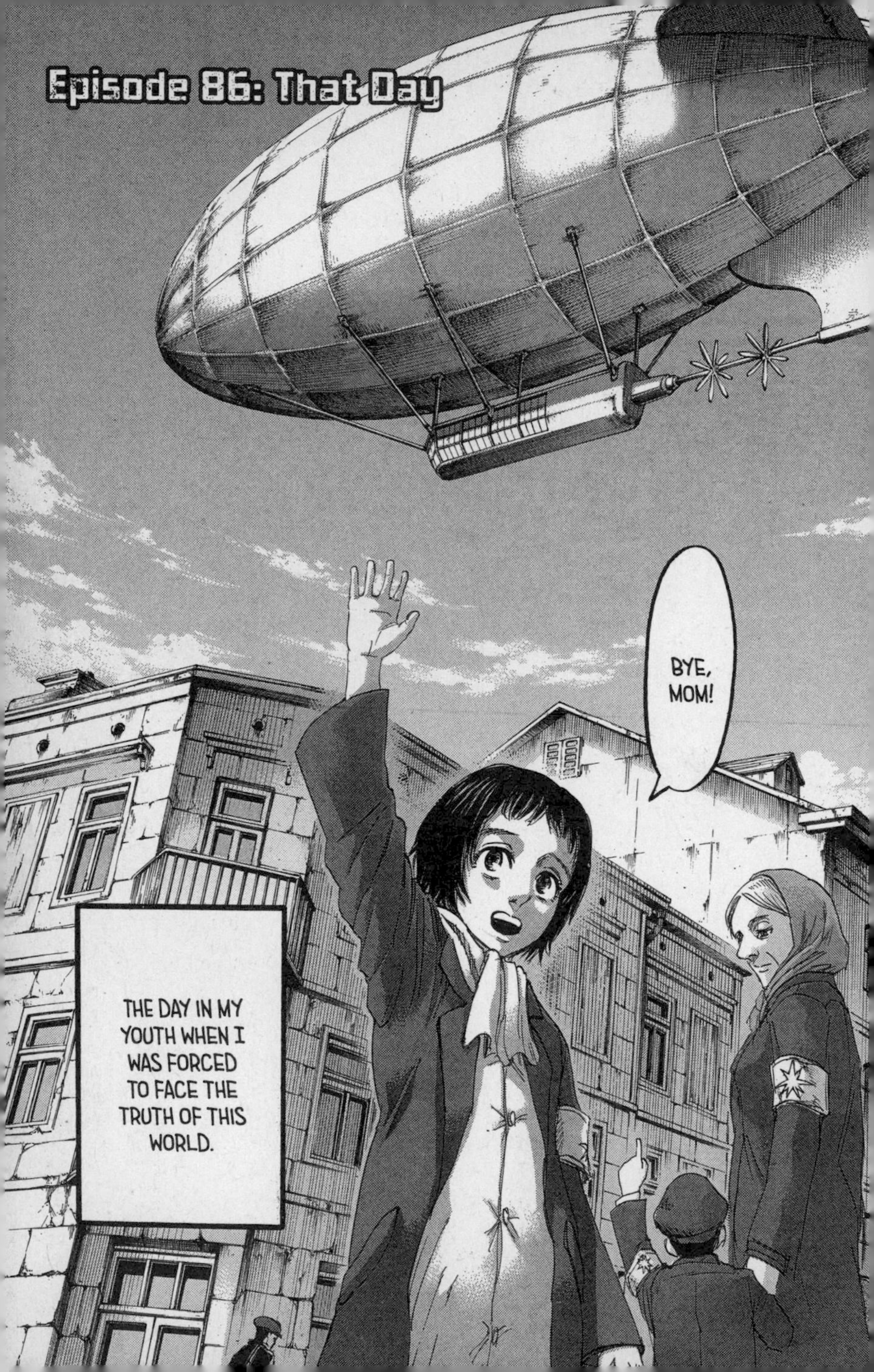
Episode 86: That Day
BYE, MOM!
THE DAY IN MY YOUTH WHEN I WAS FORCED TO FACE THE TRUTH OF THIS WORLD.

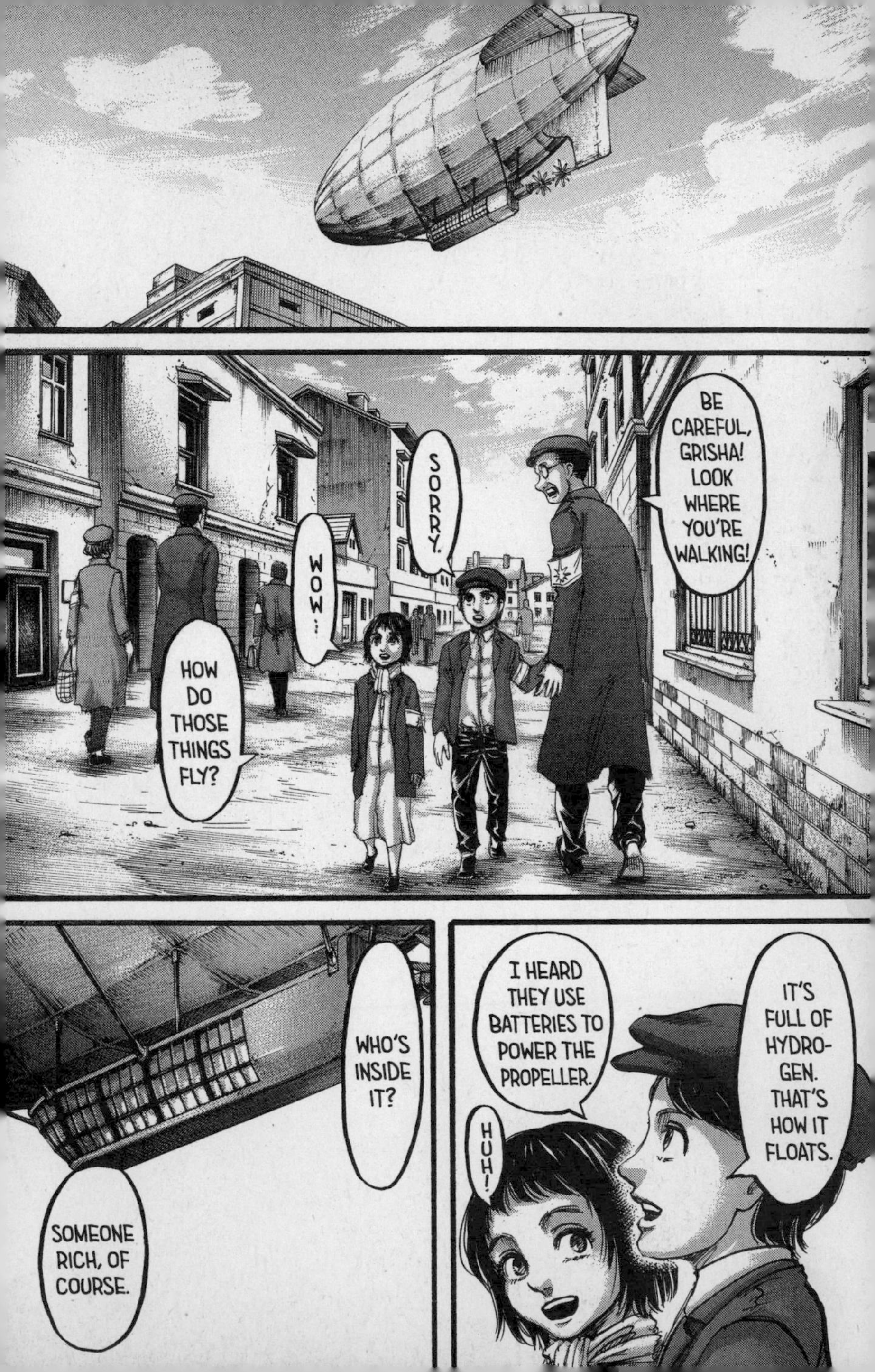
BE CAREFUL, GRISHA! LOOK WHERE YOU'RE WALKING!
SORRY.
WOW...
HOW DO THOSE THINGS FLY?
IT'S FULL OF HYDROGEN. THAT'S HOW IT FLOATS.
I HEARD THEY USE BATTERIES TO POWER THE PROPELLER.
HUH!
WHO'S INSIDE IT?
SOMEONE RICH, OF COURSE.

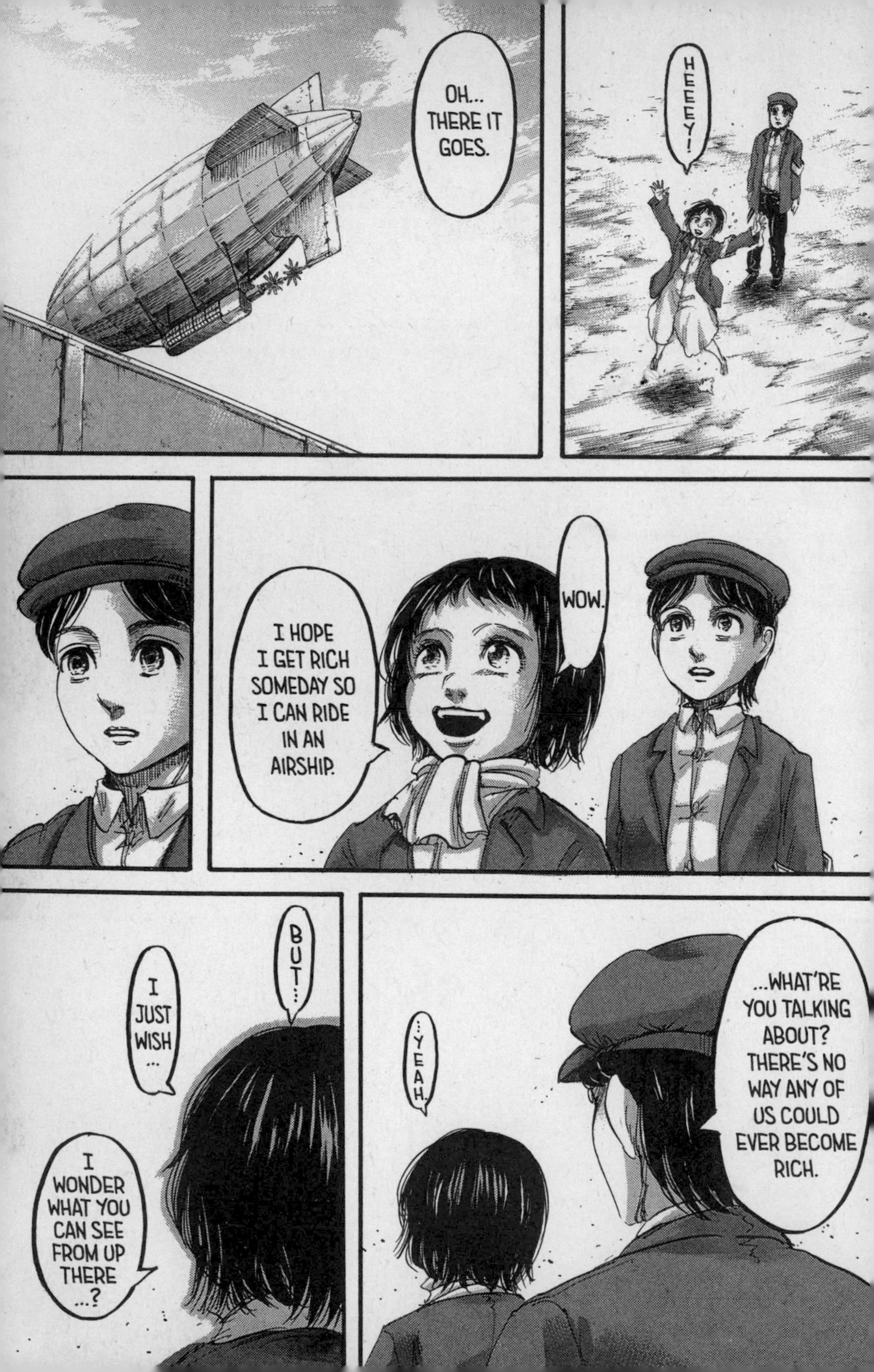
HEEEEY!
OH... THERE IT GOES.
WOW.
I HOPE I GET RICH SOMEDAY SO I CAN RIDE IN AN AIRSHIP.
...WHAT'RE YOU TALKING ABOUT? THERE'S NO WAY ANY OF US COULD EVER BECOME RICH.
...YEAH.
BUT...
I JUST WISH...
I WONDER WHAT YOU CAN SEE FROM UP THERE...?

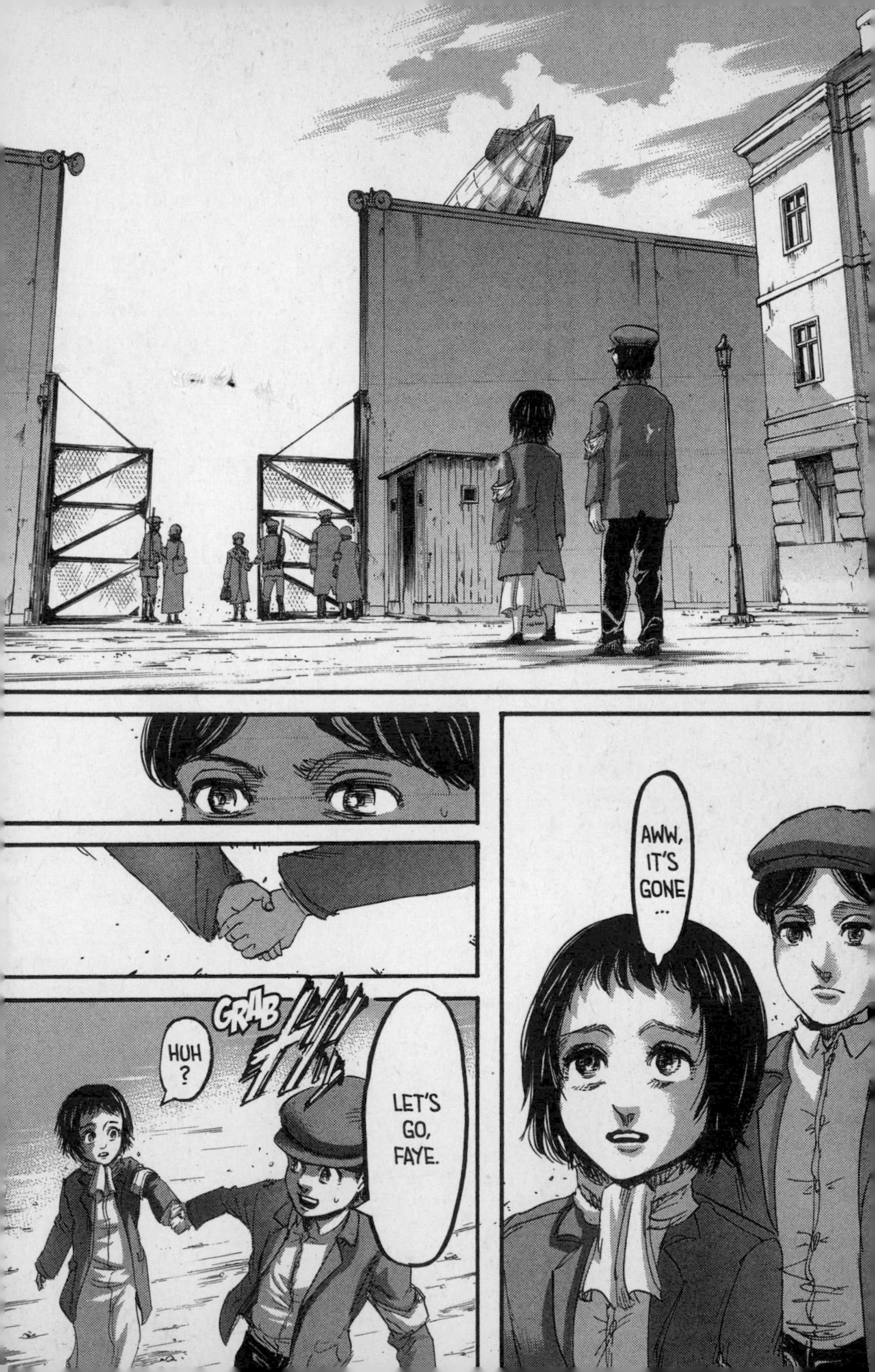
AWW, IT'S GONE ...
GRAB
LET'S GO, FAYE.
HUH ?

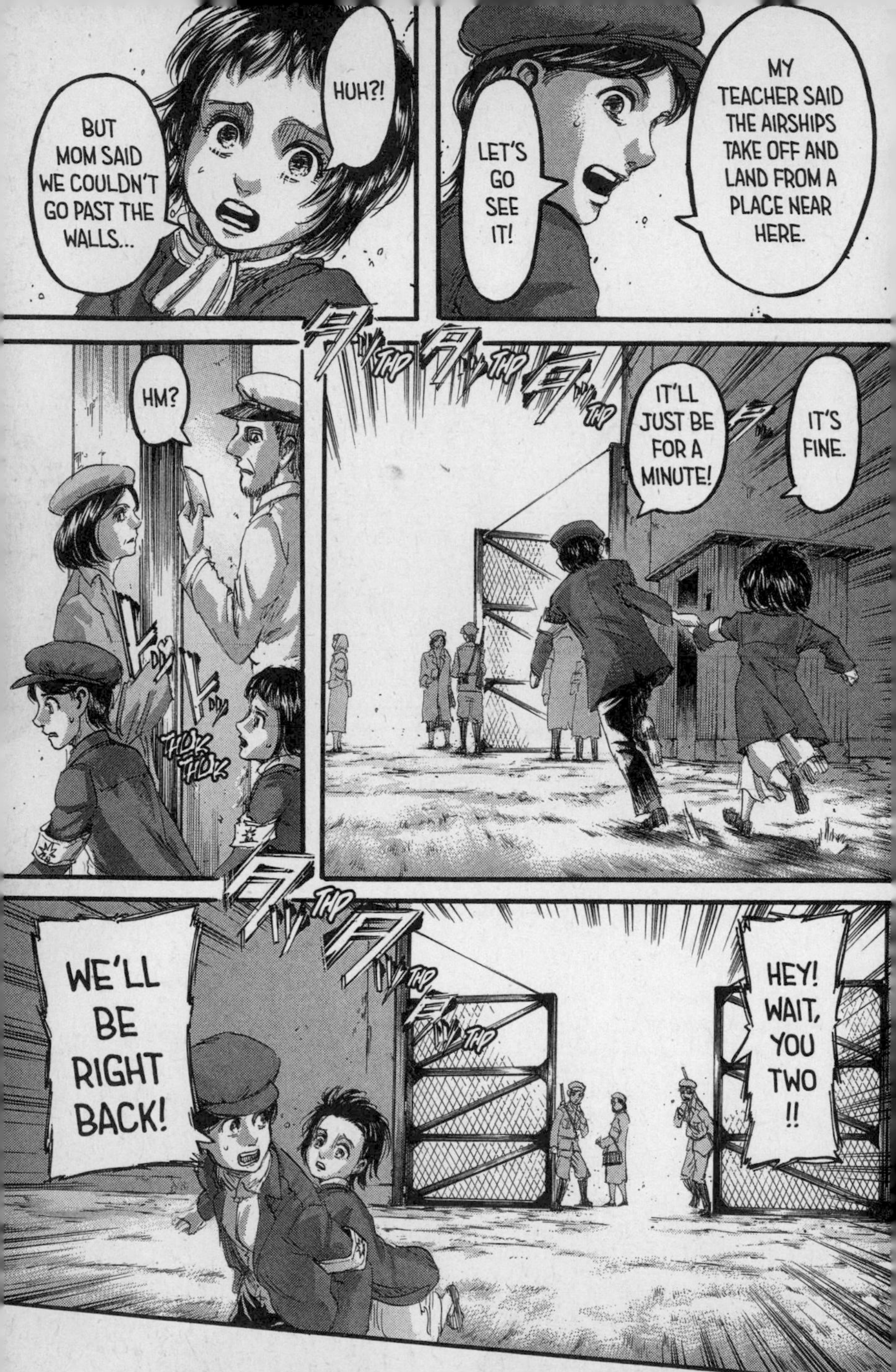
MY TEACHER SAID THE AIRSHIPS TAKE OFF AND LAND FROM A PLACE NEAR HERE.
LET'S GO SEE IT!
HUH?!
BUT MOM SAID WE COULDN'T GO PAST THE WALLS...
THP
THP
THP
IT'S FINE.
IT'LL JUST BE FOR A MINUTE!
HM?
THOK THOK
THP
THP
THP
HEY! WAIT, YOU TWO!!
WE'LL BE RIGHT BACK!

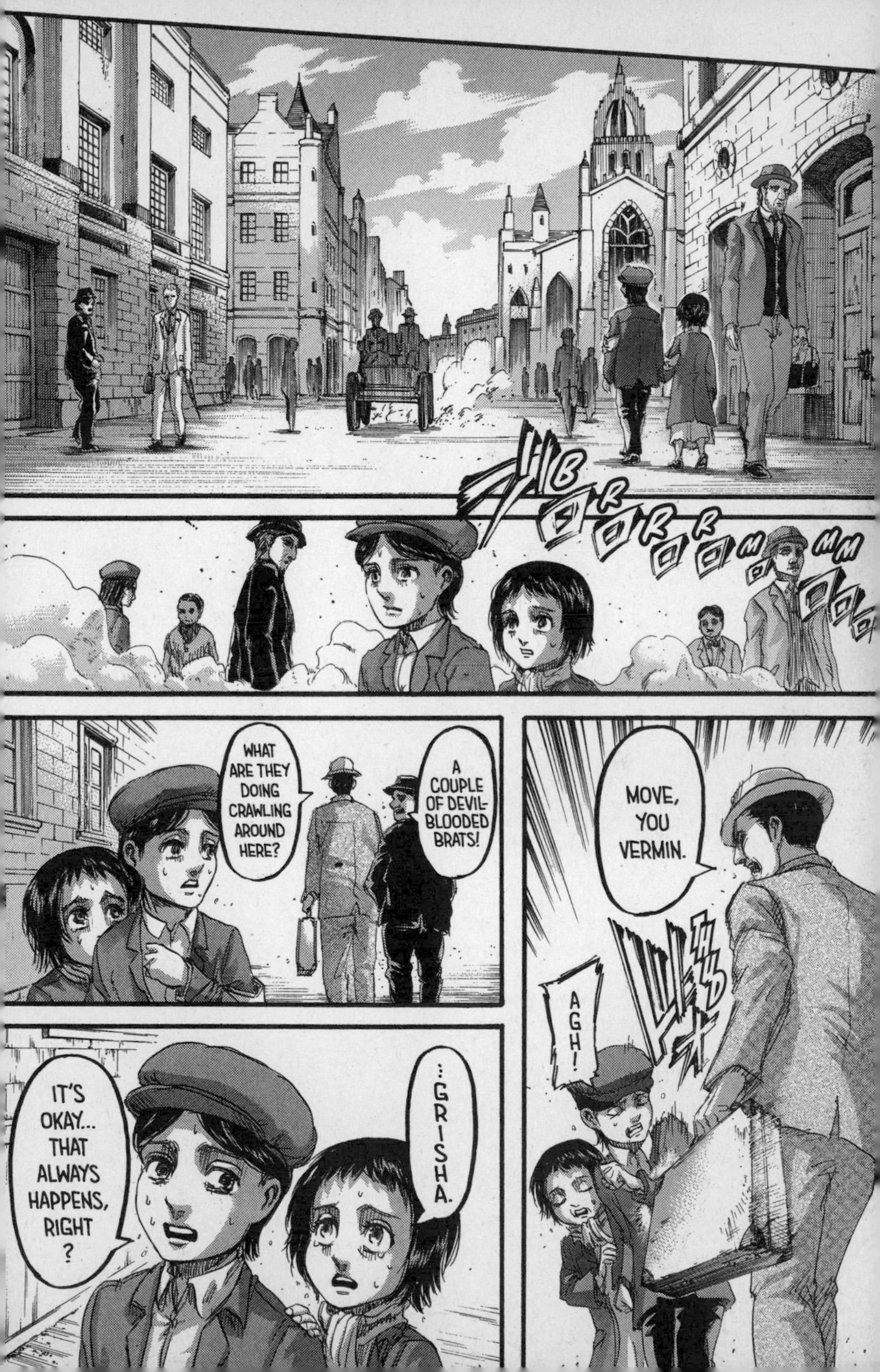
MOVE, YOU VERMIN.
AGH!
A COUPLE OF DEVIL-BLOODED BRATS!
WHAT ARE THEY DOING CRAWLING AROUND HERE?
...GRISHA.
IT'S OKAY... THAT ALWAYS HAPPENS, RIGHT?

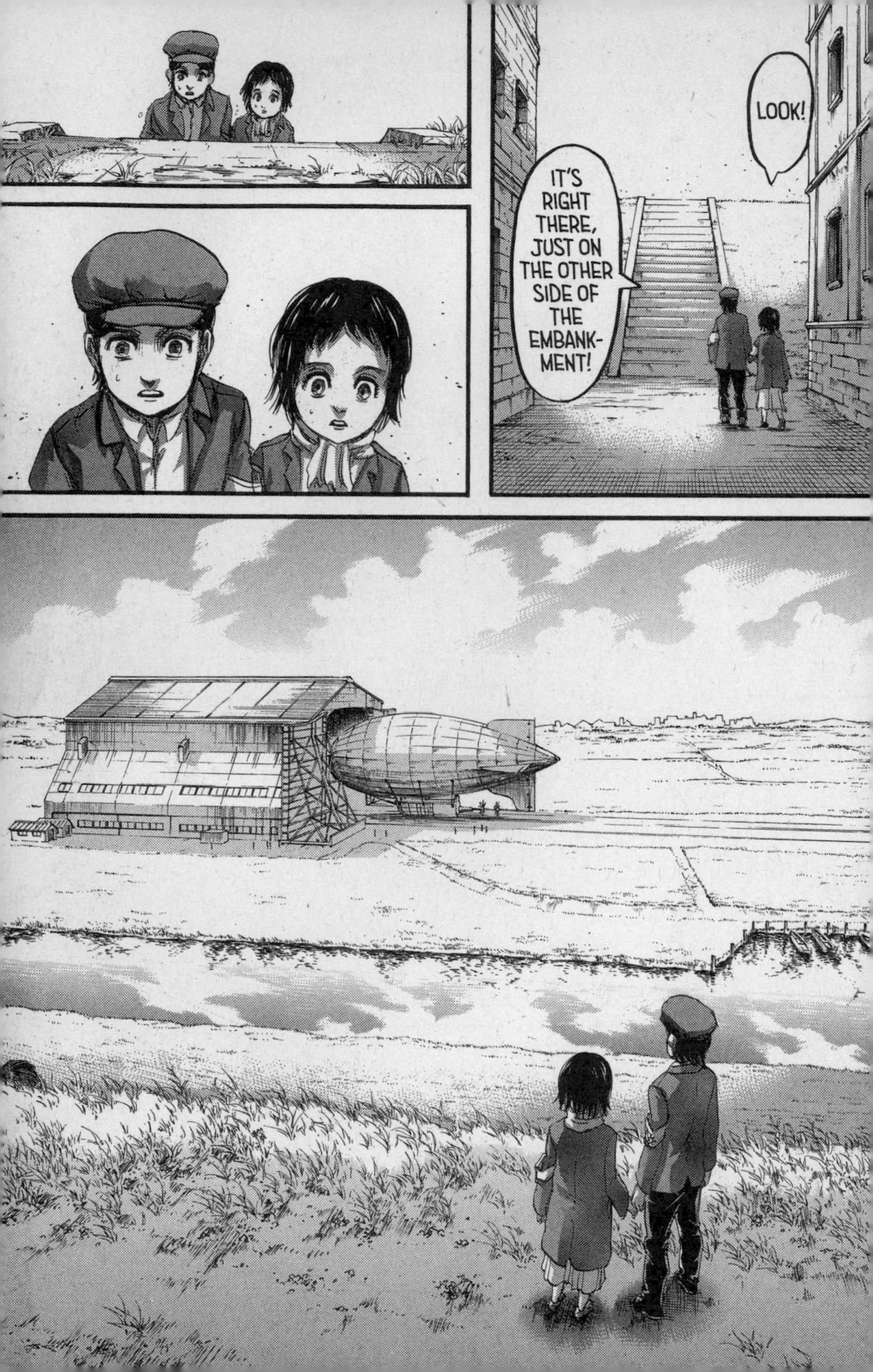
LOOK!
IT'S RIGHT THERE, JUST ON THE OTHER SIDE OF THE EMBANKMENT!

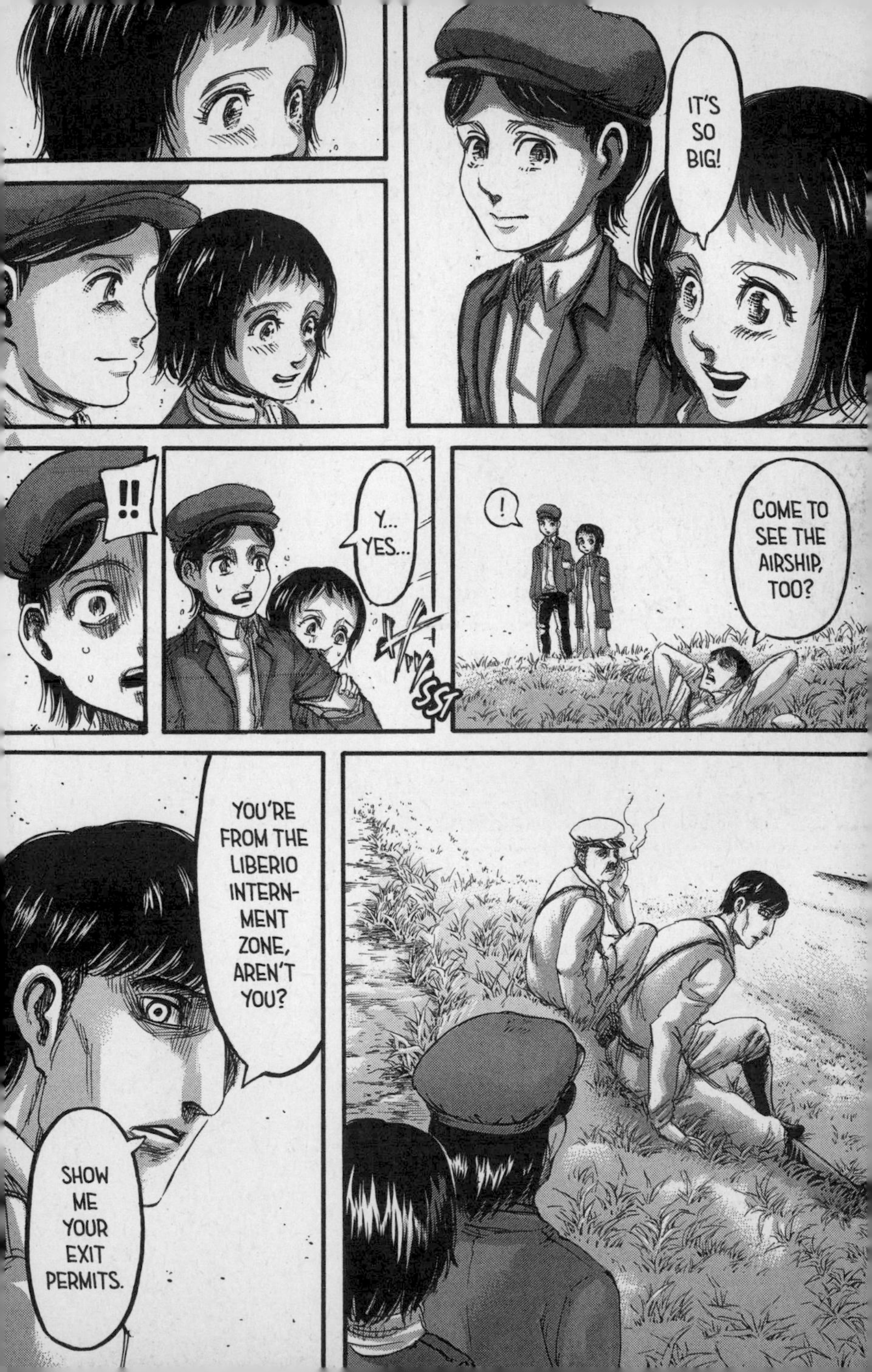
IT'S SO BIG!
COME TO SEE THE AIRSHIP, TOO?
!
Y... YES...
!!
YOU'RE FROM THE LIBERIO INTERNMENT ZONE, AREN'T YOU?
SHOW ME YOUR EXIT PERMITS.

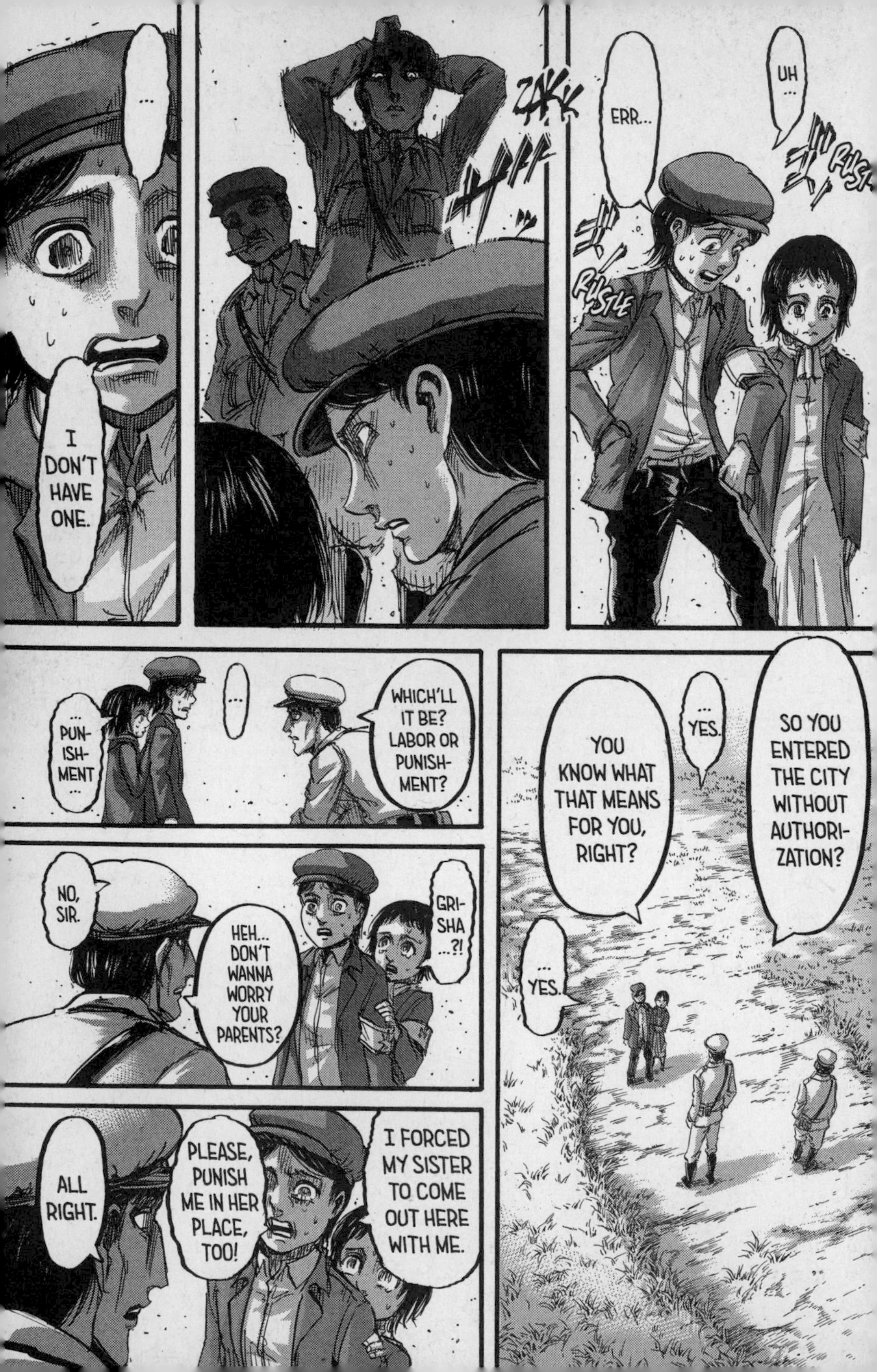
UH ...
RUSTLE
ERR...
RUSTLE
ZAKK
...
I DON'T HAVE ONE.
SO YOU ENTERED THE CITY WITHOUT AUTHORIZATION?
... YES.
YOU KNOW WHAT THAT MEANS FOR YOU, RIGHT?
... YES.
WHICH'LL IT BE? LABOR OR PUNISHMENT?
...
... PUNISHMENT ...
GRISHA ...?!
HEH... DON'T WANNA WORRY YOUR PARENTS?
NO, SIR.
I FORCED MY SISTER TO COME OUT HERE WITH ME.
PLEASE, PUNISH ME IN HER PLACE, TOO!
ALL RIGHT.

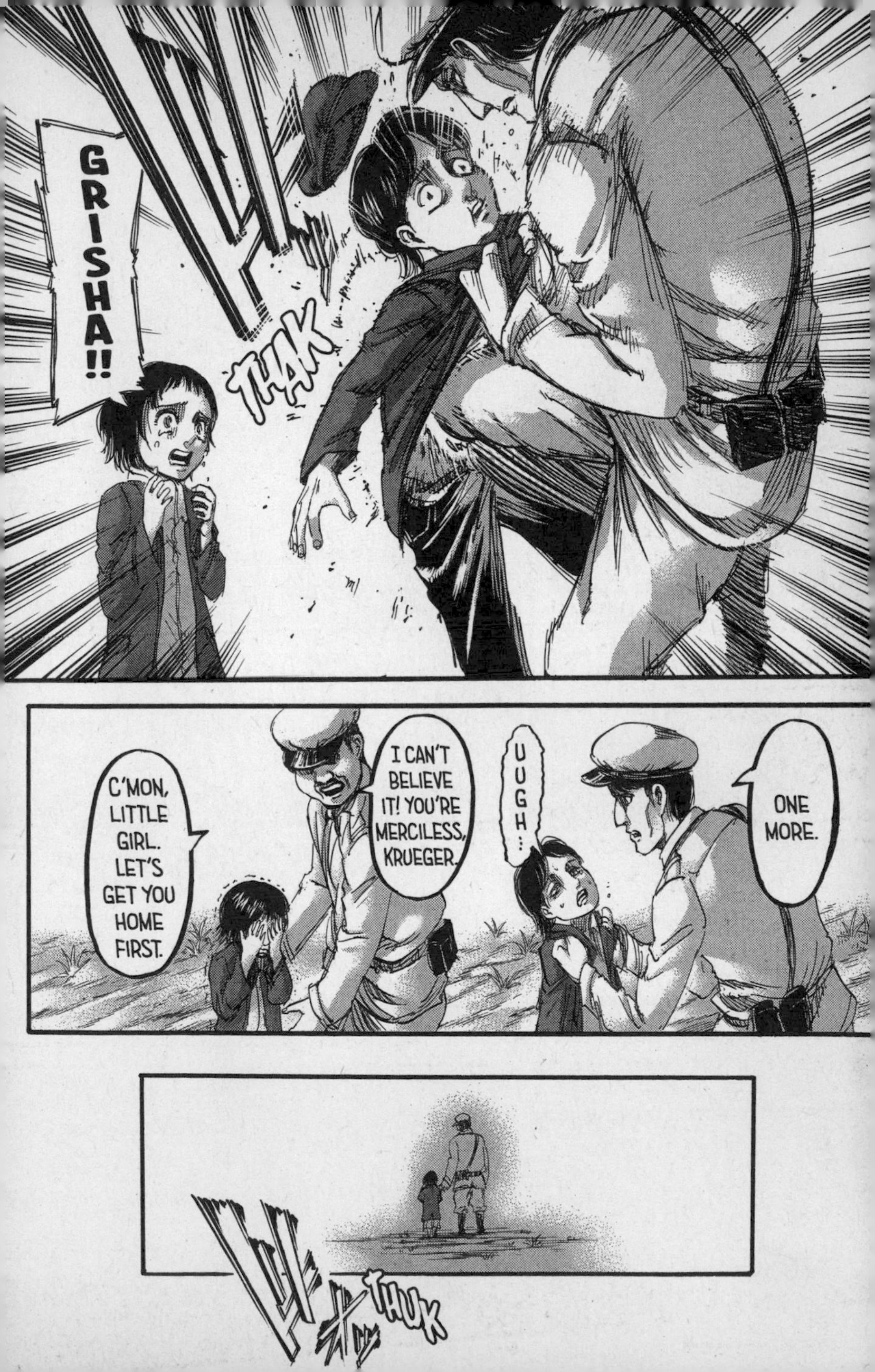
THAK
GRISHA!!
ONE MORE.
UUGH...
I CAN'T BELIEVE IT! YOU'RE MERCILESS, KRUEGER.
C'MON, LITTLE GIRL. LET'S GET YOU HOME FIRST.
THUK

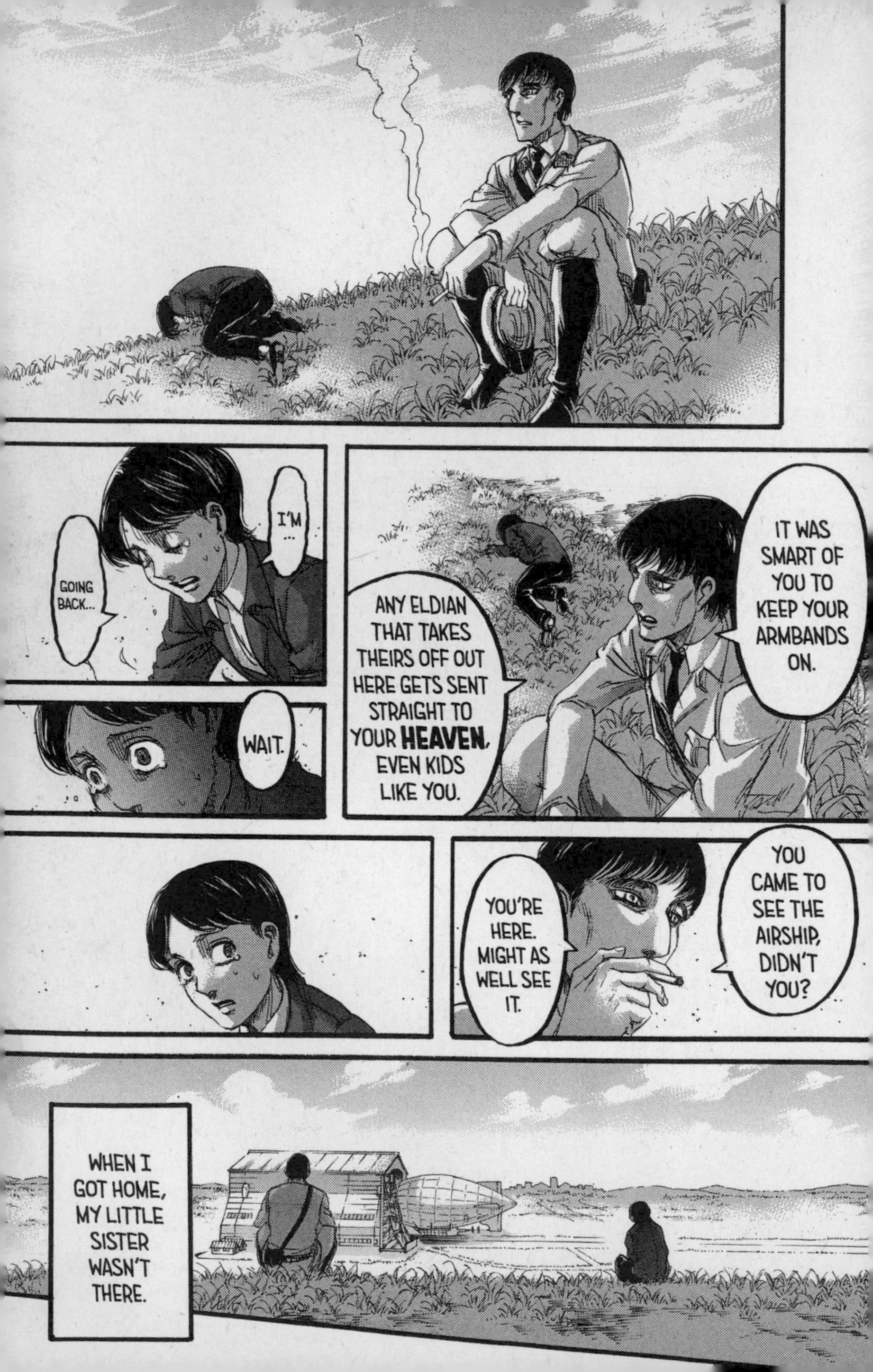
IT WAS SMART OF YOU TO KEEP YOUR ARMBANDS ON.
ANY ELDIAN THAT TAKES THEIRS OFF OUT HERE GETS SENT STRAIGHT TO YOUR **HEAVEN**, EVEN KIDS LIKE YOU.
I'M ...
GOING BACK...
WAIT.
YOU CAME TO SEE THE AIRSHIP, DIDN'T YOU?
YOU'RE HERE. MIGHT AS WELL SEE IT.
WHEN I GOT HOME, MY LITTLE SISTER WASN'T THERE.

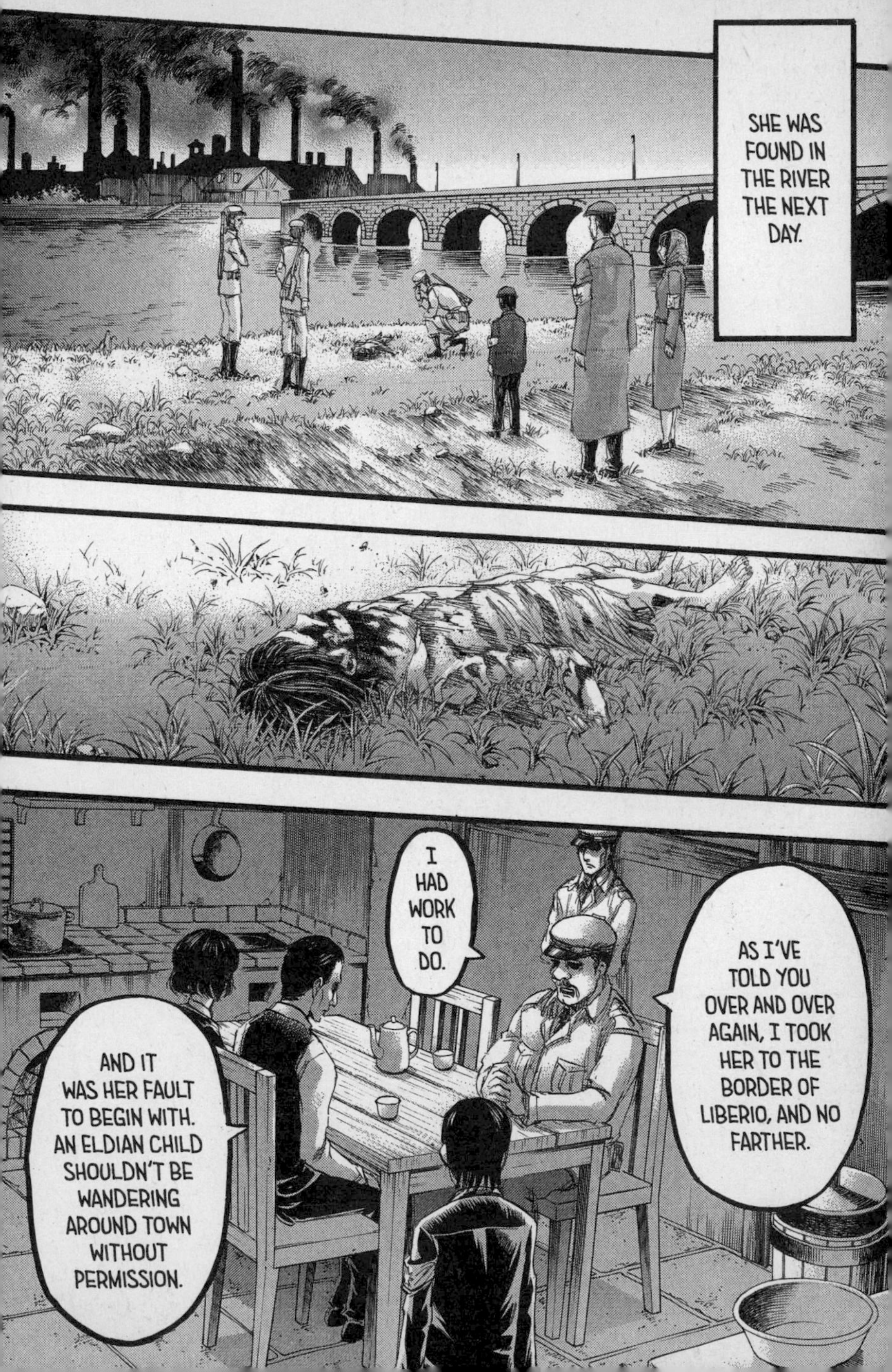
SHE WAS FOUND IN THE RIVER THE NEXT DAY.
AS I'VE TOLD YOU OVER AND OVER AGAIN, I TOOK HER TO THE BORDER OF LIBERIO, AND NO FARTHER.
I HAD WORK TO DO.
AND IT WAS HER FAULT TO BEGIN WITH. AN ELDIAN CHILD SHOULDN'T BE WANDERING AROUND TOWN WITHOUT PERMISSION.

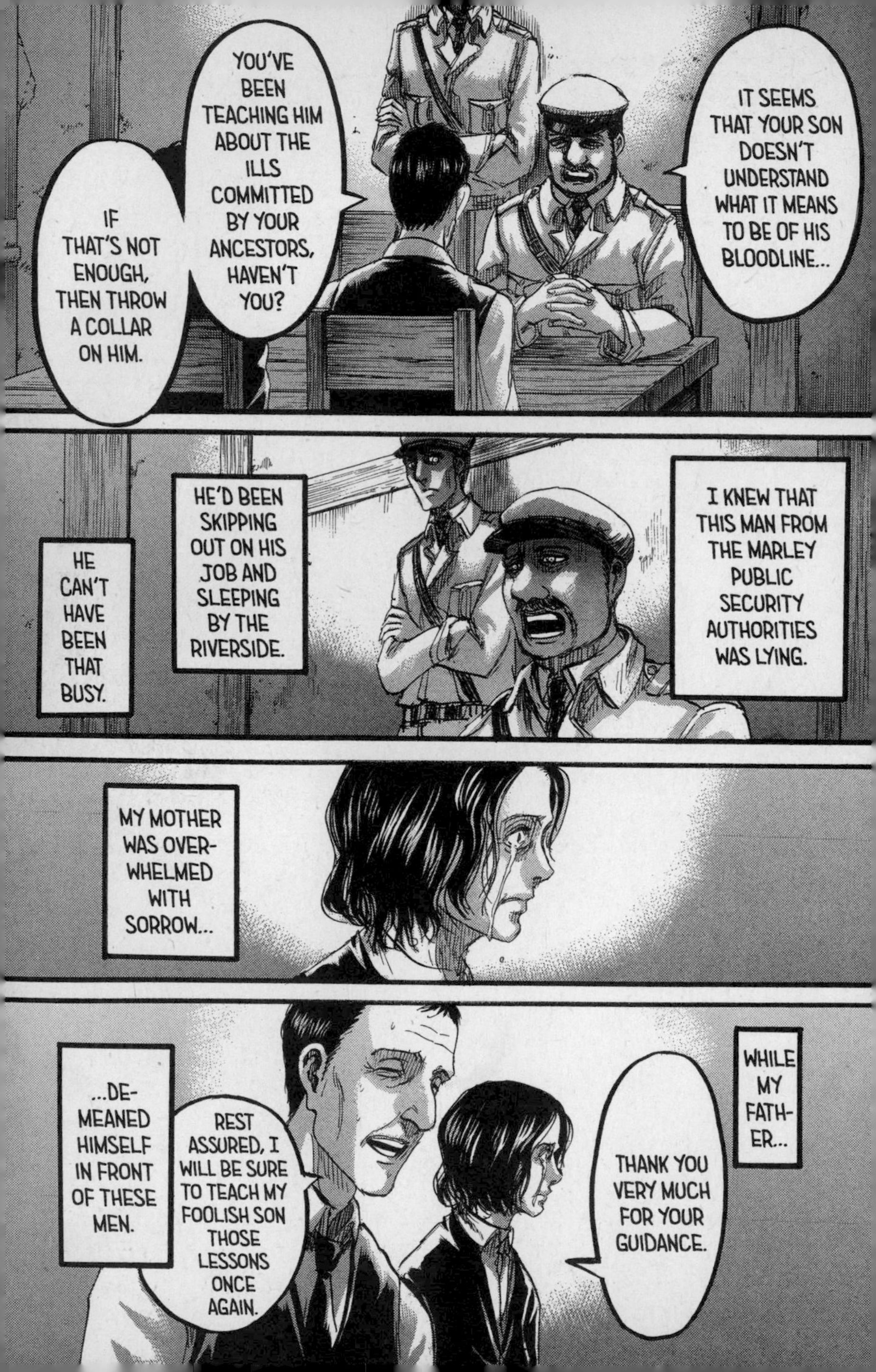
IT SEEMS THAT YOUR SON DOESN'T UNDERSTAND WHAT IT MEANS TO BE OF HIS BLOODLINE...
YOU'VE BEEN TEACHING HIM ABOUT THE ILLS COMMITTED BY YOUR ANCESTORS, HAVEN'T YOU?
IF THAT'S NOT ENOUGH, THEN THROW A COLLAR ON HIM.
I KNEW THAT THIS MAN FROM THE MARLEY PUBLIC SECURITY AUTHORITIES WAS LYING.
HE'D BEEN SKIPPING OUT ON HIS JOB AND SLEEPING BY THE RIVERSIDE.
HE CAN'T HAVE BEEN THAT BUSY.
MY MOTHER WAS OVERWHELMED WITH SORROW...
WHILE MY FATHER...
THANK YOU VERY MUCH FOR YOUR GUIDANCE.
REST ASSURED, I WILL BE SURE TO TEACH MY FOOLISH SON THOSE LESSONS ONCE AGAIN.
...DEMEANED HIMSELF IN FRONT OF THESE MEN.

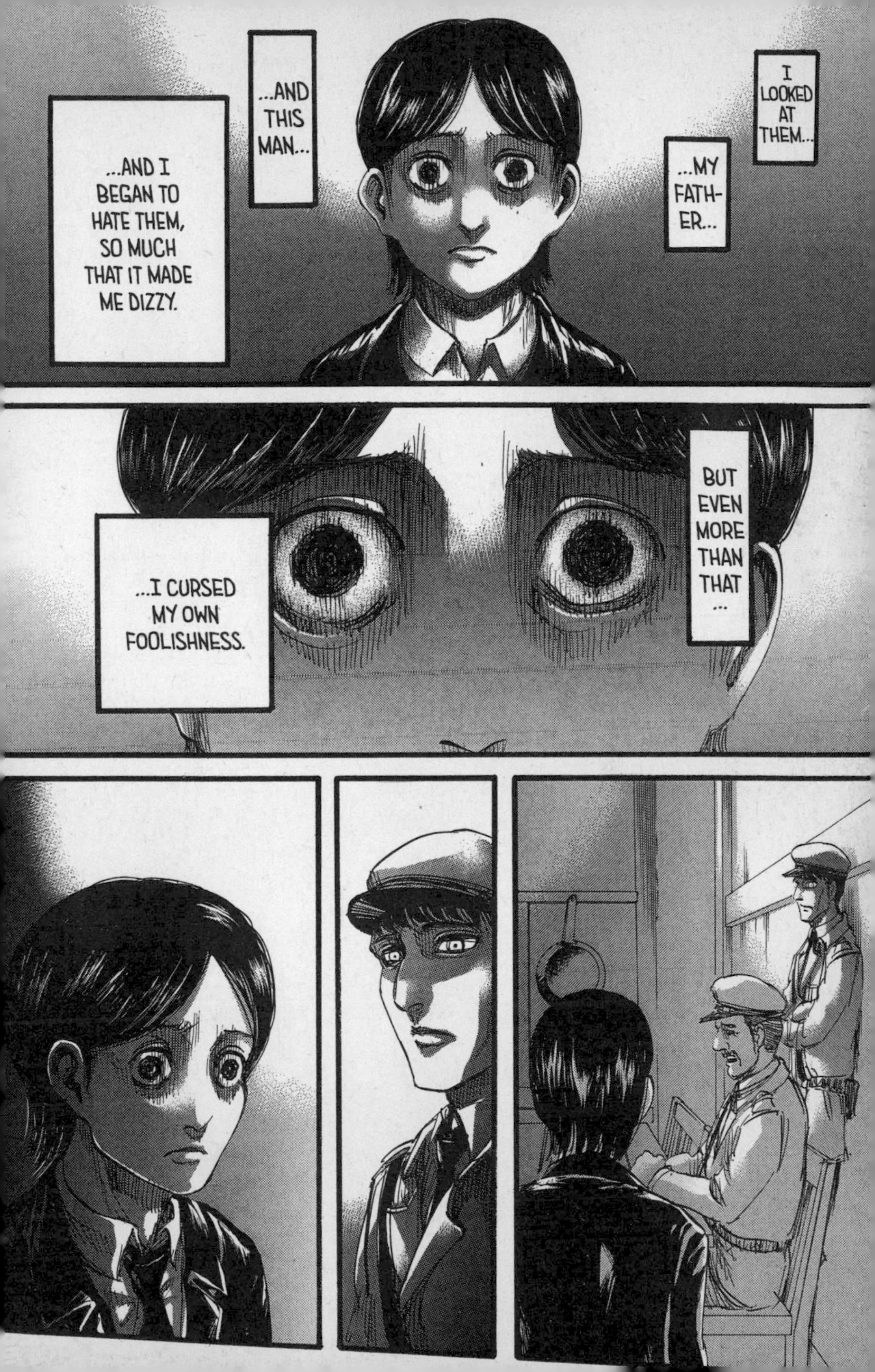
I LOOKED AT THEM...
...MY FATH-ER...
...AND THIS MAN...
...AND I BEGAN TO HATE THEM, SO MUCH THAT IT MADE ME DIZZY.
BUT EVEN MORE THAN THAT...
...I CURSED MY OWN FOOLISHNESS.

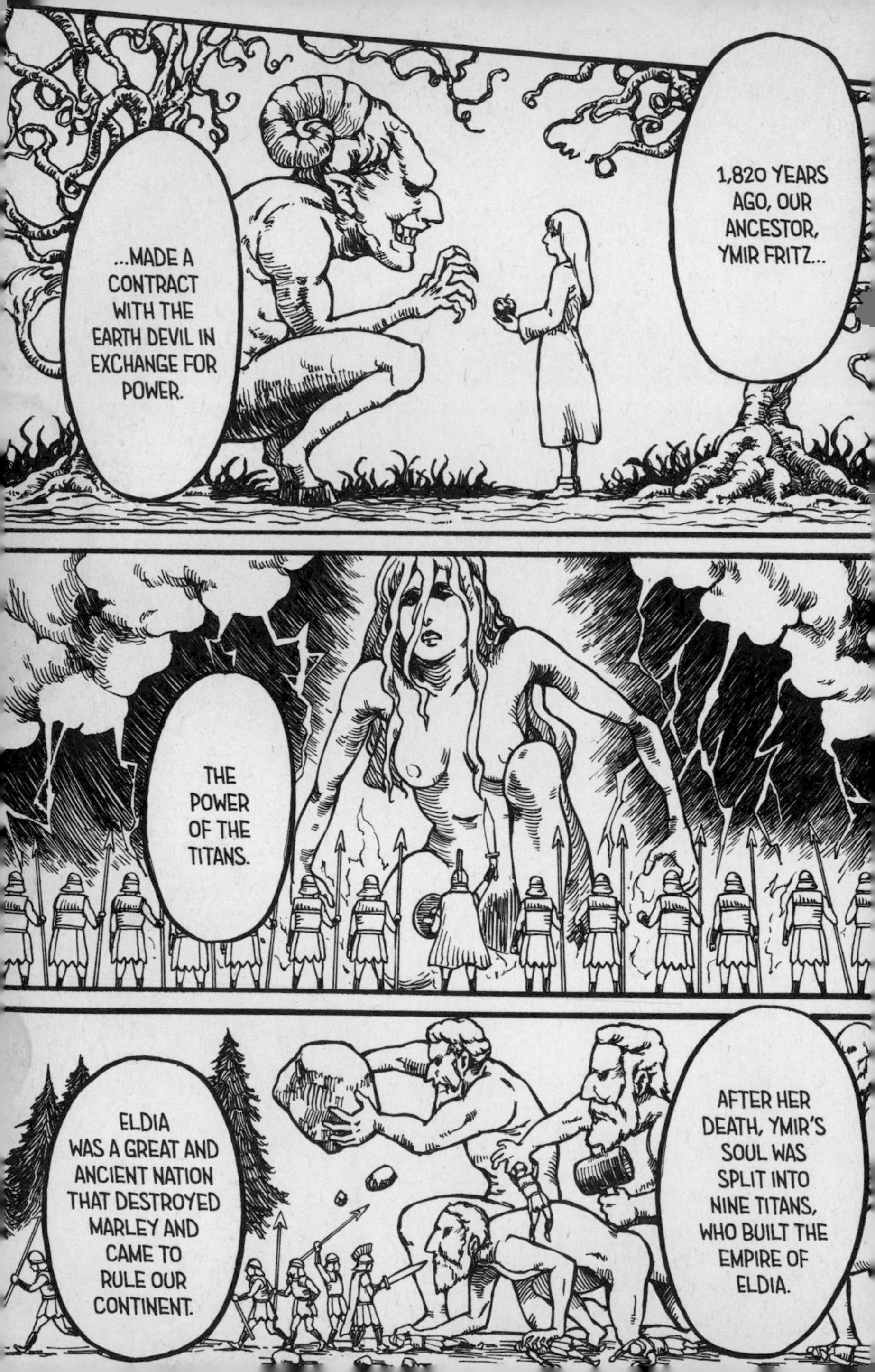
1,820 YEARS AGO, OUR ANCESTOR, YMIR FRITZ...
...MADE A CONTRACT WITH THE EARTH DEVIL IN EXCHANGE FOR POWER.
THE POWER OF THE TITANS.
AFTER HER DEATH, YMIR'S SOUL WAS SPLIT INTO NINE TITANS, WHO BUILT THE EMPIRE OF ELDIA.
ELDIA WAS A GREAT AND ANCIENT NATION THAT DESTROYED MARLEY AND CAME TO RULE OUR CONTINENT.

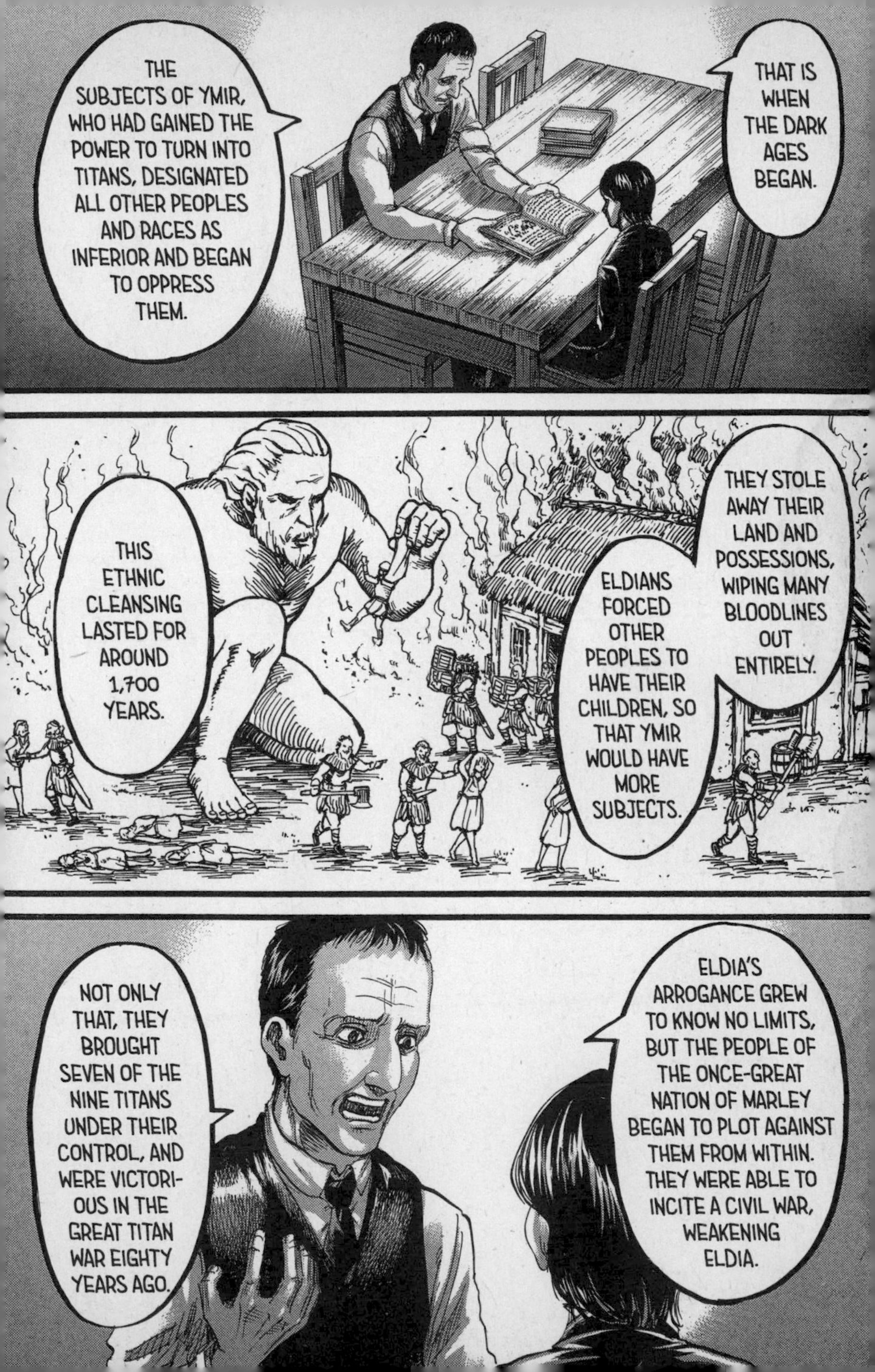
THAT IS WHEN THE DARK AGES BEGAN.
THE SUBJECTS OF YMIR, WHO HAD GAINED THE POWER TO TURN INTO TITANS, DESIGNATED ALL OTHER PEOPLES AND RACES AS INFERIOR AND BEGAN TO OPPRESS THEM.
THEY STOLE AWAY THEIR LAND AND POSSESSIONS, WIPING MANY BLOODLINES OUT ENTIRELY.
ELDIANS FORCED OTHER PEOPLES TO HAVE THEIR CHILDREN, SO THAT YMIR WOULD HAVE MORE SUBJECTS.
THIS ETHNIC CLEANSING LASTED FOR AROUND 1,700 YEARS.
ELDIA'S ARROGANCE GREW TO KNOW NO LIMITS, BUT THE PEOPLE OF THE ONCE-GREAT NATION OF MARLEY BEGAN TO PLOT AGAINST THEM FROM WITHIN. THEY WERE ABLE TO INCITE A CIVIL WAR, WEAKENING ELDIA.
NOT ONLY THAT, THEY BROUGHT SEVEN OF THE NINE TITANS UNDER THEIR CONTROL, AND WERE VICTORI-OUS IN THE GREAT TITAN WAR EIGHTY YEARS AGO.

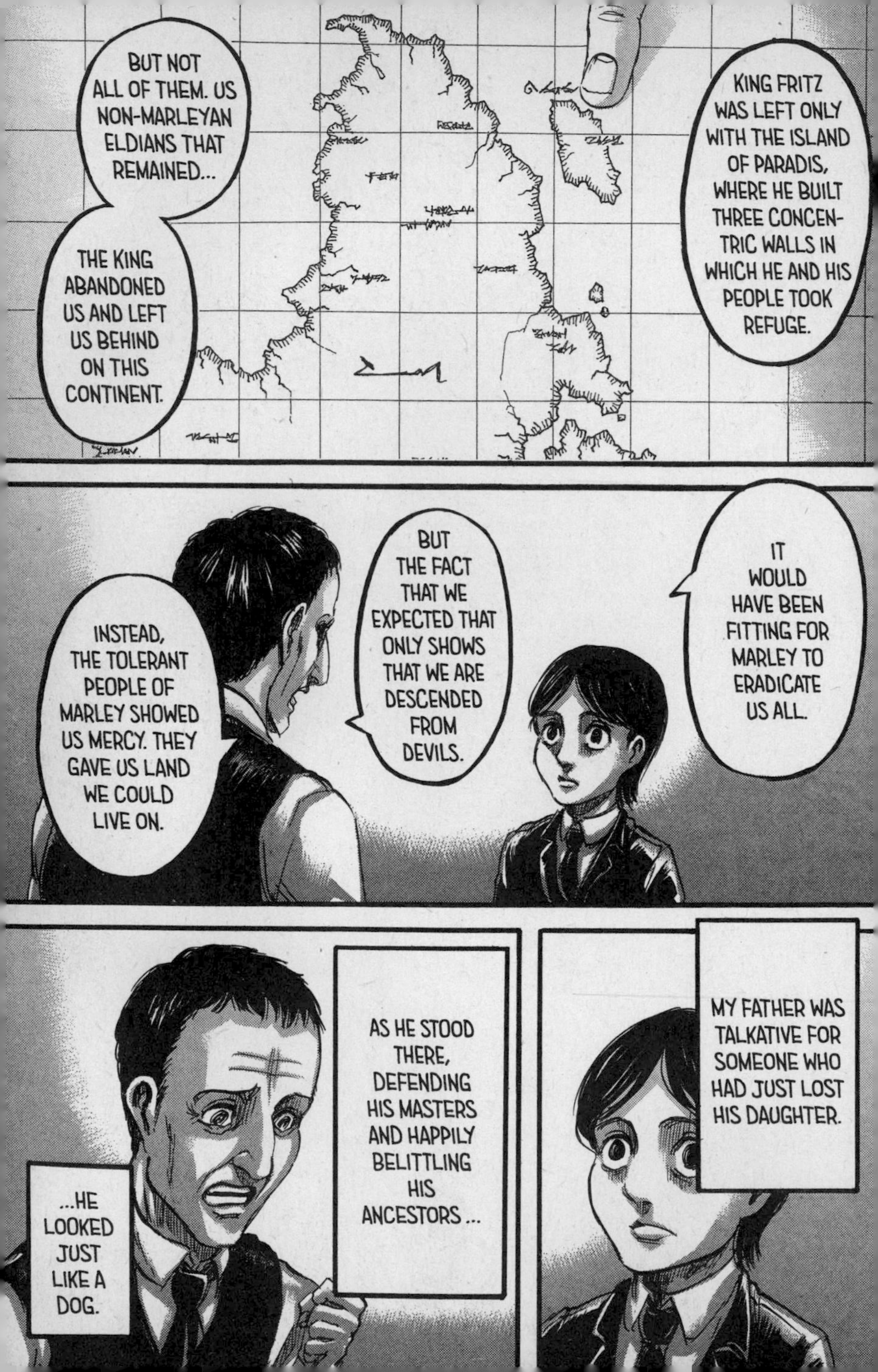
KING FRITZ WAS LEFT ONLY WITH THE ISLAND OF PARADIS, WHERE HE BUILT THREE CONCEN-TRIC WALLS IN WHICH HE AND HIS PEOPLE TOOK REFUGE.
BUT NOT ALL OF THEM. US NON-MARLEYAN ELDIANS THAT REMAINED...
THE KING ABANDONED US AND LEFT US BEHIND ON THIS CONTINENT.
IT WOULD HAVE BEEN FITTING FOR MARLEY TO ERADICATE US ALL.
INSTEAD, THE TOLERANT PEOPLE OF MARLEY SHOWED US MERCY. THEY GAVE US LAND WE COULD LIVE ON.
BUT THE FACT THAT WE EXPECTED THAT ONLY SHOWS THAT WE ARE DESCENDED FROM DEVILS.
MY FATHER WAS TALKATIVE FOR SOMEONE WHO HAD JUST LOST HIS DAUGHTER.
AS HE STOOD THERE, DEFENDING HIS MASTERS AND HAPPILY BELITTLING HIS ANCESTORS...
...HE LOOKED JUST LIKE A DOG.

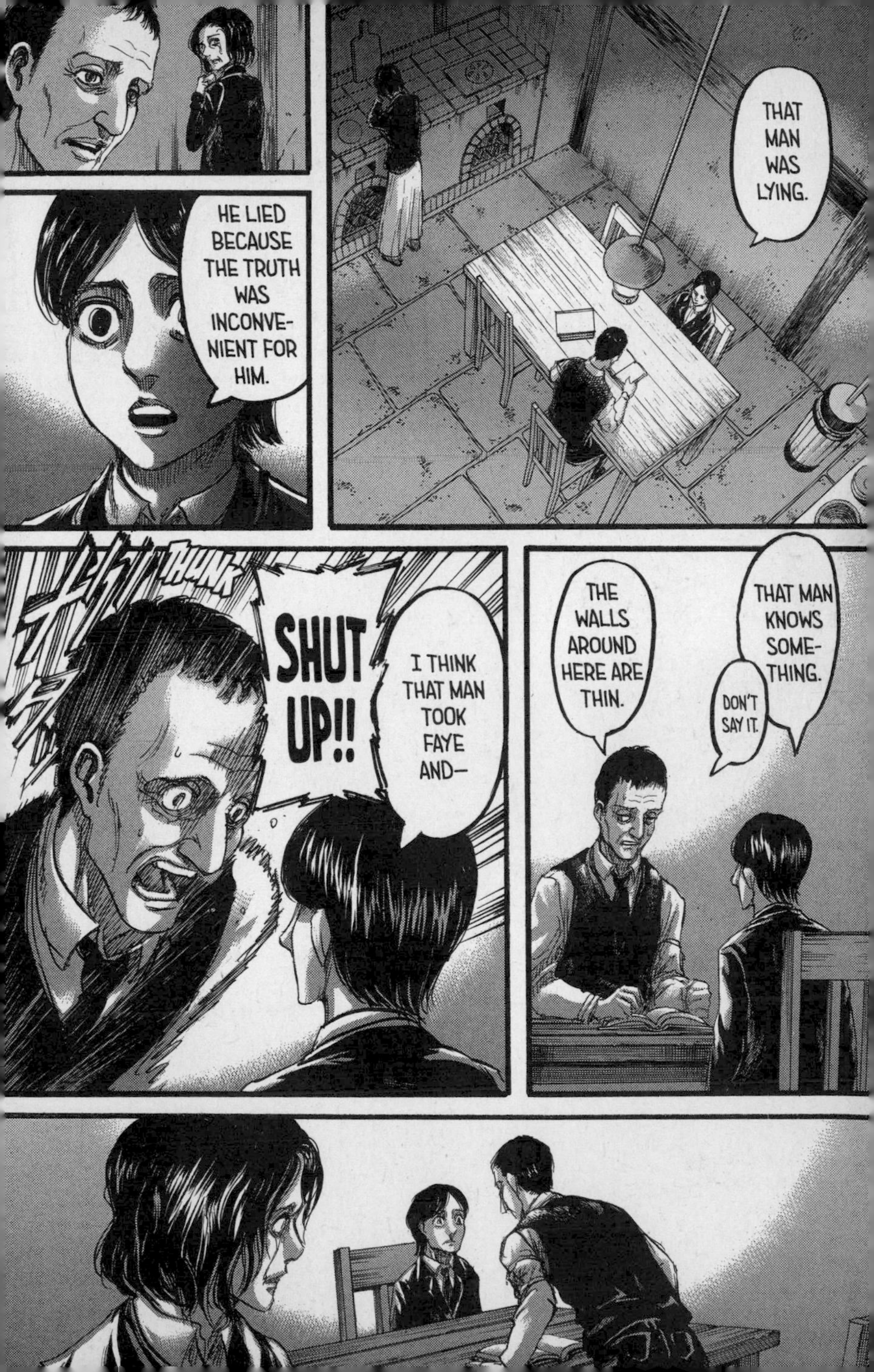
THAT MAN WAS LYING.
HE LIED BECAUSE THE TRUTH WAS INCONVENIENT FOR HIM.
THAT MAN KNOWS SOMETHING.
THE WALLS AROUND HERE ARE THIN.
DON'T SAY IT.
I THINK THAT MAN TOOK FAYE AND—
SHUT UP!!
THUNK

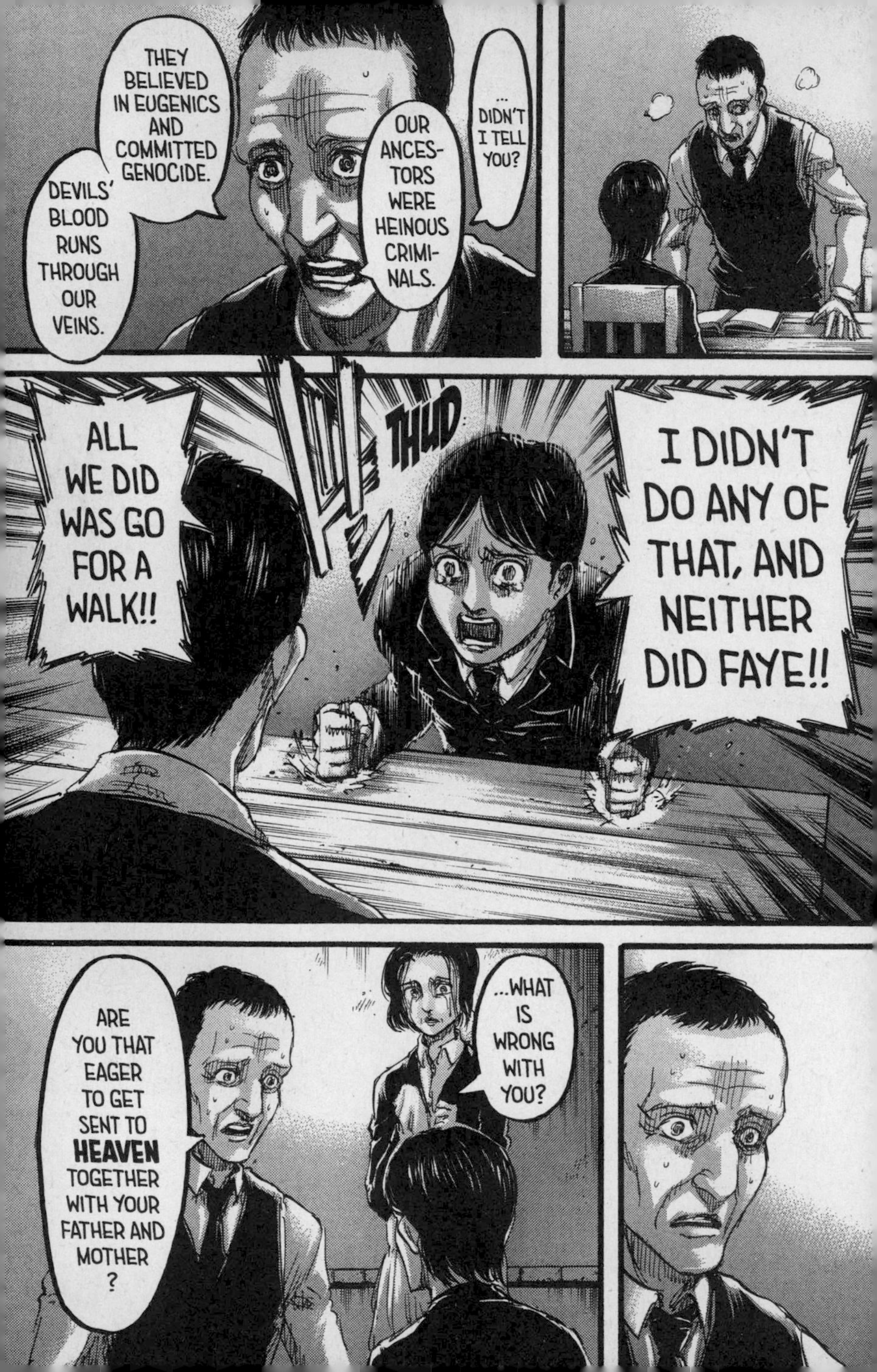
...DIDN'T I TELL YOU?
OUR ANCES-TORS WERE HEINOUS CRIMI-NALS.
THEY BELIEVED IN EUGENICS AND COMMITTED GENOCIDE.
DEVILS' BLOOD RUNS THROUGH OUR VEINS.
I DIDN'T DO ANY OF THAT, AND NEITHER DID FAYE!!
THUD
ALL WE DID WAS GO FOR A WALK!!
...WHAT IS WRONG WITH YOU?
ARE YOU THAT EAGER TO GET SENT TO **HEAVEN** TOGETHER WITH YOUR FATHER AND MOTHER?

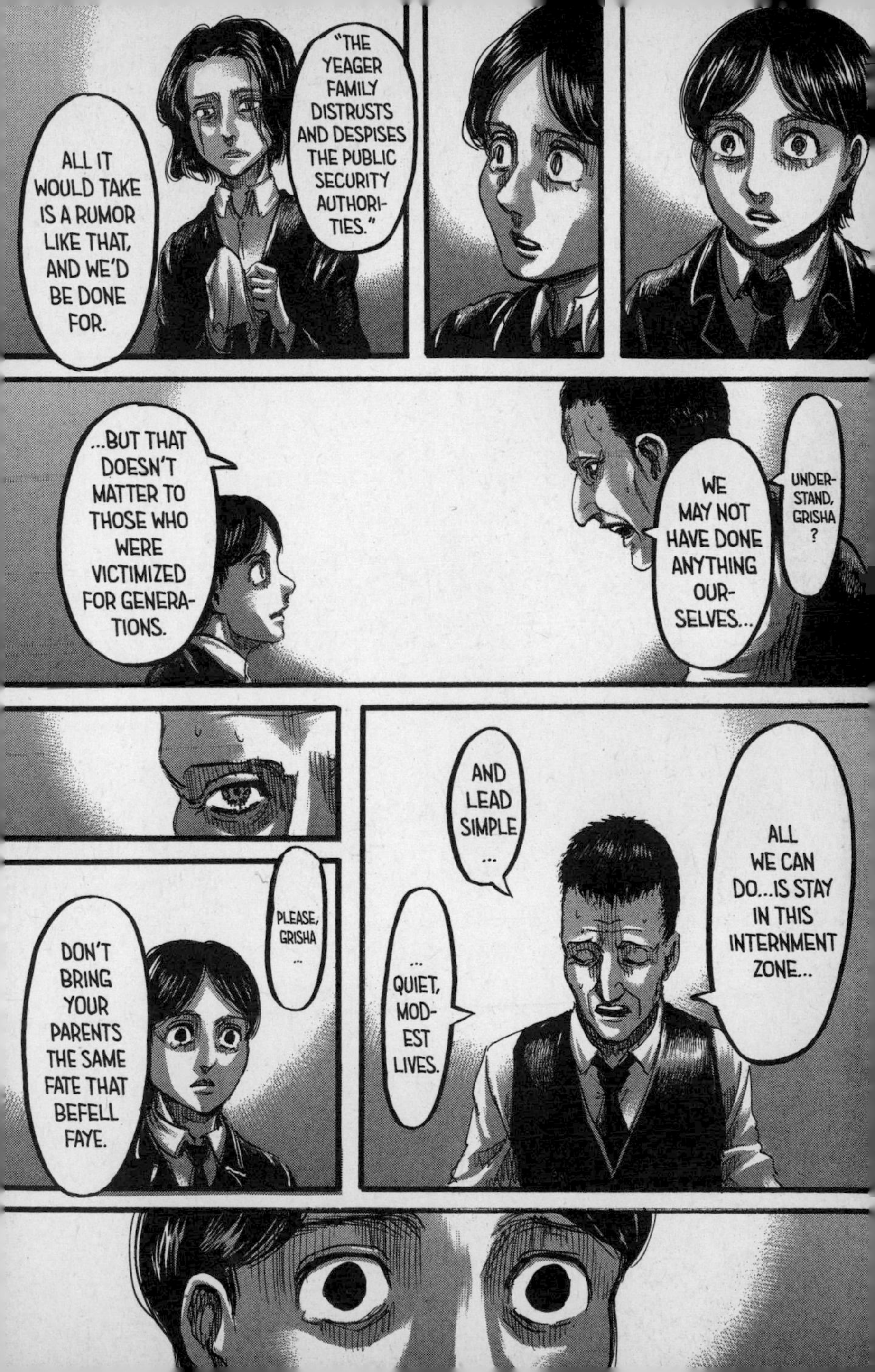
"THE YEAGER FAMILY DISTRUSTS AND DESPISES THE PUBLIC SECURITY AUTHORI-TIES."
ALL IT WOULD TAKE IS A RUMOR LIKE THAT, AND WE'D BE DONE FOR.
UNDER-STAND, GRISHA?
WE MAY NOT HAVE DONE ANYTHING OUR-SELVES...
...BUT THAT DOESN'T MATTER TO THOSE WHO WERE VICTIMIZED FOR GENERA-TIONS.
ALL WE CAN DO...IS STAY IN THIS INTERNMENT ZONE...
AND LEAD SIMPLE ...
... QUIET, MOD-EST LIVES.
PLEASE, GRISHA ...
DON'T BRING YOUR PARENTS THE SAME FATE THAT BEFELL FAYE.

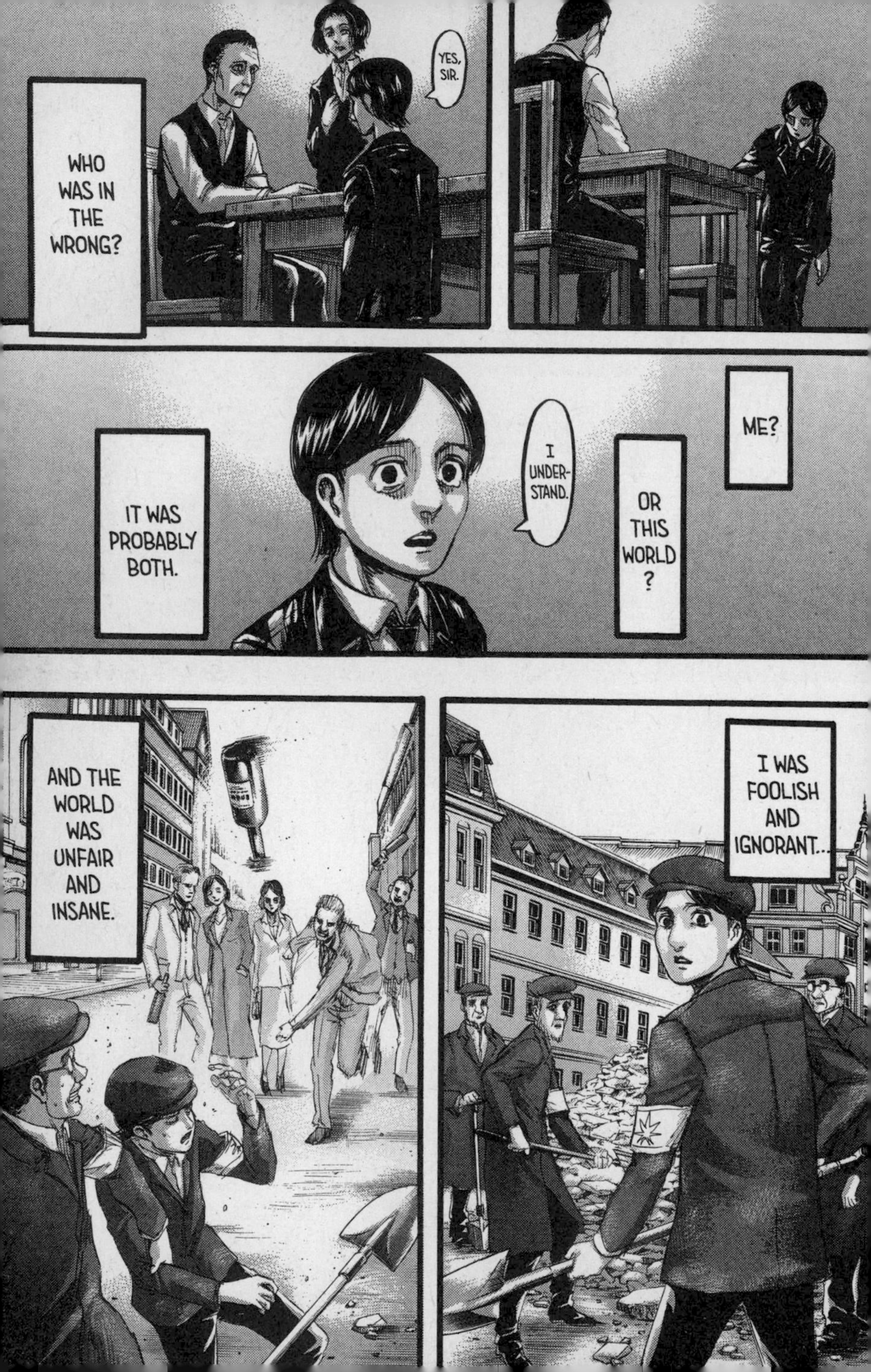
YES, SIR.
WHO WAS IN THE WRONG?
ME?
OR THIS WORLD?
I UNDER-STAND.
IT WAS PROBABLY BOTH.
I WAS FOOLISH AND IGNORANT...
AND THE WORLD WAS UNFAIR AND INSANE.

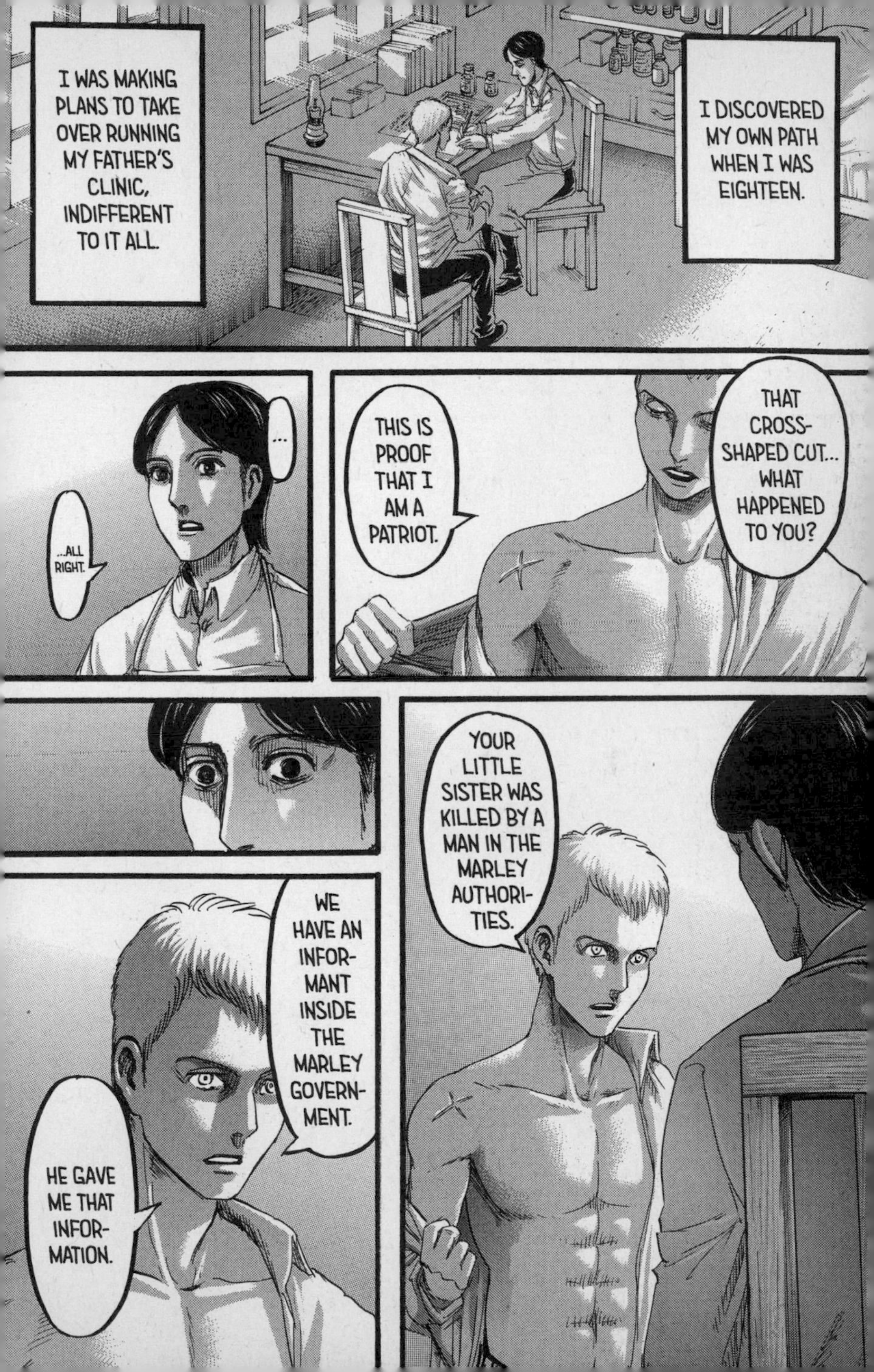
I DISCOVERED MY OWN PATH WHEN I WAS EIGHTEEN.
I WAS MAKING PLANS TO TAKE OVER RUNNING MY FATHER'S CLINIC, INDIFFERENT TO IT ALL.
THAT CROSS-SHAPED CUT... WHAT HAPPENED TO YOU?
THIS IS PROOF THAT I AM A PATRIOT.
...
...ALL RIGHT.
YOUR LITTLE SISTER WAS KILLED BY A MAN IN THE MARLEY AUTHORITIES.
WE HAVE AN INFORMANT INSIDE THE MARLEY GOVERNMENT.
HE GAVE ME THAT INFORMATION.

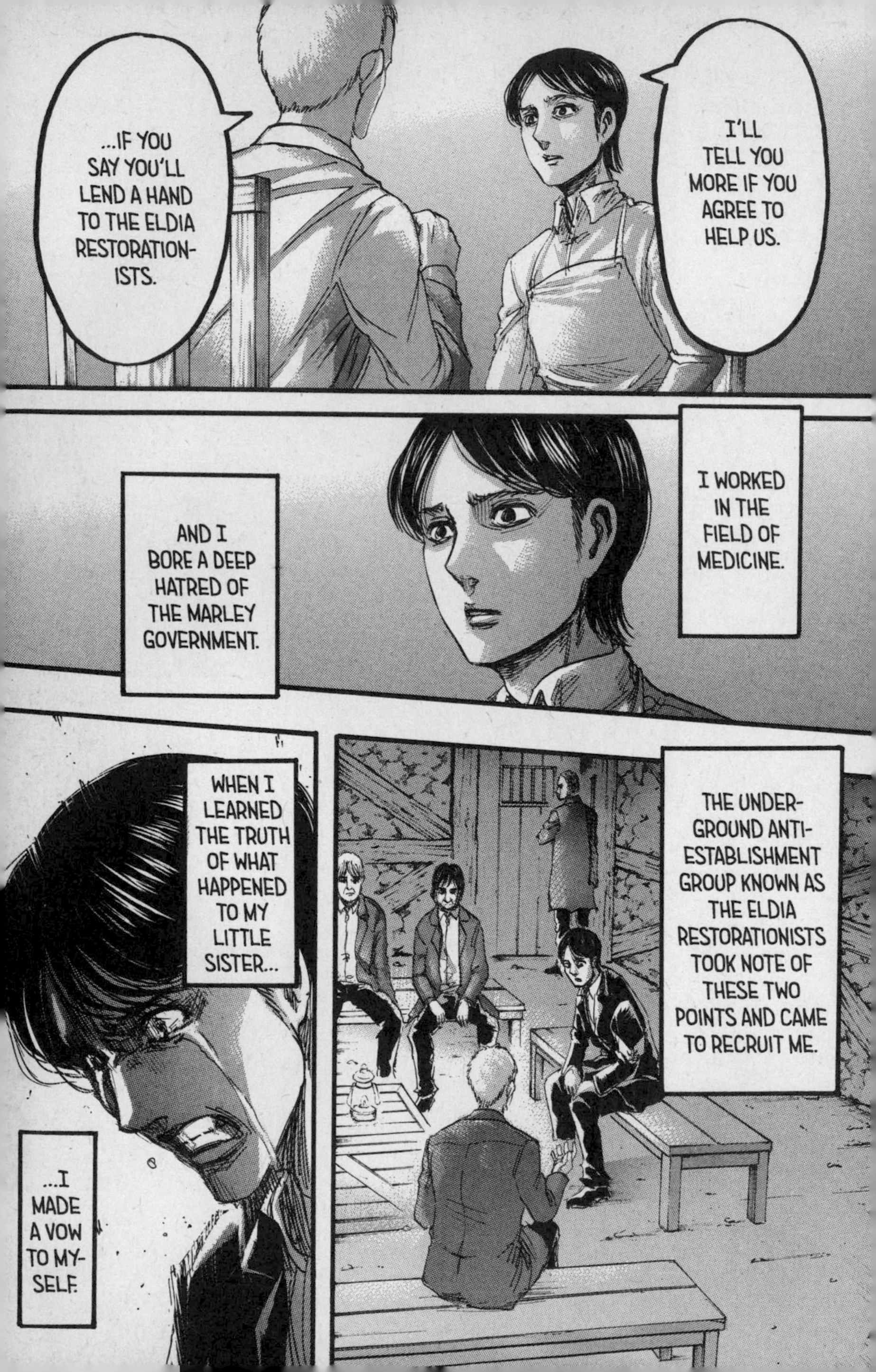
I'LL TELL YOU MORE IF YOU AGREE TO HELP US.
...IF YOU SAY YOU'LL LEND A HAND TO THE ELDIA RESTORATIONISTS.
I WORKED IN THE FIELD OF MEDICINE.
AND I BORE A DEEP HATRED OF THE MARLEY GOVERNMENT.
THE UNDERGROUND ANTI-ESTABLISHMENT GROUP KNOWN AS THE ELDIA RESTORATIONISTS TOOK NOTE OF THESE TWO POINTS AND CAME TO RECRUIT ME.
WHEN I LEARNED THE TRUTH OF WHAT HAPPENED TO MY LITTLE SISTER...
...I MADE A VOW TO MYSELF.

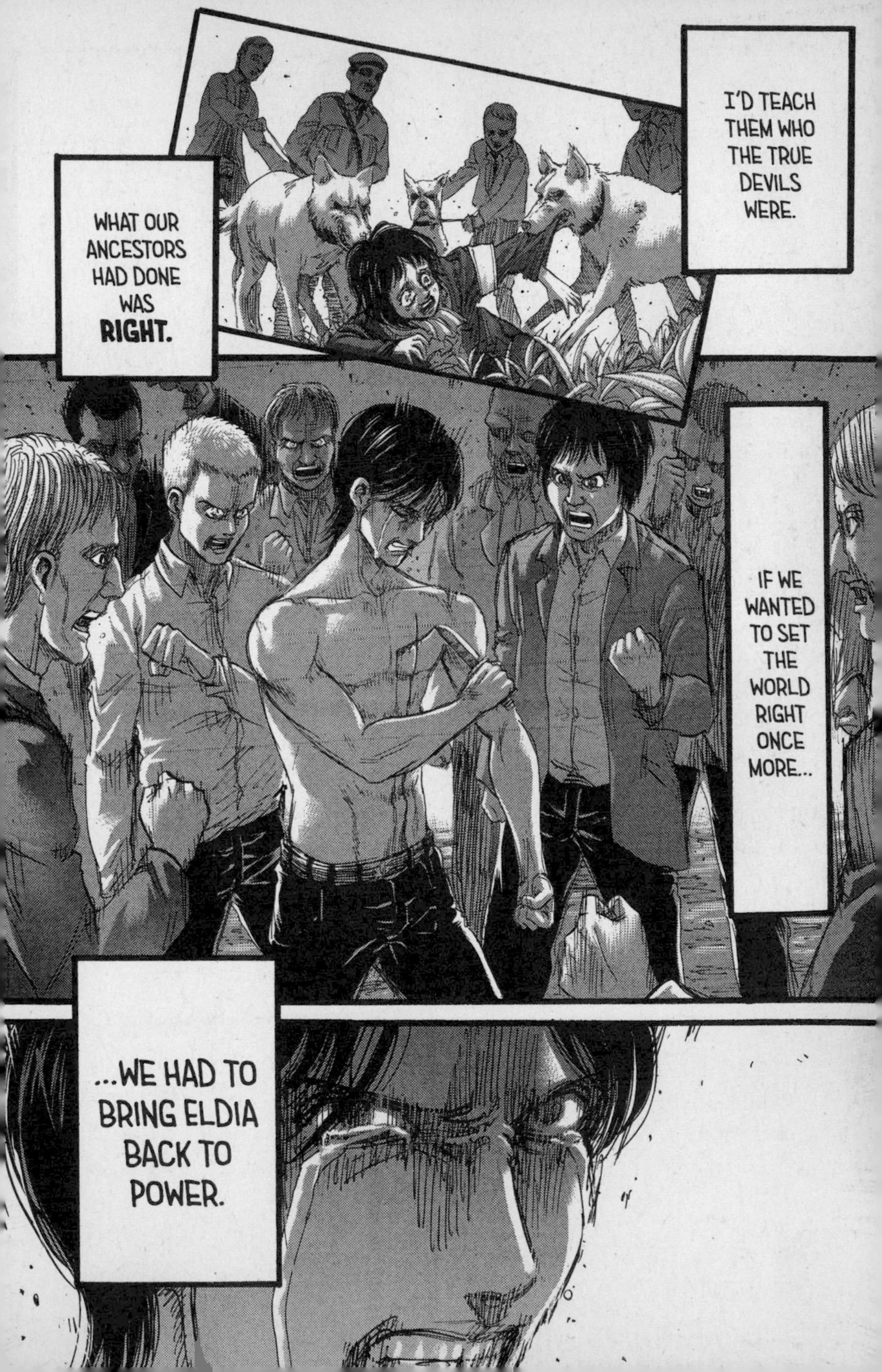
I'D TEACH THEM WHO THE TRUE DEVILS WERE.
WHAT OUR ANCESTORS HAD DONE WAS **RIGHT.**
IF WE WANTED TO SET THE WORLD RIGHT ONCE MORE...
...WE HAD TO BRING ELDIA BACK TO POWER.

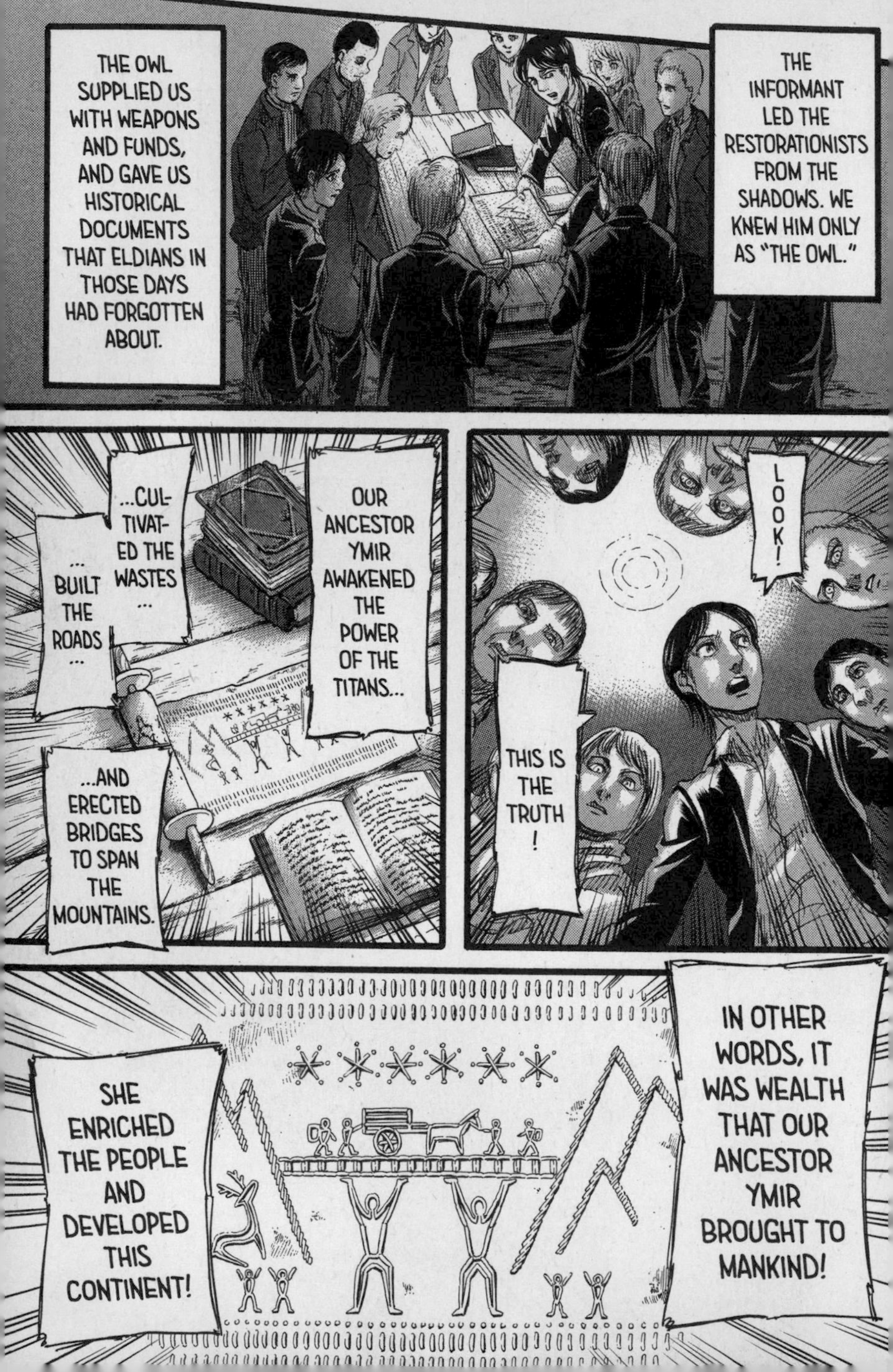
THE INFORMANT LED THE RESTORATIONISTS FROM THE SHADOWS. WE KNEW HIM ONLY AS "THE OWL."
THE OWL SUPPLIED US WITH WEAPONS AND FUNDS, AND GAVE US HISTORICAL DOCUMENTS THAT ELDIANS IN THOSE DAYS HAD FORGOTTEN ABOUT.
LOOK!
THIS IS THE TRUTH!
OUR ANCESTOR YMIR AWAKENED THE POWER OF THE TITANS...
...CULTIVATED THE WASTES...
...BUILT THE ROADS...
...AND ERECTED BRIDGES TO SPAN THE MOUNTAINS.
IN OTHER WORDS, IT WAS WEALTH THAT OUR ANCESTOR YMIR BROUGHT TO MANKIND!
SHE ENRICHED THE PEOPLE AND DEVELOPED THIS CONTINENT!

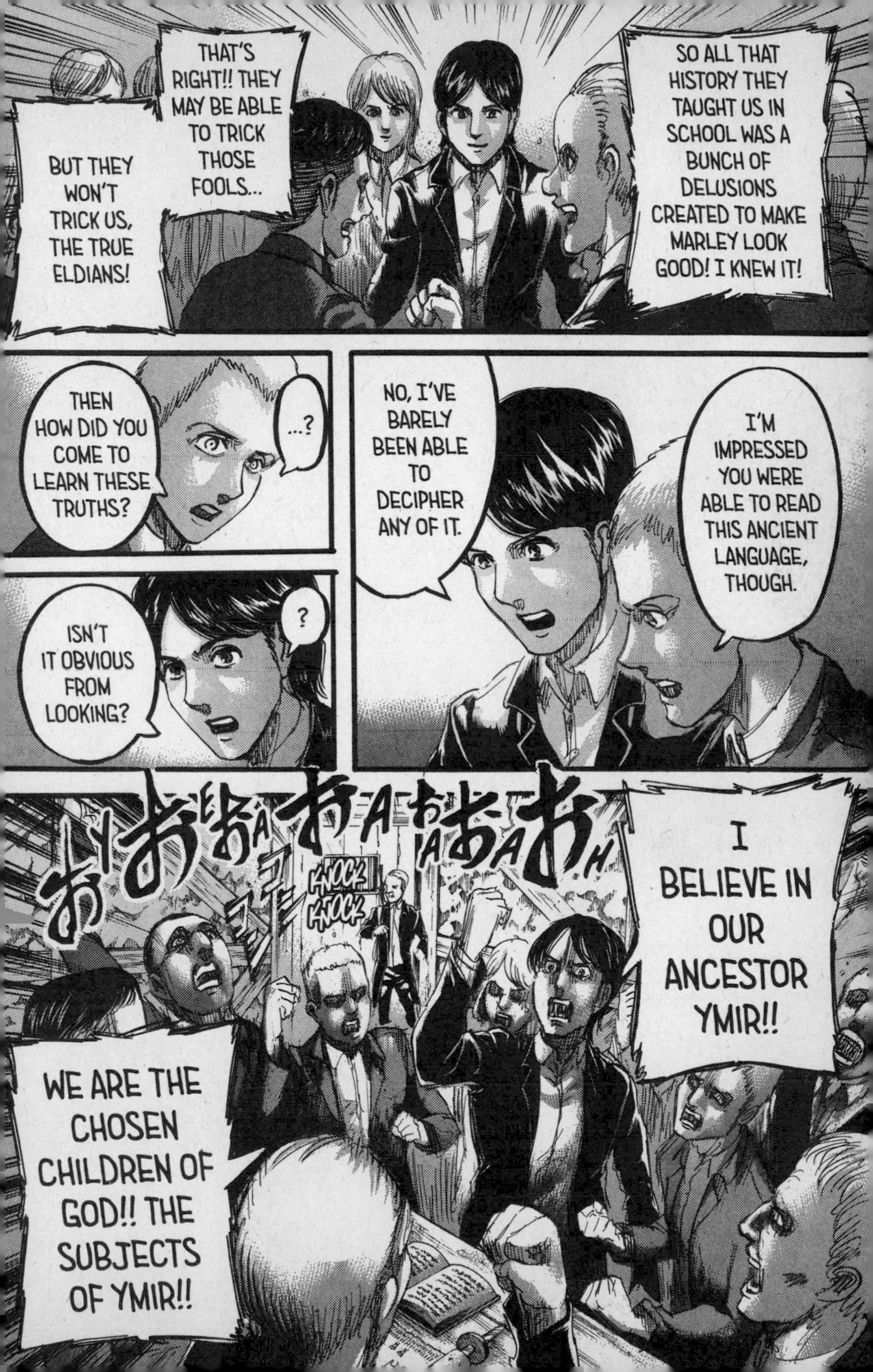
SO ALL THAT HISTORY THEY TAUGHT US IN SCHOOL WAS A BUNCH OF DELUSIONS CREATED TO MAKE MARLEY LOOK GOOD! I KNEW IT!
THAT'S RIGHT!! THEY MAY BE ABLE TO TRICK THOSE FOOLS...
BUT THEY WON'T TRICK US, THE TRUE ELDIANS!
I'M IMPRESSED YOU WERE ABLE TO READ THIS ANCIENT LANGUAGE, THOUGH.
NO, I'VE BARELY BEEN ABLE TO DECIPHER ANY OF IT.
...?
THEN HOW DID YOU COME TO LEARN THESE TRUTHS?
?
ISN'T IT OBVIOUS FROM LOOKING?
I BELIEVE IN OUR ANCESTOR YMIR!!
KNOCK KNOCK
WE ARE THE CHOSEN CHILDREN OF GOD!! THE SUBJECTS OF YMIR!!

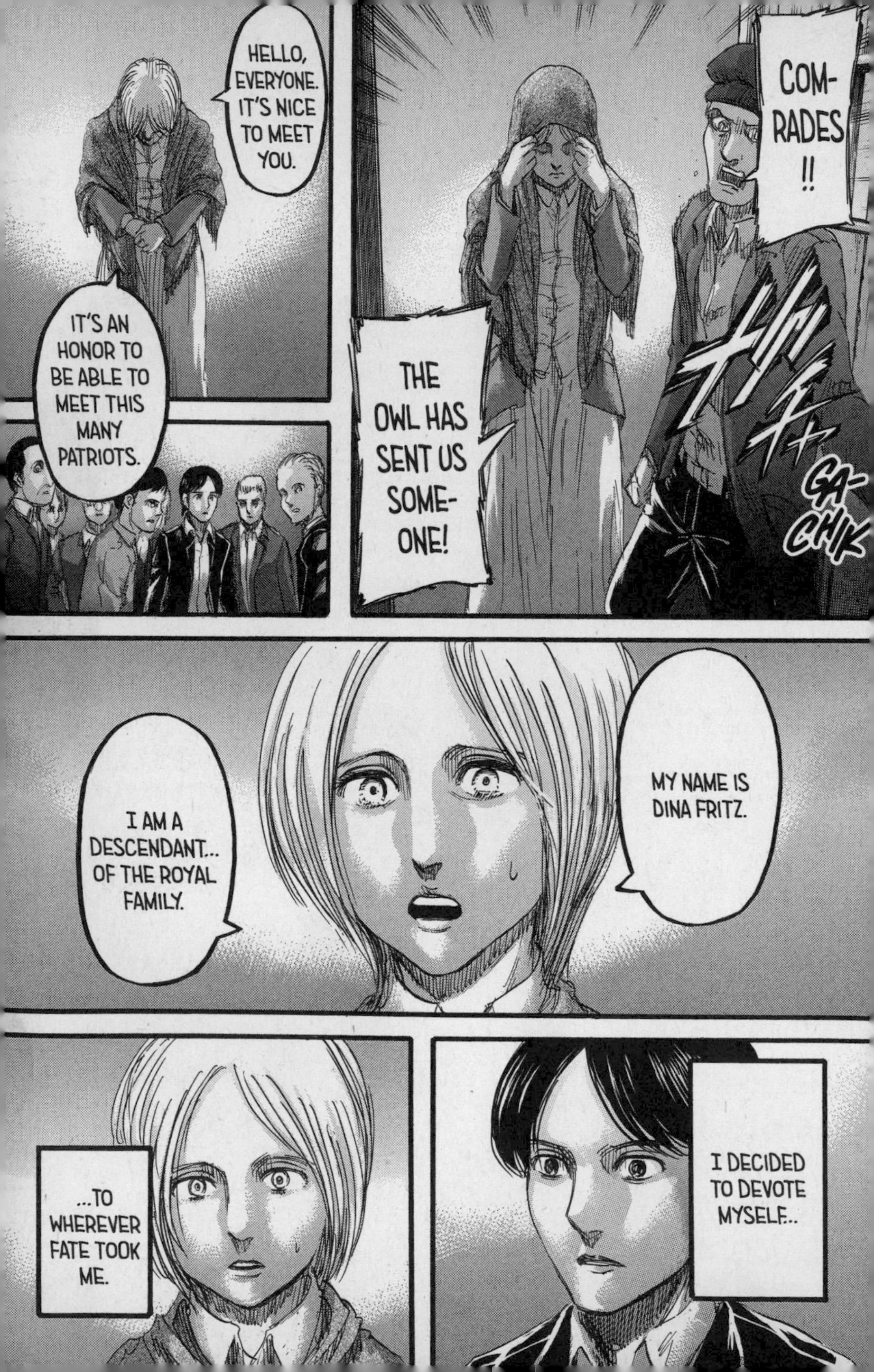

COM-RADES!!
THE OWL HAS SENT US SOME-ONE!
GA-CHIK
HELLO, EVERYONE. IT'S NICE TO MEET YOU.
IT'S AN HONOR TO BE ABLE TO MEET THIS MANY PATRIOTS.
MY NAME IS DINA FRITZ.
I AM A DESCENDANT... OF THE ROYAL FAMILY.
I DECIDED TO DEVOTE MYSELF...
...TO WHEREVER FATE TOOK ME.

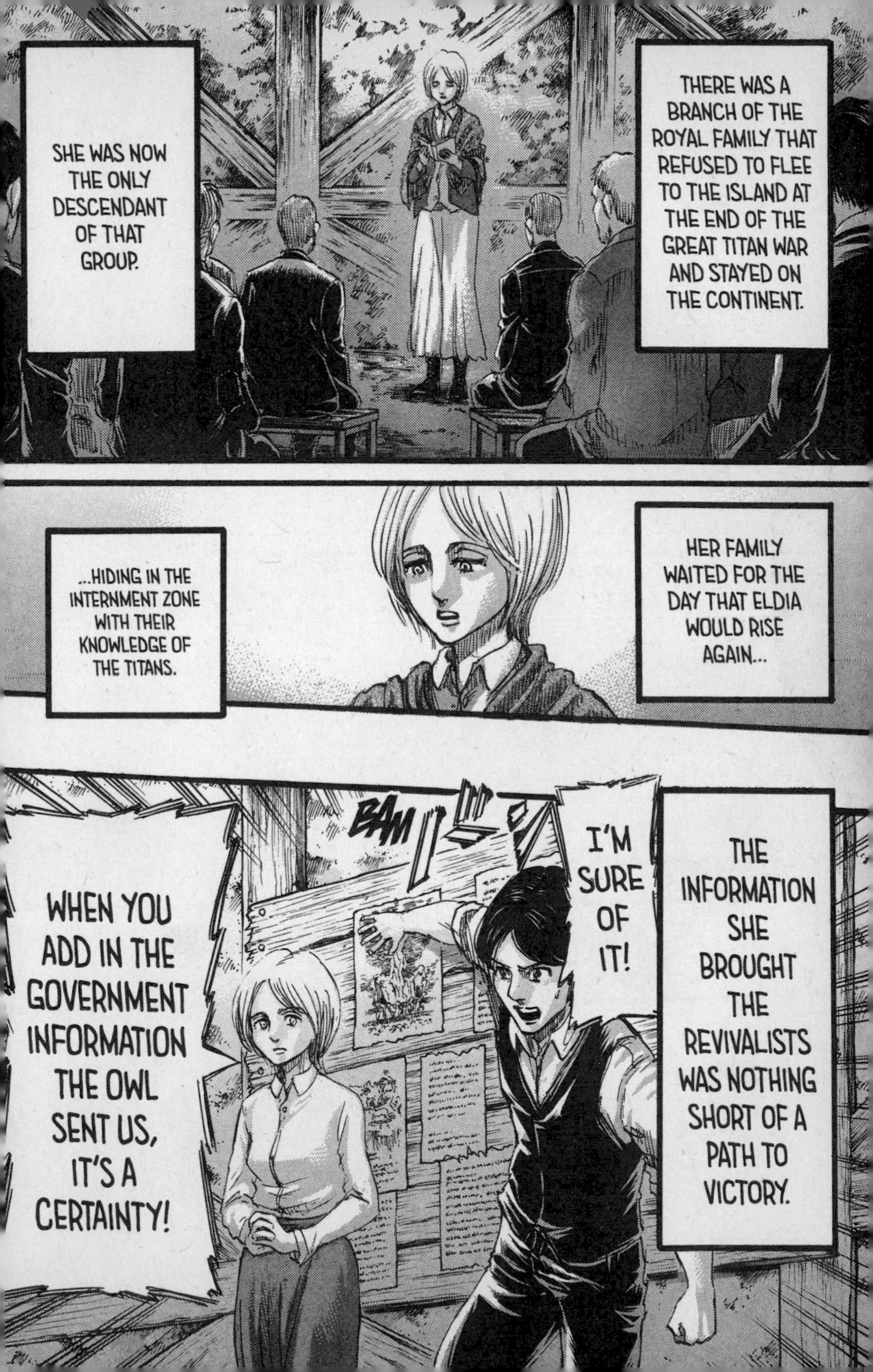
THERE WAS A BRANCH OF THE ROYAL FAMILY THAT REFUSED TO FLEE TO THE ISLAND AT THE END OF THE GREAT TITAN WAR AND STAYED ON THE CONTINENT.
SHE WAS NOW THE ONLY DESCENDANT OF THAT GROUP.
HER FAMILY WAITED FOR THE DAY THAT ELDIA WOULD RISE AGAIN...
...HIDING IN THE INTERNMENT ZONE WITH THEIR KNOWLEDGE OF THE TITANS.
THE INFORMATION SHE BROUGHT THE REVIVALISTS WAS NOTHING SHORT OF A PATH TO VICTORY.
I'M SURE OF IT!
BAM
WHEN YOU ADD IN THE GOVERNMENT INFORMATION THE OWL SENT US, IT'S A CERTAINTY!

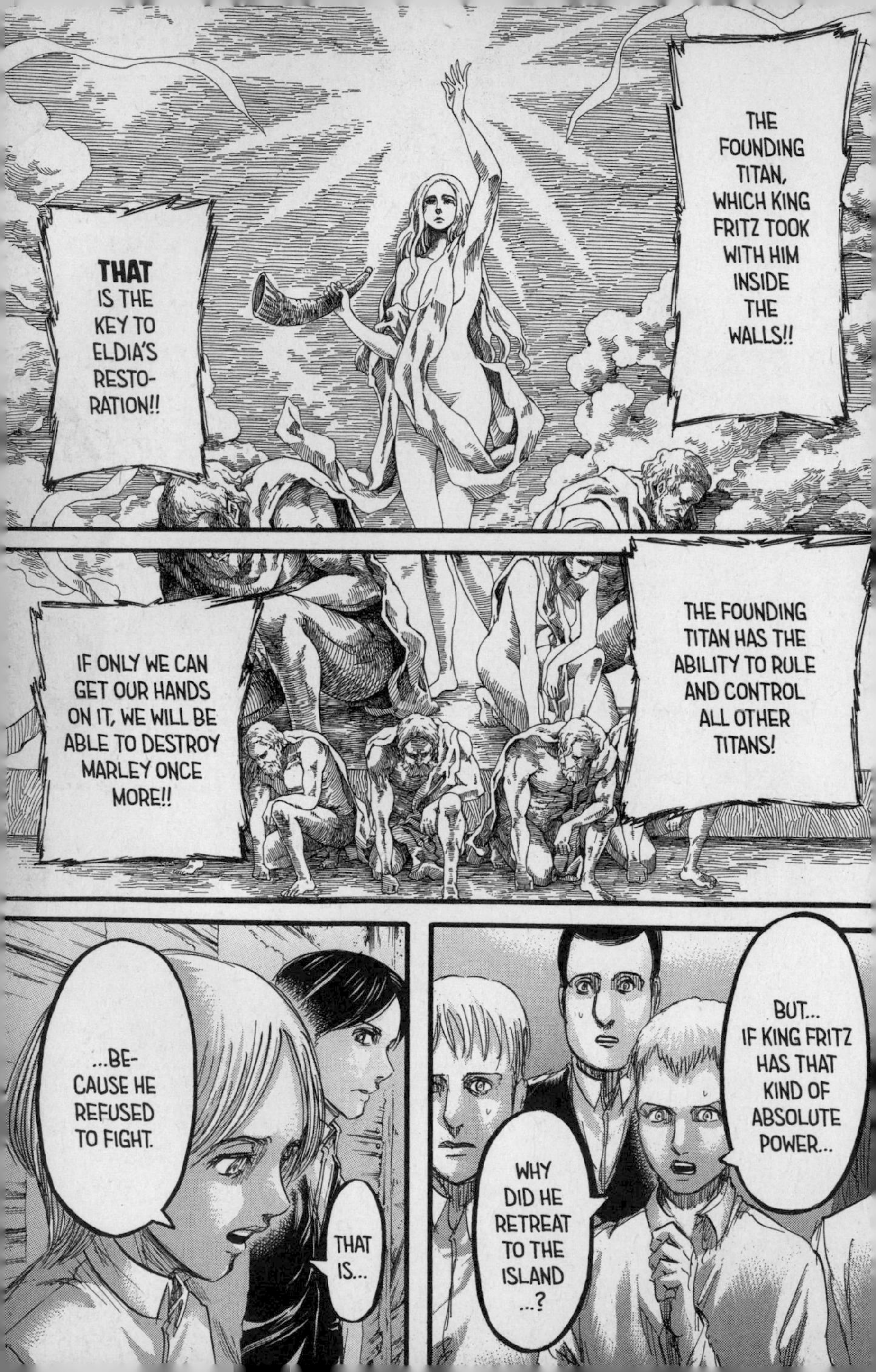
THE FOUNDING TITAN, WHICH KING FRITZ TOOK WITH HIM INSIDE THE WALLS!!
THAT IS THE KEY TO ELDIA'S RESTO-RATION!!
THE FOUNDING TITAN HAS THE ABILITY TO RULE AND CONTROL ALL OTHER TITANS!
IF ONLY WE CAN GET OUR HANDS ON IT, WE WILL BE ABLE TO DESTROY MARLEY ONCE MORE!!
BUT... IF KING FRITZ HAS THAT KIND OF ABSOLUTE POWER...
WHY DID HE RETREAT TO THE ISLAND ...?
THAT IS...
...BE-CAUSE HE REFUSED TO FIGHT.

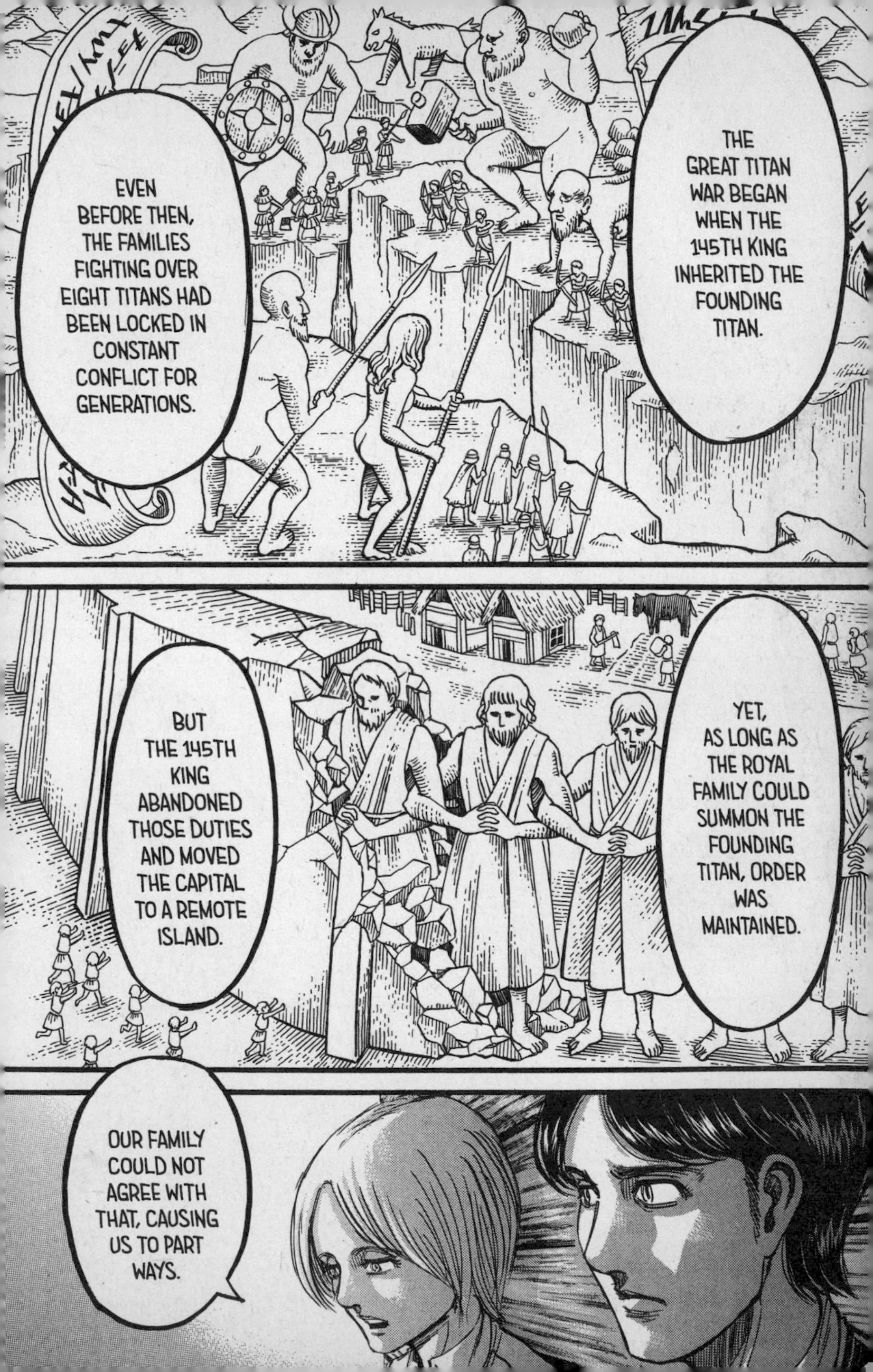
THE GREAT TITAN WAR BEGAN WHEN THE 145TH KING INHERITED THE FOUNDING TITAN.
EVEN BEFORE THEN, THE FAMILIES FIGHTING OVER EIGHT TITANS HAD BEEN LOCKED IN CONSTANT CONFLICT FOR GENERATIONS.
YET, AS LONG AS THE ROYAL FAMILY COULD SUMMON THE FOUNDING TITAN, ORDER WAS MAINTAINED.
BUT THE 145TH KING ABANDONED THOSE DUTIES AND MOVED THE CAPITAL TO A REMOTE ISLAND.
OUR FAMILY COULD NOT AGREE WITH THAT, CAUSING US TO PART WAYS.

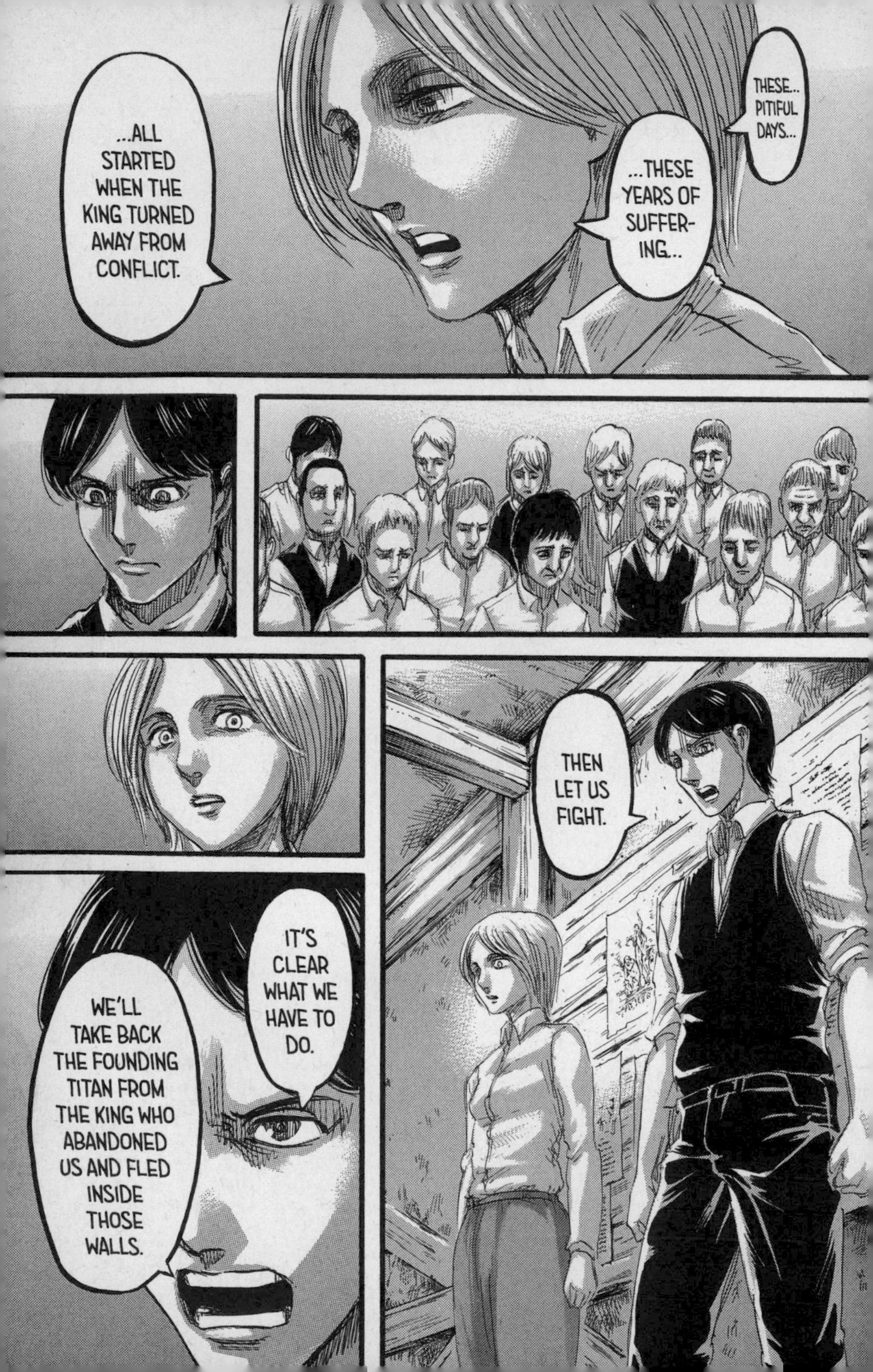
THESE... PITIFUL DAYS...
...THESE YEARS OF SUFFER-ING...
...ALL STARTED WHEN THE KING TURNED AWAY FROM CONFLICT.
THEN LET US FIGHT.
IT'S CLEAR WHAT WE HAVE TO DO.
WE'LL TAKE BACK THE FOUNDING TITAN FROM THE KING WHO ABANDONED US AND FLED INSIDE THOSE WALLS.

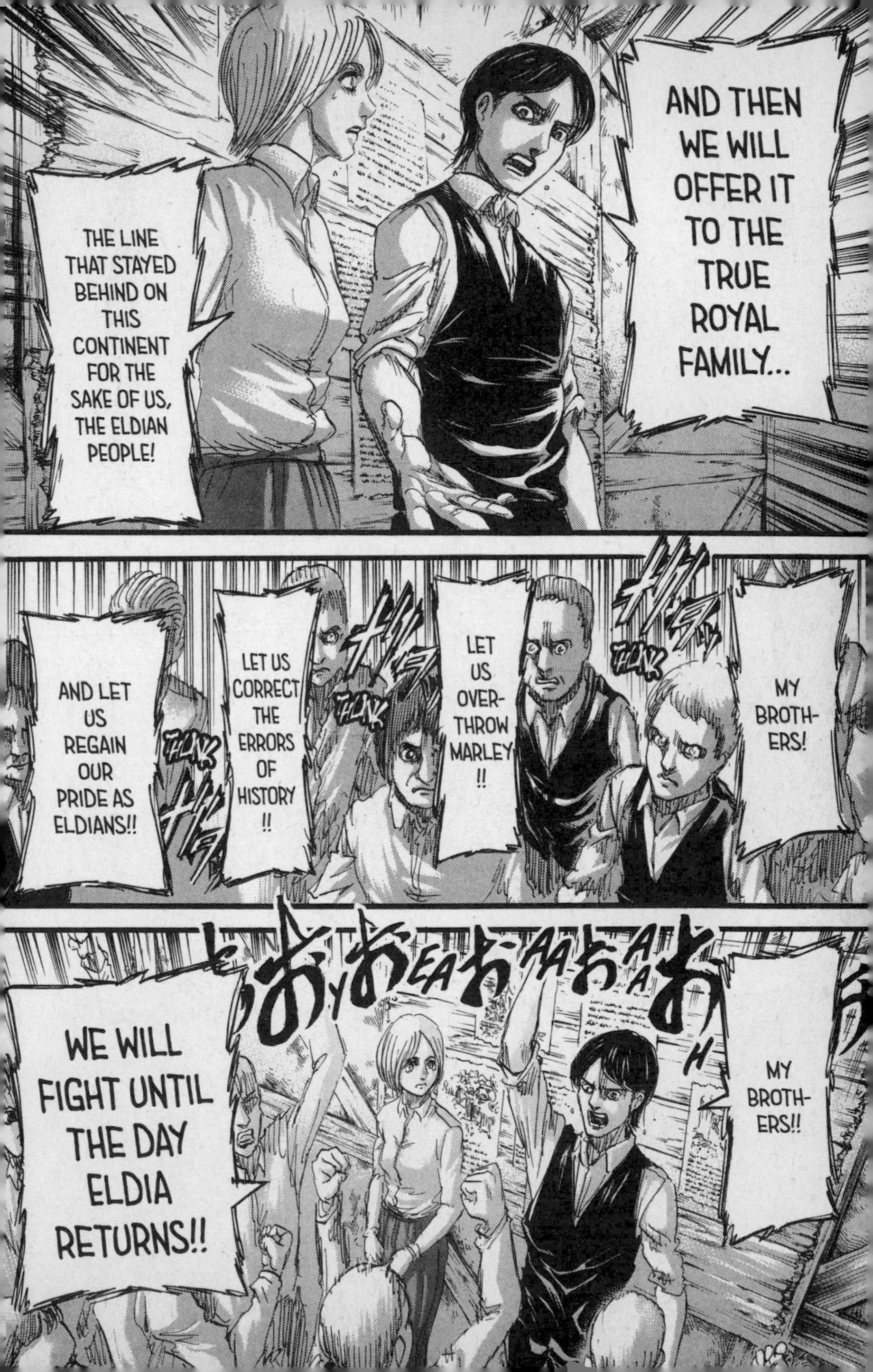
AND THEN WE WILL OFFER IT TO THE TRUE ROYAL FAMILY...
THE LINE THAT STAYED BEHIND ON THIS CONTINENT FOR THE SAKE OF US, THE ELDIAN PEOPLE!
MY BROTHERS!
THUNK
LET US OVERTHROW MARLEY!!
THUNK
LET US CORRECT THE ERRORS OF HISTORY!!
THUNK
AND LET US REGAIN OUR PRIDE AS ELDIANS!!
MY BROTHERS!!
YEAAAAAH
WE WILL FIGHT UNTIL THE DAY ELDIA RETURNS!!

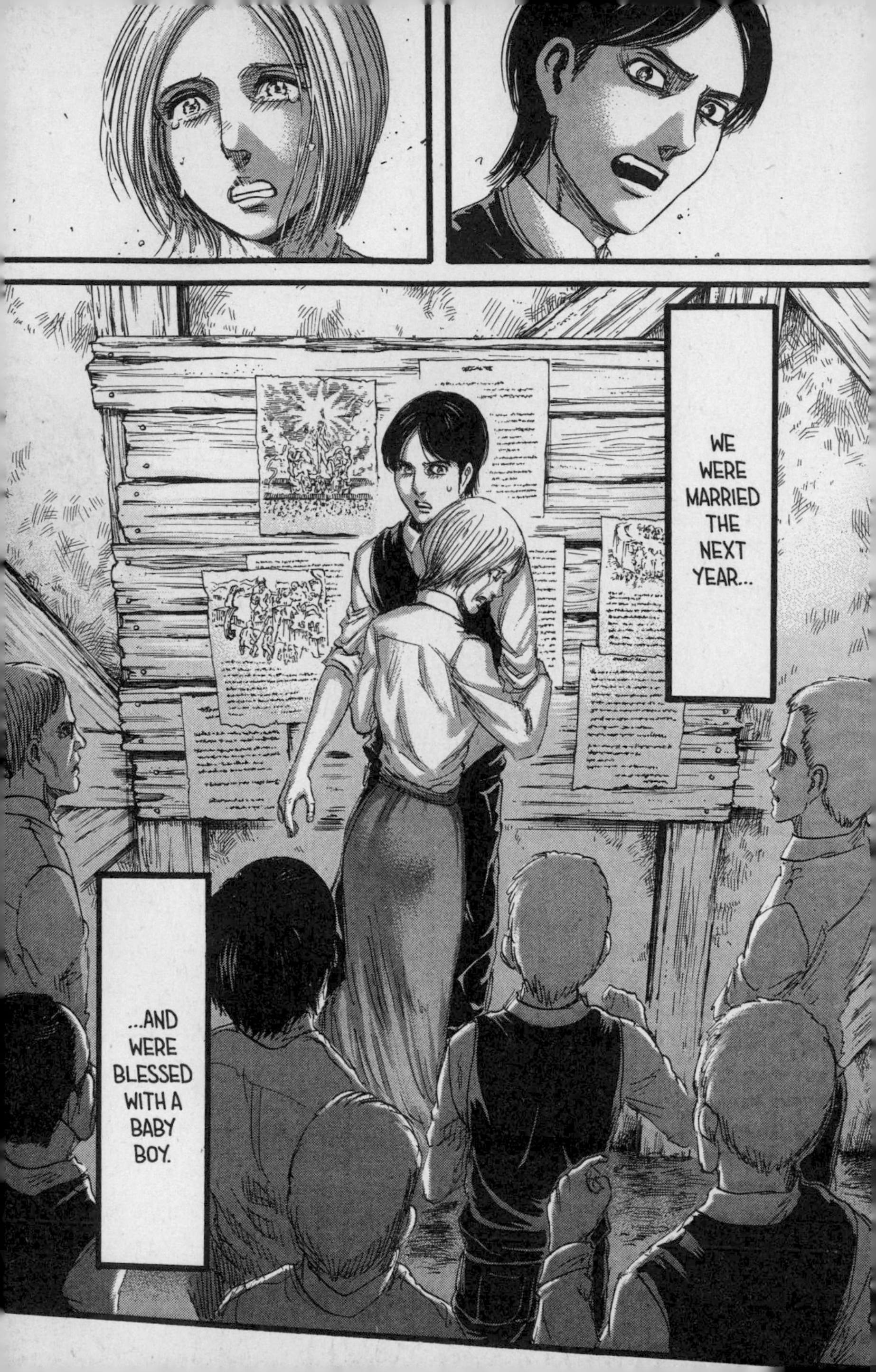
WE WERE MARRIED THE NEXT YEAR...
...AND WERE BLESSED WITH A BABY BOY.

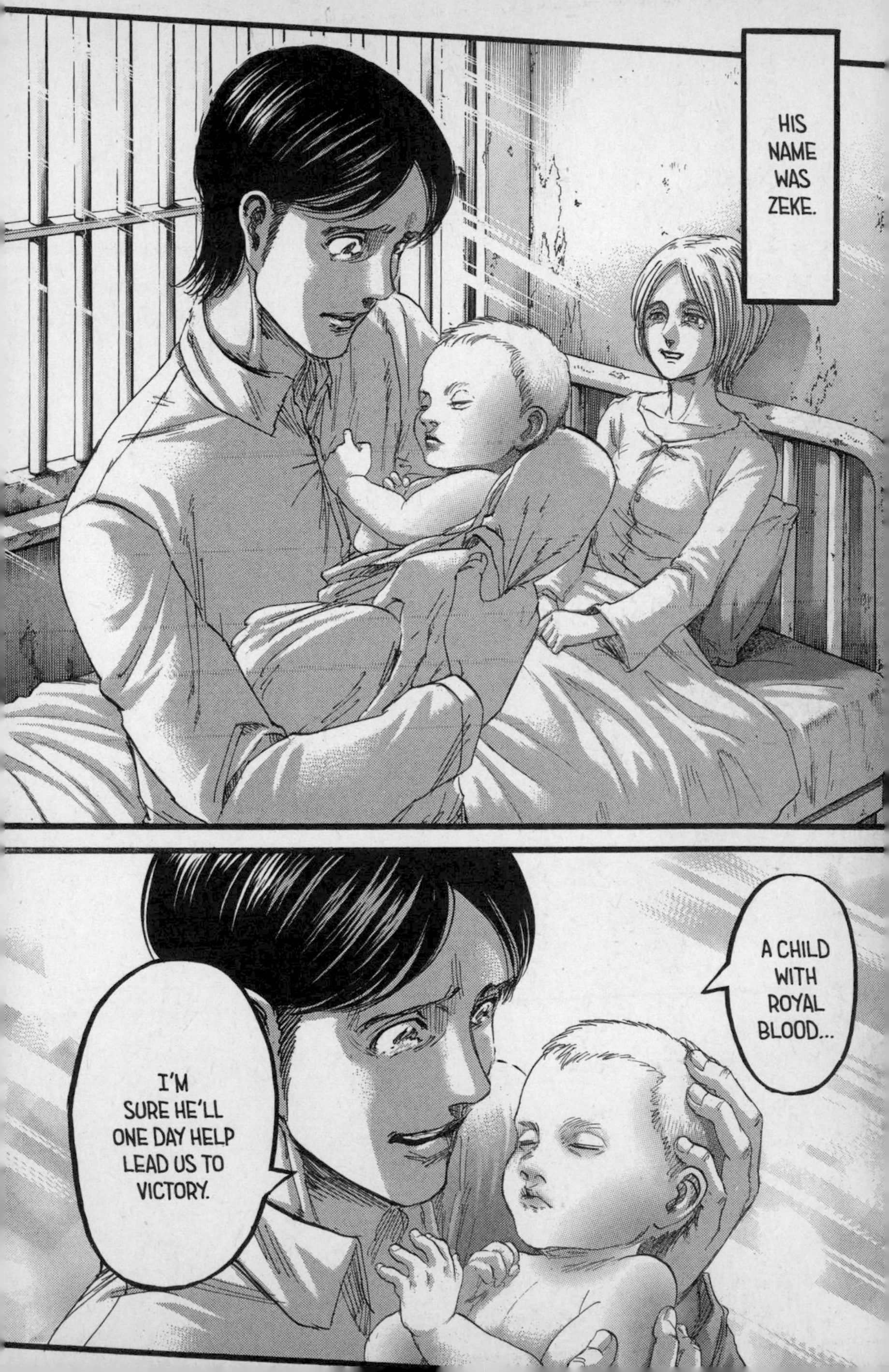
HIS NAME WAS ZEKE.
A CHILD WITH ROYAL BLOOD...
I'M SURE HE'LL ONE DAY HELP LEAD US TO VICTORY.

ONE AGE TURNED TO ANOTHER...

...AND PEOPLE CHANGED.

JUST AS THE WORLD WAS GROWING RAPIDLY...

...A TURNING POINT CAME FOR THE ELDIA RESTORATIONISTS.

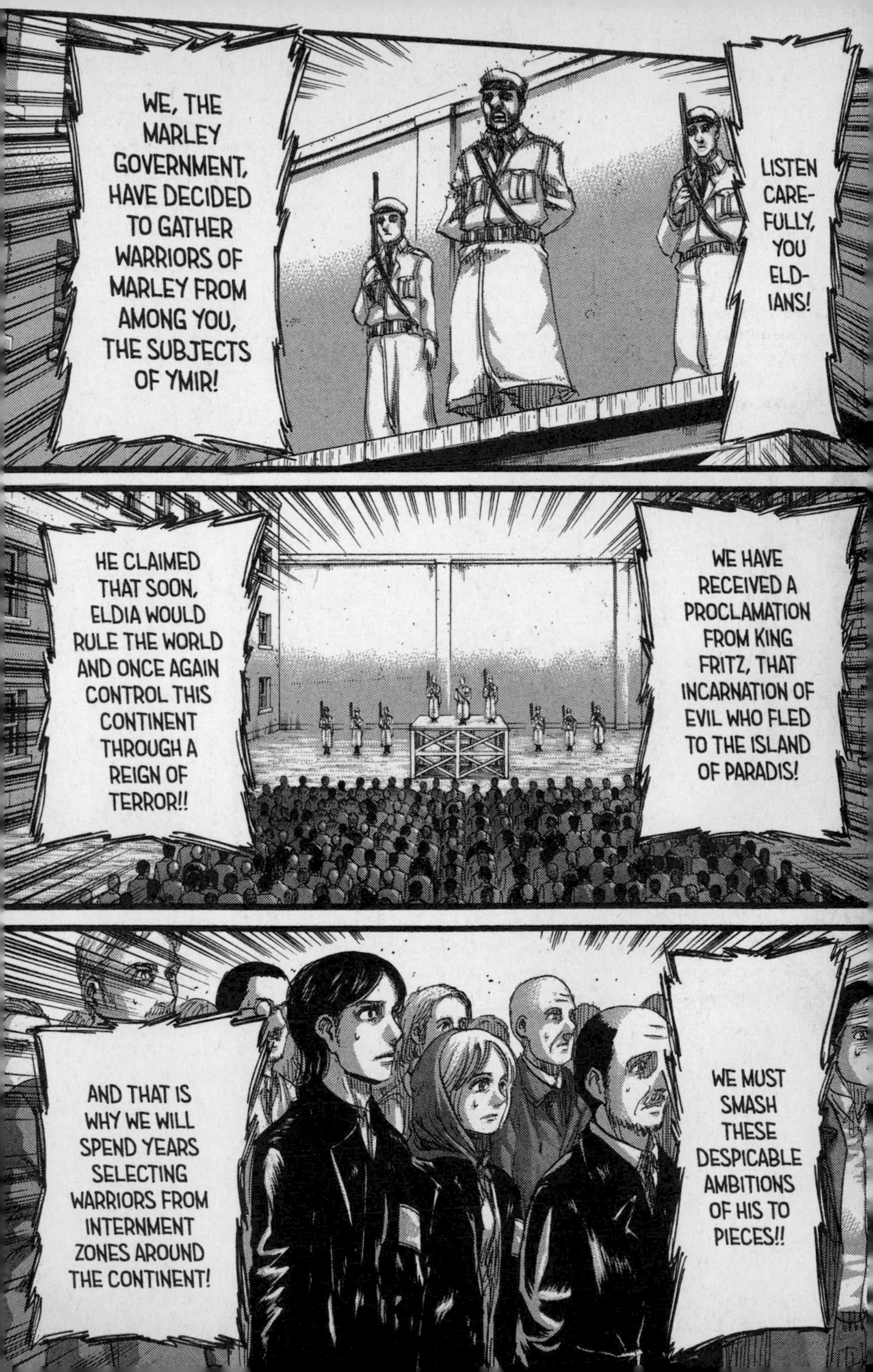
LISTEN CAREFULLY, YOU ELDIANS!
WE, THE MARLEY GOVERNMENT, HAVE DECIDED TO GATHER WARRIORS OF MARLEY FROM AMONG YOU, THE SUBJECTS OF YMIR!
WE HAVE RECEIVED A PROCLAMATION FROM KING FRITZ, THAT INCARNATION OF EVIL WHO FLED TO THE ISLAND OF PARADIS!
HE CLAIMED THAT SOON, ELDIA WOULD RULE THE WORLD AND ONCE AGAIN CONTROL THIS CONTINENT THROUGH A REIGN OF TERROR!!
WE MUST SMASH THESE DESPICABLE AMBITIONS OF HIS TO PIECES!!
AND THAT IS WHY WE WILL SPEND YEARS SELECTING WARRIORS FROM INTERNMENT ZONES AROUND THE CONTINENT!

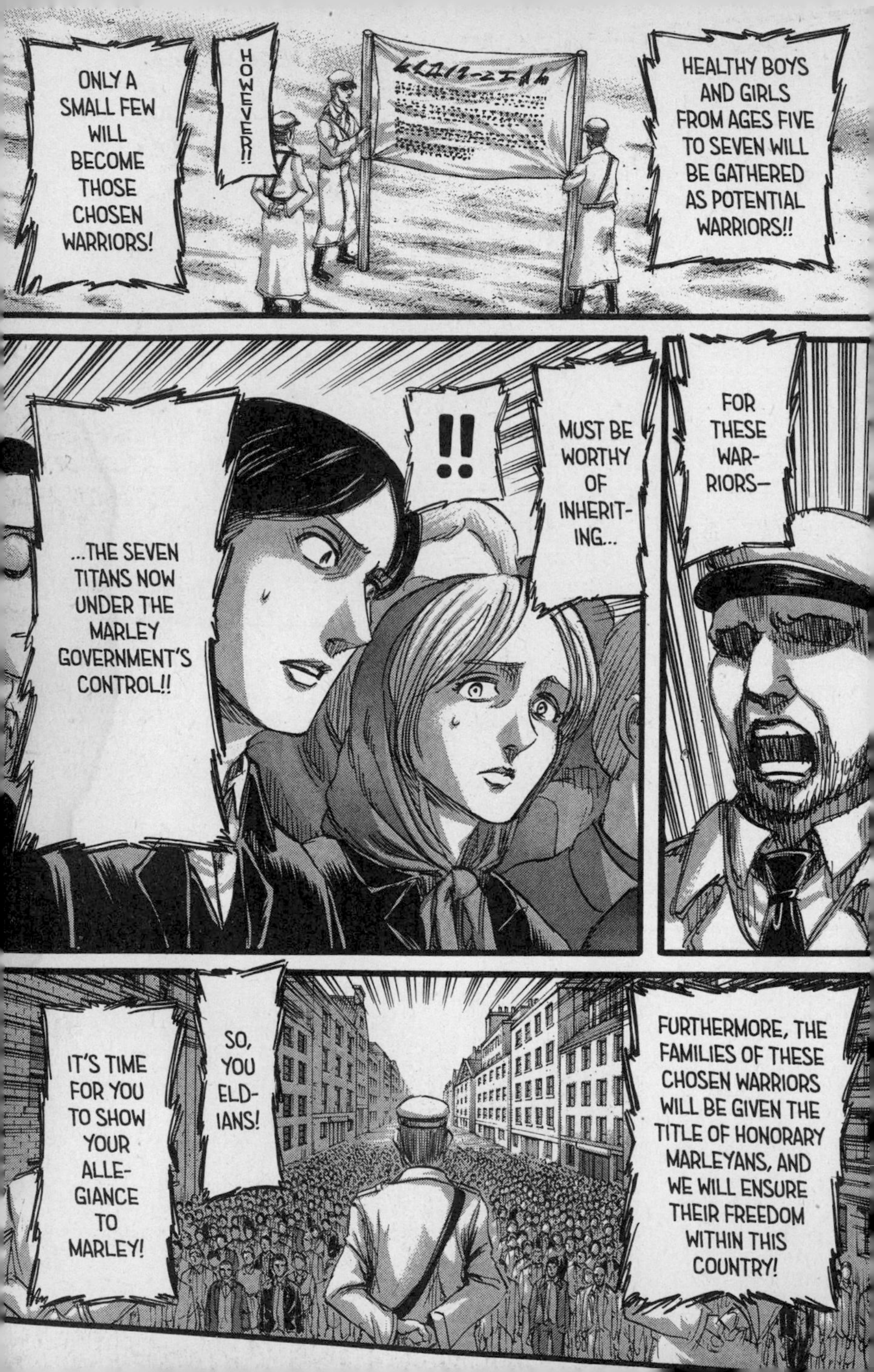
HEALTHY BOYS AND GIRLS FROM AGES FIVE TO SEVEN WILL BE GATHERED AS POTENTIAL WARRIORS!!
HOWEVER!!
ONLY A SMALL FEW WILL BECOME THOSE CHOSEN WARRIORS!
FOR THESE WAR-RIORS—
MUST BE WORTHY OF INHERIT-ING...
!!
...THE SEVEN TITANS NOW UNDER THE MARLEY GOVERNMENT'S CONTROL!!
FURTHERMORE, THE FAMILIES OF THESE CHOSEN WARRIORS WILL BE GIVEN THE TITLE OF HONORARY MARLEYANS, AND WE WILL ENSURE THEIR FREEDOM WITHIN THIS COUNTRY!
SO, YOU ELD-IANS!
IT'S TIME FOR YOU TO SHOW YOUR ALLE-GIANCE TO MARLEY!

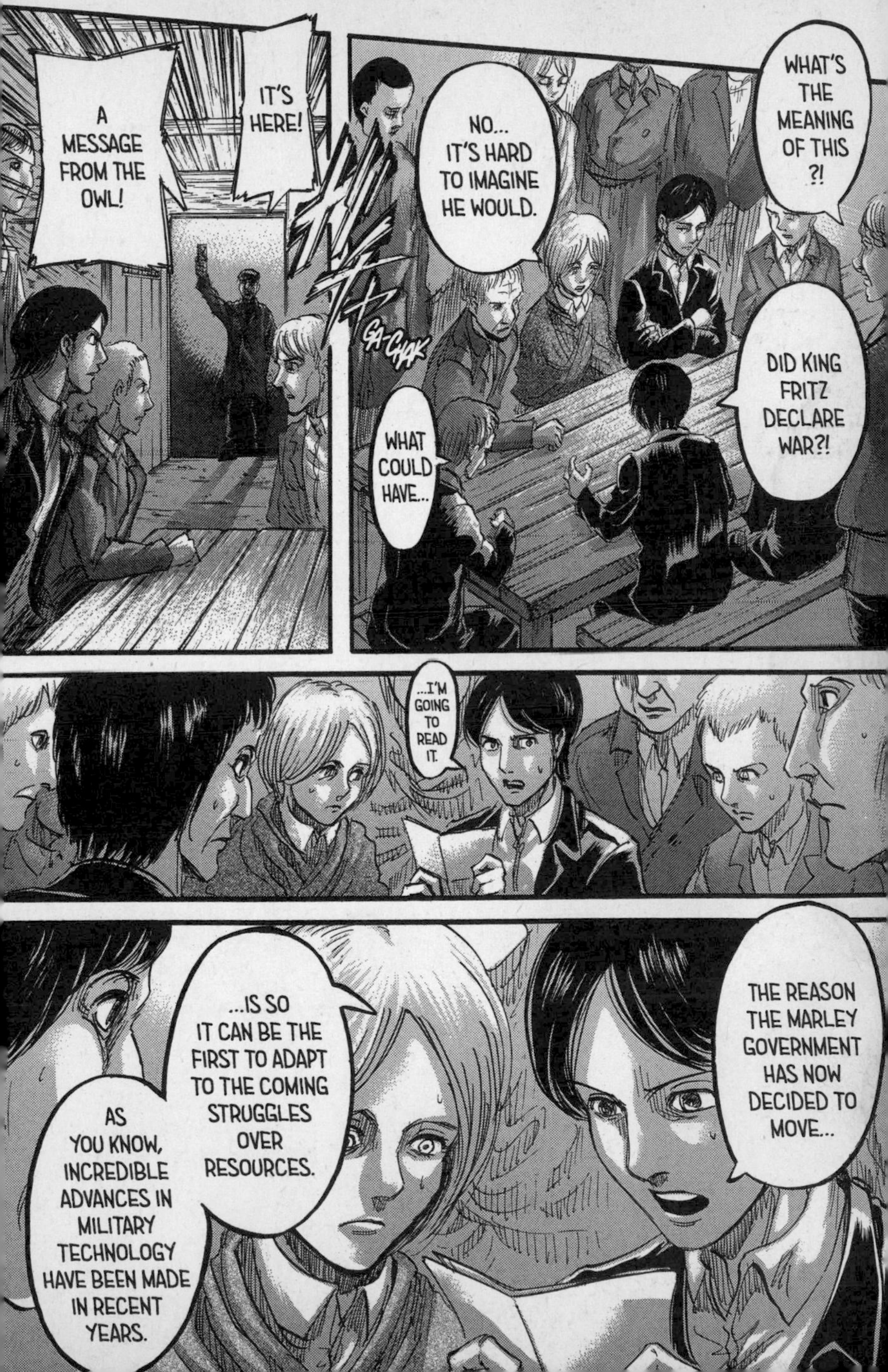
WHAT'S THE MEANING OF THIS?!
DID KING FRITZ DECLARE WAR?!
NO... IT'S HARD TO IMAGINE HE WOULD.
WHAT COULD HAVE...
GA-CHAK
IT'S HERE!
A MESSAGE FROM THE OWL!
...I'M GOING TO READ IT.
THE REASON THE MARLEY GOVERNMENT HAS NOW DECIDED TO MOVE...
...IS SO IT CAN BE THE FIRST TO ADAPT TO THE COMING STRUGGLES OVER RESOURCES.
AS YOU KNOW, INCREDIBLE ADVANCES IN MILITARY TECHNOLOGY HAVE BEEN MADE IN RECENT YEARS.

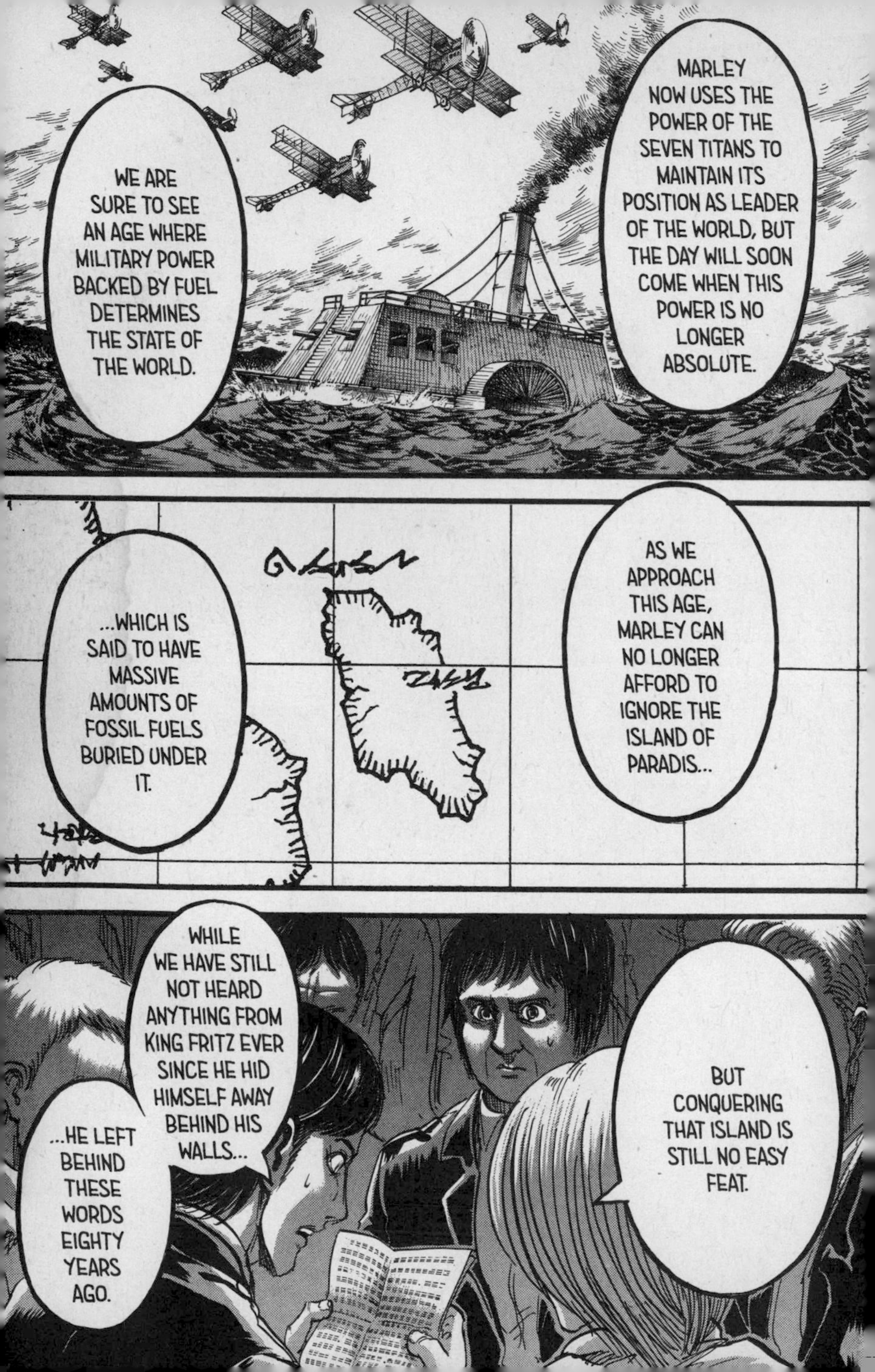
MARLEY NOW USES THE POWER OF THE SEVEN TITANS TO MAINTAIN ITS POSITION AS LEADER OF THE WORLD, BUT THE DAY WILL SOON COME WHEN THIS POWER IS NO LONGER ABSOLUTE.
WE ARE SURE TO SEE AN AGE WHERE MILITARY POWER BACKED BY FUEL DETERMINES THE STATE OF THE WORLD.
AS WE APPROACH THIS AGE, MARLEY CAN NO LONGER AFFORD TO IGNORE THE ISLAND OF PARADIS...
...WHICH IS SAID TO HAVE MASSIVE AMOUNTS OF FOSSIL FUELS BURIED UNDER IT.
BUT CONQUERING THAT ISLAND IS STILL NO EASY FEAT.
WHILE WE HAVE STILL NOT HEARD ANYTHING FROM KING FRITZ EVER SINCE HE HID HIMSELF AWAY BEHIND HIS WALLS...
...HE LEFT BEHIND THESE WORDS EIGHTY YEARS AGO.

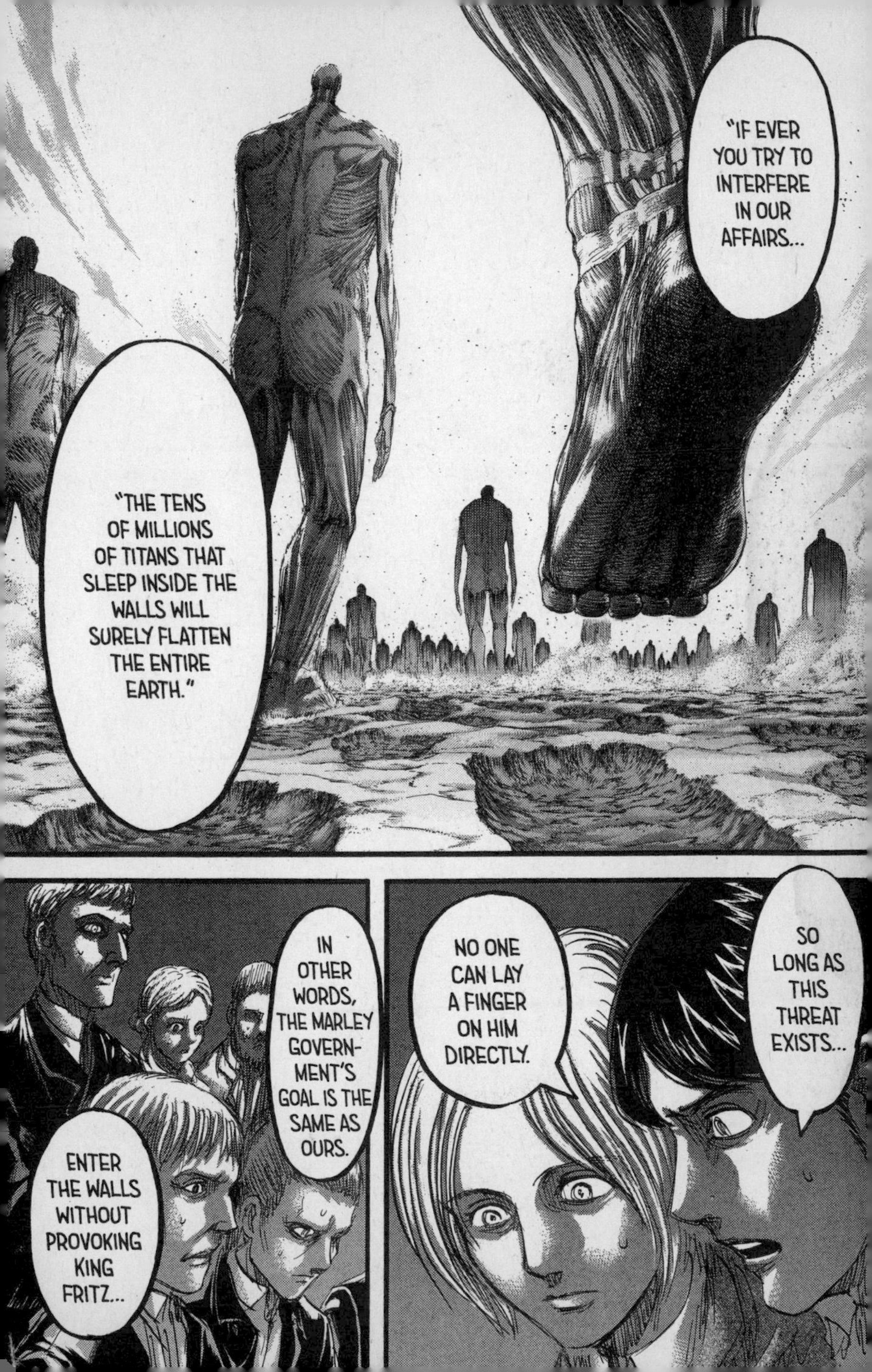
"IF EVER YOU TRY TO INTERFERE IN OUR AFFAIRS...
"THE TENS OF MILLIONS OF TITANS THAT SLEEP INSIDE THE WALLS WILL SURELY FLATTEN THE ENTIRE EARTH."
SO LONG AS THIS THREAT EXISTS...
NO ONE CAN LAY A FINGER ON HIM DIRECTLY.
IN OTHER WORDS, THE MARLEY GOVERNMENT'S GOAL IS THE SAME AS OURS.
ENTER THE WALLS WITHOUT PROVOKING KING FRITZ...

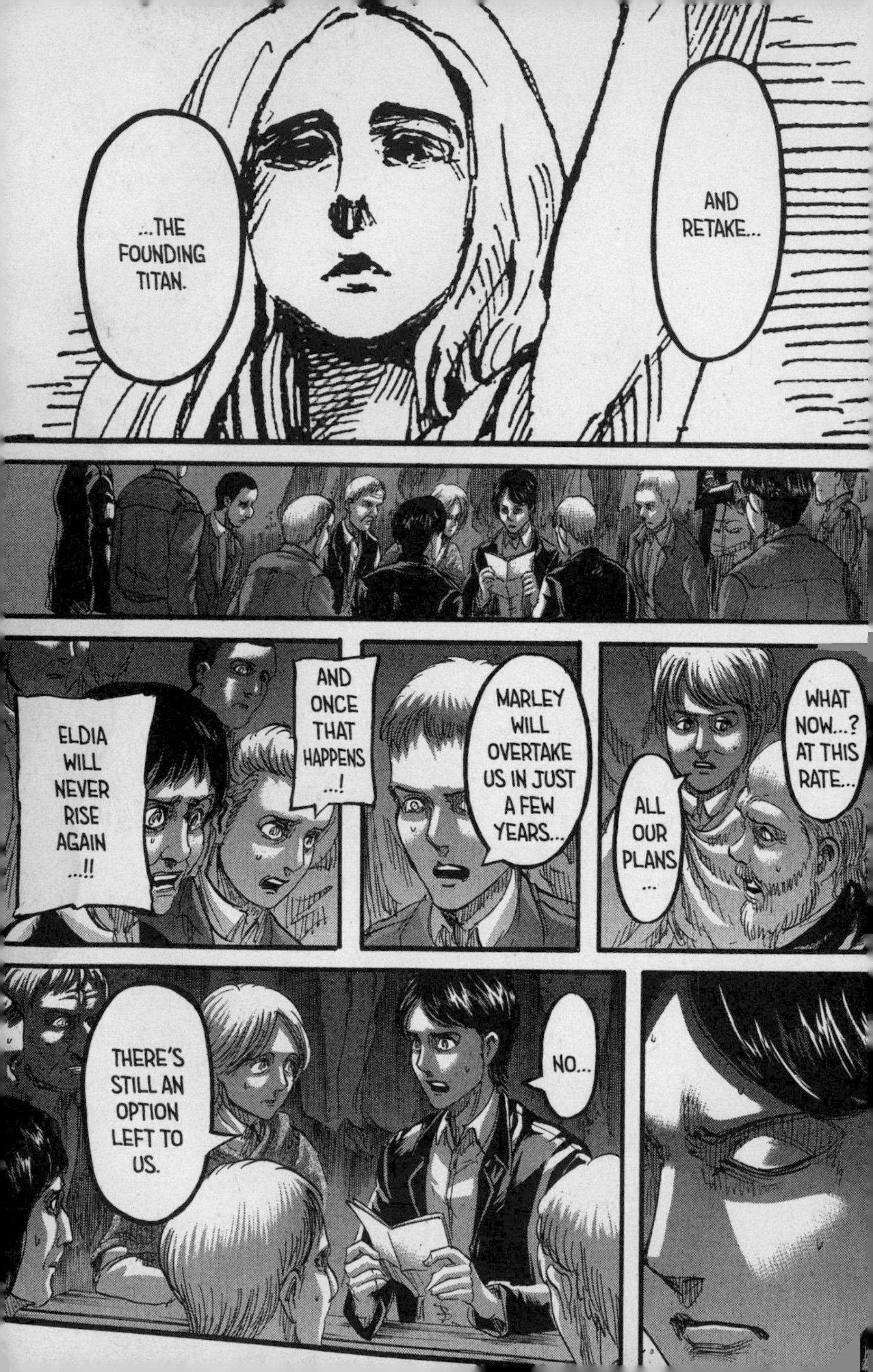
AND RETAKE...
...THE FOUNDING TITAN.
WHAT NOW...? AT THIS RATE...
ALL OUR PLANS ...
MARLEY WILL OVERTAKE US IN JUST A FEW YEARS...
AND ONCE THAT HAPPENS ...!
ELDIA WILL NEVER RISE AGAIN ...!!
NO...
THERE'S STILL AN OPTION LEFT TO US.

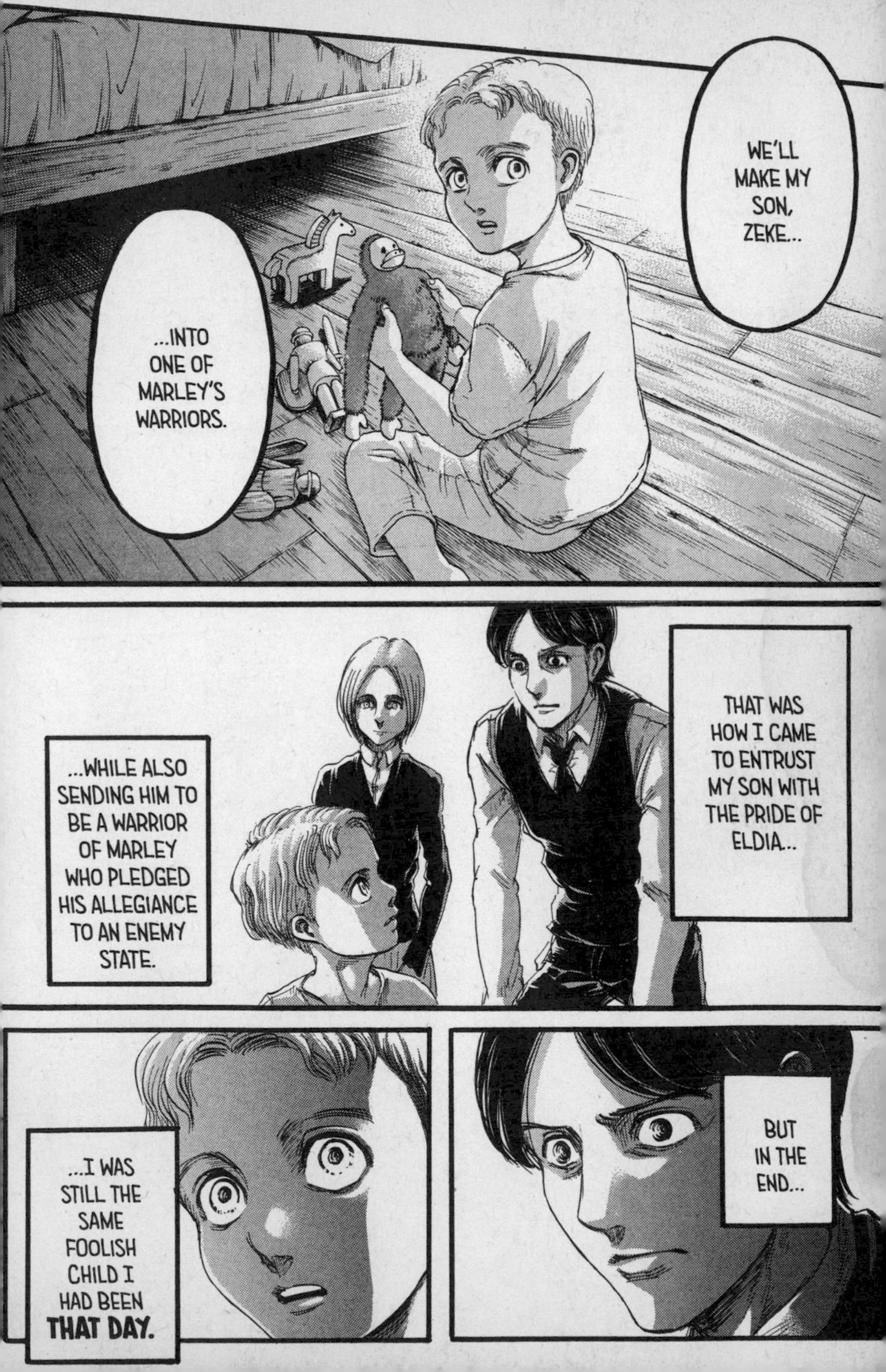
WE'LL MAKE MY SON, ZEKE...
...INTO ONE OF MARLEY'S WARRIORS.
THAT WAS HOW I CAME TO ENTRUST MY SON WITH THE PRIDE OF ELDIA...
...WHILE ALSO SENDING HIM TO BE A WARRIOR OF MARLEY WHO PLEDGED HIS ALLEGIANCE TO AN ENEMY STATE.
BUT IN THE END...
...I WAS STILL THE SAME FOOLISH CHILD I HAD BEEN **THAT DAY.**

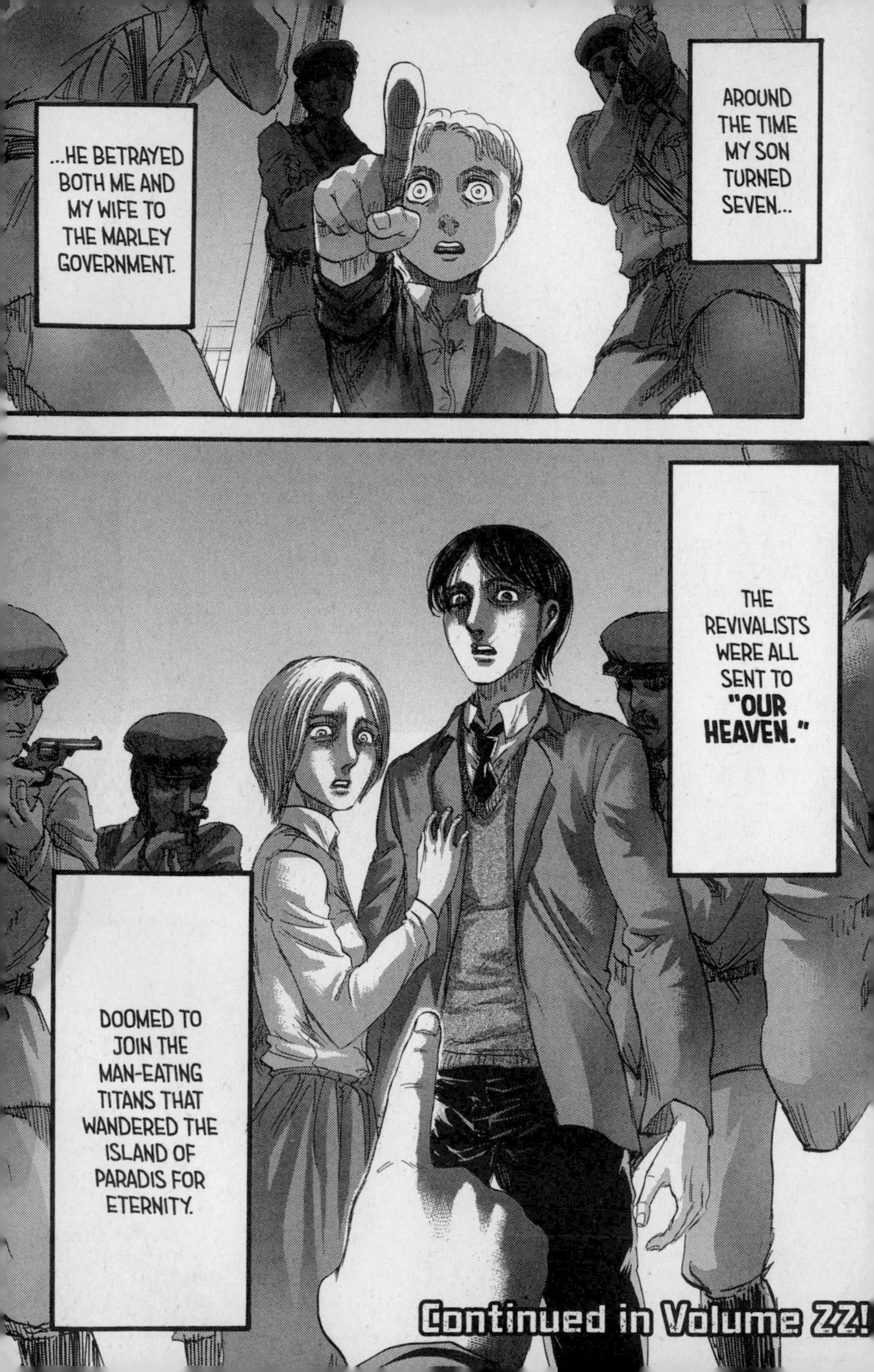
AROUND THE TIME MY SON TURNED SEVEN...
...HE BETRAYED BOTH ME AND MY WIFE TO THE MARLEY GOVERNMENT.
THE REVIVALISTS WERE ALL SENT TO **"OUR HEAVEN."**
DOOMED TO JOIN THE MAN-EATING TITANS THAT WANDERED THE ISLAND OF PARADIS FOR ETERNITY.
Continued in Volume 22!

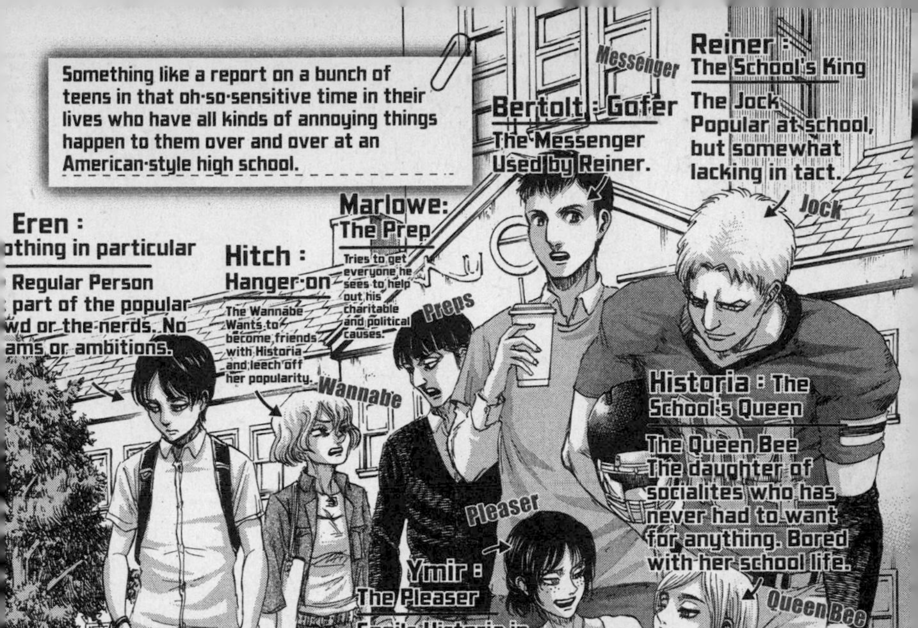
Something like a report on a bunch of teens in that oh-so-sensitive time in their lives who have all kinds of annoying things happen to them over and over at an American-style high school.
Reiner : The School's King
The Jock Popular at school, but somewhat lacking in tact.
Jock
Messenger
Bertolt : Gofer
The Messenger Used by Reiner.
Marlowe: The Prep
Tries to get everyone he sees to help out his charitable and political causes.
Preps
Hitch : Hanger-on
The Wannabe Wants to become friends with Historia and leech off her popularity.
Wannabe
Eren :
othing in particular
Regular Person
part of the popular
wd or the nerds. No
ams or ambitions.
Historia : The School's Queen
The Queen Bee The daughter of socialites who has never had to want for anything. Bored with her school life.
Queen Bee
Pleaser
Ymir : The Pleaser
Spoils Historia in hopes of making herself seem indispensable.

WHAT ARE SCHOOL CASTES?

The hierarchical relationships observed between students within the society that is a school can be seen as a caste system. This system is most notable in middle schools and high schools, and is an important element in regulating friendships and romantic relationships. As the lower castes can easily become targets for bullying, one's place within the class can sometimes become a matter of life and death.

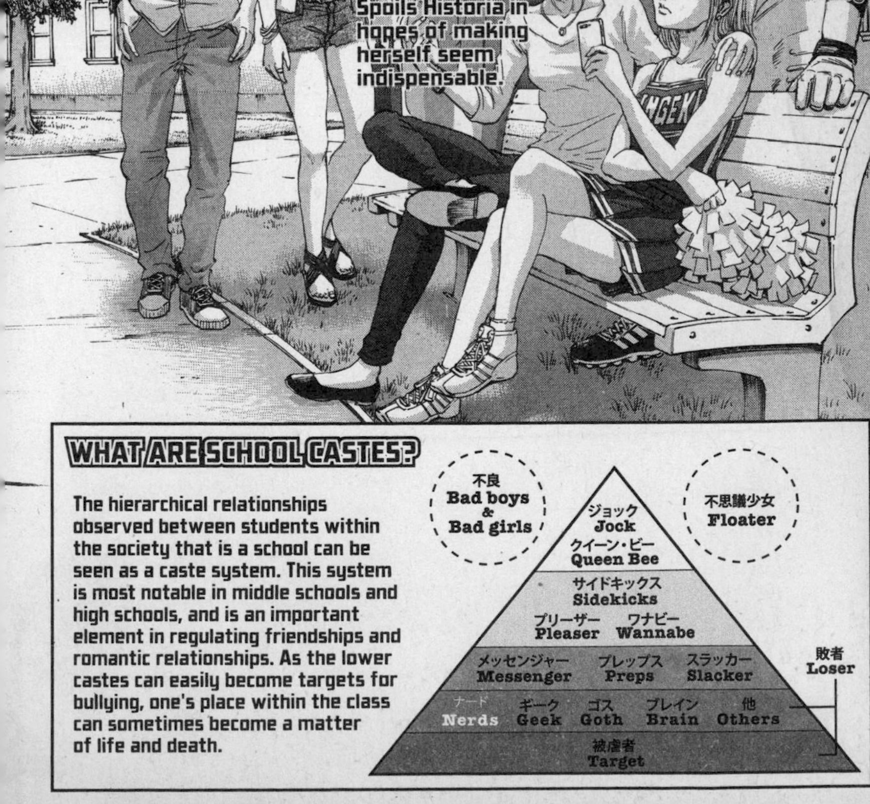
不良
Bad boys & Bad girls
不思議少女
Floater
ジョック
Jock
クイーン・ビー
Queen Bee
サイドキックス
Sidekicks
プリーザー
Pleaser
ワナビー
Wannabe
メッセンジャー
Messenger
プレップス
Preps
スラッカー
Slacker
敗者
Loser
ナード
Nerds
ギーク
Geek
ゴス
Goth
ブレイン
Brain
他
Others
被虐者
Target

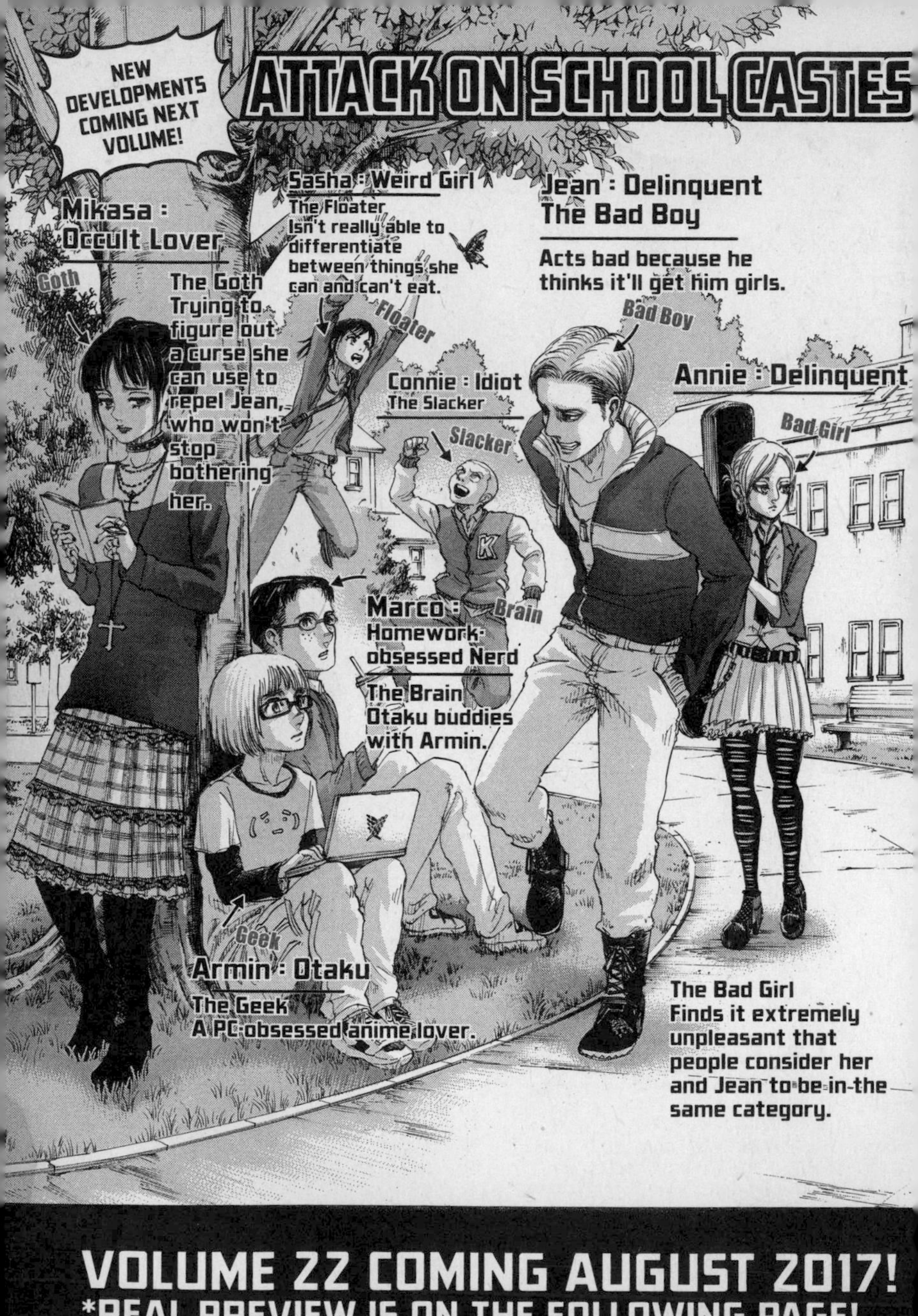
ATTACK ON SCHOOL CASTES
NEW DEVELOPMENTS COMING NEXT VOLUME!
Jean : Delinquent
The Bad Boy
Acts bad because he thinks it'll get him girls.
Bad Boy
Sasha : Weird Girl
The Floater
Isn't really able to differentiate between things she can and can't eat.
Floater
Mikasa : Occult Lover
The Goth
Trying to figure out a curse she can use to repel Jean, who won't stop bothering her.
Goth
Annie : Delinquent
Bad Girl
Connie : Idiot
The Slacker
Slacker
Marco : Homework-obsessed Nerd
The Brain
Otaku buddies with Armin.
Brain
Armin : Otaku
The Geek
A PC-obsessed anime lover.
Geek
The Bad Girl
Finds it extremely unpleasant that people consider her and Jean to be in the same category.

VOLUME 22 COMING AUGUST 2017!

***REAL PREVIEW IS ON THE FOLLOWING PAGE!**

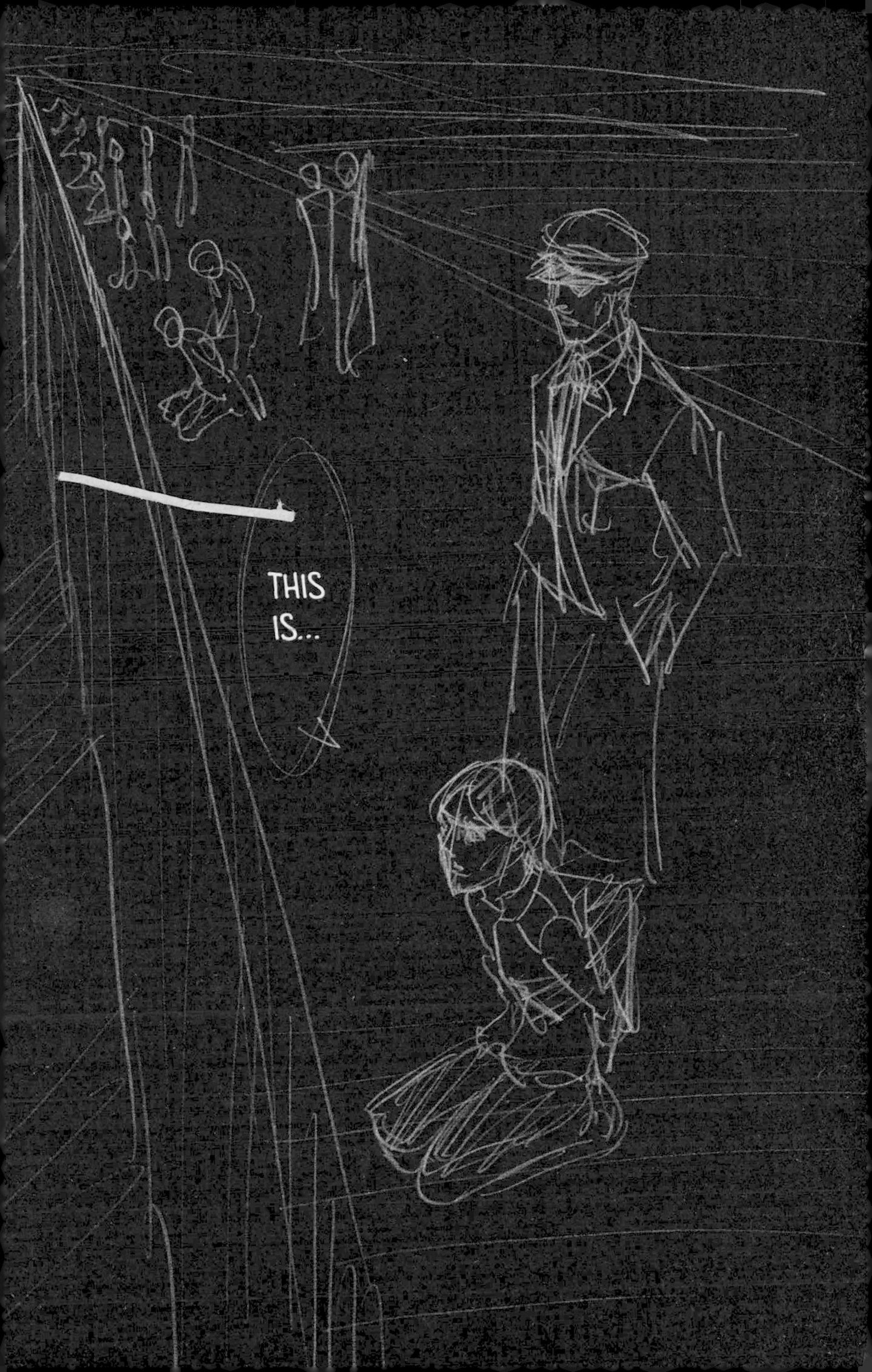
THIS IS...

THE CRUEL STORY OF THE WALLED WORLD AND THE YEAGERS BEGINS.

VOLUME 22 COMING AUG. 2017!

Attack on Titan 21 is a work of fiction. Names, characters, places, and incidents are the products of the author's imagination or are used fictitiously. Any resemblance to actual events, locales, or persons, living or dead, is entirely coincidental.

A Kodansha Comics Trade Paperback Original

Published in the United States by Kodansha Comics, an imprint of Kodansha USA Publishing, LLC, New York.

Publication rights for this English edition arranged through Kodansha Ltd, Tokyo.

First published in Japan in 2016 by Kodansha Ltd., Tokyo as *Shingeki no kyojin*, volume 21.

ISBN 978-1-63236-327-5

Original cover design by Takashi Shimoyama (Red Rooster)

Printed in the United States of America.

www.kodanshacomics.com

9 8 7 6 5 4 3 2 1
Translation: Ko Ransom
Lettering: Steve Wands
Editing: Ben Applegate
Kodansha Comics edition cover design by Phil Balsman